D1709935

Legal Blame

The LAW AND PUBLIC POLICY: PSYCHOLOGY AND THE SOCIAL SCIENCES series includes books in three domains:

Legal Studies—writings by legal scholars about issues of relevance to psychology and the other social sciences, or that employ social science information to advance the legal analysis;

Social Science Studies—writings by scientists from psychology and the other social sciences about issues of relevance to law and public policy; and

Forensic Studies—writings by psychologists and other mental health scientists and professionals about issues relevant to forensic mental health science and practice.

The series is guided by its editor, Bruce D. Sales, PhD, JD, University of Arizona; and coeditors, Stephen J. Ceci, PhD, Cornell University; Norman J. Finkel, PhD, Georgetown University; and Bruce J. Winick, JD, University of Miami.

* * *

Legal Blame

How Jurors Think and Talk About Accidents

Neal Feigenson

AMERICAN PSYCHOLOGICAL ASSOCIATION

WASHINGTON, DC

Copyright © 2000 by the American Psychological Association. All rights reserved. Except as permitted under the United States Copyright Act of 1976, no part of this publication may be reproduced or distributed in any form or by any means, or stored in a database or retrieval system, without the prior written permission of the publisher.

Published by
American Psychological Association
750 First Street, NE
Washington, DC 20002

Copies may be ordered from
APA Order Department
P.O. Box 92984
Washington, DC 20090-2984

In the U.K., Europe, Africa, and the Middle East, copies may be ordered from
American Psychological Association
3 Henrietta Street
Covent Garden, London
WC2E 8LU England

Typeset in Goudy by EPS Group Inc., Easton, MD

Printer: Edwards Brothers, Inc., Ann Arbor, MI
Cover Designer: Berg Design, Albany, NY
Technical/Production Editor: Eleanor Inskip

The opinions and statements published are the responsibility of the authors, and such opinions and statements do not necessarily represent the policies of the APA.

Library of Congress Cataloging-in-Publication Data
Feigenson, Neal.
        Legal blame : how jurors think and talk about accidents / Neal Feigenson.
            p. cm.—(The law and public policy)
        Includes bibliographical references and index.
        ISBN 1-55798-677-0
        1. Jury—United States.   2. Judicial process—United States.   3. Accident law—Psychological aspects.   I. Title.   II. Series.

    KF8972.F45 2000
    347.73'52—dc21

                                                                    00-020770

British Library Cataloguing-in-Publication Data
A CIP record is available from the British Library.

Printed in the United States of America
First Edition

For Ellen, Gabby, and Tom

CONTENTS

PREFACE

A book about common sense and law should speak to several audiences. I have written for legal scholars and law students who want to know more about how laypeople create tort law when they sit on juries, and about the psychology of jury decision making in general. I have also written for social psychologists who want to see how attribution theory and other familiar concepts apply in an important, pragmatic domain: the determination of legal responsibility for accidents. I have addressed practicing lawyers, setting out the psychological principles that explain what they may already know intuitively, but have never systematically articulated, about successful advocacy. And I have written for members of the general public who are interested in learning more about the American tort law system and the place of juries in it. I have written as simply as I can, so that lawyers can understand the psychology, psychologists can understand the law, and the general audience can understand both.

My interest in the role of common sense in legal decision making began when I attended the Lawyering Theory Colloquium at New York University Law School in the spring of 1991, conducted by Tony Amsterdam, Peggy Davis, and Jerome Bruner. The multidisciplinary readings they assigned and the fascinating discussions they led inspired the thinking and research that resulted, in 1995, in the publication of an article titled "The Rhetoric of Torts," a psychological analysis of lawyers' closing arguments in accident cases. Bruce Sales, editor of the American Psychological Association series "Law and Public Policy: Psychology and the Social Sciences," read that article and invited me to develop it into a book. I am grateful to him for giving me the opportunity to integrate my qualitative studies of legal discourse with quantitative research on lay decision making.

I thank the publishers of the following articles for the permission to adapt them for use in this book: "The Rhetoric of Torts: How Advocates Help Jurors Think About Causation, Reasonableness, and Responsibility," which appeared in volume 47 of the *Hastings Law Journal* (1995) and which, in revised form, is excerpted in chapters 2 and 5 of this book; "Effect of Blameworthiness and Outcome Severity on Attributions of Responsibility and Damage Awards in Comparative Negligence Cases" (with Jaihyun Park and Peter Salovey), which appeared in volume 21 of *Law and Human Behavior* (1997), and on which I draw in chapter 3; "Sympathy and Legal Judgment: A Psychological Analysis," which appeared in volume 65 of the *Tennessee Law Review* (1997), and which I excerpt, as revised, in chapter 3 and the Appendix; and "Accidents as Melodrama," which appeared in the *New York Law School Law Review* (1999), and parts of which reappear in this book in chapters 4, 5, 6, and 8.

I am much indebted to all of those who read and commented on those previous publications: Jeremy Blumenthal, Richard Lipman, Gregory Loken, Leonard Long, Philip Meyer, Elayne Rapping, Peter Salovey, Elyn Saks, Richard Sherwin, Christina Spiesel, Sheila Taub, John Thomas, and Benjamin Zipursky. I am especially grateful to my Quinnipiac College School of Law colleagues Brian Bix, Steve Gilles, Sandy Meiklejohn, and Linda Meyer, and to Brian Bornstein of the Louisiana State University Department of Psychology, all of whom read and commented not only on those articles but also on portions of the manuscript of this book. I have benefited as well from the guidance of Judy Nemes, my editor at APA Books, and from the comments of the anonymous reviewers whom APA Books consulted. The case studies in the second half of the book could not have been written without the cases to study, and I thank those who provided me with the raw data: attorneys Steven Errante (trial transcript in *Butler*, chapter 5), Robert Neuberger (trial transcript in *Faverty*, chapter 6), and David Wenner (mock jury videotapes, chapter 7), and Professor William Nelson of New York University Law School (trial transcript in *Guilietti*, chapter 5). Quinnipiac Law School reference librarians Tina DeLucia and Larry Raftery and interlibrary loan specialist Linda Holt helped me to locate secondary materials. Generous research support from Dean Neil Cogan helped make it possible to complete the book.

Two people deserve special thanks. Peter Salovey of Yale University has taught me psychology by allowing me to collaborate with him and Jaihyun Park on our studies of lay judgments in negligence cases, by welcoming me to audit his Psychology of Emotions seminar in the fall of 1995, and by freely sharing his time and expertise in countless discussions and e-mail exchanges during the last several years. If I am now able to write at all competently about the psychology of legal decision making, it is largely due to him. And for guiding my inquiries into the intersections of law, common sense, and popular culture, criticizing my work so perceptively, and leading by the example of his own scholarship, I thank my friend Richard Sherwin of New York Law School.

Finally, to my wife Ellen and our children, Gabby and Tom: for your love, companionship, support, and patience, my gratitude is beyond words.

Legal Blame

INTRODUCTION

This is a book about how people decide who is responsible when a person is accidentally injured or killed. It is about the habits of thought and feeling that laypeople—not judges or other legal experts—use to determine who, if anyone, is to blame and how much compensation the injured person deserves. It is also about the words laypeople use to talk about blame and what those words reveal about the ways those people think and feel. In short, it is a book about how people try to do justice in the wake of accidents.

Each year millions of Americans are injured accidentally, nearly 100,000 of them fatally (National Safety Council, 1997). These accidents produce more than $175 billion in medical, work, and other economic losses, as well as untold physical and mental suffering (Dewees, Duff, & Trebilcock, 1996; Hensler et al., 1991). On a societal level, dealing well with accidental misfortune includes compensating the injured and minimizing the amount of money spent on accidents and accident avoidance. How satisfactorily society addresses these goals of adequate compensation and efficient deterrence of risky behavior has been the subject of much empirical (e.g., Dewees et al., 1996) and theoretical (e.g., Abel, 1995) debate.

Perhaps just as important, each accident invites us to decide who is responsible for it. Making judgments about responsibility is a pervasive feature of our social existence (Weiner, 1995), and when we decide who is to blame for accidental harms, we shape many aspects of our lives. Most obviously, the American tort litigation system makes the determination of responsibility for the accident central to whether and how completely the injured person will be compensated, as well as to whether the sort of behavior that led to the harm will be deterred, and if so, at what cost.[1]

When we attribute responsibility for an accident, we also declare what is appropriate and inappropriate behavior. We define the role expectations of employers and employees, manufacturers and consumers, physicians and patients, drivers and pedestrians. We decide whether it is fair and just that someone whose behavior arguably helped to bring about the harm pay for the injured person's losses. Ultimately, we define *ourselves*: how we think and feel about what happens to us and others, and whether what happens is a matter of fate or an occasion for blaming someone.

In the American legal system, laypeople try to resolve tragedy into justice when they sit as jurors in accident trials. Jury verdict analyses tell us something about *what* juries decide, the outputs of the process (I will summarize these briefly in a moment). Legal scholars and social psychologists have devoted several excellent books (e.g., Hans & Vidmar, 1986; Kalven & Zeisel, 1966; Kassin & Wrightsman, 1988) and many hundreds of articles to the subject of *how* juries decide. Relying on this scholarship throughout the book, I hope to add to our understanding of how laypeople assign blame for accidents. I do this by connecting psychology to discourse: by showing what common-sense justice in particular accident cases sounds like and explaining why it sounds the way it does.

What is the nature of blaming for accidents that this discourse reveals? From the ongoing debate about jury performance generally (cf., e.g., Adler, 1994; Strier, 1994 [presenting largely critical views] with Daniels & Martin, 1995; Galanter, 1998; Saks, 1992; Vidmar, 1998 [reviewing and refuting claims that civil juries are "out of control"]), I draw an observation that will serve as my point of departure. Although jurors do not fare particularly well when tested on their comprehension of legal rules (Reifman, Gusick, & Ellsworth, 1992), they nevertheless tend to reach decisions that largely agree with those of legal experts (Kalven & Zeisel, 1966; Vidmar, 1995). How can it be that laypeople, who seem not to know very much about the relevant legal rules, attribute responsibility for accidents in a way that is so often, as best we can tell, correct enough by expert standards? Certainly we should expect considerable agreement between lay and expert

---

[1] Compensation and deterrence could be, and to some extent are, addressed separately from the assessment of blame for particular accidents. First-party health and other insurance covers some accident losses, and regulatory enforcement of safety rules helps deter unduly risky conduct before accidents occur. The tort litigation system combines the goals of proper responsibility attribution, compensation, and deterrence. When a court decides that one person has tortiously injured another, it attributes legal blame to the injurer, and, by compelling the injurer to pay the victim's damages, compensates the victim and discourages similar conduct by the injurer (and others similarly situated) in the future.

judgments. As Oliver Wendell Holmes wrote over a century ago, "The first requirement of a sound body of law is, that it should correspond with the actual feelings and demands of the community, whether right or wrong" (Holmes, 1881/1963, p. 36); and jurors often do understand and follow legal instructions. But *how* do jurors reach the decisions they do, and what explains the residue of conflict between lay and expert justice?

There is no simple answer to this question. One task of this book is to explain just how complex lay decision making in accident cases is. Legal blaming is *multidimensional*: It springs from common sense and is also shaped by legal rules, expert rationales, and the facts of the individual case. And common sense itself is various and contradictory, not systematic or coherent. Our common sense consists of many general habits of thought and feeling, as well as case-specific beliefs and preconceptions. Often these habits and beliefs incline jurors to view accident cases as personality-driven melodramas, in which bad outcomes are traced to that party's behavior that most deviates from salient cultural norms. Yet other aspects of common sense compete with and, in any given case, may overcome this melodramatic conception of responsibility.

If there is any overarching pattern in this complexity, it is that jurors in accident cases try to achieve what I call *total justice*. They strive to square all accounts between the parties (even though the issues the law asks them to resolve may not be framed in those terms), to consider all information they deem relevant (even if the law tries to keep them from relying on some of it), to reach a decision that is correct as a whole (even if they reach it by blurring legally distinct questions), and to feel right about their decision (even though the law discourages them from using their emotions to decide). The decisions that result are often, like common sense itself (Ross & Nisbett, 1991), "right for the wrong reasons": consistent with the law, but not necessarily the result of strict adherence to legal rules and procedures. And when a jury appears to diverge from what legal experts would have decided, we can often trace the divergence not to juror incompetence or bias (a characterization of juries in general which leading scholars reject: Hans & Vidmar, 1986; Vidmar, 1998), but rather to the same habits of thought and feeling—the urge to do total justice—that are ordinarily reliable enough but have on this occasion been pulled astray by something in the law or the facts of the case or the way in which the law or the facts were presented at trial.

Generalizations like these, however, take us only so far. To grasp how jurors use their common sense in the context of legal rules and particular facts to assign responsibility for accidents, one must turn from generalities to specific cases. This is the more original and important contribution that this book makes to the understanding of lay decision making. I examine how the words that advocates use to persuade jurors and the words the jurors themselves use to explain their decisions in several accident cases reflect the social psychology of total justice. Readers can then judge for themselves the extent to which the jurors in these cases achieved justice, and readers who believe that the jurors did not will be better able to understand why they did not.

As background for my inquiry into how laypeople think and talk about accidents, I offer a brief survey of how the legal system assigns responsibility and damages for accidental harm. I then move from the *what* to the *how* of legal blaming, explaining in more detail my approach to understanding how jurors think and talk about accidents.

BLAME AND COMPENSATION: A SNAPSHOT
OF WHAT WE DO ABOUT ACCIDENTS

As a society, we use many, often overlapping, institutions and methods to assign responsibility for accidents, distribute their costs, and compensate the injured. We can examine these institutions and methods for what they tell us about who gets blamed for accidents, and with what consequences. A complete study would include how the injured decide whether to blame someone else for their misfortune in the first place or whether simply to "lump it" (Felstiner, Abel, & Sarat, 1981; Saks, 1992); it would also include how many of those who claim redress for their injuries obtain it through some form of insurance. A thorough inquiry would then delve into the processes of "litigotiation" (Galanter, 1993): the litigated and negotiated dispositions of accident claims filed in the formal legal system. In that system, the decisions of judges and juries authoritatively assign blame, allocate accident costs to the person or persons found responsible, and, insofar as their judgments set formal precedents for courts or benchmarks for litigotiating attorneys in later cases, shape the future behavior of the responsible person or persons and others similarly situated. In addition, legislatures and administrative agencies issue rules that define permissible and impermissible behavior; the government uses these rules to attribute blame and deter unwanted conduct, both directly, by enforcing the rules against the violator, and indirectly, when the courts adopt the rules as standards of blameworthiness.

What emerges from these multiple forums and processes is a complex and partly contradictory pattern of blaming and compensating for accidents, which I survey only briefly here. According to much popular rhetoric, Americans are highly litigious, ready to sue for personal injuries at the drop of a hat, and juries are overwhelmingly biased toward plaintiffs in both their liability decisions and their damage awards. The reality, insofar as we can construct it from our admittedly imperfect knowledge (Saks, 1992), appears to be quite different (Daniels & Martin, 1995; Galanter, 1996, 1998; Saks, 1992; Vidmar, 1998).

A very small portion of all accidental injuries, about 1 in 10, results in claims for compensation of any sort, and only a fraction of these lead to lawsuits (Hensler et al., 1991). Automobile-related injuries are an exception, leading to claims for compensation (not necessarily lawsuits) 44% of the time; by contrast, only 7% of those injured at work file claims (Hensler et al., 1991),[2] and a leading study showed that only 1 of every 8 patients *negligently* injured during medical treatment filed a malpractice suit (Weiler, 1991). Of all tort cases filed,[3] about 5% or less are resolved by verdict at trial; about half of these trials are jury trials (Galanter, 1993; Gross & Syverud, 1996).[4] The remainder are settled or dismissed at an earlier stage in the proceedings.

The categories of people and entities whom legal doctrine subjects to liability for accidentally causing harm have generally expanded during the last 30 years (e.g., various municipal and institutional liabilities, especially for the acts of third parties), but in one of the most important areas of accidental harm, products liability, the wave of expanding liability has crested and even receded (Henderson & Eisenberg, 1990). The success rate of tort claimants before juries has been more or less constant for the last decade (Moller, 1996). In cases tried to juries overall, plaintiffs win about 55–60% of the time (Moller, 1996), with the success rates varying according to the type of case: over 60% for auto accidents, about 40% for products liability, and 30% for medical malpractice (Daniels & Martin, 1995; Merritt & Barry, 1999). (Keep in mind that these win rates involve the roughly two tenths of 1% of all accidental injuries that result in jury trials.) Juries decide cases the same way the judge would have about four fifths of the time (Kalven & Zeisel, 1966; Saks, 1992), and judges are more likely than juries to hold defendants responsible in products liability and medical malpractice cases (Clermont & Eisenberg, 1992).[5]

---

[2] This figure does not include workers' compensation claims or first-party insurance claims (Hensler et al., 1991, p. 109, note 1).

[3] I use *tort* here as a synonym for personal injury cases alleging accidental harm, which is not strictly accurate (e.g., defamation is a tort, and some personal injuries are intentionally inflicted), but it is not misleading in the context because more than 90% of tort cases are personal injury cases, and the vast majority of those allege unintentional injury (Galanter, 1996). The broad generalizations in the text do ignore differences between the federal courts and the state court systems, where about 98% of tort cases are filed (Galanter, 1996; Saks, 1992), as well as the considerable variations between states (Daniels & Martin, 1995).

[4] The very cursory survey in the text also elides distinctions between types of cases. For instance, because of their vastly higher rate of claiming, automobile accidents yield over 40% of all tort cases filed (Galanter, 1996) and nearly a third of all tort jury verdicts (Daniels & Martin, 1995), although as a percentage of each type of tort suit, medical malpractice cases are the most likely to reach a trial verdict (Saks, 1992).

[5] Clermont and Eisenberg (1998) stressed that this disparity is probably due to case-selection effects: For instance, if plaintiffs' lawyers believe that juries are much more favorable to their clients than judges are, they may tend to opt for jury trials when their cases are weaker; consequently, the mix of cases judges hear will be stronger for the plaintiffs, resulting in a higher percentage of plaintiff's verdicts (assuming both judge and jury are equally neutral decision makers in all important respects). More generally, no inferences can logically be drawn from data on the number of claims filed, win rates, and damage awards alone to

Compensatory damage awards to successful tort claimants are significantly correlated with the victim's medical expenses (Peterson, 1984). The noneconomic damage component of those awards (i.e., pain and suffering), which constitutes on average about half of the total recovery, is significantly correlated with the severity of the victim's injury, and in particular, with jurors' perceptions of how disabling the injury is and how much mental suffering the victim has endured (Wissler, Evans, Hart, Morry, & Saks, 1997). Less seriously injured victims are on average overcompensated and the most seriously injured are undercompensated, often by considerable amounts (Dewees et al., 1996; Kakalik, King, Traynor, Ebener, & Picus, 1988; Saks, 1992).

Punitive damages are awarded in about 5% of personal injury verdicts (Daniels & Martin, 1995; Galanter, 1996; Rustad, 1998). When they are awarded, the average amount correlates significantly with the compensatory damage award (Galanter, 1996). The mean punitive award is as much as 14 times as great as the median award, indicating that the population consists of a few, very large outlier awards and many smaller awards (Galanter, 1996; Rustad, 1998). Some experimental evidence suggests that punitive damage awards are erratic and unpredictable (Sunstein, Kahneman, & Schkade, 1998) and that jurors frequently ignore legal constraints on awarding them (Hastie, Schkade, & Payne, 1998).

Damage awards in accident cases have generally increased during the last decade, but they are not as large and have not increased as rapidly as media reports and industry rhetoric suggest, given the media's focus on anecdotes and atypical cases (Bailis & MacCoun, 1996; Daniels & Martin, 1995; Saks, 1992).[6] For instance, the median jury tort award has increased (in nominal, not constant, dollars) by about 50% in the last decade, from about $24,000 to about $35,000 in the average automobile accident case, and from about $266,000 to about $365,000 in the average medical malpractice claim (Moller, 1996; cf. Merritt & Barry, 1999). Increases in awards may be due in large part to differences in the numbers and types of cases being brought before juries, inflation, and increases in plaintiffs' medical costs, rather than to any pro-plaintiff or anti-"deep pocket" bias on the part of the jurors (Daniels & Martin, 1995; Galanter, 1996; Saks, 1992; Vidmar, 1993). Jury awards do vary considerably from place to place and from one type of accident to another, undermining efforts to describe

---

evaluative judgments about whether those filing rates, win rates, and damage awards are too high, too low, or just right. To make such judgments properly, one needs an extrinsic measure of how many injuries *ought* to result in lawsuits and plaintiffs' verdicts, and what the size of those verdicts ought to be—a difficult set of questions (Saks, 1992) which I do not address in this book.

[6] For explanations of why what Galanter (1998) called the "jaundiced view" of the civil justice system—that "out of control" jury verdicts are undermining the legal system and the American economy—persists despite substantial social scientific evidence to the contrary, see Galanter (1998) and Haltom and McCann (1998).

overall trends (Daniels & Martin, 1995). Yet the variability of jury awards is not greater than that of awards that other decision makers (e.g., attorneys) would give in the same situations (Vidmar, 1995; Vidmar & Rice, 1993), contrary to the popular image of juries as wildly unpredictable. In all, the tort liability system compensates accident victims for less than 5% of their economic losses. First-party insurance and workers' compensation make up some of the remaining losses; the victims themselves and their families absorb nearly 40% of medical costs and two thirds of lost wages (Hensler et al., 1991).

FROM WHAT TO HOW AND WHY: STUDYING HOW JURORS TALK ABOUT ACCIDENTS

Although the evidence is fragmentary and not altogether consistent, we do know a considerable amount about blame and compensation in accident cases. Yet there is still much we do not know. In particular, we know much more about outcomes (e.g., verdicts and awards)—the *what* of lay decision making about accidents—than we do about *why* and *how* those outcomes are reached (MacCoun, 1986). Judges, in their opinions, and legal academics, in treatises and scholarly articles, have offered extensive explanations of and justifications for why responsibility for accidents is attributed as it is. The thinking of other participants in and observers of the system—jurors and other nonexperts—is less well understood.

My aim in this book is to add in two ways to what we know about how society blames and compensates for accidents. First, I focus on how laypeople, rather than judges and legal scholars, think about blame and compensation. Second, to shed light not just on the outcomes (of lay decision making), but on how people get to those outcomes, I analyze the way people *talk* about blame and compensation for accidents.

The book presents three sorts of lay discourse about accidents. To begin with, I examine what laypeople themselves say in their role as jurors in accident cases. Although only a very small percentage of formal legal claims result in jury decisions, those judgments exercise a disproportionate influence on the whole system of litigotiation (Galanter, 1993; Saks, 1992) and on our cultural blaming practices in general. And while we lack direct access to what actual accident jurors say during deliberations,[7] jurors in some accident cases have disclosed in postverdict interviews what they (and other jurors) have said. We can also conduct experiments in which people who could be jurors in real cases sit as "mock jurors" deciding

---

[7] Videotapes of actual deliberations in four criminal cases are now available (Levin & Herzberg, 1986; Mason & Klein, 1997), as well as an analysis of the transcript of one contract case (Manzo, 1994), but I am unaware of any recordings of deliberations in accident cases.

simulated accident cases, and we can observe these mock jurors' deliberations. I draw on both of these sources of data in this book.

We can also learn something about how jurors think by analyzing what lawyers say to them at trial. In their opening and closing statements, the advocates for the litigants offer lay jurors alternative ways of conceptualizing the accident story before them, conceptions drawn from the advocates' extensive trial experience. The lawyers' arguments thus provide valuable, albeit indirect, evidence of the ways in which the jurors themselves may be expected to think about the case (Feigenson, 1995).

The tools I use to understand what all of this talk means—to draw inferences from what people say to what they may be thinking—are drawn primarily from social and cognitive psychology. Psychologists have uncovered much evidence about the way people make judgments: our habits of mind; how we perceive, process, and remember information; and how we bring it to bear on social problem solving. I analyze the extent to which jurors' talk about blame and compensation reflects the habits of mind that psychological research has identified.

What emerges from all of these sources of data is a more textured understanding of the way jurors think and talk about responsibility for accidents, one that adds to the largely quantitative findings derived from verdict analyses and controlled experimentation. Although the details of that understanding must wait for the chapters that follow, I summarize here two ideas that inform the individual case studies later in the book. The first is a framework for understanding lay discourse about accidents generally. The second is that lay thinking about accidents is a complex and sometimes contradictory quest for total justice.

THE MULTIDIMENSIONAL NATURE OF LEGAL BLAMING

My analyses of talk about responsibility and compensation for accidents are guided by a framework that identifies the different factors that influence thinking and talking about accidents in various contexts. The framework gives us a way to describe systematically how the discourse of jurors is likely to vary from that of, say, judges. The four components of the framework are (a) common sense; (b) the formal law, including substantive rules as well as legal procedures and institutions; (c) the thinking of experts, most relevantly for these purposes that of judges and legal scholars; and, above all, (d) the facts of the case.

I begin with people's common sense. In trying to understand, for example, why jurors often seem not to follow the instructions they are given by judges (Reifman et al., 1992), we will do well not to start with the legal rules and wonder why jurors fail to understand them completely or fail to apply them perfectly. Rather, we should invert the inquiry and try to describe the mindsets with which jurors approach the case, and then ask (as I do below) how the legal rules and procedural context may affect how jurors bring those mindsets to bear on a particular accident case.

People's judgments about fault and compensation, like other social judgments, are shaped by who we are: our life experiences and attitudes, our habits of mind, our intuitions about how the world works and how it ought to work, and our received wisdom about who is responsible for what in given situations. People's demographic characteristics—their race, gender, ethnicity, socioeconomic status, and so on—are generally not very strong predictors of their judgments in legal cases (Ellsworth, 1993; MacCoun, 1986), notwithstanding the importance that jury consultant businesses and certain high-profile cases have led the public to attribute to them. People's attitudes may be somewhat better predictors of their decisions (Diamond, Saks, & Landsman, 1998; Ellsworth, 1993), especially specific attitudes germane to the subject matter of the case, such as authoritarianism and pro-prosecution bias in criminal cases (Kassin & Wrightsman, 1983; Narby, Cutler, & Moran, 1993) or tort reform attitudes in tort cases (Moran, Cutler, & De Lisa, 1994).

People's general habits of thought and feeling, their patterns of cognitive and emotional responses, promise to tell us much more about how they are likely to make decisions about the world around them. Social psychologists (Fiske & Taylor, 1991; Nisbett & Ross, 1980; Tversky & Kahneman, 1982a) have identified many of the *cognitive heuristics*, or mental rules of thumb, that people use to make sense of things. These include the scripts and schemas that tell a person how things go and how the world is constituted. They also include the inferential tools that, augmenting or displacing normative rules of inferential reasoning, people use to go from what they think they know to what they do not know but need to: availability (relying on the information that comes most easily to mind), representativeness (reasoning by perceived resemblance), the fundamental attribution error (the tendency to attribute others' behavior to the kinds of people we think they are rather than to contingent, situational influences), and many other general habits of mind. Some mental schemas and inferential biases are content specific: For instance, people tend to think that certain sorts of injuries are more likely to have been caused by certain sorts of events (Bornstein & Rajki, 1994; Hart, Evans, Wissler, Feehan, & Saks, 1997). These cognitive habits interact with a person's emotions to shape his or her common-sense judgments about blame and compensation (Feigenson, 1997; Weiner, 1995). We should expect that people's talk about accidents will reflect these features of the way they understand their social world.

The second factor to be considered in analyzing discourse about accidents is the law. When laypeople make decisions as jurors, they do so within a highly specialized setting. The formal legal system purports to set both substantive and procedural constraints on their decisions. In greatly simplified terms, the substantive concepts that apply in accident cases include negligence and strict liability. Under a negligence rule, which the American legal system applies to most kinds of accidents, the injurer is responsible for the victim's injuries only if the injurer proximately caused those injuries by his or her fault or culpable neglect (omitting for the time being the various definitions of "fault"; Keeton, Dobbs, Keeton, & Owen, 1984). Under strict liability, the injurer is liable simply for causing the injuries, regardless of whether the injurer did so carelessly (Keeton et al., 1984). (Under strict products liability, which is something of a hybrid of traditional negligence and strict liability [Rabin, 1997], the product manufacturer is legally responsible only if a defect in the manufacture or design of the product caused the victim's injury.) Jurors are supposed to render their verdict according to the operative legal rule as explained to them by the judge; they are not supposed to find the defendant injurer liable unless they find that the plaintiff has satisfied each and every legal element of the plaintiff's case (and that the defendant has failed to establish any relevant defenses).

Jurors also decide within a particular procedural setting. They listen to testimony and observe other evidence throughout the trial; they hear the advocates' summations; they are instructed in the relevant law; then they are ordered to deliberate as a group and return either a general verdict (for the plaintiff or the defendant, and if for the plaintiff, specifying the amount of damages) or a special verdict (in which jurors also answer specific factual questions essential to the case).[8] All of these features of the official decision-making process may be expected to influence what jurors say and why they say it as they try to decide the case. And the deference generally accorded to the jury, through such devices as the general verdict and limited posttrial and appellate review, allows jurors considerable latitude to use their common sense to implement, and sometimes to oppose, the substantive legal rules.

The third type of influence on discourse about accidents comes from "expert" reasoning, whether policy oriented (instrumentalist, including law and economics) or deontological (corrective and distributive justice). These explicit rationales for assigning responsibility and awarding compensation for accidents, which may be in the form of justifications for or criticisms of broad rules or outcomes in particular cases, come from judges in their opinions and from legal scholars (including judges) in treatises and professional journals. A line of expert reasoning may be adopted by a judge in a particular accident case and thus directly become part of the official

---

[8] Again, this oversimplifies by, among other things, omitting comparative negligence (cases in which both parties are arguably at fault), counterclaims (in which both parties have been injured and each claims that the other party is responsible), and cases involving multiple defendants. Chapter 1 provides some additional detail.

law regarding accidents (which, in turn, shapes juror thinking as explained earlier). Advocates may incorporate expert reasoning, suitably translated for lay consumption, into their arguments to the jury. Or an expert rationale may be represented in the more popular press, read or otherwise absorbed by one or more jurors, and thus become a part of how those jurors think about the case.[9]

The fourth and final force shaping the way jurors talk and think about accidents, probably most important of all, is the case itself: the particular accident in question. It would not be surprising if common-sense intuitions about responsibility for accidents varied in response to the facts of the case, at least as much as in response to any general demographic, attitudinal, cognitive, or emotional biases on the part of the decision maker. Social psychological research shows that the evidence is far more important than extralegal biases in shaping juror decisions (Reskin & Visher, 1986; Visher, 1987).[10] The facts of the case are far more than the stage on which the jurors enact their role as decision makers, although far less than a script from which jurors can simply read off their judgment. We can best appreciate the multidimensional nature of legal blaming by looking closely at the facts of particular cases, which I do in the second part of the book.

THE COMMON SENSE OF ACCIDENTS: "TOTAL JUSTICE"

Three general features characterize lay judgment when it is applied to particular accident cases and filtered through the procedural and substantive constraints of the legal system. The first is that people tend to conceive of accidents as melodramas and the doing of justice as the righting of an imbalance (or the distribution of accident costs) between the good guy(s) and the bad guy(s) (Fischhoff, 1985; Wilkins & Patterson, 1987). The second is that people's common sense about accidents, like their common sense generally, is a system in dynamic tension, containing apparently contradictory impulses and susceptible to being pulled in various directions on the basis of different, sometimes relatively minor, contextual cues (such

---

[9] Although this is not a focus of this book, I should also note that common sense can influence expert discourse: Judicial and even academic experts cannot help but include common-sense thinking in the premises of their arguments and, often, in their assumptions about the world to which they apply their theories.

[10] Whether the common sense of accidents varies more systematically by case *type* (as opposed to the idiosyncratic facts of particular cases) remains to be seen, although some support for this hypothesis comes from research on media coverage of risks of accident harm: The type of hazard (e.g., arising from voluntary [recreational] activities, workaday accidents, technological hazards, or illnesses) determines how the media allocates blame for the harm (Singer & Endreny, 1993). In addition, other research indicates that only interactions between juror demographic characteristics and case type, and not juror characteristics alone, have any significant effect on juror judgments of liability and damages (see Bonazzoli, 1998; Denove & Imwinkelried, 1995). I pursue this issue further in chapter 4.

as variations in the evidence, in the lawyers' arguments, in the form of instructions, or in the decision-making process). The third is that jurors strive to give total justice, which is often consistent with, but sometimes in conflict with, the outcomes that legal rules or legal experts predict.

When people use their common sense to think about responsibility for accidents, they tend to think in simplified, personalized, moralized, and dichotomized terms. In general, people prefer monocausal explanations to multicausal ones; people are inclined to attribute conduct to "the kind of person" the actor is rather than to the circumstances in which the actor finds himself or herself; people are prone to single out as the cause of events the preceding conduct that is most morally blameworthy; and people tend to divide their simplified world of personal agency into good guys and bad guys. In short, bad outcomes such as accidents are attributed to bad behaviors, which are thought to emanate from bad people; and if one bad person caused the accident, then it follows from the principle of monocausality that no one else did. Accident stories, in this common-sense way of thinking, tend to take the shape of *melodramas*. And in building its conceptions of how accidents occur, common sense is informed not only by the evidence but also by everyday knowledge about how the world works, derived from life experience, movies, and other media, as well as from the lawyers' arguments (Feigenson, 1995; P. Meyer, 1994; Sherwin, 1994). Jurors may be inclined to think about accidents in simplified, personalized, and moralized ways because that is a predominant way in which the culture at large constructs its accounts of accidents and many other kinds of events.

The second general feature of the common sense of accidents is that it is complex and contradictory (Galanter, 1996), like common sense in general (Geertz, 1983). For instance, juror thinking and decisions appear to feature both anti-plaintiff and anti-defendant biases. Pro-plaintiff sympathy on the part of jurors is often presumed (Bovbjerg, Sloan, Dor, & Hsieh, 1991; Denove & Imwinkelried, 1995) but has been shown only infrequently (Bornstein, 1991, 1994), and evidence of anti-plaintiff sentiment is at least equally compelling (Feigenson, Park, & Salovey, 1997; Hans & Lofquist, 1992; Thomas & Parpal, 1987). A "deep pocket" effect —bias against wealthier defendants, such as physicians or corporations— has been shown in some studies (Chin & Peterson, 1985; Hammitt, Carroll, & Relles, 1985) but refuted in others (MacCoun, 1996; Vidmar, 1995; Vidmar, Lee, Cohen, & Stewart, 1994). In every case, no doubt, jurors believe that they are simply applying their common sense to the facts of the matter (Geertz, 1983), but what pushes their decisions or their decision-making methods in one direction rather than another may be the smallest of situational cues—variations in the evidence (Visher, 1987), the lawyers' arguments (Reyes, Thompson, & Bower, 1980; Sigal, Braden-Maguire, Hayden, & Mosley, 1985), or the way in which the process of deciding is structured (Greene & Loftus, 1985; Horowitz & Bordens, 1990).

By way of analogy, research on public opinion explains the great variability in responses to polls by positing that most people have ill-defined (if any) views about the subject matter on which they are questioned, so that their responses can be swayed by the form and order of questions and by whatever other relevant information is most immediately accessible to them at the time (Zaller, 1992). Similarly, jurors in accident cases are not anti-defendant or anti-plaintiff across the board, nor are they simply capable or incapable of following judicial instructions. Rather, their substantive judgments and the methods they use to reach them are highly dependent on how they construe the objects of their judgments—the parties and the story of the accident—and on the decision-making context.

Both of these features of the common sense of accidents—its tendency to melodramatize, on the one hand, and its complex and contradictory nature, on the other—are consistent with what social psychologists Lee Ross and Richard Nisbett (1991) identified as the basic descriptive principles of social judgment in general. Ross and Nisbett pointed out that people tend to attribute behavior (and hence responsibility for outcomes) to actors' dispositions rather than to situational constraints; social behavior, by contrast, is in fact greatly subject to situational factors, even quite subtle ones, so that there is generally much less individual consistency in behavior across situations than people believe. People also tend to underestimate the extent to which their own subjectivity affects their impressions of the behavior of others; instead, observers tend to believe that their interpretations of others' conduct are simple "read-offs" of an objective reality populated by people with relatively stable dispositions, rather than contingent and uncertain judgments about highly situational conduct. Third, Ross and Nisbett described individual psyches and social units as systems in dynamic tension, such that small changes in the situation can have great effects on behavior (and conversely, great changes may have little or no effect, being negated by countervailing forces of unsuspected strength).

Plainly, understanding accidents in terms of personality-driven melodramas is consistent with the bias toward dispositional accounts of others' behavior that Ross and Nisbett (1991) have identified. And the contradictory nature of jurors' thinking about accidents suggests that their common sense in this regard, like their common-sense perception of the social world generally, is a system in tension, containing conflicting impulses and intuitions that can be differently activated depending on the situation.

What happens when people's dispositional, melodramatic conceptions of accidents are filtered through the mechanisms of formal legal decision making? Let us consider an analogy to lay versus expert psychological judgment. Ross and Nisbett (1991) observed that people's social judgments in general are often right by expert standards, but for the wrong reasons.

Dispositional attributions, which give insufficient weight to the base rate or situational information on which a social scientist would depend, often yield correct enough predictions about others' behavior (indeed, were heuristic thinking not often correct, it is hard to see how it and the species would have survived). Nevertheless, lay habits of thought may lead to error when the observed situation is especially unfamiliar or complex (Margolis, 1996).

We may expect that the same would be true when lay legal judgments are compared with those of legal professionals. Jurors, despite their misunderstanding of the relevant legal rules (Reifman et al., 1992), often reason their way to judgments about responsibility and compensation for accidents that are correct enough by the expert measure of how judges would have decided (Kalven & Zeisel, 1966). Jurors' decisions are often congruent with substantive legal doctrine and the goals of tort law that experts have identified, such as optimum compensation (Dewees et al., 1996) and efficient deterrence (Baron & Ritov, 1993).

Sometimes, however, lay judgment diverges from expert standards. These apparent errors are commonly attributed to jurors' ignorance, inattentiveness, or unwarranted emotionalism (Daniels & Martin, 1995). Although these factors may play a role in some cases, most research shows that jurors take their job very seriously and are quite competent at finding facts, if not also at understanding law (Hans & Vidmar, 1986). Ross and Nisbett's (1991) work suggests a different explanation for occasional lay–expert divergence, as well as for their frequent agreement. As a summary principle, I venture that jurors strive to do *total justice* in the case before them. While total justice ordinarily leads to decisions that are justifiable in terms of formal law or expert policy, it may also lead jurors to diverge from those standards, especially when the situation is unfamiliar or complex.

By "total justice," I mean that jurors are more concerned with making things come out right than with strictly following the relevant legal rules. Perhaps a better way to put it is that jurors *try* to follow the relevant law but are guided by the total justice imperative as they do so. And total justice goes both to what jurors *think* and to what they *feel* about the verdict.

Jurors try to give a kind of justice that is total in at least five senses of the word. First, they want to *balance accounts between the parties*. They view tort liability as a contest between the plaintiff and the defendant, one of whom must be responsible (Feigenson, 1995); and they tend to think about responsibility for accidents in terms of just deserts rather than social utility (although the two may coincide; Baron & Ritov, 1993; Gilles, 1994b; Keating, 1996). In short, jurors see doing justice in the accident case as the proper response to a morality play (Stachenfeld & Nicholson,

1996), in which the good guy triumphs precisely to the extent that the bad guy gets his or her comeuppance.

Second, jurors want to give a kind of justice that is total in the sense that it incorporates *all information they think is relevant*. For instance, jurors are prone to take information about the parties and their motives into account in deciding causal responsibility (Alicke, 1992), even information that is legally irrelevant to that question. And jurors' widely noted predilection for ignoring instructions not to consider inadmissible evidence seems to apply only to information that jurors think is relevant and reliable but is being excluded on procedural grounds (Kassin & Sommers, 1997). If jurors believe that the evidence has been ruled inadmissible because it is unreliable, then they are capable of not considering it. But if they think that it adds to their knowledge of the world of the case before them, they will be inclined to use it.

Third, jurors' justice is total in the sense that they reach their decisions through a *holistic process*, eliding distinctions among elements of the case or decision-making steps that the law asks them to keep separate. Instead, jurors tend to make judgments about overall responsibility that may ignore or give improper weight to legally relevant considerations and may take into account legally irrelevant ones. For instance, jurors may "commingle" elements of the plaintiff's claim so that a very strong perception of blameworthiness somehow makes up for a weaker case on causation (Nagareda, 1998; Sanders, 1998). And they may blur distinctions between judgments of responsibility and judgments of compensation, so that the former is improperly influenced by perceptions of the severity of the injury and the latter is improperly influenced by perceptions of blameworthiness (Feigenson et al., 1997).

Fourth, jurors' justice is total in a *phenomenological* sense. Jurors want to decide the accident case in a way that reduces or eliminates the bad feelings that perceived injustice arouses (Mikula, Scherer, & Athenstaedt, 1998). They want their emotions and their thoughts to constitute a satisfying whole, and in the course of deliberations, they are concerned that not only they but also the other jurors "feel right" about their decision (Levin & Herzberg, 1986).

Fifth and finally, jurors' justice is total in an *interpersonal* sense. Jurors are guided by the group norm of appearing to be reasonable and open to persuasion, components of procedurally fair deliberations that enhance their sense of respect within the group and hence their self-esteem (H. Smith & Tyler, 1997; Tyler & Smith, 1999). Yet at least some jurors are also driven to persuade others. To reconcile this tension between the individual need to persuade and the group norm of appearing open to persuasion, jurors may strive for a common or shared discourse that creates at least the appearance of mutual respectfulness while allowing would-be persuaders to further their aims by appealing to shared mental constructs (Ruscher, Hammer, & Hammer, 1996).

Jurors' justice in accident cases is reminiscent of what has been observed in criminal cases (Fletcher, 1994), small claims court (Conley & O'Barr, 1990), and other legal arenas. Jurors use their habits of thought and feeling to seek a closure that will set things right, that will correct the imbalance that the wrongdoing of one or more parties has created. Certainly the legal system permits and to some extent even encourages this kind of holistic decision making. But even when jurors' decisions appear to conflict with the dictates of substantive law or expertise, we would do well to look for the source of the discrepancy in these same holistic habits of thought and feeling, rather than in juror incompetence or bias.

To say that jurors envision accidents as melodramas, that their intuitions are conflicting, and that they strive to do total justice is, however, to describe only part of the picture, perhaps the less interesting part. We also want to know the variations on the main themes—how the general principles play out in specific situations. How does the fundamental attribution error, for instance, lead jurors to think about responsibility for a particular accident? Which of the contradictory inclinations about justice are likely to be evoked more strongly by a given accident story? When does total justice diverge from legal (or other) norms and why? Only the close study of how jurors think and talk about blame in particular cases, to which the second half of this book is devoted, can address these questions.

THE PLAN OF THE BOOK

The first half of this book elaborates the fourfold framework for analyzing discourse about accidents, providing the background for the case studies in the second half. In chapter 1, I discuss the legal rules and expert rationales pertaining to accidents. I briefly summarize the law of accidents, both substantive (negligence and strict liability) and procedural. I then sketch the leading expert justifications for accident liability (fairness and social utility). The rules and rationales will help readers to understand the context within which accident jurors reason toward decisions and will provide criteria for evaluating those decisions.

Chapters 2 through 4 present the social psychology of common-sense thinking about accidents. First I break the psychological dynamics down into their details. Chapter 2 describes the psychology of social judgment in general and surveys the habits of thought that shape people's decisions about responsibility and compensation. Chapter 3 surveys the psychology of emotions and the role of specific emotions in thinking and decision making about accidents. (Further discussion of the role of emotion on social judgments may be found in the Appendix.) Chapter 4 reassembles the pieces to construct an overview of how jurors think about accidents, integrating the three general features of the common sense of accidents noted earlier: accidents as melodrama, conflicting intuitions, and total justice.

In the second half of the book, chapters 5 through 7 present case studies of lay discourse about accidents. Together they yield a wealth of illustrations of how everyday habits of thought and feeling manifest themselves in accident talk and decision making. Chapter 5 describes the speech of advocates to juries in two workplace accident cases. The lawyers' closing arguments are valuable sources of data about the ways people think and talk about accidents, because they present ways of understanding blame and compensation that are designed to be not merely acceptable but persuasive to jurors. In the first case, a truck driver was seriously injured when he slipped and fell from the back of his flatbed truck while putting a tarpaulin onto some heavy machinery he was picking up from the defendant's plant. He sued the defendant on the ground that the defendant's employees contributed to the accident by not helping him with the tarp. In the second case, a young railroad worker was crushed to death between the boxcar on which he was riding while conducting a backup maneuver and another line of cars sitting on a different track. His estate sued the railroad, arguing that it had failed to give the worker adequate training before assigning him to conduct and had failed to mark a crucial crossover switch. In both cases, the parties agreed on the central facts but argued about questions of duty, comparative fault, and causation—all crucial elements of the negligence case. From the lawyers' arguments, we can ascertain different ways of applying everyday habits of thought and feeling to do justice in workplace accident cases.

In chapter 6, I examine not only lawyers' arguments to jurors but also the jurors' own words, and come closer to bridging the gap between the lawyers' rhetoric and the jurors' own thoughts about responsibility for accidents. My focus is a case in which the plaintiff was seriously hurt when a teenage employee of a national fast-food chain, driving home after working a midnight shift, fell asleep at the wheel and crashed into the plaintiff's truck head-on. The plaintiff sued the fast-food chain, arguing that by allowing the teenager to work until he was sleep-deprived, it unreasonably increased the risk of harm to others on the road. I try to make sense of the jurors' words by putting them in the context of the arguments the lawyers made to the jurors, showing that most jurors agreed with the plaintiff's lawyer's portrayal of this accident as a melodrama.

In chapter 7 I analyze lay talk about accidents, not after the fact but during the decision-making process. The data I use are the deliberations of mock jurors as they decide a typical claim of malpractice against a doctor for the delayed diagnosis of breast cancer. The patient's estate claimed that her doctor did not diagnose the cancer in a timely fashion. The doctor argued in response that the patient herself was to blame for not returning to his office for a scheduled follow-up visit, which prevented him from referring her for the biopsy that would have yielded a definitive diagnosis. The deliberations reveal how jurors apply their everyday habits of thought, combined with their assumptions about doctors, patients, and breast cancer, to understand the case in a way that conforms partially, but not entirely, to the responsibility judgments of medicolegal experts.

To be sure, the analysis of individual examples of discourse about accidents yields a limited basis for generalization. I present only a small number of case studies of accident talk, without any claim that these cases are typical or representative of the whole picture. Indeed, neither the experimental social psychological evidence adduced in the first half of the book nor the case studies examined in the second half *prove*, strictly speaking, that accident trials are melodramas or that jurors always or usually think in terms of total justice. Future research, which I hope this book will inspire, should test more systematically, using a broader sample of data, the conditions in which accident jurors may be more or less likely to think in melodramatic terms, or to display one or more of the characteristics of total justice. For now, I offer melodrama and total justice as suggestive constructs that illuminate what is observed in the behavior of accident jurors and the lawyers who try to persuade them. I believe, moreover, that the case and fact specificity of my analyses is a strength, not a weakness. As noted, there is convergent evidence that judgments about responsibility and damages in accident cases depend heavily on the facts of the particular accident. In that sense, there is no "typical" accident case for our purposes. And the focus on a very few cases permits the kind of lengthy and thick description of context and discourse from which a deeper understanding of ordinary thought and talk can emerge. In any event, all of the case studies in the second half of the book are set against the background of the quantitative knowledge we do have about how blame and compensation are determined.

Finally, in chapter 8, I explore some of the broader social and cultural implications of the ways jurors think and talk about accidents. Conceiving of accidents as melodramas allows us to believe that we are doing something about the pervasive risks of accidental harm in modern life even as it diverts our attention from the persistent, systemic causes of those accidents. And understanding juror justice in accident cases as total justice (including but not limited to melodrama) may permit a better appreciation of the role of juries in the civil justice system than either popular critics or social scientific defenders of the civil jury have offered.

In sum, this book is intended to show how talk about accidents reflects thoughts and feelings about accidents. The best way to approach both how jurors talk and how they think and feel is to use the tools of social psychology, which will help us to understand jurors' common-sense views. Talking and thinking about accidents is a function not of common sense alone but also of the context in which that common sense operates, a context that includes the relevant legal rules, expert reasoning, and the facts of the case. Finally, the way jurors think and talk about accidents is a complicated matter, best explored through studies of particular cases. It is my hope that these case studies will enhance our understanding of how jurors try to turn accidental suffering into justice, and of the place of common sense justice in our legal system.

1

LEGAL RULES AND EXPERT RATIONALES: ACCIDENT LAW AND PHILOSOPHY

Most of this book is devoted to explaining the influence of common-sense habits of thought and feeling and the specific factual context of the case on jurors' judgments about accidents. In this chapter I briefly discuss two other sources of "pull" on lay thinking about accidents: the formal law governing accidents and the expert justifications proffered by legal scholars and philosophers for assigning responsibility and awarding damages. Plainly these two sources would be expected to exercise much greater influence on how judges and legal scholars reason about accidents than on how nonexperts do. Yet to understand how laypeople think and talk about accidents when they sit as jurors, one must take the formal law of accidents, both substantive and procedural, into account. It will also be interesting to examine the degree to which ordinary people's reasoning about blame and compensation matches the discourse of jurisprudes.

I intend only the most cursory summary of the rules and rationales of tort law, merely to provide some background for nonlawyers and to flesh out the fourfold framework of analysis sketched in the introduction. Lawyers, law professors, and law students may wish to skip this chapter and go directly to the social psychology of thinking about accidents in chapters 2 through 4. For those who desire more detail than this brief chapter provides, I mention in the course of the chapter a number of accessible condensations of the vast corpus of works on the rules and rationales of accident law.

THE LAW OF ACCIDENTS—SUBSTANCE

Under the common law, that is, the law declared by judges in the absence of applicable statutes, regulations, or other enacted law, one who unintentionally injures another person may, in general, be held liable to the injured person if and only if he or she causes the injury carelessly. This is the doctrine of *negligence*. In certain circumstances, the injurer may be liable even if the harm occurred despite his or her careful behavior; in such situations, the law of *strict liability* applies. Even if the injurer is *prima facie* liable under either of these theories of recovery, his or her liability may be reduced or eliminated if he or she can prove one or more *defenses*, usually based on some conduct by the victim that contributed to the accident. Any of these basic rules may be modified or replaced in any given case by a relevant statute or other enacted law.

Negligence

Most legal historians believe that, in Anglo-American common law until the early 19th century, those who unintentionally injured others were usually liable even if they acted carefully, unless the harm was an "inevitable accident" (Gilles, 1994a). Since about the middle of the 19th century, negligence has been the basic rule of legal responsibility for unintentional harm, although, as we will see below, there are many exceptions.

To recover on a claim of negligence, according to textbook tort law, the plaintiff must show that the defendant (a) owed the plaintiff a duty to take reasonable care for the plaintiff's safety, (b) breached that duty by acting carelessly, and thereby (c) caused (d) the injuries for which the plaintiff seeks recovery (Keeton et al., 1984). I briefly discuss each of these elements of the *prima facie* case of negligence. The discussion is, of course, highly simplified, ignoring for the most part the depths and complexities of each element and the interrelations among the elements.

Duty

Whatever we are doing, the law obligates us not to do it in a way that puts others at unreasonable risk of harm. By contrast, we generally have no obligation to keep others from coming to harm from sources other than ourselves. That is, the common law does not require us to help those in harm's way—to be Good Samaritans—although statutes in a number of states impose limited duties to help others (e.g., to render reasonable assistance at the scene of an automobile collision; Epstein, 1995). In recent decades, the duty to act carefully has been expanded to make certain persons or entities legally responsible for harms directly caused not by them, but by third persons, in circumstances in which the defendant knew or should have known that his or her own conduct unreasonably increased the risk of harm from the third party. For instance, those who provide alcohol to people they know or should know are too drunk to drive safely may be held legally responsible to persons injured or killed by the intoxicated driver (*Vesely v. Sager*, 1971). Liability is also imposed where the defendant is held to have a "special relationship" with either the third party or the potential victim that triggers a duty to take reasonable steps to control the risk to the potential victim (American Law Institute, 1965). So, for instance, a commercial landowner may be liable to a tenant or guest assaulted on its property by a third party if the landowner has not taken reasonable security precautions to protect tenants and guests from such assaults (*Kline v. 1500 Massachusetts Avenue Apartment Corp.*, 1970).

Breach

The law has developed several different ways for judges and juries to determine just what constitutes careless (or careful) behavior under the circumstances. One is to compare the party's behavior with that of a hypothetical *reasonable person*, who acts in an ordinarily prudent fashion to avoid putting others at undue risk of injury (e.g., F. James, 1951). Indeed, the standard jury instruction (see below) is phrased in these terms (Devitt, Blackmar, & Wolff, 1987; Gilles, 1994b). But this definition is so open-ended that judges have sought to clarify the notion of reasonable care in other ways (although they do not routinely incorporate these clarifications in their instructions to jurors).

One such conception defines reasonable behavior as *cost-effective accident avoidance*. The basic idea is that the law should encourage people to behave (and reasonable people do behave) in an economically rational way —maximizing scarce resources by taking care to avoid accident losses, but only up to the point at which extra care costs no more than the additional losses thereby avoided. Defining reasonable care in cost–benefit terms gives potential injurers an incentive to act in the desired fashion, by finding them negligent (and therefore potentially liable for the losses they cause) if and only if they could have avoided the accident (whether by implementing safety devices or just by paying more attention) at a cost lower than the expected cost of the accidents that would have occurred *without* the precautions. Thus, where B = the burden or cost of taking precautions, P = the likelihood of an accident without the precautions, and L = the cost of any such accident, the person who causes injury is negligent if and only if he did not spend B when B < P × L. (This definition of reasonable care as economically optimal care is often referred to as the "Learned Hand test," after the federal judge who explained it in an opinion half a century ago; *United States v. Carroll Towing Co.*, 1947.) I will have a little more to say about this cost–benefit conception of negligence below, when I discuss expert rationales for tort liability. For now, readers may note that the idea of reasonable care as cost-efficient accident avoidance overlaps considerably with the traditional conception of the "reasonable person," and that many judicial opinions predating Judge Hand's construed reasonable care in what look to us today like cost–benefit terms (Epstein, 1995).

A third way in which reasonableness is understood in accident law is by reference to the behavior that is *customary* for a given industry or type of activity. The underlying assumption is that those whose livelihood depends on engaging in a regular course of activity are most familiar with that activity and will strike the most sensible balance between safety and profits. For the most part, however, the law does not simply defer to industry to set its own standard of care. As the same Judge Hand wrote elsewhere, "in most cases reasonable prudence is in fact common prudence; but ... a whole calling may have unduly lagged in the adoption of new and available devices" (*The T.J. Hooper*, 1932, p. 740). Thus, conformance to custom is generally strong but not dispositive evidence of reasonable behavior. A leading exception is medical care, with respect to which customary practice is reasonable practice (Weiler, 1991). In all activities, acting *less* safely than is customary is strong evidence of carelessness (Keeton et al., 1984).

Finally, reasonable care under the circumstances of the case may be defined partly or entirely by *statute*. Where the legislature has identified certain conduct as posing an undue risk of harm, courts will defer to the legislature's judgment. Hence, generally speaking, if a person violates a statute (or regulation) enacted to protect a class of people from a certain sort of harm and thereby brings about the kind of injury the legislature sought to avoid by enacting the law, the person is considered "negligent *per se*" and, in the absence of legitimate defenses, is liable to the victim (Keeton et al., 1984).

Causation

For an injurer to be liable to the accident victim, the injurer's careless act must actually cause the plaintiff's harm. This is known as *cause-in-fact*. A negligent act is considered the cause-in-fact of the harm if the act was *necessary* to bring about the harm, that is, if the harm would not have occurred "but for" the negligent act. Because determining this requires engaging in counterfactual speculation (what would have happened if the act had *not* occurred; see discussion in chapter 2), courts often accept the somewhat less rigorous showing that the negligence "probably" caused the plaintiff's harm (Epstein, 1995).

In unusual cases in which two independent acts or events, neither a "but for" cause in itself, unite to injure the plaintiff, liability will attach to the negligent act if it was *sufficient* to bring about the harm. For example, a railroad that negligently set a fire that joined with another fire of unknown origin to burn the plaintiff's property was held liable to the plaintiff Either fire alone could have destroyed the property, so neither was a necessary cause of the harm, but each alone was sufficient (*Kingston v. Chicago & N.W. Ry.*, 1927). In addition, some states have abandoned the "but for" requirement to allow a patient who receives negligent medical care to receive compensation even if it was more likely than not that the patient *would not have survived* had the physician used proper care, so long as the plaintiff can prove that the defendant's negligence deprived the patient of a substantial *loss of chance* of recovery (*Herskovits v. Group Health Cooperative*, 1983; for further discussion of this rule, see chapter 7).

In other cases of joint causation, in which the plaintiff was injured by the act of one or more of several defendants but is not in a position to determine which, courts may relax the requirements still further, not obligating the plaintiff to prove that an identifiable defendant caused his or her injuries. For instance, women who claimed to have suffered ovarian cancers and other ailments as a result of their mothers' ingestion of a miscarriage-preventative drug decades earlier were permitted to recover by showing that the defendant drug companies in the aggregate accounted for a "substantial share" of the market in the drug; each company's liability was limited to its share of the market (*Sindell v. Abbott Laboratories*, 1980).

Every act sets in motion or continues an infinite chain of consequences. Those who act carelessly are not, however, held responsible for every outcome that would not have occurred but for their negligence; at some point, it becomes unfair or impractical to burden people with vast repercussions for merely careless conduct. Instead, the law holds negligent actors liable only for the *proximate* effects of their negligence. There are two dominant (and overlapping) ways of determining when the defendant's negligence is a proximate cause of the plaintiff's harm. Under one, defendants are held responsible only for the *foreseeable* consequences of their negligence; that is, when the kind of injury that the defendant caused was the sort of thing that the defendant should have foreseen might result from its actions and was one of the reasons for describing the defendant's conduct as careless in the first place (*Palsgraf v. Long Island R.R.*, 1928).[1] Under the other, defendants are held responsible whenever their negligence leads

---

[1] Because one ordinarily owes a duty to others only to avoid putting them at risk of harms that could reasonably be foreseen as a result of one's acts, the "foreseeability" conception effectively collapses the proximate cause inquiry into the duty element of negligence, as Judge (later Justice) Benjamin Cardozo argued in *Palsgraf*.

by a *direct* causal chain to the harm, regardless of whether that harm was reasonably foreseeable (*In re Polemis & Furness, Withy & Co.*, 1921).[2]

In most cases, the plaintiff's injuries follow both directly and foreseeably upon the defendant's negligent act, and so the defendant is unable to avail himself or herself of either proximate cause limitation on liability. The carelessness of someone who drives too fast and is therefore unable to stop in time to avoid the car in front, for instance, both foreseeably and directly contributes to the harm to that car and its occupants; there is no reason *not* to hold the careless driver responsible for the damages he or she has caused. In unusual circumstances, however (and torts casebooks are full of these), in which the defendant's negligence brings about the plaintiff's injuries only through the intervention of some peculiar and unexpected chain of events, the defendant may not be liable even though the plaintiff would not have been harmed but for the original negligent act.[3] In general, both conceptions of proximate cause are sufficiently vague to allow judges and juries in these odd circumstances to hold the defendant responsible or not, as their sense of justice dictates.

Injury

Accident victims may in general recover for all losses proximately caused by the injurer's carelessness, including medical expenses, lost wages, and pain and suffering. Where the injurer's conduct is not merely careless but reckless or worse, the plaintiff also may recover punitive damages. *Survival* and *wrongful death statutes* in most jurisdictions allow the estate or

---

[2] According to the widely recognized approach to legal causation adopted by the *Restatement of the Law (Second): Torts* (American Law Institute, 1965), the defendant is liable if his or her negligence was a *substantial factor* in bringing about the plaintiff's harm. The substantial factor inquiry looks more like a determination of cause-in-fact (for instance, it includes the requirement of "but for" causation and the exceptions thereto discussed in the text), but it also includes considerations corresponding to proximate cause. Specifically, the Restatement generally adopts the directness rather than the foreseeability rule (except with regard to intervening causes).

[3] So, for instance, the owner of a ship that carelessly discharged oil into a harbor was held not liable to the owner of a dock when the dockworkers, repairing another ship, let molten metal fall onto a rag in the water, setting the now oily water aflame and burning the dock (*The Wagon Mound [No. 1]*, 1961). It was argued that the dock fire, though certainly caused in fact by the defendant's negligent discharge of oil, and perhaps also a sufficiently "direct" result of that negligence, was not a reasonably foreseeable consequence of that negligence, and thus not a loss to be charged to the defendant. In a later case arising from the same incident, the owner of the ship that released the oil into the harbor *was* held liable to the owner of another ship that was consumed in the same fire (*The Wagon Mound [No. 2]*, 1967). Certainly the harm in this case was no more direct a result of the negligence than in the first case. The different outcome was probably due to the fact that the plaintiff in the second case, the owner of the destroyed ship, presented the court with better evidence that furnace oil may burn when spread on water. The owner of the destroyed ship did so in response to the first court's adoption of a foreseeability test, and because he, unlike the dockowner in the first case, need not have feared that the foreseeability argument would be turned around to his disadvantage (i.e., in the first case, if the defendant shipowner could have foreseen that furnace oil on water could cause a fire, why shouldn't the dockowner have foreseen this as well before he recommenced the welding that directly led to the fire?).

beneficiaries of a fatally injured accident victim to recover damages, including the income that the decedent would have generated throughout his working life. Many states also allow recovery for the loss of the decedent's companionship and the like (Keeton et al., 1984).

Strict Liability

In certain situations, a person may be held legally responsible for unintentionally injuring another even if he has acted with reasonable care. The conduct of *abnormally dangerous* (or *ultrahazardous*) activities furnishes an example. Strict liability for the accidental escape of fire, animals, and other potentially dangerous things one might bring onto one's property dates back several centuries, the classic exposition of the rule being the mid-19th century English case of *Rylands v. Fletcher* (1868).[4] The best contemporary examples of strict liability for abnormally dangerous activities are blasting and crop-dusting. The underlying rationale for strict liability arising from these sorts of activities seems to be that when one chooses to engage in an activity that is so disproportionately risky to others—that puts others in harm's way even when the activity is carefully done—one should have to bear the risk of any harms that result (Keeton et al., 1984).

Around the middle of the 20th century, another important category of strict liability arose: *products liability*. Generally speaking, a manufacturer, seller, or distributor of a product is legally responsible for injuries caused by a *defect* in its product. A particular item may be considered defective if it fails to conform to the manufacturer's own standards (a *manufacturing* or *production* defect), regardless of whether the defect could have been avoided by the exercise of greater care in manufacturing. In addition, a product made and marketed as intended may be considered defective if the foreseeable risks of harm it poses could have been avoided by adopting a reasonable alternative design (a *design* defect) or if adequate instructions or warnings would have reduced foreseeable risks of harm (a *warning* defect; American Law Institute, 1997). The basic rationales for strict products liability are that in modern society, consumers often have little practical control over the features of the products they use, and hence over their exposure to accident risks from the product, and that the manufacturer is

---

[4] In *Rylands*, the defendant had independent contractors construct a reservoir on his property to provide water for a mill. Underneath the reservoir were abandoned mine shafts, which led toward the neighboring property, on which the plaintiff was mining coal. The reservoir, half-filled, gave way, and the water flooded through the abandoned shafts and into the plaintiff's mine shafts, damaging the mining operations. The court held that although the defendant was not at fault for not knowing about the abandoned shafts or for choosing the contractors (who themselves were negligent for not taking steps to avoid the risk of flooding), he was liable to the plaintiff because the construction of the reservoir and the ensuing accumulation of water was a "nonnatural" use of his property, which he undertook at his own risk.

in a better position than the consumer to decide whether additional investments in product safety are worthwhile in terms of accident costs avoided. Many aspects of products liability law, as well as the justifications for that law, are matters of continuing controversy.

Another, traditional form of strict liability deserves brief mention: the liability of an employer (or "master") for the tortious conduct of its employees (or "servants") done within the scope of their employment. This form of *vicarious* liability is commonly referred to by a Latin phrase, *respondeat superior* ("let the master answer [for the behavior of the servant]"). Note that although the *employer's* liability is strict, in the sense that the plaintiff need not prove that the employer was negligent in hiring, training, or supervising the employee (any of which could also be the basis of a claim against the employer), the plaintiff must still prove that the *employee's* negligence caused the injury of which he or she complains. The best contemporary justifications for *respondeat superior* are that, as a matter of policy, business enterprises should internalize the costs of employees' torts to outsiders as a cost of doing business (the employer is in a better position than the injured person to spread the costs of such accidents through increased prices or insurance; Keeton et al., 1984), and that it is unfair for an enterprise to avoid the costs its activities cause to others by delegating their performance to subordinates less likely to be able to pay those costs.

Affirmative Defenses

Defendants in accident cases, like those in any other civil case, may seek to avoid liability not only by arguing that the plaintiff cannot prove one or more essential elements of his or her claim(s), but also by showing *additional* facts that relieve the defendant of responsibility for the plaintiff's injuries. These are called *affirmative defenses*. Here I mention only the two that derive from the plaintiff's own accident-related behavior: contributory fault and assumption of risk.

Contributory Fault

In many cases, the plaintiff's own carelessness may have helped to bring about the accident. Traditionally, an accident victim whose own lack of reasonable care contributed in any way to his or her injuries was completely prevented from recovering damages from the defendant for those injuries. This was the doctrine of *contributory negligence*. Almost all states today, however, whether by common (i.e., judge-made) law or by statute, have adopted the doctrine of *comparative negligence*: The plaintiff's recovery is reduced in proportion to his or her own negligent contribution to the accident. Comparative negligence rules take one of two forms. One is *pure* comparative negligence, in which the plaintiff may recover some portion of the damages from a culpable defendant regardless of how blameworthy the plaintiff himself or herself is. The second, and more common, is *limited* comparative negligence, in which the plaintiff may recover his or her proportionately reduced share of damages only up to the point at which his or her carelessness equals that of the defendant. If the plaintiff's negligence contributed more to the accident than the defendant's (in some jurisdictions, as much as the defendant's), then the plaintiff recovers nothing, just as under contributory negligence.

Contributory fault is generally not a defense to a claim of strict liability. Thus, a consumer who is injured using a product in other than its intended fashion is not barred from recovery unless the misuse is "unforeseeable" or "rare and unusual" (Keeton et al., 1984).

Assumption of Risk

A person who knowingly and willingly puts himself or herself at risk of injury from the defendant's conduct cannot recover if that risk is realized. The plaintiff has, in effect, *consented* to the possibility of being hurt by the defendant. A spectator at a baseball game who has the opportunity to buy a seat in a protected portion of the stadium but instead chooses to sit in an unscreened section cannot recover if he or she is hit by a batted ball (Keeton et al., 1984). Someone who contracts lung cancer from smoking cigarettes cannot recover from the cigarette manufacturer if the judge or jury determines that the smoker willingly smoked despite knowing the risk of disease. As both of these examples illustrate, the court may infer knowledge of the risk from the circumstances. "Everyone knows" that baseballs are hit into the stands, and knowledge of the warning label on packs of cigarettes sold in the last 30-odd years will be imputed to smokers regardless of whether they have actually read or understood the label. By the same token, suspicion that the plaintiff did not undertake the risk in a truly knowing or voluntary fashion may defeat the assumption of risk defense. Smokers, for example, may show that they became addicted to nicotine before the warning labels were required, and therefore that they did not knowingly and willingly encounter the risk of cancer (Nagareda, 1998).[5]

---

[5] Assumption of risk is distinct from contributory fault; the same behavior by the plaintiff may constitute negligence, assumption of risk, both, or neither. For instance, it may be quite reasonable for a person to proceed in the face of a known risk already created by the defendant—for example, to walk across a sidewalk covered with construction debris in order to reach an important appointment on time—in which case the person will be held to have assumed the risk of being injured by tripping on the debris but not to have behaved in a contributorily negligent fashion. Of course, conduct can be negligent without constituting assumption of the risk. An inattentive driver who veers over the center line certainly puts himself or herself at risk of being struck by an oncoming vehicle, but surely does not knowingly and willingly encounter that risk.

Multiple Tortfeasors

Many cases feature more than a single defendant: for example, the doctor and the hospital in a medical malpractice case or, in the case of a person injured by an intoxicated driver, the driver and the owner of the bar who served the driver alcohol. (Multiple plaintiffs present no special problem of substantive law; each is entitled to full compensation for his or her injuries, assuming he or she can prove the elements of his or her claim and is not subject to any affirmative defense.) At common law, multiple defendants are generally *jointly and severally liable* to the plaintiff, which means that the plaintiff can recover any part or all of the damage award from any one defendant or any combination of them. Many states, often as a part of "tort reform," have enacted *several liability* rules that limit the liability of each defendant, either on a pro rata basis, in proportion to each one's contribution to the harm, or in some other fashion.

THE LAW OF ACCIDENTS—PROCEDURE

The procedure of the accident case is for the most part similar to that of other civil cases. It follows the same pattern of "litigotiation" (Galanter, 1993), in which the accident victim, perhaps after demanding compensation from the defendant or the defendant's insurer, files a formal complaint and the defendant files a formal answer, but the parties continue to seek a negotiated settlement.[6] The parties then try to obtain factual information to support their claims and defenses, both through their own informal investigations and from each other through what is known as *discovery*. Should the case not settle or be dismissed during this stage, it will be among the small percentage of cases that go to trial (Galanter, 1993). The case may be tried to a jury if either party has properly requested a jury trial (a right guaranteed by federal and state constitutions); otherwise, the case will be tried to the judge sitting without a jury in a "bench trial." Jury trials constitute a little more than half of all trials (Galanter, 1993; Gross & Syverud, 1996), although in personal injury cases in federal court, jury trials outnumber bench trials by seven to one (Clermont & Eisenberg, 1992).

In the following, highly simplified summary, I assume that the case is tried to a jury, and I focus on those aspects of trial procedure that are especially important to jurors' decision making.

---

[6] If the defendant has also been injured by the plaintiff's actions (e.g., a typical two-car collision), the defendant may file a *counterclaim* against the plaintiff for damages. His or her claim is then subject to all relevant substantive and procedural rules that pertain to the plaintiff's claims; that is, for purposes of the counterclaim, the defendant becomes the "plaintiff" and vice versa.

Jury Selection

Adult members of the community are chosen at random and summoned to appear at the courthouse on a particular date. On the basis of qualification forms completed before or after they arrive in court, a group of those not exempted or disqualified from jury service (typically 15 to 40, although sometimes many more) are sent to the courtroom in which a particular case is scheduled for trial. This group of prospective jurors is known as the *venire*. Then, during *voir dire*, the judge and the lawyers question the prospective jurors to eliminate those who are perceived to be biased. (In federal court, judges usually conduct *voir dire*; lawyers generally have more leeway to ask questions in state court.) Any number of prospective jurors may be challenged *for cause* on grounds of evident bias (e.g., employment by a party). Each party may also strike a limited number of prospective jurors through *peremptory* challenges, for which no reason need be given.[7] While the systemic interest is in obtaining an impartial jury, each party, of course, desires a jury that will be favorably disposed to its side of the case. Eventually a *petit jury* of between 6 and 12 persons (depending on the applicable rules), with a number of alternate jurors, is empaneled and the trial begins (Mauet, 1992).

Order of Trial

In most jurisdictions, the trial begins with opening statements, in which the lawyers for each party present their theories of the case, previewing how the evidence that will be presented establishes their respective clients' legal claims. As in other types of cases, the claimant (plaintiff) presents his or her evidence first, followed by the defendant. The lawyers determine, within constraints imposed by the rules of evidence as applied by the judge, what information the jurors will hear and see. In most cases, all issues that the claims and defenses raise are tried in a single proceeding. Occasionally, however, in particularly complex cases, proceedings may be *bifurcated* so that the issue of the defendant's liability (say) will be tried first, and only if the defendant is found liable will there then be a separate trial on damages. Experimental research shows that plaintiffs win more often but receive lower damage awards (when they do win) in unitary trials than they do in separated trials (Horowitz & Bordens, 1990; cf. Diamond et al., 1998).

It is the judge's job to decide what general legal rules apply to the

---

[7] The Supreme Court has ruled that litigants in federal civil cases cannot use peremptory challenges to strike prospective jurors on the basis of race because doing so violates the equal protection rights of the challenged jurors (*Edmonson v. Leesville Concrete Co.*, 1991). If a party's use of peremptories indicates a pattern of racial bias, the party must justify its peremptories on nonracial grounds.

case at hand, and whether the evidence presented on each claim and defense is sufficient for a reasonable juror to find in favor of the party asserting that claim or defense. It is the jurors' job to decide whether the party has persuaded them, by a preponderance of the evidence, that the facts satisfy the elements of that claim or defense as the judge has defined it. So, for instance, the judge determines what *in general* constitutes negligence; the jurors determine whether the defendant or the plaintiff or both acted negligently under the circumstances *in this case* (Keeton et al., 1984).

Instructions

After all of the evidence has been presented, if the judge has not dismissed the case for want of supporting evidence, the lawyers deliver closing arguments (first the plaintiff, then the defendant; the plaintiff is usually permitted a brief rebuttal). In these arguments each lawyer once again attempts to tie the relevant law to the evidence in a way that supports the client's claims or defenses and refutes those of the opposing party. The judge then *instructs* the jurors in the applicable law. The instructions are often couched in formulaic language that is difficult for ordinary people to comprehend (Charrow & Charrow, 1979). With rare exceptions, the jurors have only the judge's oral explanation of the law at the end of the case to work with; if they need additional guidance, they may notify the judge in writing but are likely to get in response only a reiteration of the original instructions (Strier, 1994). Despite considerable psychological research showing that rephrasing the instructions in simpler language, allowing jurors to see the instructions in writing, and other reforms improve jurors' understanding of the law (e.g., Elwork, Sales, & Alfini, 1982; Severance & Loftus, 1982; for reviews, see Lieberman & Sales, 1997; J. A. Tanford, 1990), relatively few states have changed the methods of jury instruction (J. A. Tanford, 1991). As a result, jurors consistently fare poorly on tests of their comprehension of the judge's instructions (e.g., Reifman et al., 1992).

Deliberations

The jurors then leave the courtroom to deliberate until they reach a verdict.[8] As noted, the size of the jury in civil cases varies from 6 to 12 people, depending on the jurisdiction. The *decision rule*—how many jurors must agree to reach a verdict—also varies: Some states require unanimity, others a supermajority (say, 5 out of a 6-person jury or 9 out of a 12-person

---

[8] In a recent experimental reform, Arizona civil jurors have been allowed to discuss the evidence during the trial instead of waiting until the end of the trial to deliberate (see Hans, Hannaford, & Munsterman, 1999).

jury). Research shows little effect of jury size or decision rule on outcomes[9] (on limitations of these findings, see Hans & Vidmar, 1986) but does show that the larger the jury, the more complete the recall and consideration of evidence and the longer the deliberations (Saks & Marti, 1997). Research also shows that the stricter the decision rule (i.e., the greater the number of votes required for a verdict), the greater the amount of discussion during deliberations (Hastie, Penrod, & Pennington, 1983). The gender composition of the jury, the identity and participatory style of the foreperson, the jurors' initial verdict preferences, the size of the majority faction, the length of deliberations, and other factors may affect the content and outcome of deliberations (Hastie et al., 1983; for a survey, see Stasser, Kerr, & Bray, 1982). In addition, individual jurors vary in the extent of their participation in deliberations (R. James, 1959; Kassin & Wrightsman, 1988; Marder, 1987; Strodtbeck, James, & Hawkins, 1957), in their persuasiveness (Shestowsky, Wegener, & Fabrigar, 1998), and in their propensity to be persuaded (Kruglanski, Webster, & Klem, 1993). In general, research shows that jurors consider the evidence very carefully during deliberations (Ellsworth, 1989) and are "remarkably competent" at finding the facts of the case (Hastie et al., 1983, p. 230).[10]

Verdicts

Most often the jury is required to give only a *general verdict*: a statement of whether the defendant is liable to the plaintiff (for each count of the complaint) and, if so, for what amount of damages. In many cases, however, the jury is asked to return a *special verdict* or a general verdict accompanied by *jury interrogatories*, providing answers that address the specific elements or components of the claims or defenses in the case (Wiggins & Breckler, 1990; Wright & Ankerman, 1993). Limited research thus far has failed to show that the choice between general and special verdict forms affects jurors' verdicts or, perhaps surprisingly, their comprehension of the legal issues in the case (Wiggins & Breckler, 1990).

After the Verdict

The jury's verdict is often not the final word in the accident case. The trial judge may reject the verdict if he or she determines that it is

---

[9] However, the larger the jury, the less the variability in damage awards (Diamond et al., 1998).

[10] This general claim can be qualified in several ways. Research shows, for instance, that jurors typically and impermissibly consider the impact of attorney's fees on the plaintiff's recovery (Hans, Mott, & Simpson, 1998) and that, in deliberating about punitive damages, jurors often disregard one or more legally required elements and consequently reach decisions at variance from the law (Hastie, Schkade, & Payne, 1998). Anecdotal evidence indicates that deliberations are sometimes captured by a single juror who misunderstands the law and persuades other jurors to do likewise (Brill, 1982).

contrary to law (in which case, the judge will give judgment for the party that lost the verdict) or against the great weight of the evidence (in which case, the judge will order a new trial). If the judge agrees with a jury verdict for the plaintiff but believes the damage award is much too high or too low, he or she may order a new trial unless the plaintiff or the defendant, as the case may be, accepts a downward (*remittitur*) or upward (*additur*) modification of the award (F. James, Hazard, & Leubsdorf, 1992). Finally, the losing party at trial may appeal the decision, and the appellate court may modify or reverse the lower court's judgment. Research indicates that between one quarter and one half of jury verdicts that are not overturned are adjusted, usually downward and by an average of about a third of their value, although the rate of reduction varies widely by jurisdiction (Galanter, 1996; Shanley & Peterson, 1987; Vidmar, Gross, & Rose, 1998). And at any point, of course, the parties may negotiate a settlement of the dispute.

EXPERT DISCOURSES ABOUT ACCIDENTS

Scholars and judges recognize three broad goals of any system for allocating the costs of accidents: compensating victims, doing justice, and encouraging safety. Innumerable judicial opinions, treatises, and scholarly articles explore how well tort law and procedure, in general or as applied to individual cases, serve these goals. Compensation, within the context of the individual lawsuit, is a relatively simple matter; it is furthered to the extent that liability is imposed on someone other than the victim. The interesting issues regarding compensation concern the impact of insurance and whether the current litigation system, in which many accident victims recover much less than they have lost or often nothing at all, might be improved on (e.g., Dewees et al., 1996). These questions, however, are beyond the scope of this book.

The goal of doing justice has generated discussions among experts about whether compelling the defendant to pay for the plaintiff's losses is *fair*. Often this is couched in the language of *corrective justice*: In what circumstances is it morally right to compel the defendant to make good the plaintiff's losses that the defendant has accidentally caused? The goal of safety has generated discourse among experts about whether requiring the defendant to pay the plaintiff's damages is *socially useful*. The most prevalent way in which experts talk about social utility in accident cases is by using the language of *economic efficiency*—by asking how tort rules and outcomes in particular cases can be shaped to create incentives for people to behave so that the total social cost of accidents plus precautions is as low as it can be.

Both fairness talk and efficiency talk can be used to explain why the law *is* (or was) what it is (or was) (*descriptive* jurisprudence) and to argue why the law *ought* to be a particular way (*prescriptive* or *normative* jurisprudence).[11] In addition, both fairness and efficiency arguments may justify either negligence or strict liability. How well the American system of tort litigation, under either negligence or strict liability, accomplishes any of its professed goals of justice and safety are much-disputed questions that this book will not address (e.g., Abel, 1995; Bell & O'Connell, 1997; Dewees et al., 1996).

Fairness

Following Aristotle (1934), I divide the deontological rationales for accident liability into those that support *corrective justice* and those that support *distributive justice*. Corrective justice pertains to *whether* the defendant should be liable at all; distributive justice, to the *apportionment* of accident losses among multiple parties.

Corrective Justice

Fairness or justice can be used to gauge the appropriateness of outcomes in tort as in any other area of law or human relations (Walker, 1980). In tort law, including the law of accidents, one relevant species of justice is corrective justice, which means that one who has unjustifiably inflicted a loss on another must "correct" the wrong by restoring the injured party to the status quo ante (Aristotle, 1934). Accordingly, fairness may require the defendant, who has accidentally injured the plaintiff, to compensate the plaintiff for his or her losses.

Corrective justice may support either negligence or strict liability, depending on the specification of the background conditions and expectations with regard to which the defendant's conduct is evaluated (Epstein, 1999). If each person is entitled to expect more or less complete freedom from harm accidentally inflicted by others, then *any* such harm constitutes an unjustifiable departure from the status quo, and corrective justice requires liability (Epstein, 1973). If, however, each person is entitled to expect freedom only from accidental harms that result from others' *wrongful* conduct—say, conduct that does not conform to a general standard of ordinary care—then corrective justice requires liability only for negligence. The latter is the more common view among scholars today. Plainly, each version of corrective justice rests on a somewhat different ideal of social relations: a different conception of the degree of liberty with which people should be entitled to carry on their activities versus the degree of security

---

[11] Indeed, each kind of justification has been collapsed into the other: It has been argued, for instance, that economic efficiency entails corrective justice (Posner, 1981).

others should be entitled to expect from the harm those activities inflict (Coleman & Ripstein, 1995).

There are many theories of corrective justice in tort law, the details and analyses of which are beyond the scope of this chapter (for a brief review, see L. Meyer, 1997). Suffice it to point out here that although corrective justice may be the most important criterion of fairness in tort law, striving for corrective justice may actually produce conflicts with the other major goals of accident law. To limit compensation to those accident victims who can prove that their injuries were caused by the negligence of identifiable defendants, for example, is to leave many blameless victims suffering catastrophic loss. Furthermore, to hold accountable only those careless actors whose bad fortune it is to cause harm to others, and to measure the damages they must pay by the extent of the plaintiff's injury rather than by the egregiousness of their behavior, scarcely seem likely to provide rational, systematic deterrence of undesirably risky conduct (Weiler, 1991).

Distributive Justice

Although most expert talk about justice as a basis of liability for accidents is about corrective justice, distributive justice is also relevant to the attribution of responsibility. Distributive justice concerns the "fairness of the distribution of the conditions and goods that affect individual well-being" (Deutsch, 1985, p. 1). One dominant theme since the time of Aristotle (1934) is that distributive justice consists of an allocation in *proportion* to some relevant input. (This notion is the basis of the social psychological concept of *equity theory*; Walster, Walster, & Berscheid, 1978.)

Distributive justice concerns not only goods such as wealth and other resources but also "bads," such as the losses arising from an accident. Thus, the doctrine of pure comparative negligence, according to which the plaintiff's recovery is reduced by the percentage that the plaintiff's own carelessness contributed to the accident, is best justified in terms of distributive justice (*Li v. Yellow Cab Co. of California*, 1975; G. Schwartz, 1978).

Social Utility: Economic Efficiency

Consequentialist philosophies urge us to behave or adopt rules of behavior that seem likeliest to lead to some desirable end, such as maximizing society's fund of some good (e.g., utility or happiness). With regard to accidents, contemporary consequentialist talk most commonly takes the form of *economic efficiency*: Accidents should be dealt with in a way that will maximize society's scarce economic resources. In other words, the goal of accident law should be to reduce the total cost of accidents. Calabresi (1970) further subdivided economic efficiency objectives into three types: *primary* accident cost reduction is the minimization of the sum of resources spent on accidents and accident avoidance; *secondary* accident cost reduction is the minimization of the social dislocation of catastrophic accident costs through loss spreading; and *tertiary* accident cost reduction is the minimization of the transaction costs of administering whatever regime of rules and institutions is developed to address primary and secondary cost reduction.

Perhaps the simplest way to understand economic efficiency reasoning about accidents is in terms of the Learned Hand cost–benefit test. Recall that this test treats as negligent an injurer who fails to take safety precautions (B) that cost less than the expected accident costs (P × L). In theory, this rule leads to efficient (optimal) behavior (in terms of primary accident cost avoidance) because it gives potential injurers an incentive to avoid all and only those accidents worth avoiding. If B > P × L, the injurer is not liable under the Learned Hand test for not spending on safety, and that is efficient because safety (B) costs more than the accidents that spending on safety would have avoided (P × L). If, on the other hand, B < P × L, then the rational potential injurer will spend B to avoid liability for the greater amount (P × L), and once again, the expenditure of the lesser amount maximizes society's wealth.[12]

Although the Learned Hand test uses economic efficiency to define negligence, cost–benefit reasoning can also be applied in support of a strict liability rule (Calabresi & Hirschoff, 1972). It can readily be seen that, all other things being equal, both negligence and strict liability provide the same incentives to the would-be injurer, who will in any event take precautions only when they cost him or her less than the expected accident costs for which he or she can anticipate being held liable (Posner, 1992). The difference between the two rules is, in theory, purely distributional. The victim pays for accidents not worth avoiding under a negligence rule, and the injurer pays for them under strict liability.[13] Indeed, a single question—which party is the "cheapest cost-avoider," the one who *could* have avoided the accident at the least expense—may be at the root of both negligence and strict liability, although negligence asks in addition whether the cheapest precautions would have been optimal, that is, whether they

---

[12] Of the many simplifying assumptions built into this extremely basic model of behavior, readers might note that spending on B is assumed to avoid P × L completely. In real life, of course, it is rarely desirable or even feasible to eliminate the possibility of a given type of accident. Economic efficiency therefore prescribes that society spend the *lowest total amount* on safety precautions and the losses from the accidents that remain.

[13] Under negligence, the victim pays for accidents not worth avoiding (i.e., where B > P × L), because the rational injurer will not spend B and will not be liable for the P × L that results. Under strict liability, the injurer pays for accidents not worth avoiding because the injurer pays in any event.

should have been taken (Gilles, 1992). Whether strict liability or negligence is the more efficient rule as applied to a given activity depends on a number of factors, including whether the likely victims or likely injurers are in a better position to avoid accidents worth avoiding by modifying not only their level of precautions but also the level at which they engage in the activity (Polinsky, 1983; Posner, 1992).

The economic analysis of accident law has been refined and criticized in many ways that are beyond the scope of this summary (for a brief review, see Bix, 1996). I note only one criticism here. Like social utility justifications for rules or practices in other domains, economic efficiency talk about accidents presumes that people in the real world can modify their behavior in predictable ways in response to the incentives that legal rules create. Many accidents, however, are due to mere inadvertence, of a kind that is unlikely to be amenable to behavioral modification through legal rules or other feasible incentives (Shuman, 1993; Weiler, 1991; but cf. Bruce, 1984).

When lay talk about blame and compensation for accidents is discussed in the second half of the book, readers will certainly not expect to find the sorts of references to corrective justice and optimal care that judges and legal academics use. Readers may, however, find considerable overlap between people's common-sense notions of reasonableness and responsibility and the more philosophical explanations to be found in expert discourses. In chapters 5 through 7, I explore both the similarities and the differences between lay and expert analyses of the reasons to hold a defendant liable for a plaintiff's accidental injuries. I also examine how the law and procedure of the accident trial help to shape those common-sense notions into verdicts. Before I do that, I discuss common sense, the focus of the next three chapters.

2

THE SOCIAL PSYCHOLOGY OF JUROR JUDGMENTS I: COGNITIVE FRAMEWORKS AND HEURISTICS

In this and the next chapter, I review the research in social and cognitive psychology that bears on how people think about responsibility and compensation for accidents. This chapter focuses on the habits of mind people use when they believe they are thinking as best they can—trying to reach decisions calmly and logically, without being influenced, as far as anyone can tell, by self-serving perceptions or strong emotional impulses (what social psychologists call "hot" cognitions, as opposed to the "cold" ones surveyed in this chapter; Nisbett & Ross, 1980). In the next chapter I review the literature on the role of emotions in decision making about accidents.[1]

---

[1] Nonemotional "hot" or motivated cognitions are discussed where relevant throughout the next two chapters and elsewhere. These include various *ego-defensive biases*, such as attributional biases (e.g., to retain peers' social approval, adolescents may ascribe personal failure to lack of effort when communicating with peers but to lack of ability when communicating with teachers and adults; Weiner, 1995), or *defensive attribution* (Shaver, 1970 discussed in chapter 3) and the *optimism bias* of believing that one is less susceptible to health problems and other negative events than is the average person (Weinstein, 1984, 1987). They also include *epistemic motivations*, such as the need for closure (Kruglanski, 1989) or personal need for structure (Neuberg & Newsom, 1993), discussed in connection with monocausality later in this chapter. Many observed effects in social cognition have been attributed to both nonmotivated ("cold") and motivated ("hot") thinking. Following Nisbett and Ross (1980), I

In both this chapter and the next, my concern is with those *general* features of cognition and judgment that are relevant to how jurors[2] interpret the facts and the law in accident cases. I do not focus on differences among individual jurors, which are the subject of scientific jury selection (Bonazzoli, 1998) and which tend to capture much of the attention the public pays to jury behavior. There are several reasons for this choice of emphasis. First, despite popular impressions to the contrary, research shows that individual juror demographic characteristics (such as race, gender, and socioeconomic status) are generally weak predictors of juror judgments (Hastie et al., 1983; MacCoun, 1986), although the links between certain attitudes and judgments are somewhat stronger (Diamond et al., 1998; Ellsworth, 1993; Kassin & Wrightsman, 1983; Moran et al., 1994).[3] I prefer, therefore, to focus on those influences on judgment that may be shared among jurors (to varying extents, to be sure) whatever the jurors' demographic characteristics. Second, and perhaps again contrary to popular belief, the research consensus is that the evidence in the case is by far the most important influence on legal judgments, much more so than "extralegal" factors such as the personal characteristics of the litigants (Reskin & Visher, 1986; Visher, 1987). Consequently, I am most concerned with those habits of thought and feeling that are likely to affect directly jurors' understanding of the evidence and the lawyers' arguments, even though jurors may apply some of these habits to extralegal factors as well. Third, and purely pragmatically, the data I present in the second half of this book as examples of talk about accidents (transcripts of closing arguments in accident cases, written records of interviews with jurors, and transcripts of mock jury deliberations) lend themselves to inferences about decision mak-

---

look first to nonmotivated explanations (those discussed in this chapter), because they are plentiful enough, and if they suffice to explain the phenomenon in question, it is unparsimonious to seek in addition a motivated account. Note, however, that research also indicates certain interactions between heuristic thinking and epistemic motivation; for instance, Pelham and Neter (1995) found that high levels of motivation to do well on various judgmental tasks facilitated performance of easy tasks but reduced accuracy on difficult tasks by increasing the erroneous use of heuristic thinking. Thus, explaining juror cognition is not necessarily a matter of preferring one account to the other.

[2] The focus in this and the next chapter is on *juror*, as opposed to *jury*, cognitive and emotional responses to accident cases. Individual juror judgments about a case are, after all, strong predictors of the decision the jury will reach collectively (Kalven & Zeisel, 1966; S. Tanford & Penrod, 1986). Group decisions may, of course, differ from (the average of) the predeliberation decisions of the individuals constituting the group; group judgments may be less or, more frequently, more biased than individual judgments, depending on many factors (e.g., Schkade, Sunstein, & Kahneman, 1999; for a review, see Kerr, MacCoun, & Kramer, 1996). Most of the research on cognitive and emotional factors in social judgment, moreover, addresses individual rather than group thinking and deciding. Elsewhere in the book, I mention briefly some of the literature on how individual jurors' perceptions and judgments may be translated into group decisions (see references in chapters 1, 4, and 7).

[3] Moreover, considerable experimental research has found no significant differences in liability decisions or damage awards between college students and participants more demographically representative of the jury pool (for a review, see Bornstein, 1999), suggesting that jurors' demographic characteristics are less important to their decision making than commonly believed.

ers' generally shared habits of thought and feeling. In most instances, I lack sufficient information about the jurors' and other speakers' demographic characteristics and attitudes, and so cannot speculate about how these may have affected their judgments. Nevertheless, no student of juror decisions should ignore the other factors that may affect the kinds of judgments accident jurors must make, including not only individual jurors' demographic characteristics (e.g., Bornstein & Rajki, 1994; Denove & Imwinkelried, 1995; Diamond et al., 1998; Ford, 1986), cognitive styles (Graziano, Panter, & Tanaka, 1990; Kuhn, Weinstock, & Flaton, 1994), and other personality traits (e.g., Moore, Smith, & Gonzalez, 1997), but also other aspects of the trial process, including pretrial publicity (Greene, 1990; Kramer, Kerr, & Carroll, 1990; Otto, Penrod, & Dexter, 1994; Wilson & Bornstein, 1998), attorney gender (Sigal, Braden-Maguire, Hayden, & Mosley, 1985), litigant demographic characteristics (Dane & Wrightsman, 1982), litigant appearance (Kulka & Kessler, 1978), and judicial demeanor (Blanck, Rosenthal, & Cordell, 1985).

In this chapter, then, I review some of the voluminous research on the social psychological dynamics that describe how people reason their way through the law and the facts to make judgments about accidents. These mental habits include the availability and representativeness heuristics, prototype effects (including content-specific schemas and beliefs), monocausality, norm theory (counterfactual thinking), culpable causation, the fundamental attribution error (correspondence bias), hindsight bias, the severity effect, anchoring and adjustment, prospect theory, and biases in the comprehension of statistical information. I describe each habit of thought generally and then briefly discuss applications to decision making in accident cases. These patterns of thinking and judgment, and those to be discussed in chapter 3, are the tools I use to dissect the various examples of talk about accidents in the second half of the book.

Most of the research identifying these various habits of thought has been conducted in the form of controlled experimentation. Participants are typically asked to make a decision (e.g., in a test of the hindsight effect, to estimate the *ex ante* [before the fact] likelihood of a given event); the researcher manipulates one or more features of decision-making context, such as the information available to the participants (this is the *independent variable*, e.g., participants in one *condition* of the experiment are told whether the event actually occurred; participants in the other, "control" condition are not); the effects of the manipulation are then measured (this is the *dependent variable*, e.g., whether participants provided with outcome information judge the likelihood of that outcome to have been greater). If the changes in the independent variable make a difference when they ought not to, according to relevant scientific (or legal) norms of rational decision making (e.g., outcome information should not affect judgments about how probable the outcome seemed from an *ex ante* perspective, before anyone knew whether the outcome would occur), then the results indicate a "bias" relative to those norms (see Funder, 1987). How far these experimental results *generalize* to decision making by real jurors in actual cases (the *external validity* of the research), in which the decision-making context may differ in several respects from that of the experiment, is a matter of ongoing discussion (e.g., Bray & Kerr, 1982; Diamond, 1997). Most of the effects discussed in this and the next chapter have been replicated often enough, using enough different sorts of participants, stimuli, independent variables, and dependent variables, that psychologists have considerable confidence in the generalizability of the results.

It should be emphasized that these habits of mind usually serve people very well, leading to judgments and decisions that conform to norms of scientific decision making (Gilovich, 1991; Nisbett & Ross, 1980). Common sense must be largely adaptive, or else humans probably would not have survived as a species while using it. The time and mental effort we save by taking shortcuts is often worth the increased chance of error, and everyday life often provides feedback that reduces the negative consequences of any mistakes (Fiske & Taylor, 1991; Funder, 1987). And even to the extent that these habits of thought do lead to bias or error, they do not completely govern jurors' judgments about responsibility and compensation for accidents, to the exclusion of the rules and decision-making processes the law prescribes. Rather, as indicated in the introduction, these habits of thought and the law each exercise a pull on how jurors evaluate the evidence in the case. Research shows that jurors sometimes follow the law quite well. For instance, in two experiments, mock jurors correctly varied their judgments of injurers' responsibility for negligence in accordance with the cost of precautions, the likelihood of harm if the precautions are not taken, and the severity of the harm if it occurs—precisely the Learned Hand test for reasonable care discussed in chapter 1 (E. Green, 1968; Karlovac & Darley, 1988). Moreover, despite the frequent criticism that juries' awards for pain and suffering are wildly unpredictable, even random, research shows that most of the variance in awards corresponds to the severity and duration of the plaintiff's harm—the factors that ought to drive pain and suffering awards (Wissler et al., 1997).

Nevertheless, the evidence that common-sense social judgments, including judgments about responsibility and compensation for accidents, may systematically diverge from legal (and/or scientific) norms is overwhelming. Moreover, research indicates that jurors have a hard time "debiasing" or correcting for the biases to which their intuitive habits of thought lead them, especially when, as is typically the case, they are unaware of the magnitude of the bias and lack a set of procedures for avoiding its improper influence (Wilson & Brekke, 1994).[4] The next two chapters

---

[4] Wilson and Brekke (1994) argued that judgmental bias due to what they label "mental

explain some of the sources of these divergences between common sense and legal and/or scientific norms.

KNOWLEDGE STRUCTURES AND INFERENTIAL HEURISTICS GENERALLY

Jurors who decide an accident case must make judgments. According to standard doctrine, the most important of these are typically the following: Did this defendant and/or this plaintiff behave reasonably? And if not, did the defendant's and/or the plaintiff's carelessness cause the plaintiff's injuries? What makes these judgments difficult, even under the best of decision-making conditions, is that they are uncertain. The juror may know to a greater or lesser extent what the defendant did but not whether to characterize it as blameworthy; the juror may know more or less "what happened" but not why it happened. The juror must go "beyond the information given," in Bruner's (1973) famous phrase, to infer a conclusion.

Cognitive and social psychologists have found that people intuitively use two general classes of mental tools to make such judgments. People define and interpret information in terms of *knowledge structures*, and they use *judgmental heuristics* to make inferences from what they know to what they do not know (Nisbett & Ross, 1980). Without knowledge structures to organize one's perceptions, memories, and expectations, thought would be nearly inconceivable; one's mental life would be anarchic and unintelligible (Fiske & Taylor, 1991). Without judgmental heuristics or simple rules of thumb, one would be unable to reduce complex inferential tasks to relatively simple, feasible operations. Together, these ways of organizing and using information allow people to make, without psychic overload, the innumerable interpretations and decisions necessary for everyday functioning. People typically use these mental tools to make relatively rapid, even

---

contamination," that is, ordinarily unconscious and uncontrollable influences, can be corrected properly only if the person making the judgment is (a) made aware of the unwanted processing; (b) motivated to correct the bias; (c) aware of the direction and magnitude of the bias; and (d) able to exert mental control to adjust his or her response. Wilson and Brekke's model helps explain why the psychological research on debiasing (or bias correction) has reached sometimes conflicting results. Bias is more easily corrected when it is due to the failure to know or correctly apply normative inferential rules (Nisbett, 1993; Schaller, Asp, Rosell, & Heim, 1996) than when it is due to automatic processing or confusion about the source of the mental response (Wilson & Brekke, 1994). Importantly, research shows that people can adjust their judgments once their attention is called to the possible influence of biasing factors (Petty & Wegener, 1993; Wegener & Petty, 1995) or if they detect bias from the context in which judgments are made (Stapel, Martin, & Schwarz, 1998) but that the adjustments accord with their own theories of how the factors may influence such judgments, whether or not those theories are accurate and whether or not the bias is really present (Petty & Wegener, 1993; Wegener & Petty, 1995). Indeed, inaccuracy in naive theories about factor influence, mistakes about the presence of bias, and mistaken perceptions about the magnitude of bias (Petty, Wegener, & White, 1998; Schul & Goren, 1997) all may lead to *overcorrection* for perceived bias.

"automatic," judgments, but they are also involved in the more deliberate thinking that characterizes at least some juror decision making (Sherman & Corty, 1984).

Knowledge Structures

People perceive, store, and retrieve what they know using knowledge structures, such as theories, schemas, scripts, and cultural models, that describe how the world is and how it works (Cantor & Kihlstrom, 1987; Holyoak & Gordon, 1984; Singer & Salovey, 1991). For instance, people have a schema for "dog" with certain features that allows them to decide whether the source of a given, potentially ambiguous set of stimuli is a dog. And if they decide that it is, that decision creates a set of expectations, inferences about other, as yet unknown features of the animal (Nisbett & Ross, 1980).

A script, similarly, is a mental structure for a social event or series of events. By prescribing one or more scenarios for how things typically happen, and thus defining the social roles involved, the script guides how people perceive and remember actual events, classify and understand the participants' behavior, and judge whether that behavior is normal or deviant. It also guides how people infer missing information from what is explicitly provided (Schank & Abelson, 1977). Suppose, for instance, that someone says only: "John went to a restaurant. He asked the waitress for *coq au vin*. He paid the check and left." The "restaurant script" allows the listener to infer that John ate the food he ordered—an event not mentioned in the account (Schank & Abelson, 1977). A cultural model for a complex concept such as "marriage" may combine schemas (for what constitutes a marriage) and scripts (for how marriages are supposed to proceed) into an implicit framework that allows people to make sense of marital successes, difficulties, and dissolutions (Quinn, 1987).

Inferential Heuristics

People also use inferential shortcuts, or heuristics, to go from what they know to what they need to learn in order to classify, predict, or attribute responsibility. When making many kinds of decisions—for instance, which candidate to vote for in the local elections or, less momentously, which restaurant to go to this weekend—people often lack information they would like to have in order to decide with great confidence, and may decide not to devote the time and effort necessary to acquire that information. So people may resort to shortcuts. Two of the most important are that people (a) tend to rely on the information that comes most readily to mind and (b) tend to categorize things on the basis of the perceived resemblance between what they think they know of the target (Candidate

A) and what they think they know of the relevant category (good politician).

These two inferential shortcuts, each of which I discuss below, are the *availability* and *representativeness* heuristics. Both are important in their own right. Both, as well as the knowledge structures mentioned above, are also important as features of other cognitive habits relevant to jurors' evaluations of accident cases, to be discussed later in the chapter.

Availability

Using the availability heuristic, people estimating the frequency or predicting the likelihood of certain events tend to be influenced by the ease with which instances of that class of events can be brought to mind (Tversky & Kahneman, 1982a, 1982b). Those who estimate that accidents cause as many deaths as does disease, when in fact 16 times as many people die from disease, are basing their estimate on the disproportionate availability of reports of fatal accidents in the media (Slovic, Fischhoff, & Lichtenstein, 1982). When each spouse routinely overestimates his or her own contributions to joint household chores, it may be because each pays more attention to and spends more time thinking about his or her own efforts, making those efforts more available for later recall (Taylor, 1982). Those who guess that more words begin with *r* than contain *r* as the third letter do so because it is easier to conduct a mental search of words by the first letter than by the third, so it is easier to think of instances of the former class of words, even though instances of the latter are far more numerous (Tversky & Kahneman, 1982a).[5]

The availability heuristic often guides people to accurate judgments about frequency and likelihood. Often, it is easier to think of examples of one category (causes of death, tasks that a person has done, words beginning with a certain letter) than another because there really are more instances of the first category, and it is easier to think of instances of larger than smaller categories. The factors that make some information more available than other information, however, may have nothing to do with objective frequency, and in these cases, the availability heuristic can lead people astray. For example, items tend to be more accessible to perception, memory, and imagination when they are more salient, that is to say, more distinctive or vivid. Concrete information is more readily understood and remembered than abstract information (Nisbett & Ross, 1980; Taylor, 1982), recent perceptions tend to loom larger than more distant ones (Tversky & Kahneman, 1982b), and events in which a person has partic-

---

[5] More recent research has disambiguated two senses of availability—the subjective ease with which information comes to mind and the numerical amount of information that comes to mind (Schwarz et al., 1991)—and has explored the conditions under which one or the other type of availability influences judgments (Rothman & Hardin, 1997).

ipated are more accessible than ones in which he or she has not (Dawes, 1998; Taylor, 1982). The media play a major role in providing information about events beyond one's personal experience; hence, because fatal accidents (especially catastrophic ones) are generally considered more newsworthy than routine deaths from disease, information about the former tends to be more available, leading people to overestimate the relative frequency of deaths by accidents. Certain events may also be more accessible if less mental effort is required to retrieve them; thus, because it is easier to generate instances of words beginning with r than words with r in the third position, people erroneously judge the former to be more frequent (Tversky & Kahneman, 1982a, 1982b).

Representativeness

The representativeness heuristic refers to people's habit of reasoning by perceived resemblance. We see a tree with trunk, branches, and leaves of a particular shape, compare those features to our schema for "oak," and, on that basis, conclude that what we have before us is an oak tree. Representativeness is "a legitimate, indeed absolutely essential, cognitive tool" (Nisbett & Ross, 1980, p. 27). It often yields correct classifications, especially when a person's knowledge of important category features is accurate and complete and members of the category are more or less invariant with regard to those features, so that (as in the case of the oak tree, at least for nonspecialists) to know one member of the category really is to know them all.

Like other cognitive tools, however, representativeness can lead to error when used inappropriately. It can fail a person, as reasoning on the basis of ethnic stereotypes often does, when a person's supposed knowledge of category features is inaccurate or when members of the category vary considerably. Given substantial variation, one cannot reliably infer from the fact that a person who has one feature presumed to be characteristic of the category that the person also has other features presumed to be characteristic of the category (Nisbett & Ross, 1980).

Reliance on representativeness may also lead to erroneous judgments because it encourages people to disregard basic principles of statistical inference. Consider a classic example from Kahneman and Tversky (1973). Some participants were told that personality tests had been given to a group of 100 persons consisting of 70 engineers and 30 lawyers; others, that the group consisted of 30 engineers and 70 lawyers. All participants were asked to estimate the likelihood that a person selected at random from the group of 100 was an engineer, on the basis of the following personality profile: "Dick is a 30-year-old man. He is married with no children. A man of high ability and high motivation, he promises to be quite successful in his field. He is well liked by his colleagues." Participants judged the probability that Dick was an engineer to be about 50%, *regardless* of whether the group from which he had been randomly selected consisted of 70% engineers or 30% engineers. Thus, participants based their judgments on Dick's perceived resemblance to their idea of an engineer (because the information provided was diagnostically worthless, it is perhaps unsurprising that the estimated probabilities were about 50%), ignoring the base rate information that made it much more (or less) likely that Dick was an engineer than a lawyer.

Similarly, consider people's belief that effects must resemble their causes (another instance of representativeness; see Gilovich, 1991; Sim & Morris, 1998), and in particular, that *any* sample of outcomes, however small, generated by a random process must itself appear random. An example is the "gambler's fallacy" that after a run of heads, the next flip of the coin is more likely to be tails because a sequence including heads and tails better matches the random process of flipping the coin (Tversky & Kahneman, 1982b). Actually, of course, a fair coin is statistically certain to yield close to a 50-50 split of heads and tails only after a sufficiently large number of tosses (the *law of large numbers*); in a short sequence, an uneven distribution of heads and tails—one that "doesn't look random" —may be quite likely (Gilovich, 1991; Tversky & Kahneman, 1982b).

This example also shows how representativeness may produce decisions at odds with those that the application of scientific norms would produce, by leading people to ignore basic statistical rules. Availability may do the same; the person who gives equal weight to a friend's anecdote and *Consumer Reports* in evaluating a car is ignoring the significance of base rate information. The published report is likely to be based on dozens or even hundreds of (probably better-informed) anecdotes and studies, the friend's on only one (Nisbett & Ross, 1980). I take up this point again briefly at the end of the chapter.

PROTOTYPE EFFECTS

We tend to think about responsibility for accidents by using implicit models of how stories go and how people should behave in given situations. Prototype theory explains how people use those models to categorize knowledge. Many of one's concepts about people and situations are not organized according to classical set theory, as lists of those qualities or characteristics necessary and sufficient for a person or thing to be a member of the set. Instead, many social concepts are "fuzzy sets," structured around prototypes (Cantor & Kihlstrom, 1987; Lakoff, 1987). The prototype may be represented by exemplars or best instances of the category (e.g., the category "national political figure" as exemplified by President Bill Clinton) or by a summary consisting of features abstracted from individual instances (e.g., considerable experience in high office, well-established political machine, actual or potential personal scandal). Prototype theory then posits a judgmental heuristic: When confronted with the task of classifying a person or event, the person making the judgment will compare features of the person or event with the characteristic features of the prototype and will classify the person or event as a member of the target category if it sufficiently resembles or corresponds to the prototype (Cantor & Kihlstrom, 1987). Classification on the basis of prototypes is thus an instance of the representativeness heuristic (Nisbett & Ross, 1980). This process is subject to *assimilation and contrast effects* (Schwarz & Bless, 1992): Contextual information made salient at the time of the judgment may incline people to treat a person or event as belonging or not belonging in the target category, depending on various factors.

Some research using simulated criminal cases supports the hypothesis that mock jurors reason by using prototypes. They judge guilt or innocence on the basis of how the evidence corresponds to their preexisting prototypical conceptions of the offense, rather than by strictly adhering to the verdict categories the law defines. Mock jurors' prototypes partially conform to the law, and to that extent jurors should reach the same results whether they use prototypes or legal definitions; where the two diverge, however, mock jurors seem to rely on prototypes. In a series of experiments, V. Smith (1991) began by showing that people have naive or lay conceptions of various crime categories. They organize these conceptions prototypically rather than in terms of a set of necessary and sufficient elements. For instance, two experimental scenarios might each equally satisfy the *legal* definition of "robbery" as the taking of property from the victim by force or threat of force, yet one contains more features popularly associated with robbery—say, that the perpetrator is armed. Smith showed that the more such features there are in the scenario, the more people identified the scenario as a robbery. She next showed that in most cases, scenarios more closely corresponding to the layperson's prototypical crime yielded higher conviction rates than did less prototypical scenarios. Finally, Smith showed that participants who heard the judge's instructions on the actual elements of the crime before reading the fact scenarios reached the same verdicts as those who did not. Thus, the mock jurors relied on their preexisting prototypes instead of the judge's instructions in determining guilt (V. Smith, 1991; Wiener, Habert, Shkodriani, & Staebler, 1991). Later research has largely confirmed that mock jurors rely on these prototypes not only in choosing verdicts (V. Smith, 1993) but also in finding facts (V. Smith & Studebaker, 1996). English and Sales (1997), however, have criticized both the methodology and theoretical bases of these studies, arguing that Smith's mock jurors may very well have been drawing on a more general "common sense" rather than on specific prototypes of crimes when they made their decisions. Smith, moreover, has found that explicitly instructing jurors that certain features of the prototype are not legal elements of the crime does improve jurors' ability to conform their judgments to the law (V. Smith, 1993).

Other research shows that jurors have case-specific schemas that they use in making judgments in accident cases. For example, Bornstein and Rajki (1994) presented participants with three versions of a products liability case, holding constant everything except the alleged cause of the plaintiff's ovarian cancer: a chemical from a nearby dump that had leaked into her water supply, her birth control pills, or a special ink she used in calligraphy. The allegation regarding the source of the injury influenced participants' ratings of causation and their verdicts. They were most likely to find that the cancer had been caused by the chemical manufacturer, less so the drug manufacturer, and least of all the ink company. Thus, participants' judgments were influenced not only by the evidence but by their preconceptions about what causes what.

Prototypes also influence damage awards. Researchers first observed that participants had schemas for certain kinds of accidents: how they typically occur and the sorts of injuries they typically produce. Thus, the prototypical car accident involves being broadsided and results in whiplash or other spine and neck injuries; the typical fall results from a slip on ice and leads to a broken bone. Researchers then found that mock jurors' pain and suffering awards were both larger and more variable when produced by an atypical than by a typical accident (Hart et al., 1997).

MONOCAUSALITY

People tend to prefer simple explanations for events or behaviors to complex ones. A century and a half ago, John Stuart Mill identified "the assumption . . . that a phenomenon cannot have more than one cause" (Mill, 1864, p. 469). People tend to be "satisficers," content to rely on what first strikes them as a plausible sufficient cause for an event, guided consciously by simple schemas for "how things go" or unconsciously by the mere availability of causal candidates (Nisbett & Ross, 1980). And even though people can sometimes generate multiple possible causes of their own or others' behavior, they tend to *act* as if causation were "hydraulic," a zero-sum game, such that the presence of one sufficient cause reduces the tendency to attribute causal force to any other factor (Nisbett & Ross, 1980).[6]

---

[6]For instance, providing extrinsic incentives for behavior (e.g., rewards for helpful conduct) can *decrease* people's willingness to engage in such behavior later (Batson, 1998). This would not occur unless actors believed that their willingness to help must be caused by *either* the reward *or* an intrinsic cause (i.e., inherent altruism); they act as if they understand their own behavior in monocausal terms ("If I got a reward for helping, I must not be helpful by

This preference for simple causal explanations may derive from the need to conserve scarce cognitive capacity (Fiske & Taylor, 1991). Accordingly, people are

> primarily motivated to seek a single sufficient explanation for any event, rather than one that is the best of all possible explanations. That is, individuals may exert more cognitive effort in seeking an adequate explanation when none has yet come to mind than they do in seeking for further (and possibly better) explanations when an adequate one is already available. (Kanouse, 1972, p. 131)

The preference for monocausality may also be traced to the *need for closure* (as a personality trait or under the circumstances): The stronger the need for closure, the more inclined a person will be to choose a monocausal account (Kruglanski, 1989; Kruglanski & Mayseless, 1988).[7]

---

nature"). Similarly, in a famous experiment, children presented with an extrinsic motivation (a reward) for engaging in an activity that they could very well find intrinsically motivating (playing with markers) later engaged *less* in that activity when the reward was taken away than did children who had never been given the extrinsic motivation in the first place. The children who had been rewarded later acted as if they found drawing less intrinsically interesting; apparently they had inferred that the reward, not the intrinsic interest of drawing, had been the reason for engaging in the activity the first time around (Nisbett & Ross, 1980). To similar effect is research showing that surveillance leads overseers to distrust those whom they have been asked to oversee. Apparently the overseers come to attribute conscientious behavior by their charges to their surveillance, thus preferring a monocausal explanation for that behavior ("they're behaving well because I'm watching them") to more complex alternatives (Nisbett & Ross, 1980). This process has been described in the literature as the *discounting* of alternative causes (Kelley, 1973; Morris & Larrick, 1995). For a recent review and analysis of research articulating the conditions under which people are likely to discount or not to discount alternative causes, see McClure (1998).

[7] On epistemic motivation and causal attributions, see Kruglanski (1989). According to Kruglanski's model of lay epistemics, "[a] 'need for closure' refers to the striving for clear-cut knowledge on a given topic, and the intolerance of confusion and ambiguity. This particular need is assumed to inhibit the formulation of alternatives to a given hypothesis, as these introduce confusion and hence undermine existing closure" (Kruglanski & Mayseless, 1988, p. 9). And for some people, the (closely related) *personal need for structure* leads them to prefer relatively simple cognitive structures in making social and nonsocial judgments (Neuberg & Newsom, 1993). Need for closure is also associated with simplified thinking in the form of stereotype-consistent recall and judgment (Dijksterhuis, van Knippenberg, Kruglanski, & Schaper, 1996), as well as increased commission of the fundamental attribution error and other instances of insufficient adjustment from early cues or anchors (Kruglanski & Webster, 1996).

The need-for-closure construct could very well apply to juror decision making in accident cases because jurors would appear to desire what Kruglanski described as "nonspecific" closure, that is, a resolution of their attributional task, but not any particular one (Kruglanski & Webster, 1996). Jurors want closure because they are legally obligated to decide the case before them (although real juries may hang) and, presumably, would like to do so as quickly as their other goals (e.g., deciding fairly) permit. Jurors want *nonspecific* closure because, presumably, they are not committed in advance to any particular outcome (those jurors who give indications of such bias before or at *voir dire* are likely to be excluded for cause).

"[T]he need for nonspecific closure is assumed to effect an initiation of attributional activity and its quick freezing, once a plausible hypothesis has been generated and found consistent with extant evidence" (Kruglanski, 1989, p. 77). Jurors are generally likely to "freeze" their attributions of fault as soon as they have found one party responsible for the accident (assuming that that judgment is consistent with the evidence, as it is almost certainly likely to be, because few cases in which neither party can plausibly be assigned legal responsibility are likely to make it to trial), and not to be inclined to pursue the matter further.

Conversely, it could be argued that real as opposed to mock jurors' decision-making context

NORM THEORY AND COUNTERFACTUAL THINKING

Norm theory (Kahneman & Miller, 1986) posits that people trying to identify the cause or causes of some outcome imagine (or simulate) scenarios other than the one that actually occurred by "undoing" or "mutating" one or more of the events that preceded the outcome. They imagine: "If only *x* had been different, the outcome would have been different." The more readily they can construct an alternative, counterfactual scenario (i.e., the easier it is to imagine a particular change in the events preceding the outcome), the more probable they judge that alternative to have been, and the more likely they are to think that the actual outcome need not have occurred. The cause of the actual event becomes the prior occurrence that is changed in the alternative story.[8]

In Kahneman and Tversky's (1982) classic experiment that uncovered this phenomenon (which they labeled the *simulation heuristic*, referring to the mental simulation of counterfactual scenarios), some participants read a story about a man who left his office at the usual time but drove home by an unusual route; others read a version in which he left early but took the usual route. In both stories, the man braked hard to stop at a yellow light, although he could easily have gone through. When the light changed, he started through the intersection, only to be rammed and instantly killed by a teenager driving a truck while under the influence of drugs. Participants were asked how the man's family, dwelling on the accident, completed the sentence stem, "If only. . . ." Those who read the "unusual route" version most often responded that if only the man had taken his usual route, the accident would not have occurred. Those who read the "unusual time" version most often responded that changing the time of departure from the office would have avoided the accident.

This and other research shows that people most readily imagine the alternative scenario that changes (and thus locates as the actual cause) some event in the actual story that stands out as surprising or deviant. They "normalize" that event by mutating it to conform to the expected,

---

discourages closure in the relevant sense. The adversarial context and the judge's instructions would encourage jurors to listen to both sides of the case and to entertain competing hypotheses; the process of deliberation would lead jurors to believe that it is appropriate to consider alternative points of view; and real jurors have plenty of time to reach a decision that they tend to take quite seriously. For all of these reasons, real jurors would seem to be less likely to rely on a "satisficing" mode of thought and more likely to have an incentive, or at least opportunity, not to rest with the first plausible attribution of responsibility.

Other personal differences in epistemic motivation also affect causal attributions. For instance, individuals' *need for cognition* (Cacioppo, Petty, Feinstein, & Jarvis, 1996) may inspire them to scrutinize message content carefully rather than to process it heuristically (Petty & Cacioppo, 1986), which may lead them to contemplate more complex causal attributions.

[8]Not all research identifies counterfactual thinking with causal attributions. Mandel and Lehman (1996) distinguished judgments of preventability from judgments of causation and reported findings that counterfactual content is associated with the former but not the latter. N'gbala and Branscombe (1995) concluded that mental simulation and causal attribution are separate and distinct processes.

routine scenario (hence, "norm" theory), in which bad outcomes do not occur. In the "unusual route" story, the man's choice of route is deviant; in the "unusual time" version, the deviance is his decision to leave the office early. The experiment also shows that people tend to imagine an alternative scenario that changes some feature of the main object of attention or concern: the behavior of the protagonist (in this case, the man), rather than that of a third party. (For neither group of participants was undoing the teenager's conduct the most common response.) It follows that the more readily jurors can imagine a person acting differently and thus avoiding the accident, the more likely they are to find that the person's actual conduct caused the accident (Kahneman & Tversky, 1982).[9]

Further research on the social psychology of counterfactual thinking, although its findings are not entirely consistent, has largely confirmed and expanded Kahneman and Tversky's (1982) early results (for reviews, see D. Miller, Turnbull, & McFarland, 1990; Roese, 1997; Roese & Olson, 1995). Deviance in many senses—conduct that varies from a routine, stands out from the perceptual background (i.e., salience), or is perceived to be infrequent—has been shown to characterize the prior event that people mutate when they imagine how things might have been otherwise (Roese & Olson, 1995).[10] In addition, research shows that controllable antecedents are more mutable than uncontrollable ones (Roese & Olson, 1995; C. Williams, Lees-Haley, & Price, 1996). This may explain why relatively few participants in Kahneman and Tversky's experiment targeted the driver who was under the influence of drugs as the event that could have been otherwise: From the protagonist's perspective, there was nothing

---

[9] Hastie (1999) reported recent research using think-aloud protocols which indicate that mock jurors mentally mutate various antecedents and, if they believe that the difference between the probability of the consequent event with and without the antecedent is great enough, identify the antecedent as the cause of the event.

This review of norm theory or counterfactual thinking should not be understood to imply that the person whose action is most easily imagined otherwise will always be blamed the most (D. Miller & Turnbull, 1990). Where only the defendant can plausibly be held legally responsible, the defendant's liability will be enhanced where the *victim's* behavior is deviant. In one experiment, for instance, participants read a story of a woman who walked to work along either her normal or an unusual route. In both scenarios, she passed a building under construction, and a piece of scaffolding fell and struck her on the back. Participants who read the unusual-route version found the scaffolding company more negligent and awarded greater damages to the woman (Macrae, 1992). In a similar study, participants read about a woman who dined at either her usual restaurant or one she had never tried before. In both cases she got food poisoning. The latter restaurant was found more negligent. Both studies are analyzed in Macrae and Milne (1992).

[10] Ritov and Baron (1994) found that participants awarded greater compensation to a passenger hurt by the sudden stopping of the train in which the passenger was riding when the stop was due to exceptional circumstances (the failure of a mechanical device or a human engineer, either of which is expected to be successful in avoiding accidents, to stop the train before it hit a fallen tree) rather than routine circumstances (the device or the engineer succeeded in stopping the train before it struck the tree, but did so suddenly enough to injure the passenger). Note also that exceptionality may be a function of the conversational context of the causal inquiry; depending on the purpose of the inquiry, the search for a cause may assume away certain "background conditions" and focus attention on whatever may be exceptional, given those conditions (see Hilton, 1990).

he could do about the teenager's presence on the road. Furthermore, acts are usually easier to "undo" than omissions, and they are therefore more likely to be targeted as the cause of an accident (Kahneman & Miller, 1986; but cf. Roese & Olson, 1995).

Use of norm theory often yields accurate causal attributions (G. Wells & Gavanski, 1989). As with other instances of the availability heuristic, the most accessible information may in fact be the most valid basis for the inference to be made. But norm theory thinking can bias causal judgments because people do not necessarily change the prior event that was least likely to happen and thus most likely to have "made the difference" between what happened and what could have happened.[11]

When people engage in counterfactual thinking of the sort norm theory describes, judgments about fault and compensation, as well as causation, follow. In one set of experiments, participants read about a case in which a construction worker painting the rafters at a shopping mall was injured when he fell from scaffolding. The defendant mall had asked its warehouse manager to order safety lines to secure the scaffolding, but none had been available. Participants who mentally undid the accident by imagining that the mall had obtained the safety lines found that the defendant's conduct was more abnormal and more negligent, and were more likely to decide for the plaintiff, than participants who did not mutate the story in this way (Wiener, 1993). In a follow-up experiment, participants who read a version of the case that prompted them to think that the shortage of safety lines was unusual were more likely than those not so prompted to imagine that the defendant could have avoided the accident, that its conduct was abnormal, and that it should be liable (Wiener & Pritchard, 1994). In another set of studies, similarly, participants who read a description of a two-car traffic accident and then heard a closing argument in which the lawyer told them in effect that "if only Driver A had acted otherwise, the accident could have been avoided" assigned a greater percentage of fault to Driver A than did participants who heard a counterfactual that focused on what Driver B could had done otherwise to avoid the accident or those who

---

[11] For instance, in the experiment described in the text, no participants chose to undo the event with the lowest prior probability: the man's reaching the intersection precisely when he did, instead of a few seconds sooner (in which case he would have gone through). Kahneman and Tversky (1982) observed "The finding is typical: Events are not mentally undone by arbitrary alterations in the values of continuous variables" (p. 205).

It can readily be seen, moreover, that causal analysis using norm theory may diverge from the *scientific* model of causal analysis, because the heuristic yields judgments similar to those promoted by the logical fallacy of *post hoc, ergo propter hoc* ("after which, therefore on account of which"), with the abnormal event identified as "hoc." The same method of causal reasoning by *post hoc, ergo propter hoc* applies to positive outcomes (and not only to negative ones, like injury-producing accidents) and leads many laypeople to attribute causal efficacy, for instance, to any medical intervention, however worthless. "When an intervention is followed by improvement, the intervention's effectiveness stands out as an irresistible product of the person's experience," even though the body's own healing processes are likely to yield the improvement without any intervention at all (Gilovich, 1991, p. 128).

heard that even if Driver A had acted otherwise, the accident would have occurred anyway (Branscombe, Owen, Garstka, & Coleman, 1996).[12]

In sum, the more unusual or deviant jurors perceive some event preceding the accident to be, the more likely the jurors are to think not only that the accident need not have occurred, but that it *should* not have occurred and that the person causally responsible for the accident is also to be blamed for it.[13] To some extent, this way of thinking is consistent with the legal definition of negligence as conduct that deviates from custom (see chapter 1), although perceptions of deviance, and hence blameworthiness, need not be confined to the evidence of customary behavior that the law deems relevant.

CULPABLE CAUSATION

Mock jurors attribute greater causal significance to acts, and greater responsibility to those who perform them, the more morally blameworthy those acts are, even though the relative degree of perceived moral blameworthiness is causally irrelevant to the result (Alicke, 1992). In one experiment, for instance, participants more often identified a driver's speeding as the cause of an accident and held the driver more responsible for the accident when the driver was rushing home to hide a vial of cocaine from his parents than when he was rushing home to hide an anniversary present

---

[12] Ease of counterfactual simulation has also been invoked to explain the "Wells effect" (G. Wells, 1992): Jurors are more likely to find a defendant liable when presented with 80% reliable evidence that the defendant committed the act in question than they are when presented with (completely reliable) evidence that there is an 80% chance that the defendant committed the act in question. Niedermeier, Kerr, and Messé (1999) showed that jurors in the latter situation can more easily simulate a counterfactual scenario in which the defendant is innocent and are therefore more reluctant to hold the defendant liable.

[13] Note, finally, that the apparent conflict between the prototype effect studies (Bornstein & Rajki, 1994; V. Smith, 1991, 1993), which show that prototype-*consistent* facts lead to more guilty or liability verdicts, and norm theory studies, which show that abnormal or deviant, that is, norm-*inconsistent* facts lead to more liability verdicts, can be reconciled. Notwithstanding superficial resemblances, the two kinds of research deal with two different processes. Smith's work on intuitive prototypes of crimes, for instance, asks participants to engage in a matching task: (How well) does this set of facts match the (legal) definition of a given crime? Norm theory thinking also involves a contrast between given facts and a norm, but it responds to a different question: Why did the event happen? The "if only" thinking that this question engenders triggers an affective response that drives the ultimate judgments (as is discussed in chapter 3) that is missing from the matching task in the prototype studies.

Note also that although Bornstein and Rajki's (1994) study superficially resembles norm theory research in that it asked participants to rate how likely it was that the defendant's product caused the plaintiff's injuries, those participants were really engaged in a matching task. Bornstein and Rajki preinstructed participants that the experiment was going to test how people decide whether or not a certain kind of product is capable of causing a certain sort of injury. They then told participants that the plaintiff alleged that the defendant's product had caused the harm, gave participants expert testimony going both ways, and asked them: Do you think the defendant's product caused the harm? So they were not really asking participants to identify the cause of the plaintiff's harm. True norm theory work measures the effect of factual variations from perceived normalities or regularities. Bornstein and Rajki were, in effect, asking about the regularities themselves: Does a product of this sort lead to this sort of injury?

he had bought for them. A possible explanation for these results is that participants react with greater negative affect to those who act in a morally objectionable fashion, "staining" the actor's character, and then seek to validate that stain by attributing to the actor greater responsibility for the negative outcome (Alicke, 1992). (Other examples of this sort of relationship between negative affect and attributions of responsibility will be explored in chapter 3.)

FUNDAMENTAL ATTRIBUTION ERROR

Every human behavior is situated in its surrounding circumstances, and so is *a priori* attributable to both the actor and the situation. Yet people tend to attribute the behavior of others to the others' corresponding personality traits or dispositions rather than to situational constraints, even where the circumstances explain the behavior quite adequately. Psychologists call this habit of thought the *fundamental attribution error* (Nisbett & Ross, 1980; Ross & Anderson, 1982) or *correspondence bias* (Gilbert, 1998; Gilbert & Malone, 1995).

In one classic experiment, for instance, listeners assumed that speakers' pro-Castro remarks corresponded to the speakers' private opinions even though the listeners knew that the speakers were obeying the experimenter's explicit request to make those remarks. That is, the listeners attributed the pro-Castro remarks to the actors' pro-Castro dispositions rather than to situational factors that practically demanded pro-Castro behavior (Ross & Anderson, 1982). In another experiment, basketball players randomly assigned to shoot free throws in poorly lit gyms were judged as less capable than were players randomly assigned to shoot free throws in well-lit gyms. Observers chalked up the relatively poor shooting to the players ("can't shoot") rather than to the situation ("bad lighting"; Gilbert & Malone, 1995). As these and many other examples illustrate, attributions of behavior to the actor's traits rather than to the circumstances are often erroneous because there is in fact much less correlation between dispositions and behavior across markedly different situations than commonly believed (Ross & Nisbett, 1991).

The fundamental attribution error reflects both the availability and representativeness heuristics. It derives from availability because, in social settings, actors tend to appear more salient, and hence are more available, than situational elements and are thus more likely to be seen as causal agents (Nisbett & Ross, 1980; Taylor, 1982). (By contrast, people tend to attribute their own behavior to the circumstances rather than to their [perceived] dispositions, because from the actor's point of view, it is the circumstances that are more salient. This distinction between attributions for the behavior of self and others is known as the *actor–observer* effect;

Nisbett & Ross, 1980.[14]) The fundamental attribution error also derives from overreliance on representativeness because it treats behavior as representative of the dispositional state it resembles (Nisbett & Ross, 1980; Sherman & Corty, 1984).

Although the fundamental attribution error is one of the most robust of social psychological phenomena, it has also been qualified and criticized in various ways.[15] Two points are worth mentioning here. First, dispositional attributions for others' behavior are not inevitable; people tend initially and even automatically to understand others' conduct in this way but may, on reflection, modify or correct those initial impressions to incorporate more situational factors (Gilbert, 1998).[16] Second, the habit of making dispositional attributions may properly be termed an "error" when compared with social scientific norms of causal explanation but perhaps not when the observer has good reason to focus on the actor's contribution to events—for instance, when the observer's epistemic goal is to pass legal judgment on the actor (Gilbert, 1998; Hamilton, 1980).[17]

---

[14] For an introduction to the large and complex topic of attributions for things that one does or that happen to oneself, see Weiner (1995).

[15] Some social psychologists have questioned the cogency and even the existence of the fundamental attribution error, arguing that more recent research has not established that people display a general predilection to attribute causes to dispositions rather than to circumstances, has failed to substantiate the systematic differences between actor and observer attributions on which the fundamental attribution error is partly based, and has failed to demonstrate that attributions to the person are any more likely to be erroneous than attributions to the circumstances (Ajzen & Fishbein, 1983; Harvey & McGlynn, 1982; Harvey, Town, & Yarkin, 1981; Monson, 1983). Others have sought to explain the fundamental attribution "error" as reflecting participants' understandable observance of the *conversational norms* (Grice, 1989) governing the experimental situation. Participants "incorrectly" rely on normatively irrelevant information (e.g., in the essay-writing scenario, they draw inferences from the content of the essay to the writer's dispositions regarding the essay topic even when told that the writer was ordered to express that point of view in the essay) because the experimenter has provided them with the information about essay content and, consistent with Grice's maxim of relevance, participants assume they are supposed to use that information in reaching their judgments (Funder, 1987; N. Schwarz, 1996; Turnbull & Slugoski, 1988).

Cross-cultural research, moreover, indicates that the bias toward dispositional attributions may derive from broader cultural meaning systems, for example, the Western emphasis on individualism, rather than from more or less universal cognitive processes (Choi & Nisbett, 1998; Hamilton & Sanders, 1992; Menon, Morris, Chiu, & Hong, 1999; J. Miller, 1984; see also discussion in chapter 8).

[16] Leyens, Yzerbyt, and Corneille (1996) explained what they call the *overattribution bias* as a process of anchoring and adjustment (cf. Quattrone, 1982) that can lead people to attribute behavior to any sort of dispositional or situational factor depending on what kind of concept (e.g., personality-based, sociological) the experimental instructions activate in participants' minds, so long as the participants perceive that concept to be applicable to their judgmental task. (Other applications of anchoring and adjustment are discussed elsewhere in this chapter.)

[17] Hamilton (1980) argued that participants in the classic experiments cited to support the fundamental attribution error can be considered to have committed error only in terms of the model of scientific reasoning about causes. These participants, however, may have been acting not as "intuitive psychologists" but instead as "intuitive lawyers," and thus have understood the experimental question to require the attribution of responsibility instead of the explanation of causation. Attributions to the person rather than to the circumstances in these cases are "fully plausible as assessments of responsibility," Hamilton argued (1980, p. 770), because the actors in the experiments could have acted otherwise.

Hamilton's (1980) analysis may be sound with respect to voluntary behavior, which was the context of the experiments referred to, and to the *correspondent inference* theory of attribution

The fundamental attribution error suggests two implications for jurors' decisions in accident cases, at least for those cases in which the plaintiff argues negligence as a theory of recovery. First, jurors are likely to assume that accidents do not happen unless someone was negligent. Second, they are likely to attribute causation (and, hence, fault and responsibility) on the basis of the parties' personal dispositions to decide that the plaintiff or defendant acted as he did because "he's that kind of guy." Let me explain each of these in turn.

The fundamental attribution error should dispose jurors to find that accidents are due to someone's negligence, that "someone's to blame." Assume that no one is responsible for the accident, in the sense that no one is at fault. The accident "just happened." This amounts to saying, of each party, that there is no good reason to expect that party to have acted differently to avoid the accident. Under the circumstances, anyone else would have behaved the same way. The fundamental attribution error, by contrast, attributes the actor's behavior to his or her personality, to something "in" the actor, rather than to the circumstances. This is tantamount to saying that some substantial percentage of others would have acted differently under the circumstances. (If most others would have acted the same way as the actor did, then the attribution, logically, would have to be to the circumstances, because nothing "in" the actor led him or her to act differently from the norm.) But if the actor's conduct is different from that of the "ordinary prudent person," a standard most jurors are likely to identify with how they think most people behave,[18] then the actor is negligent (Keeton et al., 1984).[19] So committing the fundamental attribution error is inconsistent with the assumption that no one is responsible for the accident.[20]

---

on which she drew (Fiske & Taylor, 1991). According to Heider (1958), at the fourth level of responsibility, people are held responsible for their voluntary actions, unless there is a sufficient external justification. But Hamilton's critique of the fundamental attribution error does not apply to the negligence case, in which the test is not solely whether the actor could have acted otherwise, but whether he or she *should* have. Thus, Hamilton's (1980) observation that "[t]he fact that everyone else acted the same way in response to the experimenter's instructions [in an early attribution error experiment] is . . . useful causal information but is less relevant morally or legally" (p. 770) is not germane, because in the negligence case, distinguishing a party's behavior from what others would have done is generally very important to a finding of legal responsibility.

[18] According to textbook law, discussed briefly in chapter 1, behavior in accordance with custom is usually strong but not conclusive evidence that the behavior is reasonable; thus, compliance with customary behavior does not absolve a party from responsibility if the custom of the entire industry is careless. Conversely, a divergence from custom usually establishes carelessness but does not conclusively do so. Generally speaking, however, the "reasonably prudent person" corresponds to how (the jurors think) people other than the actor (i.e., an idealized version of themselves) would have behaved in similar circumstances; at the very least, the textbook law of negligence allows jurors great latitude to equate "reasonable behavior" with "how most people behave."

[19] Unless, of course, the party exercised *greater* care than the reasonably prudent person would have under the circumstances. This possibility is not at issue in many cases, including those studied in the second half of this book, and thus can be safely ignored for the present purposes.

[20] The fundamental attribution error concerns judgments about the causes of behavior, not

Thus, the fundamental attribution error should lead jurors to attribute both the cause of and the responsibility for an accident to someone's fault rather than to the circumstances. Accidents don't happen unless someone is negligent.[21] The question jurors in a negligence case are actually asked

about responsibility for outcomes, which is the question jurors must decide. In the psychological research, people commit the fundamental attribution error when asked the question: Why did the person act that way—was it the circumstances or his personal disposition? Jurors deciding accident cases confront what appears to be a very different question: Is the actor responsible for the accident? And this latter question ought to break down into two further distinct inquiries: whether the act caused the accident and whether the person acted as he or she did because he or she was careless. The hypothesis that the fundamental attribution error yields the presumption that "someone's to blame" thus seems to confuse the attribution of causation (of the behavior) with the attribution of responsibility (for the outcome). I will explain why it is nevertheless appropriate to conflate, as does my argument in the text, attributions of causation and responsibility in this context.

Many social psychologists are careful to observe that attributions of causation and responsibility are different matters (Fincham & Jaspars, 1980; Shaver, 1985). Specifically, an attribution of causation is ordinarily necessary (Fincham & Jaspars, 1980) but not sufficient for an attribution of responsibility. Responsibility without causation may indeed arise when a person in a certain relationship to one who causes harm is held answerable, for example, vicarious liability of an employer for acts by employees within the scope of employment (see chapter 1). But attributions of responsibility ordinarily involve not only causation but also other factors, such as the extent to which the actor was *free* to act and whether he or she should have *foreseen* the likely consequences of his act (Fiske & Taylor, 1991; Heider, 1958; Shaver, 1985). (Even an actor with control over his or her behavior who should have foreseen the consequences may be judged not responsible for those consequences if another cause intervened; Schultz, Schleifer, & Altman, 1981.)

Notwithstanding these distinctions between attributions of causation and responsibility, the fundamental attribution error is relevant to attributions of responsibility for accidents for at least three reasons. First, the distinction between behavior and outcomes diminishes in jurors' minds because, on the basis of norm theory, jurors should already be likely to attribute the cause of the accident to one or more acts or omissions of a party, especially precautions taken or forgone. Thus, an inquiry into the cause of the behavior in question will appear to jurors to be an inquiry into a possible cause of the accident. Second, the two requirements beyond causation for attributing responsibility for outcomes, control and foreseeability, are also implicitly satisfied in the context of the accident case. The law regards the actor as free to act in the absence of evidence of mental incapacity, compulsion, or unavoidable accident (Keeton et al., 1984), and the hindsight bias (see discussion later in this chapter) implicitly furnishes the foreseeability dimension of responsibility. Taken together, the assumptions that the actor could have behaved differently and should have foreseen the consequences of his or her behavior lead under hornbook negligence law to the conclusion that the actor is at fault for not acting differently (Casper, Benedict, & Perry, 1989; Loftus & Beach, 1982). Third, the judgmental context may make the causal attribution tantamount to an attribution of responsibility, because jurors are likely to make causal attributions with the socially governed consequences—a judgment of responsibility and liability—in mind (Lloyd-Bostock, 1983). For all of these reasons, the fundamental attribution error should bias jurors' attributions of responsibility for accidents, and not merely their attributions of the causes of behavior.

Some experimental research confirms that people conflate attributions of causation and responsibility. In terms of Heider's (1958) typology of levels of responsibility, the greatest marginal increase in attribution of responsibility occurs when causation, and not merely association, is present (Fincham & Jaspars, 1979). Accident victims offer additional support: Whether they identify themselves or others as the cause of the accident, more than 85% attribute fault to the person identified as the cause (Hensler et al., 1991). (Other research showing how jurors conflate causation and fault is referenced in chapter 4.)

[21] The doctrine of negligence, of course, recognizes a class of cases in which the defendant's fault may be implied from the mere fact of an accident: *res ipsa loquitur* ("the thing speaks for itself"). The first element of *res ipsa* requires that the accident be of a kind that ordinarily does not occur without negligence (Keeton et al., 1984). (The other elements, that the instrumentality of the accident be within the defendant's exclusive control and that the plaintiff not contribute to the accident, do not concern us here.) But what distinguishes the cases that meet this criterion from those that do not? None of the usual doctrinal

to confront is, "Who, if anyone, is responsible for the accidental injury?" But given the fundamental attribution error, jurors may reformulate this question as, "Who among the parties before the court is responsible?" Because the accident must have been caused by someone's carelessness, the jurors' task is simply to determine whose.

Who are jurors, prone to commit attribution error, likely to think is responsible for the accident? The second and more obvious implication of the fundamental attribution error for juror decision making in negligence cases is that jurors would be expected to attribute responsibility for the accident on the basis of the sort of person a party is.[22] The fundamental attribution error links behavior and traits; and while psychological research participants inferred traits from behavior, lawyers can exploit the connection in the other direction: X is a good (careful, deserving) person, and therefore could not be responsible for a bad outcome (the accident).

I am unaware of any research specifically testing the effects of fundamental attribution error on decision making in accident cases, but experimental support for its application to accident cases may be found elsewhere. In criminal cases, evidence that the defendant has been convicted of other crimes in the past is sometimes admitted for the limited purpose of impeaching the defendant's credibility as a witness. The admission is accompanied by an instruction that jurors not consider the prior convictions as evidence of the defendant's guilt in the case at bar. Much experimental research confirms that mock jurors are unable to adhere to this limiting instruction. Those who sit on mock trials in which the priors are admitted with the cautionary instruction convict at a higher rate than

---

interpretations of "does not ordinarily occur without negligence" accurately captures the only valid basis in probability theory for inferring negligence from the fact of the injury: that the probability of negligence, given the injury, be greater than half (Kaye, 1979). The verbal vagueness and statistical incoherence of this element of *res ipsa* doctrine suggest that what divides the cases satisfying the element from the cases that do not is merely a rough distinction between the accidents people are expected to put up with in the absence of proof that the defendant is negligent (e.g., a passenger who slips and falls while getting on a bus), and those, on the other hand, that stand out from the ordinary run of events (e.g., the pedestrian who, while walking in front of the defendant flour dealer's building, is hit by a falling barrel of flour [*Byrne v Boadle*, 1863]). In any event, the cases studied in this book do not appear to meet the standard definition of *res ipsa* (e.g., in *Butler*, discussed in chapter 5, the judge did not instruct jurors on *res ipsa* even though he speculated that *res ipsa* might be necessary to send the case to the jury without any evidence of how Butler fell [B. 64.4–22, 4/25/90]).

[22] The standard negligence instruction encourages jurors to ask whether each party is "the kind of person (who would act negligently)," because the instruction is phrased in terms of how the reasonable "person" would act. By also referring to the circumstances, the instruction (and other instructions on the relative nature of "ordinary care" and "quantum of care"; Devitt et al., 1987) might appear to avoid the fundamental attribution error. But the focus on the "reasonable person" (as opposed to, say, reasonable behavior) directs jurors' attention to the individual rather than the circumstances. Moreover, the instruction posits a stable personality, that of the reasonable person, which would exacerbate the tendency to attribute causation (and responsibility) to enduring dispositions of the actor—to personality and attitude—rather than to the circumstances. Thus, the instruction may lead jurors to define fault differently than does standard tort doctrine, according to which negligence should be understood purely in terms of conduct, as the creation of unreasonable risks, and not as a state of mind (Keeton et al., 1984).

those who do not learn about the priors (e.g., Wissler & Saks, 1985). While not excluding other explanations, researchers frequently speculate that the fundamental attribution error may account for this effect: The priors lead jurors to conclude that the defendant is the sort of guy who commits crimes like this.[23]

In addition, anecdotal evidence suggests that the fundamental attribution error plays a large role in juror thinking. The advocate's strategy of seeking to persuade the jury that the other party is the sort of person who would be responsible for the accident, and that his or her client is not, is well recognized in the literature of the psychology of legal argument and in the profession.[24] It would indeed make sense for lawyers to argue this way, to exploit the "illusion of validity" that results from internal consistency among inputs (Saks & Kidd, 1980). The more the inputs (e.g., aspects of defendant's character) seem "of a piece," the more confidence a lay decision maker will have in the accuracy of the inference from those inputs. Hence, "The skillful attorney may trade on this defect of intuition by trying to paint a consistent personality picture of a party to a case" (Saks & Kidd, 1980, p. 136).

HINDSIGHT BIAS

The hindsight bias is the tendency to overestimate the probability of a known outcome and the ability of decision makers to have foreseen it (e.g., Fischhoff, 1975, 1982b). In short, when informed of the outcome of a series of events, people are prone to think that "I knew it would happen" (Fischhoff & Beyth, 1975). The hindsight bias is one of the most consistently replicated effects in the cognitive psychology literature and has proved fairly resistant to attempts to reduce its impact ("debiasing"; Fischhoff, 1982a; for reviews, see Hawkins & Hastie, 1990; Rachlinski, 1998).

The best explanation for the hindsight bias seems to be Fischhoff's

---

[23] Relatedly, research on how people's implicit theories of social reality affect their social judgments shows that "entity" theorists, who (like people prone to the fundamental attribution error) look to stable traits as causes of behavior, are more likely than "incremental" theorists, who look for more dynamic explanations for others' behavior (e.g., in terms of those others' goals or needs), to base judgments of guilt or innocence in a simulated criminal case on (legally irrelevant) personal information about the defendant and are likely to recommend harsher punishments (Levy & Dweck, 1998; Levy, Plaks, & Dweck, 1999).

[24] For instance, as Judge Richard Posner wrote in granting summary judgment in an age discrimination case:

> This part of the affidavits [proffered by the plaintiff, Visser] is amateur psychoanalysis. They do not report primary facts from which a reasonable person in [affiants'] position would infer that one of Packer's [the employer's] motives was to deprive Visser of most of his pension. They construct a psychological model of Packer and deduce from it that he must have wanted to do Visser out of a pension. He was that kind of guy. This is the kind of argumentation one expects in a closing argument. (*Visser v. Packer Engineering Assoc.*, 1991, p. 659)

(1975) idea of "creeping determinism." Once people know the outcome of a sequence of events, they assimilate the outcome and the prior events into a coherent whole; and in making sense of that whole, they tend to attribute greater causal significance to some of those events than those events seemed to warrant in foresight. In addition, several researchers have identified a connection between the counterfactual thinking that underlies norm theory and the hindsight bias. Counterfactual thinking enhances the hindsight bias by providing the observer with an explanation for why things occurred as they did, which hardens the observer's certainty that things were bound to have occurred as they did (Roese, 1997; Roese & Olson, 1996; C. Williams, Lees-Haley, & Brown, 1993; but cf. Robbennolt & Sobus, 1997).

Support for the hindsight bias comes from many areas of the law (see Rachlinski, 1998). For example, mock jurors' damage awards in a civil suit against a police officer for an allegedly illegal search and seizure were significantly affected by whether and what the jurors knew about the outcome of the search, even though this information should have been irrelevant to their decisions (Casper, Benedict, & Perry, 1989). Those who were informed that the search had turned up contraband gave lower awards than did those in a neutral condition who were not provided any outcome information.

The hindsight bias has obvious relevance to accident cases tried under a negligence theory. As explained in chapter 1, fault or lack of reasonable care is an essential element of negligence liability, and reasonable care means taking steps to avoid foreseeable risk of harm. So negligence liability hinges on foreseeability: the perceived likelihood of the harm *ex ante*, before the accident occurs. But jurors decide the case after the accident has already occurred. Therefore, they are making an *ex post* (after the fact) judgment about that *ex ante* possibility. The hindsight bias predicts that jurors will overestimate the foreseeability of the accident and tend to hold the injurer liable for not foreseeing that his or her conduct would lead to harm.

Research bears out this hypothesis. In one study (Kamin & Rachlinski, 1995) based on an actual case, participants were asked to decide whether a town should have taken the precaution of hiring an operator for its drawbridge during the winter when the bridge was not in use. The risk was that if ice built up and the river flooded, ships might be dislodged and float toward the bridge, damaging it if the drawbridge could not be raised to let the ships through. Some participants were placed in an *ex ante*, foresight condition (before any such accident had occurred) and were asked whether the city should hire the operator. Other participants were placed in *ex post*, hindsight conditions (after such an accident had occurred) and were asked whether the town should be held responsible in negligence for not hiring the operator. (One hindsight condition group was simply made aware of the accident; the others also heard an instruction designed to counter any hindsight bias.) Less than a quarter of those in the foresight condition decided that an operator should be hired, but more than half in the hindsight conditions decided that the operator should have been hired. (There was no significant difference between those who heard the debiasing instruction and those who did not.) In another experiment, participants were asked to determine the reasonableness of a psychotherapist's conduct under the *Tarasoff* rule, which imposes on psychotherapists a duty to take reasonable steps, including warning, to protect the foreseeable victims of a patient's violence after release. Participants who were told that the patient did commit violence after release were more likely to decide that the psychotherapist should have foreseen the violence and was negligent for not doing so than were participants who were not given any such outcome information (LaBine & LaBine, 1996).

In sum, the hindsight bias would be predicted to increase jurors' attributions of responsibility to the parties in accident cases—most obviously to defendants whose acts lead to injuries to plaintiffs, but also to plaintiffs who are alleged to have been contributorily negligent.

SEVERITY EFFECT

Information about the extent of an accident victim's injuries may affect judgments about causality and responsibility. In an early, often-cited experiment, Walster (1966) presented two groups of participants with nearly identical scenarios. In both, a man left his car parked on a hill, and after he left, the car rolled down the hill. One group was told that the car hit a tree stump; the other was told that the car struck and injured a person. The second group found the car owner more responsible for the accident than did the first group. This is known as the *severity effect* or *outcome severity effect* (Robbennolt, in press).

Data concerning the severity of the consequences cannot affect the overall judgment of responsibility if the decision makers observe the demarcations between the doctrinal categories of breach, causation, and injury (see chapter 1). Strictly speaking, the extent of the injury should be irrelevant to the determinations of fault and causation (although it is, of course, relevant to the measure of damages, assuming responsibility is established). Yet Walster's (1966) participants "bent" their judgments in the direction of a more global conception of responsibility for the accident, a prototype in which responsibility increases as the consequences become more serious.

A "cold" cognitive explanation for the severity effect is the hindsight bias, discussed above. Jurors who know that a person's conduct led to serious consequences will be prone to believe that the person should have foreseen those consequences and is responsible for not doing so and not taking steps to avoid them. "Hot" or motivated explanations for the effect are discussed in chapter 3.

The severity effect has been the subject of considerable psychological research (for a review and meta-analysis, see Robbennolt, in press). In general, the effect is significant but its strength depends in part on how the effect is measured (e.g., in terms of judgments of liability, responsibility, blame, or punishment), with the weakest effects on judgments of liability (Robbennolt, in press).

ANCHORING AND ADJUSTMENT

People who have to make a numerical estimate on the basis of un-certain or incomplete information may select a reference point or initial estimate, an *anchor*, and then *adjust* the initial figure up or down to reach their judgment (Jacowitz & Kahneman, 1995; Tversky & Kahneman, 1982b; cf. Strack & Musweiler, 1997). The anchoring and adjustment bias leads people to give undue weight to irrelevant and even arbitrary anchors, insufficiently adjusting them to reach the final estimate. In a striking il-lustration, participants were asked to estimate various quantities, such as the percentage of African countries in the United Nations. An anchor between 0 and 100 was provided by spinning a wheel of fortune, and par-ticipants saw the wheel being spun. Participants were asked first to indicate whether the number on the wheel was higher or lower than the value to be estimated, and then to estimate that value by moving up or down from the number. These evidently arbitrary starting points unduly influenced partic-ipants' final estimates. For example, those given an anchor of 10 estimated the percentage at issue as 25%; those given an anchor of 65 estimated it at 45% (Tversky & Kahneman, 1982b). The same anchoring phenomenon also affects nonnumerical judgments, for example, the *prior hypothesis bias* or the undue staying power of first impressions (Arkes, 1989).

The obvious application of anchoring and adjustment to accident cases is in the determination of damages, especially pain and suffering dam-ages and punitive damages, as to the determination of which the judge provides jurors with little if any meaningful guidance (Greene, 1989; Hastie et al., 1998; Wissler et al., 1997). A number of studies have indeed shown that when mock jurors are provided with an anchor in the form of the *ad damnum* or amount requested by the plaintiff's attorney, their damage awards are biased toward that anchor (Chapman & Bornstein, 1996; Greene, 1989; Hastie, Schkade, & Payne, 1999; Malouff & Schutte, 1988), although one study found no such effect (Greene, Downey, & Goodman-Delahunty, 1999). In addition, Raitz, Greene, Goodman, and Loftus (1990) found that expert testimony on damages can exert an anchoring effect on jurors' awards: When the plaintiff's expert specified an amount representing the plaintiff's lost wages, mock jurors' most frequent award was precisely that amount. Both compensatory (Hinsz & Indahl, 1995) and punitive (Robbennolt & Studebaker, 1999) damage awards may be anchored by statutory award limits, which may thus actually increase the average size of those awards, contrary to the intentions of those who enacted the limits. It is interesting to note that Chapman and Bornstein (1996) also found that anchoring had a *cross-modality effect*, such that anchors on damage awards influenced mock jurors' judgments about whether the defendant caused the plaintiff's harm, and causal anchors affected damage awards. The anchor, moreover, can be provided by jurors' own prior beliefs as well as by the attorneys' arguments, expert witnesses, or other aspects of the case. Greene, Goodman, and Loftus (1991) found that mock jurors who believed that million-dollar verdicts in personal injury cases were common tended to award greater compensatory damages than those who did not.

DECISION FRAMING (PROSPECT THEORY)

Contrary to the assumptions of rational choice theory (on which normative law and economics relies, for example), the way people make choices regarding uncertain outcomes often depends on how those choices are posed to them or framed. The most robust finding in this literature is that people are generally risk-averse when a choice is framed as a potential gain and risk-preferring when the mathematically identical choice is framed as a potential loss (Kahneman & Tversky, 1984; Tversky & Kahneman, 1981).

In Tversky and Kahneman's (1981) classic experiment, participants were told that the outbreak of an unusual disease threatened to kill 600 people in the United States, and they were presented with a choice between two programs to combat the disease. One program would certainly save 200 people; the other presented a 1 in 3 chance of saving 600 and a 2 in 3 chance of saving no one. Nearly three quarters of participants preferred the first program. In the next phase, other participants were presented with the same threatening disease scenario, but a choice between two other programs. One would certainly result in 400 people dying; the other, a 1 in 3 chance that no one would die and a 2 in 3 chance that 600 would die. More than three quarters of these participants selected the second program. It is clear that the sets of programs in the two phases of the experiment are identical mathematically. The only difference is that the first pair of programs is framed in terms of lives saved, whereas the second pair is framed in terms of lives lost.

Subsequent experiments by Tversky and Kahneman as well as others have confirmed this asymmetry in attitudes toward risk. A unit of possible loss is disvalued more than the identical amount of possible gain is valued, or *loss aversion* (Kahneman & Tversky, 1984). A related anomaly in people's reasoning about valuing gains and losses is the *endowment effect*: People often demand more to give up an object than they are willing to pay to acquire it (Kahneman, 1994; Kahneman, Knetsch, & Thaler, 1991).

Decision framing is relevant to judgments of both liability and compensation for accidents. How a risk is framed *ex ante* may determine how seriously people view the risk and whether they think precautions should be taken to avoid the risk (Margolis, 1996), and this, in turn, via the hindsight bias, influences *ex post* perceptions of responsibility for not taking those precautions, should a bad outcome occur. More specifically, if people see incurring a risk as a loss from the status quo rather than seeing avoiding the risk as a gain, they are more likely to fear the risk and believe steps should be (or have been) taken to avoid it. Because most any risk can be framed either way (as a new danger and thus as a loss from the status quo, or as part of a broader class of dangers people already face, the elimination of which is therefore a gain), framing alone can affect judgments of responsibility (Margolis, 1996).

Framing also affects compensation awards. McCaffery, Kahneman, and Spitzer (1995) showed that when pain and suffering damages are framed as the amount the plaintiff needs to be made whole once the injury has already occurred (the *ex post* perspective), awards are significantly lower than when they are framed as the amount the plaintiff would have to have been paid to suffer the injury in the first place (the *ex ante* perspective). This makes perfect sense in terms of loss aversion, because from an *ex ante* perspective, the injury is a loss from the status quo and is thus valued more than compensation is from the *ex post* perspective, in which being compensated is a gain relative to the status quo. (One can also think of this in terms of the endowment effect. People demand more to "sell" their uninjured status than, already injured, they would pay to "buy" it.) The law formally discourages the *ex ante* perspective, but many lawyers are familiar with its use (McCaffery et al., 1995).[25]

BIASES IN COMPREHENSION OF STATISTICS

Finally, I mention a phenomenon well known to students of lay judgment: When estimating likelihood or frequency, people tend not to understand basic principles of probability and statistics and to violate those principles in systematic ways (Nisbett & Ross, 1980; Tversky & Kahneman, 1982a, 1982b). Many of these errors, as noted earlier, are due to the use of the availability and representativeness heuristics. Recall that people tend to judge the frequency of a class of events on the basis of the ease with

---

[25] Framing also affects other aspects of law, such as litigation and settlement strategies (for original research and a review of the literature, see Rachlinski, 1996) and message persuasiveness (S. Smith & Petty, 1996).

which instances of the class come to mind (availability), which may or may not correspond to the objective frequency. And people tend to make judgments of likelihood (e.g., that a target person or event is a member of a class) by relying on the perceived degree of resemblance between known features of the target and features presumed to be characteristic of the class (representativeness), thereby giving insufficient weight to base rate information (i.e., prior probabilities), sample size, and other factors on which correct statistical inferences ought to depend (Tversky & Kahneman, 1982b). Indeed, they do so even when the information provided about the target is diagnostically worthless, as in the engineer–lawyer experiment mentioned earlier (Kahneman & Tversky, 1973). Ignoring base rate information may also reflect the availability heuristic: Lay decision makers may emphasize anecdote at the expense of prior probabilities because the latter information tends to be less vivid, and therefore less available, for making judgments (Nisbett & Ross, 1980).

As with other judgmental biases, using availability and representativeness rather than following sound statistical principles may very well make sense for lay decision makers in general, because people need to conserve their scarce "on-line" cognitive capacity (Fiske & Taylor, 1991) and often have little incentive to take the time and effort needed to refine their everyday judgments. And as with other judgmental biases, reasoning by availability and representativeness often yields judgments of likelihood and probability that are correct enough. Moreover, people may simply lack the expertise needed to follow normative rules of statistics, although research indicates that they can be taught to improve their statistical reasoning (Nisbett, 1993). Yet, as with other cognitive biases, the habits of thought people use to estimate likelihoods and probabilities can lead to judgments that diverge from objective fact. In the context of assigning responsibility and determining compensation for accidents, as well as other aspects of the trial process, those divergences take on increased significance (Saks & Kidd, 1980).

In any given accident case, jurors may use, and advocates may invite them to use, any or all of these habits of thought. We will see in the second half of the book how lawyers' and jurors' talk reflects these ways of thinking. I conclude the first half of the book, in chapter 4, by trying to draw some of these habits of thought together to suggest certain broader characteristics of jurors' common sense about accidents. Before reaching that point, however, I consider jurors' habits of *feeling* as well as their ways of thinking, and examine how emotion and cognition interact in shaping jurors' judgments. This is the topic of the next chapter.

3

THE SOCIAL PSYCHOLOGY OF JUROR JUDGMENTS II: EMOTIONS AND LEGAL JUDGMENT

That emotions play some role in how people think about responsibility and compensation for accidents is intuitively obvious, but what part they play is not at all clear. There is considerable disagreement in the psychological literature about just what emotions are and whether a psychobiological, cognitive, or cultural approach, or some combination, is the most fruitful way to study them. Furthermore, although the effects of emotional or motivated thinking, so-called "hot" cognitions, on the sorts of social judgments involved in deciding accident cases have been the object of much research in the last two decades, we still know much less about them than we do about the "cold" cognitive phenomena discussed in chapter 2. Finally, the emotional and nonemotional aspects of one's judgment processes may seem inextricable from each other, and teasing out the distinct contributions of emotion to judgment is therefore quite difficult.

In this chapter, I outline some of the psychological research on affective states and their influences on social, and specifically legal, judgment. I discuss some of the emotions that seem most relevant to jurors' judgments about accidents—sympathy, anger, and anxiety (or fear)—and, as appro-

The full text of this article appeared originally at 65 TENN.L.REV.1 (1997); the portions included here, edited by the author, are adapted by permission of the Tennessee Law Review Association, Inc.

priate, I elaborate in connection with each the emotional dimensions of the habits of thought already discussed in chapter 2. (Research on the influence of moods, as opposed to specific emotions, on social judgment is summarized in the Appendix.) First, however, I offer some general findings from the growing and conflicting body of emotion theory and research on the topics of emotion in general, emotion and reason, and emotional regulation. For readers unfamiliar with the psychological study of the emotions, this brief, basic survey will prove useful. Those who are more knowledgeable about the psychology of the emotions may prefer to turn directly to the second part of the chapter.

EMOTIONS IN GENERAL

The psychological literature on emotions includes widely varying theories and diverse findings, so any attempt to provide a capsule description of what emotions are is bound to be problematic (see Russell & Barrett, 1999). Given that caveat, *emotion* may be defined as

> a complex set of interactions . . . mediated by neural/hormonal systems, which can (a) give rise to affective experiences such as feelings of arousal, pleasure/displeasure; (b) generate cognitive processes such as emotionally relevant perceptual effects [and] appraisals . . . ; (c) activate widespread physiological adjustments to the arousing conditions; and (d) lead to behavior that is often, but not always, expressive, goal-directed, and adaptive. (Plutchik, 1994, p. 5)

That is to say: (a) Emotions incline or ready a person to change in certain ways; (b) those ways include feelings and thoughts, brain and body states, and actions; and (c) emotions may be triggered by both external and internal events. Thus, emotions combine cognitive, affective, and action-oriented features (Lazarus, 1991a, 1991b; Scherer, 1984, 1993). The capacity to experience emotion, moreover, is genetic (LeDoux, 1996); people do not make up their ability to experience and respond emotionally, although they certainly learn display rules and ways of understanding what emotions mean.

The primary function of emotions is to signal changes in the environment that are important to the person experiencing the emotion (Lazarus, 1991a, 1991b) and to help that person to choose among and to coordinate competing goals, objectives, and values (Damasio, 1994; Plutchik, 1994). To perform these functions effectively, at least some emotional responding occurs rapidly, beneath the threshold of consciousness (Ekman, 1994a; LeDoux, 1996; M. Robinson, 1998). For instance, fear in the presence of a threatening object (say, a wild animal) adjusts a person's priorities and triggers physiological changes that ready him or her to act accordingly (run or fight!). For the fear response to serve its purpose, the fear-provoking stimuli are processed directly through the amygdala, in a manner not available to consciousness, as well as through the more circuitous cortical pathway, which may then provide additional feedback to the amygdala (Le-Doux, 1996). The feelings and related thoughts of which people are aware are the conscious output of this (partly) unconscious process.

Yet, according to the cognitive theorists of the emotions (e.g., Lazarus, 1991a; Ortony, Clore, & Collins, 1988) on whose work much of my analysis depends, to observe that part of humans' emotional processing is subconscious is perfectly consistent with the claim that emotions are fundamentally *cognitive*. Each emotion depends on an (implicit) *appraisal* of the significance for the person of changes in that person's environment (Clore, 1994), and emotions (or groups of them) can be differentiated from one another on the basis of the general cognitive structures of these appraisals (Ortony et al., 1988; Roseman, Antoniou, & Jose, 1996; C. Smith & Ellsworth, 1985). For instance, to be angry is to have perceived "a demeaning offense against me and mine" (Lazarus, 1994, p. 164). People's emotional lives, moreover, encompass not just the initial appraisal but also extensive reflection, evaluation, and modification of their own and others' emotions. In short, cognition (in a broad sense) infuses the experience of emotion, even though it does not exhaust that experience.

Many psychologists consider some emotions to be more "basic" than others (see, e.g., Ekman, 1992; Plutchik, 1994), and some believe that certain emotions are universal, in part because of evidence that facial displays of different emotions are recognizable across cultures (Ekman, 1973, 1994b; cf. Carroll & Russell, 1996; Russell, 1994, 1995). Others, however, insist that emotions are social constructions (Averill, 1983; Harré, 1986), a view that emphasizes intercultural and even intracultural variations in how emotions are experienced, displayed, and construed (Lakoff, 1987; Scherer, 1997; Shweder, 1994).

EMOTION AND REASON

To raise the topic of emotion and legal judgment is to confront the common view that emotions are irrational and that emotional decision making is therefore very different from rational decision making. This view takes several forms: emotions have no rational content; emotional responding is rapid and (therefore) non-reflective; emotional arousal interferes with rational deliberation; emotions arise from subconscious sources and hence are incorrigible (e.g., Solomon, 1990). As a preliminary matter, it will help us to understand how emotions may influence legal judgment if we see the extent to which these general presumptions are either unsubstantiated or, at any rate, much less descriptive of some emotions than of others.

First, it is true that emotions begin as neurological events—the operation and, to some extent, consequences of which are unavailable to the conscious mind. In this sense, at least part of a person's emotional life is not "rational" (LeDoux, 1996; Zajonc, 1980). But the emotions relevant to legal judgments about accidents are not *only* subconscious; they also have conscious content. It is widely accepted that the vast majority of emotions are not merely irrational urges or preferences. Rather, as noted above, emotions involve cognitive appraisals of changes in the individual's relation to his or her environment (Frijda, 1986; Lazarus, 1991a, 1991b; Ortony et al., 1988). Emotions thus involve beliefs as well as feelings (de Sousa, 1987; Greenspan, 1988; Harré, 1986; Nussbaum, 1995; Rorty, 1980; Solomon, 1990). If the underlying belief or appraisal is shown to be mistaken, the emotion itself may be judged inappropriate or wrong (Kahan & Nussbaum, 1996).

Second, emotions *as they participate in the legal decision-making process* need not be so unreflective as to undermine reasoned deliberation. While it may be true that the primary function and virtue of some emotions is to permit quick, nondeliberative processing of information and to prepare the person experiencing the emotion to act immediately (Ekman, 1994a; Plutchik, 1994), this is generally not true of many other emotions (including, e.g., sympathy). These other emotions are best conceived as processes rather than as immediate responses to environmental stimuli (Scherer, 1984, 1993), and (as we see below) they may be modified by reappraisal of the environment and in other ways (Ellsworth, 1994). Given the context of decision making at trial—the duration of the process, as well as the requirement of deliberation and the norm encouraging it—there is plenty of opportunity to reevaluate and modify even such emotions as anger and fear.

Third, we must consider whether emotions are likely to be irrational in the sense that they disrupt reasoned deliberation. Certainly the arousal produced by very strong emotions may disrupt complex information processing (Petty, Gleicher, & Baker, 1991; Yerkes & Dodson, 1908; Zillmann, 1994). The potential interference of emotional arousal with complex judgment, however, depends on the emotion. A typically less strongly valenced (less strongly felt as positive or negative) emotion such as sympathy, which tends to produce less arousal than many other emotions (Eisenberg & Fabes, 1990), may interfere less than do other emotions that play a role in legal judgment, such as anger (Zillmann, 1994). And once again, the time-consuming processes of legal proof and decision making seem likely to reduce or prevent the interference that emotional arousal might produce in other settings (Kaplan, 1991).

Fourth, while emotions do arise from unconscious sources and therefore may influence legal judgment in ways one cannot know, and hence cannot fully address or control (LeDoux, 1996; Plutchik, 1994), the same is true of many non-emotion-based judgment processes. People are often unaware of what has given rise to the schemas, scripts, and other implicit and intuitive knowledge structures discussed in chapter 2, which can influence subsequent perceptions and judgments. Moreover, research in belief perseverance, for instance, which shows that people tend to persist in their beliefs in the face of both new data that should lead them to modify those beliefs and information that discredits the original basis for them (Ross & Anderson, 1982), applies regardless of whether those beliefs arose through emotional or nonemotional cognitions. And although the intractability of certain deep emotional disorders indicates that some emotions are less subject to conscious modification than are (some) non-emotion-based knowledge structures, other emotions, especially highly cognitive ones such as sympathy (Feigenson, 1997), need not be.

In sum, to say that emotions may figure in common-sense thinking about accidents is not to say that those thoughts are somehow "tainted" by, much less given over to, irrationality. I proceed to consider what the psychological literature has to say about *how* emotions shape the judgments that enter into common-sense thinking about accidents. First, however, I consider the extent to which decision makers can *regulate* the effect of recognized emotions on their judgments, as the law generally urges them to do (Feigenson, 1997).

EMOTIONAL CONTROL

Broadly speaking, emotional experience itself can be regulated, in theory and sometimes in practice, by monitoring one's own emotions and moods and attempting to discern their causes; one can then try to adjust one's surroundings to relieve negative moods or maintain positive ones (Salovey, Hsee, & Mayer, 1993; Salovey & Mayer, 1990). A person experiencing a negative emotion may try to cope with it (Lazarus, 1991a) by action directed at the stimulus producing the emotion, by reappraising the significance of the stimulus (Isen, 1984; Lazarus, 1991a), or by actively recruiting positive memories to counteract negative moods (Josephson, Singer, & Salovey, 1996). People can also, to some extent, control the behavioral consequences of the emotions they experience (Emmons, King, & Sheldon, 1993; Lazarus, 1991a).

There are, of course, limits to people's ability to control their emotions. People differ in their "emotional intelligence"—their ability to monitor, evaluate, and regulate emotions in themselves and in others (Goleman, 1995; Salovey & Mayer, 1990; but cf. Davies, Stankov, & Roberts, 1998). Emotions result in part from unconscious processes, which may frustrate or prevent attempts consciously to modify them (LeDoux, 1996). Indeed, efforts to control one's moods under cognitive strain may produce an "ironic" result of mood change in a direction opposite to that intended (Wegner, 1989; Wegner, Erber, & Zanakos, 1993). Similarly, instructions to mock jurors to disregard emotion-provoking evidence actually increased the influence of that evidence on jurors' verdicts and sentences in a simulated criminal case (Edwards & Bryan, 1997). Finally, efforts to control certain strong emotions through suppression may have adverse consequences for the physical health of the individual (Pennebaker, 1989; Petrie, Booth, & Pennebaker, 1998).

Once again, the amenability of emotional influence on judgments to self-regulation may very well depend on the emotion in question. Some fears and anxieties may be "emotionally remembered" in the amygdala, and thus impervious to attempts at conscious retrieval, much less extinction or alteration (LeDoux, 1996). This should be much less true of sympathy, however, because of its highly cognitive nature (Feigenson, 1997). Indeed, there is evidence that even the (often) strong emotion of anger can be (at least partially) regulated (Averill, 1994; Tice & Baumeister, 1993), which suggests that the usually less arousing emotion of sympathy can be as well.

Finally, the decision-making context may modify the influence of emotions on judgment. For instance, accountability may attenuate the role of emotions: People who believe that they will be held accountable in some sense for their decisions tend to be less prone to heuristic mental processing (Tetlock, 1985), including the use of their emotions as cues to judgment (J. Lerner, Goldberg, & Tetlock, 1998).

PARTICULAR EMOTIONS AND EMOTIONAL EFFECTS

I now examine more closely the particular emotions that may be expected to figure most prominently in jurors' decision making about accidents: sympathy, anger, and anxiety (or fear).[1] I define each emotion, identify the factors associated with the arousal of that emotion (the "inputs" to emotion in the social judgment process), and survey the emotion's effects on judgment (its "outputs"). I also explain relationships between each emotion and the habits of thought discussed in chapter 2. I begin with, and devote the most extended discussion to, sympathy because it is the emotion most frequently supposed to influence juror judgments (Feigenson, 1997).

Sympathy[2]

Sympathy is a heightened awareness of the suffering of another and the urge to alleviate that suffering (Mercer, 1972; Wispé, 1991). The

---

[1] Other emotions, for example, disgust (W. Miller, 1997), may also be relevant to juror judgments in accident cases.
[2] *Sympathy* is often used synonymously with *compassion*, *pity*, or *empathy*. Philosophers, psychologists, and legal commentators have used each of the latter three terms to refer to what I call sympathy. Sympathy should, nevertheless, be distinguished from all three. For an

awareness of the other's suffering is both thought and felt, and is accompanied by the desire to do something about the suffering (Wispé, 1991)— the *action tendency* (Lazarus, 1991a) associated with the emotion. Sympathy involves the ability to imagine oneself in the sufferer's predicament and, in some sense, to feel the other's pain (Batson, 1991; Davis, 1994). It also requires the ability to discriminate between feeling one's own pain and sympathizing with another's pain, because "only action driven by the recognition of others' pain *as theirs*, and the urge to relieve it *in them*, qualifies as sympathetic helping" (Wispé, 1991, p. 158). The ability to sympathize, like the capacity to experience and act on other emotions, varies by individual (Lazarus, 1991a).[3]

---

observation of the overlap and the need to clarify the confusion among sympathy, empathy, pity, and compassion, see, for example, Lazarus (1991a).

Sympathy is perhaps closest to *compassion*. Solomon's (1990, p. 231) definition of *compassion* —"to be concerned, to wish fervently that the suffering would cease, and to want (perhaps desperately) to do what will bring this end about"—is virtually the same as my conception of sympathy. In ordinary usage, however, compassion seems to require a higher threshold of the other's suffering.

Sympathy is also similar to *pity*, at least in the classical sense of fellow feeling for a suffering other who is not at fault for his or her own significant misfortune (Nussbaum, 1992). Some psychologists use the word *pity* to describe what I mean by sympathy; a leading example is Weiner (Schmidt & Weiner, 1988). Pity in contemporary culture, however, need not include the (significant) fellow feeling that characterizes sympathy; pity may be associated with disdain or contempt, with a distancing of the pitier from the person pitied, and may thus be quite consistent with the assignment of blame (Greenspan, 1988).

Sympathy is probably most often treated as synonymous with *empathy*. For examples of psychological research conflating sympathy and empathy and discussions of that conflation, see Batson (1991), Eisenberg et al. (1994), and Wispé (1986). Empathy is usually defined as the ability to share the emotional response of another to the other's situation, whatever the other's emotion may be (Eisenberg & Fabes, 1990). Thus, in contemporary parlance, one may empathize with another's joy (or any other emotion), but one may properly sympathize only with another's suffering (Adam Smith [1759/1982] observed this distinction long ago but defined sympathy "to denote our fellow-feeling with any passion whatever," while reserving pity and compassion for what I mean by sympathy.)

Sympathy and empathy have in common, therefore, the taking of the sufferer's perspective and the sharing of his or her affect (although perspective-taking in itself need not lead to either emotion; i.e., perspective-taking is necessary but not sufficient for both sympathy and empathy; Eisenberg & Fabes, 1990). (Davis, 1994, further offered the helpful clarification that role- or perspective-taking characterizes the *process* of what he called empathy, whereas the observer's affective response refers to the *outcome* of empathy.) But only sympathy includes the cognitive appraisal that the sufferer does not deserve his or her suffering and the desire to help relieve that suffering for the sufferer's sake (see discussion in text). This other-directedness of sympathy helps to highlight the difference between sympathy and empathic distress (Batson, Early, & Salvarani, 1997). Empathy, but not sympathy, may move the perceiver to avoid the sufferer instead of helping him or her, because one who experiences empathic distress aims primarily to relieve one's own ill-feeling, not the sufferer's (Batson, 1991).

[3] Gender differences in empathy and sympathy have been observed but may very well be a function of the method of measurement: When measured by self-reports, women appear to be significantly more empathic than men, but the differences tend to disappear when physiological or facial measures (Eisenberg & Lennon, 1983) or behavioral measures (Major & Deaux, 1982) are used. Eisenberg and Lennon speculated that the reasons for these measurement-specific differences in empathy may include internalized social expectations (i.e., that it is more acceptable for women to report empathic reactions) and differences in individuals' ways of expressing empathy (i.e., it may be that people who express empathy strongly in one way [say, facial expression] are less likely to express it strongly in other ways [say, by verbal report]). Conversely, Eisenberg et al. (1991) reported some gender differences in vicarious emotional responding as measured both by self-report and skin conductance.

Psychologists have identified several factors that govern whether and how intensely sympathy is experienced. First and perhaps most obvious is the perception of others' pain. "Empathy and sympathy depend most on the sights and sounds of the person in pain" (Wispé, 1991, p. 171). One way the perception of pain leads to feelings of sympathy is through muscle mimicry. Negative facial expressions regularly lead observers to display congruent negative facial expressions, which reflect or even produce negative emotional feeling (Niedenthal & Showers, 1991; Wispé, 1991). Similarly direct and arguably innate is the distress provoked by another's distress calls (Frijda, 1986). The perception of others' pain, however, need not be immediate or direct. Sympathy may also be aroused in the victim's absence through descriptions and representations of the victim's suffering (Hoffman, 1990).

Second, the greater the perceived similarity between observer and sufferer, the more readily sympathy is aroused (Batson, Turk, Shaw, & Klein, 1995; Davis, 1994). Similarity probably facilitates the imaginative role-taking that has long been identified as essential to sympathy (Davis, 1994; A. Smith, 1759/1982). The more similar to the sufferer the observer believes himself or herself to be, the more readily and fully he or she can imagine what the sufferer's world looks and feels like. Experimental instructions encouraging participants to imagine themselves in the victim's place —that is, to identify with the victim—have also been shown to increase sympathy (Davis, Conklin, Smith, & Luce, 1996; M. Lerner, 1980). Imagining oneself in the victim's place enhances the similarity of perspective between observer and sufferer, and this increases sympathy. Perhaps relatedly, the intensity of sympathy may be influenced by how much the perceiver likes the sufferer (Ortony et al., 1988).

Third, sympathy, like other emotional reactions, tends to be more intense the more unexpected the event that gives rise to it (Ortony et al., 1988). Evidence for this effect is provided by norm theory research, which shows that observers tend to feel greater sympathy for the victim of an accident (or a crime) that occurs under exceptional circumstances than for the victim of a typical or expected sequence of events (Macrae, 1992; Macrae, Milne, & Griffiths, 1993; D. Miller et al., 1990).

Fourth, people tend to be more sympathetic toward those whom they perceive to be suffering undeservedly. Experimental support for this inverse relationship between sympathy and control, responsibility, or blame comes from the work of Bernard Weiner and his associates (e.g., Graham, Weiner, & Zucker, 1997; Schmidt & Weiner, 1988; Weiner, 1980, 1995; Weiner, Graham, & Chandler, 1982). According to Weiner's attributional theory, when an observer perceives a person in need of aid, he or she then attempts to discern the cause of the need. If the cause is perceived to be outside the sufferer's control or responsibility, the observer reacts with sympathy and is inclined to help; if the cause is perceived to be within the sufferer's control or responsibility, the observer reacts with anger and is inclined to ignore the sufferer (Weiner, 1995).

Sympathy in the Judgment Process

Both the factors that elicit sympathy (sympathy's "inputs") and sympathy's effects (or "outputs") may be expected to shape common-sense decision making about accidents. With regard to inputs, the perspective-taking involved in sympathizing may lead jurors to attribute to the object of their sympathy (the plaintiff in an accident case, say) characteristics they believe to be true of themselves (Davis et al., 1996). And the role of both similarity to the target and the unexpectedness of the event in increasing the intensity of sympathy may lead jurors to incorporate legally irrelevant factors into their judgments about responsibility and compensation (Feigenson, 1997).

With regard to outputs, sympathetic decision makers may perceive and weigh the evidence in a biased fashion. Research on affect and social judgment (see the Appendix) shows generally that emotional feelings influence which facts decision makers will attend to, how much time they will spend poring over them, and how they will interpret and categorize them. Decision makers' feelings in response to what they first learn about the case will affect their further perceptions and evaluations of the case, because they learn the evidence over a period of time and cannot withhold their judgments until all the evidence is in (Wrightsman, Nietzel, & Fortune, 1994). Specifically, observers who are made to feel sympathetic toward a victim and then learn that the other person is no longer in need feel no more sympathy but continue to value the other's welfare as their initial emotional reaction prompted them to do (Batson et al., 1995). Thus, even after the emotion seems to be gone, observers tend to resist information about the victim's responsibility for his or her plight (Batson et al., 1997). Sympathy may also influence liability and compensation judgments, as I discuss in the next subsection.

We are now also in a position to see the interplay between sympathy and some of the judgmental habits discussed in chapter 2. First, sympathy is important to the counterfactual thinking involved in norm theory. As noted above, abnormal events provoke more intense emotional reactions in general than do normal ones (Buck & Miller, 1994; Kahneman & Tversky, 1982). In particular, many studies show that the more abnormal or deviant the event or sequence of events leading to a bad outcome is perceived to be, the greater the sympathy observers feel for the victim, the more they blame the defendant, and the more compensation they award the victim (Macrae, 1992; Macrae & Milne, 1992; Macrae et al., 1993; D. Miller et al., 1990). That is, sympathy mediates the effect of perceived abnormality on judgments of responsibility and compensation.

In addition, the inverse relationship between sympathy and blame is consistent with the fundamental attribution error. Committing the fundamental attribution error makes the observer more likely to blame the other for his or her behavior (Cohen, 1982), whereas empathically taking the other's perspective (a component of sympathy) reduces the fundamental attribution error, and hence the tendency to blame the other.[4]

Research on Sympathy in Jurors' Judgments About Accidents

Jurors are commonly thought to use sympathy in making decisions (Azevedo, 1990; Bovbjerg et al., 1991; W. Green, 1990). Considerable experimental research on how jurors decide criminal cases supports this view (Dane & Wrightsman, 1982). Relatively little research, however, has been done on civil jurors' use of sympathy. Bornstein (1994, 1998) conducted a number of studies showing that sympathy mediates mock jurors' responsibility judgments. In one set of experiments, using a variety of personal injury cases, Bornstein (1994) manipulated sympathy for the parties by varying the status of the defendant (large corporation vs. small business). He found that the greater sympathy that mock jurors had for the victim of a large corporate defendant's conduct made them more likely to find that the defendant caused the harm. In another experiment, using a product liability lawsuit against the manufacturer of a birth control pill, Bornstein (1998) manipulated sympathy for the plaintiff by varying the severity of the injury. Mock jurors who were more sympathetic to the plaintiff found the defendant liable more often.

Bornstein (1998) explained the effect of sympathy on responsibility judgments in terms of the action tendency induced by sympathy. One who feels sympathy for another's suffering is inclined to do something to alleviate that suffering, which in the context of a personal injury suit means compensating the victim. The urge to compensate may then lead jurors to impose liability on the defendant, because jurors know that legal rules prescribe compensation only in the event that the defendant is found responsible (Lloyd-Bostock, 1979, 1984).[5]

Other research indicates that sympathy plays a less important role than is commonly believed. Kalven and Zeisel (1966), surveying trial judges' views, found that jurors' sympathy for the defendant was a reason

---

[4] Similarly, *just world theory* also posits an inverse correlation between sympathy and blame (see M. Lerner, 1980). "[W]hen we blame victims to reassure ourselves about a just world, we distance ourselves from them, or dehumanize them, which defeats compassion" (Lazarus, 1991a, p. 289). The end result is that blame and sympathy are inversely correlated, but the process by which this comes about is, as Wispé (1991) explained, a "perversion" of the logic underlying the belief that justice and fairness generally prevail in the world, "transforming the belief that 'people get what they deserve' into the belief that 'people deserve what they get'" (pp. 124–125).
[5] For a more thorough analysis of the processes by means of which sympathy may affect responsibility judgments in accident cases, see Feigenson (1997).

for judge–jury verdict disagreement in about 4% of all criminal cases (i.e., in about one fifth of the roughly 20% of all cases in which the judge disagreed with the jury about the verdict). Again, far less research has been done on decision making in civil cases, but some of it also suggests that sympathy's role is limited. For instance, Hans and others have found among some actual jurors not sympathy for plaintiffs, but instead an anti-plaintiff bias; these jurors tended to denigrate personal injury plaintiffs as greedy or complaining (Engel, 1987; Hans & Lofquist, 1992).

An experiment I conducted with Jaihyun Park and Peter Salovey offers further evidence that jurors' sympathy for accident plaintiffs, if any, may be overriden by anti-plaintiff bias (Feigenson et al., 1997). We asked participants to be mock jurors and read accounts of four cases of accidental injury. In one, for example, a man resting at home heard a hissing noise in his kitchen and smelled gas; he ran outside just before his house exploded and injured him. In another, a railroad worker was riding on the back of a line of boxcars and "talking" the engineer (on the radio) through a backup maneuver; a crossover switch had been left in the wrong position, and the line of boxcars ran into another line of cars sitting on a different track, catching the worker between the cars.[6] We created eight different versions of each story, manipulating, *inter alia*, the severity of the plaintiff's injury (severe—death; or mild—e.g., a broken ankle) and the degree of the plaintiff's blameworthiness (high—e.g., the homeowner, safely outside on his front lawn, ran back into the house as it exploded; or low—e.g., the homeowner kept running away from the house).[7]

After reading about each accident, participants completed a questionnaire in which, among other things, they registered their emotional responses to the case. They also completed each of the three steps involved in a comparative negligence decision: They apportioned fault between the parties; they assessed gross damages, the amount they believed necessary to compensate the plaintiff fully; and they computed adjusted or "discounted" damages, gross damages reduced by the proportion to which they believed the plaintiff's own fault contributed to the accident (in a real case, the judge, not the jury, performs this last computation).

There were three principal findings. First, the severity of the outcome affected participants' apportionments of fault: The more severe the accident, the more fault they attributed to the *plaintiff*.[8] Second, the plaintiff's blameworthiness affected gross damage awards as well as apportionment of fault: Participants reduced gross damages when the plaintiff was highly blame-

---

[6]The real case on which this scenario is based is discussed in chapter 5.
[7]We also varied the amount of "extralegal" sympathy we expected the plaintiff to elicit (e.g., high—the railroad worker had just gotten married and had a small child; low—the worker was single). This manipulation proved ineffective, and we dropped it from our subsequent analyses of the data.
[8]$F(1, 125) = 5.65, p < .05.$

worthy,[9] thus *double discounting* the plaintiff's recovery (once contrary to law, and then as legally prescribed). Third, outcome severity affected the rate at which gross damages were adjusted: The more severe the accident, the greater the rate at which participants discounted the damage award.[10]

Taken together, these findings seem to indicate that our participants were biased against plaintiffs. Consider, first, that increasing outcome severity increased attributions of responsibility to the plaintiff. The simple fact that the plaintiff, rather than the defendant, was blamed more, when presumably both parties, with the benefit of hindsight, could have foreseen the fatal consequences of their carelessness, seems to reflect an anti-plaintiff bias. Now consider double discounting. *Any* reduction in gross damages by the victim's responsibility is an anti-plaintiff bias, because gross damages ought to represent the amount necessary to compensate the plaintiff fully for his or her injuries, regardless of fault. In addition, this double-discounting effect is traceable entirely to the high-severity condition; that is, jurors inappropriately reduce gross damages when the outcome is severe. That would seem to rule out as the source of double discounting the party-neutral explanation of failure to understand instructions, because participants in the low-severity condition had the same instructions and presumably were equally competent to understand them. Third, the fact that participants often allocated nonzero percentages of blame to victims in the low-blameworthiness condition, in which the victim's behavior was designed to be more or less blameless in a legal sense,[11] further suggests an anti-plaintiff bias.

How can one account for this anti-plaintiff effect? The mock jurors' emotional reactions to the case may provide a clue. They did feel sympathy for the accident victims whose stories they read.[12] And, as predicted, they felt more sympathy the more seriously the victim was injured[13] and less sympathy the more the victim was to blame.[14] Yet something else overcame the expected effects of that sympathy. That something else may very well have been other emotions—anger and anxiety (or fear)—and it is to these emotions that I turn next.

Anger

Anger may be found on practically every list of basic emotions (Plutchik, 1994), yet that is not to say that it is easily understood. For one

---

[9] $F(1, 125) = 4.69, p < .05$.

[10] Interaction of Blame × Severity on adjusted damages, $F(1, 125) = 10.09, p < .001$.

[11] Across all cases, the mean percentage fault assigned to the plaintiff in low plaintiff blameworthiness condition, $M = 10.25\%$; in the exploding house case (plaintiff running away from house), $M = 14.33\%$; in the railroad accident case (plaintiff obeyed all rules), $M = 21.80\%$.

[12] $M = 5.55$, on scale from 1 (*no sympathy at all*) to 7 (*very much*).

[13] $F(1, 125) = 6.24, p < .02$.

[14] $F(1, 125) = 8.88, p < .005$.

thing, psychological researchers were slow to extract the study of anger from the study of aggression (Averill, 1982, 1983). The focus on aggression is explicable, given its often devastating social and personal consequences, not to mention its own inherent complexity (Averill, 1982). But although aggression is the action tendency associated with the emotion of anger (Lazarus, 1991a), some psychologists argue that there is no necessary connection between the two: Aggressive behavior need not be driven by anger, and people are often angry without engaging in aggressive behavior (Averill, 1982, 1983). Consistent with my approach elsewhere in this chapter, I define anger in terms of its cognitive structure and then identify its antecedents (inputs) and its effects on social judgments (outputs). Keep in mind throughout, however, that anger, like other emotions, is a cognitive, physiological, and behavioral complex, the full examination of which would require us to consider personal, social, and cultural dimensions (Averill, 1994).

To experience anger is to perceive "a demeaning offense against me and mine" (Lazarus, 1991a). More broadly, it is to perceive a threat to a social norm or personal expectation (Averill, 1982), and in particular, a threat to or violation of the moral norm of individual autonomy (as opposed to the moral norms of community or divinity; Rozin, Lowery, Imada, & Haidt, 1999). A crucial component of anger is the attribution of blame (Averill, 1983). Only when people hold someone (including themselves) accountable for an unfavorable outcome will they experience anger rather than (or in addition to) other negatively valenced emotions (Lazarus, 1991a). Ortony et al. (1988) explained that anger is a compound of reproach and distress: It is the emotional response to holding another person responsible for blameworthy behavior (reproach) and being upset about the outcome (distress). (This is not, of course, to imply that the initial perception of blameworthiness may not later be considered mistaken by either the angry person or an observer; anger requires the *subjective* appraisal of blameworthiness though not necessarily its *objective* confirmation [Parrott, 1993].) Most often, anger is aroused by blameworthy conduct that is perceived to be intentional (Quigley & Tedeschi, 1996), but anger is also frequently reported as a response to accidents perceived to have been avoidable (Averill, 1982, 1983). Others have confirmed that anger is a common response to perceived injustice (Mikula et al., 1998; Solomon, 1990; Velasco & Bond, 1998).

Anger motivates one who feels it to attack the source of the anger or, if that is not possible, to displace the attack onto another object (Lazarus, 1991a). In the context of legal judgment, the tendency to attack may take the form of an urge to punish a criminal (Pillsbury, 1989) or civil defendant. If, on the other hand, the object of anger is an accident victim, then the tendency, as we have already seen in connection with Weiner's (1995) theory of emotional response to suffering, is to ignore the sufferer.

The literature on the effects of anger on social judgment is even less extensive than that on the effects of sympathy. Studies have shown that angry people rely more on heuristic cues when processing social information than do sad people (Bodenhausen, 1993; Bodenhausen, Sheppard, & Kramer, 1994). Thus, inducing anger in accident case jurors may be predicted to make them more prone to decide responsibility and compensation by using the kinds of mental shortcuts described in chapter 2.

More important, a consistent finding in the research is that people who are angry tend to blame more (Gallagher & Clore, 1985; Keltner, Ellsworth, & Edwards, 1993; J. Lerner, Goldberg, & Tetlock, 1998). Keltner et al. (1993) found that participants in whom anger had been induced (e.g., by reading an anger-provoking scenario) were more likely than sad participants to attribute hypothetical future events to human agency rather than to situational factors and to attribute responsibility for a social mishap whose cause was unclear to the people involved rather than to the circumstances. Keltner et al. reasoned that one who is angry believes that another person is responsible for some harm or offense he or she has suffered; anger thus makes salient the role of other people in causing negative events, and consequently makes the angry person more likely to attribute other negative events to human agency. Thus, anger and blame attributions can create a kind of feedback loop in which each increases the other (Quigley & Tedeschi, 1996).

Even more germane to our concerns, J. Lerner et al. (1998) found that participants who viewed an anger-provoking video clip and then read several vignettes of accident cases blamed the defendants who caused the injuries more than did participants in the control condition. Among other possible explanations for this effect, Lerner et al. speculated that, consistent with the *affect-as-information* theory (Schwarz & Clore, 1988; see the Appendix), participants may have misattributed their angry mood, actually due to the earlier stage of the experiment, to the accident vignettes; participants then interpreted that anger as informative to their judgments of responsibility for those accidents (consistently with the findings of Keltner et al., 1993, described in the preceding paragraph). Other research on the persistence of angry moods after initial anger episodes (Averill, 1982; Zillmann, 1983, 1994) makes this account plausible.

Yet another reason to believe that anger may affect attributions of blame requires us to revisit norm theory. C. Williams et al. (1996) showed that mock jurors get angrier at those responsible for accidents that occur in mutable as opposed to immutable circumstances, and that the anger is highly correlated with the fines the mock jurors are willing to impose on the perpetrators. No mediational analyses were performed, but a mediating role for anger on attributions of blame would be consistent with Averill's (1982) identification of norm violation (in the sense of a violation of the observer's normative standards, rather than or in addition to abnormality in the sense of simply violating expectations) as an antecedent of anger.

A recent study (Feigenson et al., in press), confirmed that mock jurors' anger mediated their apportionments of fault in comparative negligence cases. We asked over 200 participants to be mock jurors and to read accounts and view photographs of two accidents, both based on actual cases (the home gas explosion and railroad accident cases also used in our previous study, described earlier). We created eight different versions of each story, manipulating the severity of the plaintiff's injury (severe—e.g., serious internal damage and multiple amputation; or mild—e.g., a broken ankle), the degree of the plaintiff's blameworthiness (manipulated as in the previous study), and the degree of the defendant's blameworthiness (high —e.g., the railroad did not mark crossover switches with flags and targets, which might have enabled the plaintiff to see the crucial switch; low— e.g., the railroad marked its switches). After reading about each accident, participants completed a questionnaire in which, among other things, they registered their emotional responses to the case, apportioned fault between the parties, and assessed damages.

We found that participants' anger, toward *both* parties, played a role in some but not all of their comparative negligence decisions. Multiple regression analyses showed that anger mediated the effect of legally relevant variables (blameworthiness and outcome severity) on apportionment of fault but not on compensation; that is, blameworthiness and outcome severity have an effect on the percentage fault judgment because of the effect they have on participants' anger. Increasing the severity of the accident made participants angrier at the defendant, which led them to apportion more fault to the defendant.[15] Yet increasing the *plaintiff's* blameworthiness made participants angrier at the plaintiff, which led them to apportion more fault to the plaintiff.[16] Anger was not a significant predictor of participants' gross or adjusted damage awards. In sum, anger may be elicited by the perception of blameworthy behavior, and it may in turn influence attributions of responsibility—to *both* the plaintiff and the defendant in accident cases in which both may plausibly be blamed.

Anxiety (or Fear)

Anxiety, fear, dread, and terror are a few of the words used to identify members of a class of negatively valenced affective states, the general cognitive structure of which is displeasure about the prospect of an undesirable

---

[15] Outcome severity increased anger at defendant, $F(1, 206) = 12.83$, $p < .001$; when apportionment of fault regressed on emotional reactions, anger at defendant, $\beta = 0.28$, $p < .01$. Thus, outcome severity significantly affected anger at the defendant, which in turn was a significant predictor of the defendant's perceived fault, whereas outcome severity did not significantly predict the defendant's perceived fault. In other words, anger at the defendant *mediated* the effect of outcome severity on the percentage fault attributed to the defendant (Baron & Kenny, 1986).

[16] Victim blameworthiness increased anger at the plaintiff, $F(1, 206) = 36.24$, $p < .0001$; when apportionment of fault regressed on emotional reactions, anger at the plaintiff, $\beta = -0.39$, $p < .0001$.

event (Ortony et al., 1988). Although I do not mean to put too much weight on the distinctions among them, I focus on anxiety and fear as the emotions most likely to be relevant to jurors' judgments about accidents.

One who feels anxious perceives an uncertain, existential threat to his or her well-being (Lazarus, 1991a; Lazarus & Averill, 1972). Thus, anxiety may be distinguished from fear, which usually refers to the perceived danger of imminent, physical harm (LeDoux, 1996; Rosen & Schulkin, 1998). (We might further distinguish *dread*, which connotes a sense of the subjective certainty of the future event not necessarily included in fear [Ortony et al., 1988], and *terror*, which suggests both imminence and great undesirability.) The variables that predict the intensity of anxiety or fear are the degree to which the event that is the object of the feeling is undesirable and the perceived likelihood of the event (Ortony et al., 1988).[17]

It might seem counterintuitive that jurors' anxiety (much less their fear) should play any part in their decisions about responsibility for accidents. First, anxiety and fear are anticipatory emotions (Lazarus & Averill, 1972), but the accident on which jurors sit in judgment has, of course, already occurred. Second, anxiety and fear emotions concern the consequences of an event for the self (Ortony et al., 1988), but the accident did not happen to the jurors themselves, and they will not personally suffer the consequences of their verdict.

Yet the same capacity of imaginative projection that permits jurors to empathize with the victim, to imagine themselves in the plaintiff's position, which can lead to sympathy, can also lead to anxiety or fear. Aristotle (1942) wrote that the objective of tragedy was to elicit from the audience fear and pity for the protagonist of the drama. Pity in the classical sense, which today we call sympathy, may well be the response to the victim of the accident drama (see chapter 4). But it is not the only possible response. Jurors may also become anxious or afraid at the prospect of suffering such an accident themselves. As Aristotle (1926) wrote, what people pity when another person is the victim they fear when they think it might happen to them.

In general, anxiety or fear often results in coping by means of *defensive reactions*, whether through defensive reappraisals of the environment (Lazarus & Averill, 1972), repression of anxiety-producing cognitions (Eriksen, 1966), or biased processing of information (Biek, Wood, & Chaiken, 1996). Accordingly, the anxious or fearful juror may engage in *defensive attribution* (Shaver, 1970). Recall (from chapter 2) the severity effect, in which the defendant or injurer is found to be more at fault the more severe

---

[17]Lazarus (1991a) also discerned a close relationship between fear (or anxiety) and anger: Where the perceived threat is uncertain and thus one's confidence that one will be able to cope with the negative affect is undermined, one may react with fear or anxiety rather than anger.

the consequences of the accident. In the first of our comparative negligence experiments (Feigenson et al., 1997), outcome severity indeed affected attributed fault, but in the *other direction*: The more severe the outcome, the more mock jurors blamed the *plaintiff*. According to defensive attribution, the more seriously injured the accident victim, the more anxious jurors become about the prospect of suffering such a terrible fate themselves; as a consequence, they more readily blame the victim for the accident, to preserve their belief that they can avoid similar misfortune (e.g., Fiske & Taylor, 1991; M. Lerner, 1980). Thus, defensive attribution may help to explain the anti-plaintiff effect we found.[18]

Defensive attribution also illuminates the relationship between our mock jurors' anxiety or fear and their anger. In the same experiment, we found that increasing the plaintiff's blameworthiness significantly increased participants' anger at the plaintiff.[19] That participants reacted with anger to stories of accidents is understandable in terms of the definition of anger provided by Ortony et al. (1988): the emotional response to holding another person responsible for blameworthy behavior (reproach) and being upset about the outcome (distress). But it is very striking that participants in this experiment directed their anger primarily at the accident *victim*. A clue to the source of this intense reaction against blameworthy victims comes from the significant main effect for victim blameworthiness on the degree to which participants identified with the victim. The more blameworthy the plaintiff, the less participants were able to imagine themselves in the plaintiff's place.[20] This is a clear, indeed prototypical, indication of a defensive reaction to suffering. By blaming the victim, mock jurors distanced themselves from the victim, preserving their belief that they will not find themselves in the same position (Lazarus, 1991a; Wispé, 1991).[21]

Some psychologists have questioned the empirical support for and even theoretical coherence of the defensive attribution account for the severity effect (Fincham & Jaspars, 1980; Vidmar & Crinklaw, 1974). Many others, however, continue to find it a plausible account of why outcome severity may influence judgments of responsibility (Burger, 1981; Fiske & Taylor, 1991).

Another body of research suggesting that emotions in the fear and anxiety family may affect judgments of responsibility and compensation may be found in the literature on *risk perception*. The *psychometric* approach

---

[18] On the close relationship between defensive attribution and the *belief in a just world* (M. Lerner, 1980), see Maes (1994).

[19] $F(1, 125) = 66.13, p < .0001$.

[20] $F(1, 125) = 6.58, p < .02$.

[21] Where only one person is the cause of harm (to property), a relationship between anger toward that person and the severity effect has been shown: The greater the damage caused, the angrier observers were at the person who caused the damage and the more responsibility they attributed to him or her (van der Keilen & Garg, 1993; mediational analyses were not reported).

posits that ordinary people perceive risks to be more serious the more they dread the risk (because of their perceived lack of control over the risk, its catastrophic potential, and other factors) and the more unknown the risk is (Slovic, Fischhoff, & Lichtenstein, 1982, 1985, 1987). Jurors' perceptions about a given type of risk might, by analogy to culpable causation (see chapter 2), influence their after-the-fact judgments in accident cases involving the creation of that type of risk. The more jurors dread a risk, the greater the "stain" they may place on the person who created the risk, and hence the greater the causal and legal responsibility they will attribute to that person in order to justify the stain. That is, jurors may treat their negative affect as diagnostic of the degree of blame deserved by the risk creator (cf. Schwarz, 1990; Schwarz & Clore, 1988).[22] Note that the negative affect produced by reading about a particular kind of tragedy leads experimental participants to perceive even unrelated risks as more severe; thus, moods may have *generalized* effects on risk perception (Johnson & Tversky, 1983).

Aside from the studies of defensive attribution and risk perception, there is little research on the effect of anxiety or fear on legal judgments. Arguably relevant to this topic is research on *terror management theory* (e.g., Rosenblatt, Greenberg, Solomon, Pyszczynski, & Lyon, 1989), which shows, *inter alia*, that when people's mortality is made salient to them, they tend to punish those who transgress cultural and moral norms more harshly. Perhaps we can infer that jurors who are made to think about their own deaths (whether by the facts of the case or, as in the terror management theory experiments, by an extrinsic stimulus) would attribute more responsibility to an injurer perceived to have acted in a morally deviant fashion and award greater damages to the victim.

This survey of the possible effects of fear or anxiety on common-sense decision making in accident cases, like the preceding surveys of the effects of sympathy and anger (and the discussion of more general mood effects in the Appendix), is necessarily tentative. Insufficient research has been conducted on the role of affect in legal judgments to permit more comprehensive or confident predictions. The research that has been done, however, should assist us considerably in making sense of common-sense thinking and talking about accidents.

---

[22] Although this is pure speculation, it is possible that the psychometric approach to risk perception helps to explain the plaintiffs' verdicts and favorable settlements in the silicone breast implant litigation. Despite the lack of evidence of any causal connection between implant leakage and cancers, connective tissue disorders, and other alleged ailments suffered by the plaintiffs, jurors seemed willing to blame the implant manufacturers for not sufficiently warning the public about health risks *which did not materialize*. Possibly jurors' dread of unknown diseases caused by the injection of a foreign chemical into the body allowed them to overcome the apparent weakness of the alleged causal connection between the defendant's conduct and the injuries (cf. Nagareda, 1998, for a different explanation for the outcomes in these cases).

4

HOW JURORS THINK
ABOUT ACCIDENTS

In this chapter I attempt to integrate the various psychological phenomena discussed in chapters 2 and 3 into a more coherent view of the common sense of accidents. I make three general observations. First, several important judgmental heuristics, including monocausality, norm theory, fundamental attribution error, and culpable causation, point toward a common-sense conception of accidents as *melodramas*. Research on the role of emotions in comparative negligence judgments, which I and others have recently conducted, offers empirical support for this conception.

Second, I explore what is perhaps the most salient characteristic of common sense concerning accidents: its complex and even contradictory nature. The melodramatic conception of accidents turns out to be only part of a much more complicated picture. For instance, the research literature shows variously that jurors are sometimes biased in favor of accident plaintiffs and sometimes biased against them. I describe some of this complex picture, suggest a reconciliation of at least some of the apparent contradictions, and also explain why some contradiction is to be expected in society's common sense about accidents.

Finally, I draw from these overviews of the processes and outcomes of common-sense thinking about accidents the notion that jurors strive to achieve *total justice*. In the course of applying the law (to the best of their understanding) to the facts of the case, jurors aim for a justice that is "total" in several senses. In reaching their decision, jurors try to *square accounts* between the parties; in judging the litigants, they tend to consider *the totality of each person* or entity, rather than limiting their attention to the parties' legally relevant features; they tend to give justice by means of a *holistic process* rather than in the discrete steps the law prescribes; they want to *feel right* about their decision, so that their cognitions, emotions, and decisions yield a congruent and satisfying whole; and they want their *deliberative interactions* to reflect a just process.

I do not contend that this view of how people think about accidents, or any part of it, necessarily reflects any lasting or universal features of human thought and action. It is at most a snapshot of a particular legal system and culture (that of the United States) during a relatively brief period (roughly the last few decades of the 20th century). Although the broad observations in this chapter are, I hope, generally accurate within those limits, and perhaps beyond, readers should keep those limits in mind.[1]

ACCIDENTS AS MELODRAMAS

In chapters 2 and 3, I discussed various habits of thought and feeling that people use to make judgments under conditions of uncertainty. Here I would like to show how several of these psychological phenomena constitute a single dynamic of *normalcy and deviance*. People who think this way are inclined to believe that a bad thing like an accident probably occurred because one person did a deviant (i.e., bad) thing, and that the person behaved that way because of the sort of person he or she is. Add to this the tendency of people to prefer simple, monocausal explanations for events, and the result is that jurors would be expected to possess a common-sense schema of responsibility for accidents in which one and only one party, the "bad guy," is to blame, and the other party is more or less innocent. That is, social psychology suggests that jurors may tend to conceive of accidents as melodramas.

I begin by offering a definition of melodrama derived from literary, film, and television criticism. I then sketch some of the interrelationships among the relevant social psychological constructs, in a way that makes clear the connection between the cultural and social psychological domains. Finally, I discuss experimental research supporting the proposition that jurors are inclined to think of accidents as melodramas. In the following section, I indicate some of the limits of the melodramatic conception

---

[1] On the other hand, these three features of the common sense of accidents—melodrama, contradiction, and total justice—may very well characterize common-sense thinking in other legal domains as well. Perhaps they apply to any interaction between two or more human beings that yields a bad outcome. I welcome others to extend the ideas in the text to other areas of law and social life.

of accidents by placing it alongside other evidence of how jurors think about accidents.

A Definition of Melodrama

A melodramatic conception of an accident is a narrative in which (a) events, such as accidents, are caused by individual human agency; (b) the acts of individuals are explicable in terms of their characters; (c) the agents involved in the accident can be divided into "good guys" and "bad guys"; (d) the focus of the narrative is the accident victim and his or her suffering; and (e) the good guy wins (at trial) and the bad guy gets his or her comeuppance. I support this definition by reference to treatments of melodrama in the fields of literary, film, and media studies.

The first two features of this definition—*human agency* as the cause of events (or *personalization*) and *actions derived from character traits*—are implicit in the third, the *polarization of narrative into good versus evil*, and cannot really be understood apart from it. As Brooks (1976) wrote in his classic study, *The Melodramatic Imagination*,

> Melodramatic good and evil are highly personalized: they are assigned to, they inhabit persons who indeed have no psychological complexity but who are strongly characterized. Most notably, evil is villainy; it is a swarthy, cape-enveloped man with a deep voice. (pp. 16–17)

That is, melodrama is populated with easily recognizable character types, which are without personal idiosyncrasy and can be clearly distinguished from one another (Meisel, 1994). The point of such characterization, clearly, is to *explain behavior*; the emphasis on (simply defined) traits makes such traits (and the person-in-situation stereotypes they invoke) the leading candidate for the cause of the actor's conduct. A bad guy is a bad guy always, whatever the situation; the bad guy is a bad guy because he or she does bad things, but even before he or she does those bad things, one is cued to expect them by the bad guy's appearance. In melodramas, then, things happen because people make them happen, and the kinds of people they are determine the kinds of things they make happen.

Melodramatic *polarization* of the world into good versus evil deserves further emphasis.

> The essential action of melodrama is to polarize its constituents, whatever they may be—male and female, East and West, civilization and wilderness, and, most typically, good and evil.... [T]he melodramatic world is composed of binary oppositions. Individuals are either wholly good or wholly evil, and it is this Manichaean vision that most obviously characterizes melodrama. (Mason, 1993, pp. 16–17)[2]

---

[2] Grimsted (1994, p. 210) added: "Humans find comfort in escaping the ambiguities of personal

The melodramatic narrative is thus simplified in a third way: not only by limiting the causes of events to human agency and the causes of human action to character traits, but also by limiting the range of instrumental characters to two, the good guy and the bad guy.

The fourth feature of melodrama is a *focus on the victim and his or her suffering.* "One of the characteristic features of melodramas in general is that they concentrate on the point of view of the victim" (Elsaesser, 1987, p. 64). The victim thus becomes the central object of the audience's emotional participation in the story. The victim is the good guy but is at most a passive hero (Nowell-Smith, 1987).[3] This is important to keep in mind, in connection with the final feature of melodrama, which is that *the good guy (usually) wins.* Melodrama denotes a story that "ends on a happy or at least a morally reassuring note" (Thorburn, 1981, p. 74).[4] If the good guy is passive, he or she needs a hero to make sure that he or she wins. In the accident case, that hero is the *jury* (as we see in the case studies in chapter 5).

To be sure, this definition is oversimplified. It is something of a pastiche that elides the historical contexts in which melodramatic form originated and developed (Hays & Nikolopolou, 1996), the ideologies that melodrama has represented or combated (e.g., Gledhill, 1987), and the significance of distinctions among the various media in which melodrama may appear (Schatz, 1981).

Perhaps the most obvious way in which my conception diverges from the usual understanding of melodrama is by not emphasizing the heightened emotionality of the form. Most treatments of melodrama place "emotional shock-tactics and the blatant playing on the audience's known sympathies and antipathies" (Elsaesser, 1987, p. 44),[5] or something along those

---

and social life by entering a morally simple world of perfect virtue and total vice, the latter always painted black enough to allow even the conspicuously shoddy to see themselves as among the children of light." To the same effect, Brooks (1976, pp. 12–13) wrote, "we find [in melodrama] an intense emotional and ethical drama based on the manichaeistic struggle of good and evil."

[3] Nowell-Smith (1987, p. 72) explained that in classical tragedy, the hero also suffers, but starting in the romantic period there is "a split, producing a demarcation of forms between those in which there is an active hero, inured or immune to suffering, and those in which there is a hero, or more often a heroine, whose role is to suffer. Broadly speaking, in the American movie the active hero becomes protagonist of the Western, the passive or impotent hero or heroine becomes protagonist of what has come to be known as melodrama."

[4] Once again, Brooks (1976, pp. 11–12) wrote that melodrama requires the "persecution of the good, and final reward of virtue," and on a somewhat more ambiguous note, that "[T]he ritual of melodrama involves the confrontation of clearly identified antagonists and the expulsion of one of them" (p. 17).

[5] See, for example, Booth, 1983; Elsaesser, 1987; Thorburn, 1981, p. 74 (melodrama "makes sensational appeals to the emotions of its audience"). Melodrama elicits these emotions through plot structure, characterization, and, importantly, the actors' own displays of affect. So reliable (or "readable") is the connection between melodrama and emotion that social psychological studies have used soap operas as stimulus materials in establishing a high degree of cross-cultural agreement in recognition of emotional expressiveness. Ratings by American viewers of expressed emotions by actors in both Japanese and American soap operas (viewed

90   LEGAL BLAME

lines, at the center of the discussion. (Recent analyses of melodrama concur in the centrality of emotion to melodrama but tend to consider it positively rather than pejoratively.[6])

Let me explain why emotion figures somewhat differently in a conception of melodrama that might usefully be applied to accident cases. First, consider one obvious difference between the contexts of dramatic performance and law: By and large, the law in tort cases purports to prohibit jurors from using their emotions to decide cases (Feigenson, 1997). This does not mean that emotions—both the lawyers' and the jurors'—do not figure in accident cases. Of course they frequently do, and the research discussed in chapter 3 indicates that they do and why they would be expected to. And emotional response, specifically sympathy, is plainly invoked by the fourth element of the definition, the emphasis on the plaintiff and his or her suffering. This difference in sanctioned response between the theater (or the living room) and the courtroom does, however, suggest that extreme emotion is less likely to be integral to legal judgment than to artistic melodrama (as some of the research reviewed in chapter 3 has indicated).

Second, the presentation of a legal case is at least somewhat constrained by the evidence and the rules governing its presentation in court in a way that the scripting of a theatrical drama is not, and the constraints limit the range of both the emotions likely to be evoked and the plot devices available for evoking them.

> Melodrama utilizes material that will invariably produce strong emotional shocks for the spectator . . . : murders, large-scale thefts or forgeries, confrontation with a murdered victim, trial, sentencing, preparation for the execution, hard labor, beggary, futile efforts to earn a living, a father's curse, tragic or joyous shocks connected with sudden recognitions. (Gerould, 1991, p. 121)[7]

And the author of a melodrama composes this material into plots with unexpected, sharp reversals (Gerould, 1991), the better to provoke intense emotional response (Ortony et al., 1988). It is the rare personal injury case that permits such manipulations of the story line, even though lawyers may orchestrate witnesses and their testimony in the hope of enhancing dramatic effect.[8]

But if accident trials seem *un*melodramatic because they do not em-

---

without sound) were highly correlated with ratings by Japanese viewers (Krauss, Curran, & Ferleger, 1983).

[6] See, for example, Affron (1991).

[7] "Melodramatic narratives are driven by the experience of one crisis after another, crises involving severed familial ties, separation and loss, misrecognition of one's place, person, and propriety. Seduction, betrayal, abandonment, extortion, murder, suicide, revenge, [jealousy], incurable illness, obsession, and compulsion—these are part of the familiar terrain of melodrama" (Landy, 1991, p. 14).

[8] I thank Richard Sherwin for this observation.

phasize the expression of strong emotions and the plot devices that elicit them in quite the same way as do melodramas in film or television, certain features of melodrama can illuminate the role that emotions do play in common-sense judgments about accidents. Sympathy and anger, in particular, are strongly affected by the *attributional* features of the case (as we saw in chapter 3): namely, who appears to have *caused* the accident and *why*. By focusing on these attributional features of the case, which correspond to the first three elements of my definition of melodrama, one can better understand the place of emotions in common-sense thinking about accidents.

The Social Psychology of the Melodramatic View

As discussed in chapter 2, people tend to select as the cause of an event the prior event that deviates the most from some relevant norm (norm theory); to assign more causal responsibility to an act the more morally blameworthy the act is (culpable causation); and to attribute others' behavior to their character traits rather than to situational constraints (fundamental attribution error or correspondence bias). Furthermore, they tend to prefer simple causal explanations to complex ones (monocausality). Together, these phenomena constitute a common-sense schema of responsibility for accidents in which one and only one party, the "bad guy," is to blame, and the other party is more or less innocent. That is, social psychology suggests that jurors may tend to conceive of accidents as melodramas. Let us see how these attributional features of melodrama work together.

People's preference for simple, indeed monocausal, accounts of events points toward a melodramatic conception of accidents, in which one and only one party is to blame. But melodrama is not the only conceivable form of understanding responsibility for accidents that meets the preference for causal simplicity. To understand why the common sense of accidents might be melodramatic, I turn to the attributional habits that incline people to identify *which* single party is to blame and *why*.

Norm theory and culpable causation complement one another as accounts of how people identify the causes of accidents. According to both, the more deviant the act preceding an accident, the more likely observers are to think that the act need not have been done, and therefore, that the person who did it is responsible for the accident. The salient norm (to return to the examples given in chapter 2, e.g., the regular commute or the person who does not use drugs) provides the observer with a set of expectations for how the actors should behave and thereby highlights any variations as deviant in the moral as well as the statistical sense. These two habits of thought underscore the common-sense tendency to conceive of accidents in terms both personalized and moralized, important features of the melodramatic form.

Finally, the fundamental attribution error, the belief that another person acted the way he did because "he is that kind of guy," is plainly a central component of melodrama. In melodrama, stock characterizations of an actor as the good guy or the bad guy are offered to frame the audience's expectations regarding the actor's behavior and thus as implicit explanations for the behavior that ensues. The fundamental attribution error shows why this way of presenting stories suits people's attributional habits: People tend to trace behaviors to actors' dispositions or enduring traits, rather than to the circumstances. This is the quintessence of a personalized notion of responsibility, which is central to melodrama.

Additional support for the idea that people tend to conceive of accidents as melodramas comes from a recent experiment on the role of emotions in legal judgment (Feigenson et al., in press), which I described in chapter 3. In summary, participants read accounts and saw photographs of two accidents. The accident stories were manipulated to vary the severity of the plaintiff's injury, the plaintiff's degree of blameworthiness, and the defendant's degree of blameworthiness. After reading about each accident, participants completed a questionnaire in which, among other things, they registered their emotional responses to the case.

The most striking finding for the present purposes was that mock jurors were significantly more emotionally involved with the plaintiffs in accident cases when *one and only one* party was highly blameworthy—when attributions of blame for the accident were designed to be *unambiguous*. When the accident fit this monocausal structure—whether it was the defendant *or the plaintiff* who alone was highly blameworthy—mock jurors reported that they felt sadder and sorrier for the plaintiff and could more easily imagine themselves in the plaintiff's position.[9] This shows, I believe, that jurors respond emotionally to accident cases *as if they think the prototypical accident is structured like a melodrama.*

There are a number of reasons to interpret our findings in this way.[10]

---

[9] Sadder for the plaintiff, $F(1, 206) = 4.34$, $p < .05$; sorrier for the plaintiff, $F(1, 206) = 5.83$, $p < .02$; more easily imagine self in the plaintiff's position, $F(1, 206) = 5.21$, $p < .03$.

[10] One way to explain the melodrama effect is to turn it around and ask why, in attributionally *ambiguous* cases (i.e., those in which both parties were highly blameworthy or neither was), empathetic responses to the plaintiff were *reduced*. When it was harder for mock jurors to assign responsibility for the accident, perhaps they had to spend more time thinking about the details of the case. This cognitive effort may have tempered the jurors' initial emotional impulses to be sympathetic toward the plaintiff, and thus attenuated the amount of sympathy they reported. Other researchers have found that participants in whom a negative mood had been induced and who were then given an incentive to expend effort on a substantively unrelated cognitive task reported feeling better afterward (Erber & Tesser, 1992). The experimenters reasoned that the involving, unrelated cognitive task resulted in fewer thoughts related to the negative mood and hence a reduction in the intensity of that mood. In our experiment, similarly, task difficulty (determining responsibility in an attributionally ambiguous situation) may have occupied jurors' cognitive capacity, reducing their capacity to process and sustain thoughts that might have reinforced their initial emotional state.

First, the pattern of emotional responses we found reflects a mind-set in which the parties to an accident case are linked in a relationship of *complementarity*. That is, mock jurors' emotional reactions to the plaintiff depend not only on their perception of how blameworthy the plaintiff was (as is to be expected; as explained in chapter 3, observers tend to feel more anger at a more blameworthy sufferer but more sympathy for a less blameworthy one), but also on how blameworthy they perceive the defendant to have been. Thus, mock jurors consider *both* parties' levels of blameworthiness as relevant to their emotional responses to the plaintiff.[11]

Complementarity is further indicated by the fact that mock jurors' emotional reactions to one party were significantly correlated with their corresponding emotional reactions to the other party. The angrier participants felt toward the defendant, the more sympathy and sadness they felt for the plantiff. The angrier they felt toward the plaintiff, the greater their sympathy for the defendant.[12]

To react to accident cases as if the parties are linked in this complementary way is to conceive of the accident as a melodrama. Mock jurors' emotional reactions reflect a view of responsibility for accidents that is not only simplified but also dichotomized. Jurors seem to feel that one party is to blame just to the extent the other is not and that each party deserves an emotional response that depends on the emotional response appropriate to the other party. Thus, if one party is the "good guy," the other cannot be. This is melodrama. And the fact that this mind-set influences not all emotional response, but only empathetic responses to the plaintiff, is consistent specifically with the element of melodrama that places the plaintiff and his or her suffering at the center of the accident narrative.

Second, we can put our findings in the context of other social psychological research on *affective expectancies* to suggest that jurors respond

---

[11] If the defendant is highly blameworthy but the plaintiff is not, all information relevant to responsibility attributions indicates sympathy for the plaintiff. When, however, both parties are to blame or neither is, the signals provided by each party's blameworthiness point in opposite directions, and the jurors' emotional responses are less intense. That is, a highly blameworthy plaintiff indicates less sympathy for the plaintiff; but if the defendant is also highly blameworthy, this suggests that the plaintiff is *not* as blameworthy, which indicates *more* sympathy for the plaintiff.

Indeed, jurors seem to consider their *emotional reaction* to one party (and not only that party's degree of blameworthiness) as a cue to how they ought to feel about the *other* party. Negotiators who perceive a negotiation as a zero-sum affair feel *less* satisfied and happy if they believe that their *opponents* are happy (Thompson, Valley, & Kramer, 1995). Similarly, jurors who think that justice in comparative fault cases is a zero-sum affair—what the plaintiff wins, the defendant loses; to the extent the defendant is to blame, the plaintiff must not be—may (subconsciously) adjust their emotional responses in a complementary fashion. If, for instance, both parties are highly blameworthy, the plaintiff's behavior may trigger anger, but if jurors are also angry at the defendant, they may take that anger as a cue to reduce their anger toward the plaintiff.

[12] Anger toward the defendant was positively and significantly correlated with sympathy for the plaintiff, $r = .49$ ($N = 214$), $p < .0001$, and sadness for the plaintiff, $r = .24$ ($N = 214$), $p < .001$; anger toward the plaintiff was positively correlated with sympathy for the defendant, $r = .22$ ($N = 214$), $p < .002$.

emotionally to accident cases *as if they expect accidents to take melodramatic form*. This research shows that expectations help drive emotions (T. Wilson, Lisle, Kraft, & Wetzel, 1989), so that affective reactions are quicker when experience fits expectation; when it does not, emotional responses are slower to form (Fiske & Taylor, 1991, pp. 427–428).[13] Now, if jurors expect that accidents are caused by only one party, then cases that match the expectation by being attributionally unambiguous should evoke more strongly the affective response associated with that expectation—for instance, feeling sad for the accident victim. By contrast, cases that are attributionally ambiguous and thus do not match jurors' prior accident schema should evoke less intense responses. And this is precisely what we found. Thus, social psychological research on both cognition and emotion suggests why jurors might be predicted to think about accidents as melodramas.[14]

There is something else about (most) accident cases that may incline lay justice to take the form that it does. Many accidents, including all of those studied in the second part of this book, are caused by inadvertence or impulse rather than intentional or even reckless disregard of the safety of the actor or others (Shuman, 1993). The consequences of inattention, however, can be enormous: death or severe injury. Thus, jurors are often confronted with the task of assigning liability that could very well seem *disproportionate* to blameworthiness. To restore proportionality, a hallmark of common-sense justice (Finkel, 1995), jurors may resort to blaming habits that convert mere inadvertence into (greater) culpability, so that the cause will seem to resemble the effect (Sim & Morris, 1998) and the punishment will seem to match the offense. Melodramatic thinking is a way of doing this.

TENSION AND CONTRADICTION IN COMMON-SENSE THINKING

The second general theme to be found in the research on the social psychology of juror decision making about accidents is that it is not monolithic, reducible to any simple idea or proposition. Let me make this important point in two ways. First, having just argued that the melodramatic conception is a prominent feature of common-sense thinking about accidents, I now outline the limitations of that conception and suggest some

---

[13] Relatedly, studies of *schema-triggered affect* show that schemas carry emotional associations and that those associations will be triggered by new phenomena that are perceived to fit the schema (Fiske, 1982).
[14] Other research shows that people may develop affective responses to a target person described as a "good guy" or a "bad guy" even when they are unable to recall any of the specific information contained in the description. Thus, melodramatic characterization may be encoded in emotional memory, which then guides subsequent recognition and evaluation (Christianson, Säisä, & Silfvenius, 1995).

reasons why neither melodrama nor any other single concept can explain very much of the way people think about accidents. Second, I take a step back and survey the complex landscape of how people decide accident cases. Experimental studies and analyses of actual jury verdicts show several, sometimes conflicting biases (anti-corporate defendant, anti-plaintiff, pro-plaintiff) in judgments about responsibility and compensation for accidents. I conclude by offering some tentative explanations for the complicated and even contradictory picture that emerges.

Limitations on the Melodramatic Conception of Accidents

Despite the support for the melodramatic conception of accidents in the research on cognitive heuristics and in the emotional responses of jurors to the facts of accident cases, jurors' ultimate judgments regarding fault and compensation are not completely governed by the framework of expectations that the melodramatic narrative provides. First and most obviously, plaintiffs win only a little more than half of tort cases tried to juries: over 60% for auto accidents, about 40% for products liability, and about 30% for medical malpractice (Daniels & Martin, 1995) for an overall rate of about 55%, which has held more or less steady during the most recent decade studied (Moller, 1996). Even if jurors are sympathizing with plaintiffs or giving vent to anger against defendants, as the typical accident melodrama would incline them to do, other factors must be entering into their judgments—for instance, perceptions of the relative weakness of plaintiffs' cases or the relative strength of defendants' in those claims that are tried to juries.[15]

Second, jurors in comparative negligence cases are quite willing to apportion fault between the plaintiff and the defendant, rather than to allocate all of it to one party or the other as they would have to in the Manichaean, monocausal world of melodrama. Indeed, as discussed in chapter 3, mock jurors in Feigenson et al.'s (1997, in press) experiments tended to apportion significant percentages of the fault to plaintiffs who the facts indicate are more or less legally blameless.

Third, experimental research suggests that jurors do not simply give in to emotion, melodramatic or otherwise, in reaching their decisions. Even in the experiment in which we found the melodrama effect in jurors' empathetic responses to the plaintiff, the presence or absence of melodramatic causal structure did not significantly affect jurors' apportionments of fault

---

[15] At issue here are *case selection effects* (Clermont & Eisenberg, 1998). For instance, although in general cases that go to trial differ from cases that settle by presenting closer questions of liability or damages or both (e.g., defendants who think they have a sure loser are likelier to settle), cases tried to juries probably include weaker plaintiff's cases than cases tried to judges, perhaps (ironically) because plaintiffs' lawyers believe jurors will be more favorable to them than judges will be (Clermont & Eisenberg, 1992).

or their damage awards. Indeed, mock jurors' decision making in general does not appear to be driven mainly by their emotional responses to the case. They do respond emotionally to accidents in ways that attributional theories of emotional response predict, reacting with more sympathy to an accident victim whom they perceive not to be responsible for his or her own suffering, and with more anger to a blameworthy victim. But the jurors' anger and sympathy play only a very limited role in their ultimate judgments. As explained in chapter 3, our mock jurors did attribute more fault to more blameworthy parties because they were angrier at those parties, but their anger did not affect their damage awards, and their sympathetic reaction to seriously injured plaintiffs, although considerable, played no significant causal role in their judgments of either responsibility or damages (Feigenson et al., in press).

Jurors, then, do not simply yield to the melodrama often offered by plaintiffs' attorneys. One possible reason is that the sheer amount of attention that jurors devote to trial information and the seriousness with which they undertake their duties (e.g., Hans & Vidmar, 1986) may tend to supersede superficial understandings of the case, yielding more deliberate rather than automatic mental processing (J. A. Tanford & Tanford, 1988). Any sense of being accountable for their judgments (to other jurors or to their families and communities, if not also to the public at large) could further inhibit simplistic, heuristic thinking (J. Lerner et al., 1998). Jurors may thus have an incentive not to behave as "satisficers" for whom the first sufficient explanation of the accident is enough; instead, they may entertain more complex alternatives.

More important, the plaintiff's lawyer may not construct the case primarily as a melodrama. The lawyer may acknowledge the complexity of accident causation, decline to portray the defendant as the "bad guy," or gesture toward the larger significance of a verdict for his or her client, encouraging jurors not so much to square accounts as to "send a message" (although this last is not necessarily inconsistent with the melodramatic appeal). And even if the plaintiff's lawyer proffers melodrama, the adversarial system ensures that jurors will hear *competing versions* of the case, making it less likely that the plaintiff's version of the case will be accepted without qualification. In any given case, jurors may prefer a different account of the accident, even a different melodrama. Defendants' lawyers in accident cases often do not structure their arguments in narrative form at all (as we see in chapter 5). Frequently, as an alternative to the plaintiff's story, they offer jurors what Bruner (1986) called *paradigmatic* reasoning, an element-by-legal-element account of why the plaintiff has failed to satisfy the requirements of the prima facie case. But contemporary images of the legal system also allow defendants' lawyers to import a popular melodrama into the courtroom: the story of the greedy, undeserving plaintiff versus the good corporation that is just doing its best to give customers what they want. The currency of anti-plaintiff messages in the media (Haltom & McCann, 1998; I return to this point in chapter 8) makes it quite plausible that jurors might think about accident cases this way.

The sort of thinking encouraged by the pro-plaintiff melodrama is only part of people's multifarious common sense about responsibility for misfortune. The tendency to engage in defensive attribution—to blame the victims of rapes, muggings, or environmental disasters in order to preserve one's faith that one will not be victimized oneself—has been proven in many studies, as we saw in chapter 3; so, too, the related *belief in a just world*, the credo that people deserve what they get, which leads observers to derogate the victims of misfortune (M. Lerner, 1980). Add to this the admission that there is simply much that is not known about how jurors think (e.g., Saks, 1992), and it is not terribly surprising that melodrama cannot explain all of what jurors think and decide.

The Conflicting Pattern of Juror Biases in Accident Cases

The overall picture that emerges from research on juror decisions regarding responsibility and compensation for accidents is one in which different studies have yielded different and partially conflicting findings. The literature documents anti-corporate defendant effects, pro-plaintiff effects, and anti-plaintiff effects. It is just not true that jurors are simply biased against defendants or, for that matter, biased against plaintiffs.

In an attempt to make sense of the outcomes of juror decision making, I first survey the research, which includes studies using all sorts of methodologies: archival studies (i.e., statistical analyses of verdicts and damage awards in actual cases), surveys of actual jurors, and controlled experiments. I present the findings that support each kind of bias (anti-corporate defendant, pro-plaintiff, and anti-plaintiff) and indicate the extent to which each bias can be explained in terms of one or more of the habits of thought and feeling discussed in previous chapters. I then suggest other explanations for the complex pattern of common-sense decisions about accidents, including a claim that *case type* may moderate the effect of those habits of thought and feeling on the ultimate judgments of responsibility and compensation.[16]

First, an *anti-corporate defendant* effect seems to be a robust finding

---

[16] It might seem at first glance that anti-defendant and pro-plaintiff effects come to the same thing, and that an anti-plaintiff effect, for example, could just as easily be described as a pro-defendant effect. The distinctions are as follows. The first set of biases, the anti-corporate-defendant effect, finds that jurors judge *corporate* defendants less favorably than *individual* defendants on the same facts. The effects I call *pro-plaintiff* are driven by jurors' *sympathy for the plaintiff*, and so pro-plaintiff seems a more natural classification than anti-defendant, although the net result may very well be the same. Finally, and similarly, the anti-plaintiff effects seem to be driven by defensive attribution, the fundamental attribution error, and other processes directed *toward the plaintiff*.

across different case types (products liability, slip and fall, vehicle, workplace injuries, medical malpractice) and different research methodologies (verdict analyses, controlled experiments, surveys). Corporate defendants have been found more responsible (Hans, 1994) and held liable more often (Bornstein, 1994; MacCoun, 1996) than individual defendants on the same facts. Actual corporate and government defendants paid greater sums in compensatory damages than did individual defendants for injuries of the same type and severity, an effect which was especially pronounced when the injury was severe (Chin & Peterson, 1985). In experimental scenarios, similarly, plaintiffs received larger damage awards from corporate than from individual defendants in the same types of cases (Hans, 1994; MacCoun, 1996; but cf. Bornstein, 1994).

What might explain these anti-corporate defendant findings? It does not seem that jurors are simply anti-business; rather, people tend to hold generally positive attitudes toward businesses and the free-enterprise system (Hans, 1998). Some jurors may indeed share an "egalitarian" impulse to hold corporate defendants liable for the consequences of their profit-seeking activity (Douglas, 1992; Polisar & Wildavsky, 1989), but this does not appear to be a dominant attitude. Instead, a likely reason that corporate defendants appear to be found liable more often and for greater damages than individual defendants for otherwise similar accidents is that jurors believe that corporate defendants should be held to a higher standard than individual defendants, because corporate defendants have greater knowledge of the risks of various courses of action and can devote greater resources to learning about and managing those risks (Bornstein, 1994; Hans, 1994, 1998).

Another common explanation for the anti-corporate defendant effect is the *deep pocket* hypothesis: that jurors are biased against wealthy defendants. Whatever its prevalence in popular beliefs about juror decision making, the deep pocket hypothesis is not firmly supported in the research. The jury verdict analyses often cited in support of the deep pocket hypothesis (e.g., Chin & Peterson, 1985; Peterson, 1984) confound defendant status (corporate vs. individual) with wealth.[17] Experiments disaggregating the two variables of corporate status and wealth (Hans, 1994; MacCoun, 1996) identify the former, not the latter, as the source of bias (but cf. Darden, DeConinck, Babin, & Griffin, 1991). As Bornstein (1994) suggested, however, an anti-wealth bias could still be part of the reason for the anti-corporate defendant effect to the extent that jurors take corporate status as a proxy for wealth (i.e., if jurors believe that corporate defendants are in general wealthier than individual defendants).

The deep pocket hypothesis has also been offered to account for find-

---

[17] Peterson (1984) used the independent variable of case type (e.g., work injury, product liability), which may lead to a further confounding to the extent that different defendants may be sued for the same type of injury.

ings that jurors award more for equivalent injuries in medical malpractice than in automobile collision cases (Bovbjerg et al., 1991). However, Vidmar (1993, 1995) and his colleagues (Vidmar et al., 1994; Vidmar & Rice, 1993) have conducted a series of studies finding no such effect, and Vidmar (1993) has criticized reliance on jury verdict analyses to prove the supposed deep pocket phenomenon.

Second, a *pro-plaintiff* bias relative to legal norms has been shown by experiments using products liability scenarios. Plaintiffs who attract more sympathy because of the greater severity of their injuries win more verdicts (Bornstein, 1998); plaintiffs who attract more sympathy because of their weaker financial status or the visibility of their injuries receive greater damages (Darden et al., 1991). These findings can be adequately accounted for by the severity effect (discussed in chapter 2) and the biasing effects of sympathy (discussed in chapter 3). Note, incidentally, that in the case of medical malpractice suits, this apparent pro-plaintiff effect on responsibility attributions (or verdicts) may not really be a bias at all. One leading study of *expert* decision makers' evaluations of iatrogenic medical injuries (those caused by the health care providers themselves) found that the more seriously injured the patient, the more likely the health care providers were negligent (Danzon, 1985; but cf. Taragin, Willett, Wilczek, Trout, & Carson, 1992).

Third, in contrast to the pro-plaintiff findings above, an *anti-plaintiff* effect has been found in different sorts of cases and using different research methodologies. One measure of the effect is the finding in comparative negligence cases that the more seriously the plaintiff is hurt, the greater the percentage of fault mock jurors attribute to the *plaintiff* (Feigenson et al., 1997). Moreover, both mock jurors (Feigenson et al., 1997; Zickafoose & Bornstein, 1999) and real ones (Hammitt et al., 1985) double discount the comparative negligence plaintiff's recovery by reducing the gross damage award to take the plaintiff's fault into account. And when experimental jurors are assigned the task of computing the adjusted or final damage award (which the judge does in real comparative negligence cases), they give the plaintiff a smaller amount than warranted by their own previous apportionments of fault to the parties (Thomas & Parpal, 1987), and they discount the gross award at a higher rate the more severely the plaintiff is hurt (Feigenson et al., 1997). Still another measure of an anti-plaintiff effect is that the *same actor's* behavior is more often attributed to bad intent and negative stereotypes when the actor is the plaintiff than when he or she is the defendant (Lupfer, Cohen, Bernard, Smalley, & Schippmann, 1985). Finally, jurors in actual lawsuits against business defendants report anti-plaintiff sentiments in post-verdict interviews (Hans & Lofquist, 1992).

Anti-plaintiff effects may be due at least in part to defensive attribution (Feigenson et al., 1997), as noted in chapter 3. By blaming the victim, jurors distance themselves from him or her, preserving their belief that they will not find themselves in the same position. In addition, the fundamental attribution error may also be at work (Lupfer et al., 1985). Jurors may believe that tort plaintiffs are greedy and complaining (Engel, 1987; Hans & Lofquist, 1992), the kind of "bad people" who, according to the logic of dispositional attribution, are responsible for bad outcomes like accidents (Feigenson, 1995). Linking these two explanations may be the *belief in a just world* (M. Lerner, 1980). Jurors, striving to make sense of why the plaintiff was victimized, may believe that the plaintiff either was to blame or in some other sense "had it coming," perhaps because the plaintiff was a bad person.

What are we to make of these various and partly conflicting findings? The differences in research results do not appear to be the result of trends —perhaps because not enough studies have been conducted, or because the time frame for all of the research surveyed (early 1980s to the present) is too brief to indicate any trends. Some, but not all, of the apparent conflicts may be accounted for by differences in methodologies—in the nature of the data, the stimulus materials used, the variables manipulated, or the dependent measures. For instance, experimental work showing an anti-corporate defendant effect manipulated defendant status as an independent variable (e.g., Bornstein, 1994; Hans, 1994; MacCoun, 1996); jury verdict analyses showing an anti-corporate defendant effect regressed over corporate status as a variable (e.g., Peterson, 1984). Experimental work showing an anti-plaintiff effect in cases involving corporate defendants, by contrast, did not manipulate defendant status (e.g., Feigenson et al., 1997; Thomas & Parpal, 1987), and thus did not as readily permit an anti-corporate defendant effect to emerge.[18]

I would like to suggest another explanation for the complexity of juror decisions about responsibility and compensation in the aggregate. These apparently conflicting findings reflect at the molar level, as it were, different combinations of jurors' particular habits of mind and feeling, which variously cut against or reinforce one another at the molecular level of the individual case. Experimental research tends to isolate a few variables at a

---

[18]Note, for instance, that jury verdict analyses appear to support the deep pocket hypothesis (e.g., Bovbjerg et al., 1991; Chin & Peterson, 1985; Peterson, 1984), whereas the research refuting it is (largely) experimental (e.g., Vidmar, 1993, 1995). The major methodological differences between these two kinds of work are: (a) Real cases feature real (suffering) plaintiffs, whereas laboratory experiments do not; and (b) jurors are making real decisions in real cases but not in laboratory experiments. The first suggests that jurors' sympathy for plaintiffs—and hence their inclination to use need-based distributive justice (Feigenson, 1997) —might result in a more pronounced tendency to compensate the victims of wealthier defendants in real cases than in simulated cases. As for the second, the research on whether real versus hypothetical decision making affects outcomes is limited and inconclusive (Kaplan & Krupa, 1986; D. Wilson & Donnerstein, 1977), with no studies directly on point. Also, Vidmar (1993) argued that jury verdict analyses supposedly showing a deep pocket effect are confounded by many other variables that could explain the differences in verdicts (type of case, number of defendants, etc.).

time and cannot explore the full range of interactions that characterizes decision making in the real world. Moreover, researchers test for the effects of those variables in at most a small handful of scenarios, and although they hope that their findings can be generalized to other kinds of cases, it is always possible that different configurations of evidence, or different presentations of the same evidence by the lawyers, would elicit different patterns of response from the jurors. Thus, we see the biases to which we attach the labels of anti-corporate defendant, pro-plaintiff, and anti-plaintiff because the heuristics that yield those biases are present in the microcosms of particular cases; we see conflict at the molar level because the molecules differ from one another in so many ways.

There may, nevertheless, be greater order at some intermediate plane of analysis. Perhaps the myriad individual cases can be grouped into categories, within each of which important heuristics tend to function in similar ways and incline jurors toward similar outcomes (i.e., the kinds of "molar" biases discussed above). Let me suggest, for instance, that *case type* may *moderate* the effect of any one or more of those habits on juror judgments in accident cases.

This hypothesis is attractive for a number of reasons.[19] The idea that the effects and interactions of jurors' decision-making habits depend on the type of case being decided comports with the foundational social psychological insight into the importance of *situational* variables in social cognition and social judgment (Ross & Nisbett, 1991). It also fits with the understanding of individual jurors' (and juries') psychological makeup as a *system in tension*, in which different features drawn from the same complex of cognitive and emotional inclinations may come to the fore in response to different stimuli (Ross & Nisbett, 1991). More or less every juror has the potential to use any or all of the habits of mind and feeling discussed in chapters 2 and 3. In any given case, each may support or cancel out others, but the judgments that emerge may arrange themselves into patterns along case type lines. The case type hypothesis is also generally consistent with the importance of prototype effects on judgments of liability and damages, discussed in chapter 2.

Although there is as yet almost no research to support the case type hypothesis (see Vidmar et al., 1994), let me illustrate why I think it may be a plausible explanation for at least a portion of the pattern of results

---

[19] Before this hypothesis is tested, the idea of "case type" would have to be defined more precisely. In the text, I adopt the usage that seems implicit in the foregoing research on juror decision making. This distinguishes categories of cases based, very roughly, on the type of activity in which the plaintiff was engaged at the time of the accident and/or the instrumentality of the accident. Thus, work-related, vehicular, products liability, slip-and-fall, and medical malpractice accidents are five of the leading case types. Obviously there is some overlap among these standard classifications (consider, e.g., a vehicular accident on the job), and perhaps a better one should be developed. (An entirely different method of categorizing case types, suggested in the section of this chapter on accidents as melodrama, could be in terms of the dramatic genre or genres most readily evoked by the accident story.)

found in the literature. Generally speaking, the research shows, for instance, the *least* anti-plaintiff bias and the *most* anti-*defendant* bias in products liability and medical malpractice cases.[20] One reason may be that, on the whole, in these types of cases the plaintiff is much more readily portrayed as passive and the defendant as active than in other types of cases (e.g., workplace injuries).[21] That is important because, according to norm theory, the party most likely to be held responsible for the accident is the one who can most readily be imagined having acted otherwise (and thus having avoided the accident), and acts are generally easier to "undo" mentally than are omissions. So a type of case that disproportionately features active defendants and passive plaintiffs will, all other things being equal, feature more anti-defendant and fewer anti-plaintiff outcomes (Wissler et al., 1997). Of course, all other things may not be equal, and in any given case, the particular facts and the ways in which the lawyers present those facts to the jurors can shape how the jurors perceive the parties' passivity or activity—as we see in chapters 5 and 6.

Even if case type proves on further research to account for some of the differences in juror decision making about accidents, no doubt a good deal of complexity and even contradiction will remain, both intrapsychically (within each juror) and societally (the pattern of juror decision making in the aggregate). I believe that this complexity is to be expected, not just because the sources of information are so variegated and ultimately incomplete, but also because the very object of inquiry—common-sense decision making across accident cases—encompasses so many potential individual and group sources of variance. Still more fundamentally, complexity and even contradiction are to be expected when the object of study is common sense, which, as Geertz (1983) famously described it, is an "immethodical" collection of adages, images, and rules of thumb (see also Nisbett & Ross, 1980).

At the very least, however, the possibility of case type effects should direct the inquiry toward a more particularized examination of common sense, which presumes that the answers to how people think about accidents are more likely to be found in features of the case (i.e., the situation) than in any disposition of individual jurors or society as a whole to be biased toward plaintiffs or defendants in general. This offers another jus-

---

[20] Yet these two types of cases consistently display the *lowest* plaintiff *win rates* in actual cases (Clermont & Eisenberg, 1992; Peterson, 1984). This could very well be due to case selection effects: For example, the higher stakes in these types of cases make it worthwhile for plaintiffs' lawyers to bring relatively weaker cases, and (mis)perceptions of juries' pro-plaintiff biases lead defendants to settle more often, leaving a weaker set of plaintiff's cases to go to trial. (Note that the text refers to biases, which are measured relative to some extrinsic norm or metric, not win rates.)

[21] We see in chapter 7, however, a medical malpractice case in which jurors readily viewed the patient (the plaintiff is her estate) as well as the defendant physician as active parties who may have been responsible for the bad outcome.

tification for the bottom-up, ethnographic approach taken in the second half of this book.

TOTAL JUSTICE

Having first offered a broad claim about common-sense thinking in accident cases—that people tend to think about accidents as melodramas —and having then shown that the explanatory force of any one concept must be qualified by the complexities and contradictions of common-sense thinking, I would like to try again to capture the common sense of accidents at a still more general level. The idea is *total justice*. When jurors think and talk about responsibility and compensation for accidents, when they try to reach decisions that are just, the justice for which they strive is total justice—which sometimes may be more justice than the law recommends.

Jurors' justice in accident cases is "total" in five interrelated senses. The first is that jurors appear to think of doing justice as reaching a result that is complete, neat, with no loose ends; they think of their job as *squaring* or *balancing the accounts* between the litigants. The procedure of the lawsuit invites jurors to view tort liability as a contest between the plaintiff and the defendant, at least one of whom must be responsible for the accident that put things out of whack (Feigenson, 1995). The jurors' job is to restore proper order, to make everything come out right, by giving each party what it deserves; and in the context of the lawsuit, any realignment of one party's deserts means a corresponding adjustment to the other's. That is what jurors' emotional responses to the case indicate. The parties are linked in a complementary relationship, so that to the extent one party is perceived to be the good guy, the other cannot be; if one attracts sympathy, the other warrants anger (Feigenson et al., in press). Jurors' liability decisions mirror their emotional squaring of accounts. Doing justice in the accident case, as in any other kind of case, becomes a morality play (Stachenfeld & Nicholson, 1996; Weiler, 1991), in which jurors seek a right result by adjusting the fates of the parties to correspond to what the jurors believe each party merits (Baron & Ritov, 1993).

To some extent, this sense of justice as the squaring or balancing of accounts is exactly what the expert discourse of corrective justice (discussed in chapter 1) seems to require. The defendant has (allegedly) upset the status quo by wrongfully injuring the plaintiff (Coleman & Ripstein, 1995), and the jurors' job is to correct the imbalance to the extent it *deserves* to be corrected. Thus, jurors arguably conform to legal and expert norms when they conceive of their decision as linking the parties in a complementary way; a damage award for the plaintiff takes just that amount away from the (sufficiently solvent) defendant; a verdict for the defendant "saves" the defendant and "deprives" the plaintiff by precisely the same amount. Thinking about responsibility for accidents in terms of just deserts is also not necessarily inconsistent with the expert discourse of social utility, which jurors tend to eschew (Baron & Ritov, 1993; Gilles, 1994b; Keating, 1996), although total justice is prone to diverge from social utility goals (as explained in chapter 8).

The urge to decide the lawsuit in a way that makes everything come out right (or as right as possible) may, however, produce a result that does not comport with the applicable law. For instance, in awarding compensatory damages in wrongful death cases, mock jurors may base their awards on the survivors' economic circumstances rather than on the income stream of which the decedent's wrongful death deprived them (Goodman, Greene, & Loftus, 1989). Striving for total justice, using their power to put the survivors in the position in which the jurors think the survivors belong, the jurors may go beyond the information the law considers relevant.

This leads to a second sense in which jurors' justice in accident cases is total: Jurors want to *use all information* that they deem relevant to their decision. Many studies using many different types of cases have tended to support the common perception that jurors are reluctant or unable to follow instructions to disregard inadmissible evidence (see Kassin & Studebaker, 1998, for a review and theoretical framework). Of particular interest is the consistent finding that jurors are likelier to follow limiting instructions when given reason to believe that the evidence is being excluded for irrelevance (Golding, Fowler, Long, & Latta, 1990) or unreliability (Fein, McCloskey, & Tomlinson, 1997). They tend to ignore limiting instructions, however, when they believe the evidence is being excluded on purely procedural grounds (e.g., because the information should have been kept confidential [Golding et al., 1990]; or was obtained in violation of a party's due process rights [Kassin & Sommers, 1997]). That is, jurors are inclined to take into account whatever evidence they think will help them reach a substantively correct result.

To the same effect is jurors' susceptibility to the hindsight bias and their imperviousness to debiasing (Rachlinski, 1998). Legal rules may ask jurors to gauge the reasonableness of the parties' conduct from an *ex ante* rather than from an *ex post* perspective, but jurors have little motivation to do so. Instead, they are likely to think: "If I know the outcome of the parties' conduct, why make believe that I don't? The outcome is what really happened, and taking it into account will help me to reach a just decision about responsibility for what happened."

A particular instance of the urge to do justice on the basis of the totality of the information is that jurors tend to make judgments based on their conceptions of the *whole person* of each litigant, or at least conceptions that include features of the litigants beyond those that the formal law makes relevant to their decisions. For instance, in culpable causation research, mock jurors who were asked to determine how much a motorcyclist's speeding contributed causally to an accident took into account the moral blameworthiness of the motorcyclist's reason for speeding (Alicke, 1992). In the course of making a causal attribution, these jurors were implicitly making a judgment about the person of the motorcyclist. His unsavory conduct (in the conditions in which he was speeding home to hide a vial of cocaine) may very well have aroused negative affect, which jurors may have tried to rationalize by increased blaming (Alicke, 1992). The use of the fundamental attribution error makes this aspect of total justice even clearer. To treat behavior as emanating from dispositions, that is, permanent character traits, is to refer to the whole person when making judgments about causation and hence responsibility. (We see examples of this in all of the cases studied in chapters 5 and 6.)

Third, and relatedly, jurors' justice in accident cases is total in a *procedural* sense. Jurors are prone to decide *holistically* rather than by keeping separate the discrete steps or elements the law requires jurors to consider. They tend to merge the law's distinct elements, making a global responsibility judgment that may ignore or give improper weight to legally relevant considerations and take into account legally irrelevant ones (Feigenson et al., 1997).

There are many examples of jurors' total, that is, global, decision making in determining liability, computing damages, and reaching ultimate judgments including both liability and damages. Norm theory and culpable causation lead us to expect jurors to conflate fault and causation, legally distinct elements in negligence cases (Feigenson, 1995). Similarly, an analysis of recent litigation against makers of cigarettes and silicone breast implants argues that jurors "commingle" the elements of fault and causation so that strong beliefs in the defendants' blameworthiness make up for questionable causal links between the defendants' acts and the plaintiff's injuries (Nagareda, 1998). Furthermore, when computing compensatory damages in wrongful death cases, mock jurors often simply pick what strikes them as a reasonable figure, without bothering to compute the elements of compensation the law prescribes (Goodman et al., 1989). Finally, jurors in accident cases may also ignore the legal rules that tell them that liability and damages are independent questions. They may use compensatory damages to enforce culpability judgments (e.g., Anderson & MacCoun, 1999; Chapman & Bornstein, 1996; Greene, 1989; Kalven, 1958) or allow their judgments of culpability to be affected by the severity of the victim's injuries (Feigenson et al., 1997; but cf. Cather, Greene, & Durham, 1996).

Fourth, common-sense justice is total in a *phenomenological* sense. Jurors want to *feel right* about their decisions. People crave the sense of emotional completion and satisfaction provided by a well-resolved story (McKee, 1996), and jurors realize that it is within their power to supply that satisfying resolution to the accident story before them. (We see in chapters 5 and 6 how plaintiffs' lawyers can exploit this possibility by engaging the jurors as active decision makers.) Jurors, moreover, are prone to react to perceived injustice with anger or other negative affect (Mikula et al., 1998) and want to decide the accident case in a way that reduces or eliminates that bad feeling.

Feeling right about the decision also means molding component cognitions and associated emotions into an acceptable whole. Cognitive dissonance theory posits that being aware of conflicts between one's cognitions or between cognitions and behaviors leads to negative emotional arousal (Festinger, 1957; Pittman, 1998). This in turn motivates any number of coping mechanisms. For instance, faced with two equally desired alternatives and experiencing dissonance, a person may choose one and then reevaluate the unchosen alternative as less desirable (Jones, 1998); or the person may internalize otherwise insufficient external prohibitions regarding the unchosen alternative so that the person now believes he or she "could not" have chosen it in the first place (Jones, 1998; cf. Cover, 1975).

Jurors deciding accident cases can be expected to strive to work their emotions and their judgments into a satisfying totality. Jurors, as noted earlier, often face the task of assigning liability for harm that could seem greatly disproportionate to the inadvertence or impulse that brought the harm about; they persistently resort to melodramatic and other common-sense blaming practices in the face of contrary legal instructions because the melodramatic account makes them feel right about doing what the law requires. Some of this occurs intrapsychically and perhaps nearly automatically, as indicated by our experimental participants who "adjusted" their feelings about the plaintiff and the defendant to fit a complementary pattern (Feigenson et al., in press). The effort to harmonize emotions and cognitions proceeds during jury deliberations, as jurors encourage each other to explore whether they feel right about the decision they are reaching (Levin & Herzberg, 1986)—perhaps to enhance their own respective senses of emotional well-being, perhaps as part of a conscious strategy to bring the deliberations to a close.

The *interpersonal* nature of jury decision making adds a fifth and final sense to the notion of total justice, one that has as much to do with the language in which jurors express their thinking as with the substance of their decisions. When people believe that decision-making procedures are fair—when they perceive that *procedural* justice is being done—they experience increased self-respect within the group, which leads to greater self-esteem and an increased willingness to help the group achieve its goals (H. Smith & Tyler, 1997; Tyler, Degoey, & Smith, 1996; Tyler & Smith, 1999). That is, people value fairness in group procedures in part because fair procedures inform them that they are respected and valued group members.

Fairness and procedural justice in jury deliberations mean at least that jurors should appear to be reasonable and open to persuasion; they should appear to listen to one another's views. Yet for many jurors, presenting oneself in a way that is consistent with this group norm (Leary, 1995) may be in tension with the need to persuade others to accept one's own view of the case. Would-be persuaders may seek to enhance their sense of self-efficacy (Bandura, 1997); to generate agreement and hence social proof for the correctness of their initial position (Cialdini, 1994)[22]; to present themselves as persuaders rather than as too easily persuaded, and hence as more intelligent (Cialdini, Braver, & Lewis, 1974); and, not least, to bring about justice as they perceive it, which may depend on convincing a sufficient number of fellow jurors to think likewise. To reconcile the individual need to persuade with adherence to the group norm of appearing open to persuasion, jurors may develop a *shared discourse* for talking about the case, which allows speakers to obtain the satisfaction of conformity (Baumeister, 1982) to group speech norms (and thus to foster at least the appearance of mutual respect and hence procedural justice) at the same time as it enhances their instrumentalist goal of persuading others (see Baumeister, 1982) by grounding deliberations in shared mental constructs (Ruscher et al., 1996).[23] (There is some evidence of this interpersonal development of a common discourse in the mock jury deliberations analyzed in chapter 7.)

One can find echoes of many aspects of the notion of total justice in other areas of the law. As Fletcher (1994) observed, the success of "blame the victim" defenses in certain high-profile criminal trials in the early 1990s indicates that jurors seeking to do justice may disregard the constraints of legal rules. Jurors acquit or hung in the Lorena Bobbitt and (first) Menendez brothers trials, despite overwhelming evidence of the defendants' guilt, because the crime victims were themselves believed to be blameworthy in some respect (alleged wife abuser, alleged child abusers). According to Fletcher, these jurors were seeking to do total justice—to square all accounts—in the single case. That is, they were treating criminal cases like comparative negligence cases (Finkel, 1995). Still more broadly, ethnographic evidence indicates that laypeople conceive of the legal system as implementing "broad notions of social justice" rather than narrowly drawn legal rules (Conley & O'Barr, 1990); accordingly, they believe that the law should decide individual disputes so as to set straight social im-

---

[22] Generating social proof may also be a motive for the *group's* movement toward consensus (Ruscher et al., 1996).

[23] Ruscher et al. (1996) found that small groups motivated to achieve consensus rather than those motivated to achieve accuracy were most likely to spend time talking about shared constructs (operationalized as stereotype-consistent information). Juries, of course, are (highly) motivated to achieve accuracy *and* consensus. In the absence of an objective standard for accurate judgment, however, people may use consensus as a substitute for accuracy (Funder, 1987); thus, in the context of jury decision making, the accuracy motivation may partially collapse into the consensus motivation, strengthening the expectation that juries will spend considerable time talking about shared understandings.

balances between the parties. This, too, is total justice in the first two senses used above. And experimental evidence in criminal cases confirms that jurors commingle factually distinct charges so that the sum of their verdicts is fair to the defendant (Kerr & Sawyers, 1979)—a commingling that is consistent with the third sense of total justice.

The idea of total justice also helps us make sense of a set of facts about juror decision making that, in the aggregate, is fairly curious. Practically all serious students of jury behavior concur that jurors take their duties very seriously and go about their business very responsibly (Hans & Vidmar, 1986). Jurors themselves tend to describe their experiences in positive terms and to leave their work favorably impressed with their fellow citizens and with the justice system (e.g., Marder, 1997). Jurors take such pains with the process of decision making because they are very concerned to get things right. And usually they do: About four fifths of the time, jurors reach the same decision that the judge, the "expert" decision maker and most likely alternative were there no jury trials, would have reached (Kalven & Zeisel, 1966). This rate of agreement compares very favorably with interdecision-maker reliability in other fields (Saks, 1992). And yet somehow jurors manage this degree of competence even though they are famously poor at understanding the substantive law on which their decisions are supposed to be based (e.g., Reifman et al., 1992).

How can one account for jurors' general diligence, their high rate of "correct enough" decisions, and their lack of comprehension of the law? Those who claim that jurors are too prone to decide emotionally, too given to nullification, or just too incompetent may explain the third fact but hardly the first two. One can, however, explain all three by positing that jurors try hard to get things right, which for them means doing total justice; and that total justice often, but not always, leads to decisions consistent with the law.

The explanation is that total justice, like common sense in other domains, often, but not always, leads to results that are right by the relevant normative standards, albeit for the wrong reasons (Ross & Nisbett, 1991). In familiar, everyday contexts, people do a good enough job when they rely on common sense—for instance, the intuition that people have relatively stable personalities from which their behavior in a wide range of situations can be accurately predicted (cf. the fundamental attribution error). One habitually encounters the same people in the same situations, so often there is no practical difference between (or any practical way to disentangle) dispositional and situational attributions (Gilbert, 1998). And any mistakes one makes in predicting others' behavior are often either trivial or easily corrected (Fiske & Taylor, 1991).

Faced with the task of passing consequential judgments on strangers in an accident case, jurors have none of these safeguards, yet their common sense usually leads to correct enough results. Why? One reason is that some important features of the decision-making task are *familiar* to jurors. Jurors are adept at deciding facts—that is, at gauging the relative plausibility and persuasiveness of different stories about the accident—because they do that all the time in their everyday lives. And where the outcome of the case turns on concepts with which jurors are familiar—for instance, the notion of reasonableness—they are also likely to decide well. They are less practiced, however, at parsing legal language and responding to the kinds of questions used to measure comprehension of jury instructions. Here, the context of decision making takes them into unfamiliar territory, increasing the likelihood of divergence from legal or expert norms.

Sometimes, to be sure, jurors' decisions, and not just their understanding of the law abstracted from those decisions, diverge from legal or expert norms. Some number of divergences, of course, are to be expected given the variation in the population of juries and verdicts. Put enough jurors on enough juries and some will produce outlier decisions. In addition, I would speculate that deviations from legal or expert norms are likeliest when the facts of the case or the presentation of the evidence opens up an unusual discrepancy between total justice and judgment according to professional norms. For example, where the case for the defendant's moral blameworthiness is very strong, yet evidence that the defendant caused the plaintiff's injuries is weak, jurors' tendency to view the accident as a melodrama may lead them to cast the defendant as the bad guy, who must be held liable in order to square accounts with the suffering plaintiff (see Nagareda, 1998).

If this explanation is valid, it underscores the need to trace divergences between lay and expert decisions in accident cases to the difficulty of the decision-making context at least as much as to any intellectual or moral shortcomings on the part of the jurors. This is not, by the way, to suggest that (constitutional issues aside) jurors can or should be precluded from deciding some subset of especially complex cases. The leading research indicates that jurors are generally competent in these cases as in others (for the evidence regarding medical malpractice cases, e.g., see Vidmar, 1995), although there is certainly evidence to the contrary (Sanders, 1998; Selvin & Picus, 1987), and that with regard to jurors' systematic shortcomings, such as evaluating statistical evidence, judges (the most likely alternative decision maker) may not fare much better (Cecil, Hans, & Wiggins, 1991; Lempert, 1993; Vidmar, 1998). The point, rather, is to develop an enhanced appreciation for why jurors think as they do, including, perhaps, a more nuanced explanation for why that thinking occasionally diverges from professional norms (though much less often than commonly thought). I also might note that by underestimating the importance of the situation in which jurors act, which may include needlessly confusing presentations of evidence (Sanders, 1998) and law (Lieberman & Sales, 1997), and by underestimating the subjectivity of common wisdom regarding jury behavior (Galanter, 1998; Saks, 1992), the popular perception of (many) accident juries as prejudiced or incompetent (see Daniels & Martin, 1995; Galanter, 1996, 1998) itself reflects what has been called *naive realism*:

> the individual's unshakable conviction that he or she is somehow privy to an invariant, knowable, objective reality—a reality that others will also perceive faithfully, provided that they are reasonable and rational, a reality that others are apt to misperceive only to the extent that they (in contrast to oneself) view the world through a prism of self-interest, ideological bias, or personal perversity. (R. Robinson, Keltner, Ward, & Ross, 1995, p. 405)

In sum, the total justice notion helps us to pull together many strands of jurors' common-sense thinking about accident cases, and to do so in a way that may lend greater credit to jurors than they receive in many of the disparaging accounts of juror behavior in the media. I return to this topic at the end of the book. To say that jurors are doing total justice is not, however, to specify *what* total justice consists of in any given case. The fact-specificity of lay judgments about blame and compensation requires that one attend to the details of each case to find the particular form that total justice is taking at the moment. Those inquiries are the subject of the second part of this book.

5

THE RHETORIC OF ACCIDENTS: HOW ADVOCATES HELP JURORS THINK ABOUT LIABILITY AND DAMAGES

Having reviewed the social psychology of thinking about accidents, I now examine how people *talk* about accidents. I begin by studying examples of discourse from personal injury trials—specifically, what advocates say to jurors in their closing arguments.

The trials I examine arose out of workplace accidents. In one, a truck driver was seriously injured when he fell from the back of his flatbed truck while loading machinery. In the other, a railroad worker was crushed to death between cars while conducting a backup operation at night. How should jurors think about who is responsible for these accidents? How do jurors develop an understanding of "how things go" in these situations— about loading industrial machinery onto trucks or maneuvering a line of railroad cars back down a track to hook up with another set of cars—that will enable them to judge whether the plaintiff or the defendant behaved reasonably under the circumstances? In both cases, moreover, the victims' own behavior seems to have contributed to the tragedy. How do jurors determine whether it contributed enough so that the defendants' liability, if any, should be reduced or negated?

The words the lawyers use in their attempts to persuade jurors can shed considerable light on how the jurors themselves may have thought about the case. From the words the lawyers use, one can draw at least qualified inferences about how jurors may think about accidents: how their habits of thought and feeling affect the way they apply the law to the facts in order to reach a verdict. I look for traces of those thoughts and feelings in the lawyers' words; I ask what must be true about jurors' judgmental habits in order for what the lawyers say to make sense. And I do this within the contextual structure sketched in the introduction: the pull of the substantive law of negligence, the procedural law guiding the jurors' decision-making process, and the conventions governing the lawyers' arguments.

As a preliminary matter, let me explain why I believe that tentative inferences can be made from how lawyers argue at trial to how jurors think. Undoubtedly, the presumption that what attorneys say is strongly connected to how jurors think is problematic (Amsterdam & Hertz, 1992). The lawyers' rhetoric may suggest knowledge structures and judgmental heuristics that the jurors do not actually use, or the jurors may think in ways not prompted or encouraged by the attorneys' arguments. If, as researchers have noted (Holstein, 1985), there is reason to be cautious when drawing inferences to jurors' thinking from their own speech during mock deliberations, considerably more caution would appear appropriate in the effort to infer that thinking from what attorneys say to them.

Yet it seems reasonable to presume that the ways in which lawyers try to persuade jurors are strongly related to the ways jurors think. Lawyers and witnesses attempt to structure information in ways that will appear coherent to the jury (Holstein, 1985). This implies that the juror schemas those lawyers and witnesses try to address are shared social constructs, not purely idiosyncratic ideas of the jurors. It would surely be odd if there were no significant connections—if the speech acts of trained professionals, highly motivated to make just those connections and reputed for their success in making them, were instead irrelevant to the speakers' goals. This chapter and the next, therefore, follow in a long tradition of rhetorical analysis which presumes that what advocates say may reflect and guide, if not determine, what jurors think (Conley, 1990).

In the course of a trial, lawyers say many things that they intend jurors to hear and understand, beginning with *voir dire* and running from the opening statement to witness examinations to the closing argument (or summation). Using closing arguments as a database, therefore, does not capture all aspects of trial advocacy, but it does focus on one of the most important.[1] The summation is where the lawyer brings the entire case to-

---

[1] Three limitations of using transcripts of closing arguments to analyze trial advocacy and juror cognition should be noted and placed in perspective. First, an analysis of trial transcripts omits much about the context of the cases, including details about the parties, attorneys, jurors, and judges involved. Second, to examine only the words the attorneys use, and in transcript form

gether for the jurors, in light of the evidence actually presented rather than that which the lawyer expected to be presented. Opening arguments may have a greater persuasive impact (Lind & Ke, 1985; Pyszczynski & Wrightsman, 1981). Closing arguments, however, offer jurors a more comprehensive formulation of the case, one to which the jurors may (if the lawyer has been successful) match the conceptions they have already, but perhaps still only vaguely and incompletely, developed.

The closing argument is also the advocate's last and best opportunity to suggest to jurors a shared discourse they can use during deliberations as they seek to persuade one another en route to their verdict. We know that even the smallest semantic components of the lawyers' and jurors' common language, such as the verbs speakers use, implicitly communicate causal attributions (Brown & Fish, 1983; Rudolph & Försterling, 1997), and that advocates' use of such subtle cues in their closing arguments (Schmid &

at that, is to leave out intonation, accent, pace of speech, and other features of spoken and unspoken communication. Third, by studying only closing arguments, the analysis omits all the other phases of the case in which attorneys try to persuade jurors, such as *voir dire*, opening statements, and cross-examination.

Nevertheless, transcripts of closing arguments provide much valuable information about trial advocacy and hence about the rhetoric of negligence in particular cases. First, putting demographic and other characteristics of the jurors or the parties to the side does not undermine the project. As noted in chapter 2, most research has failed to show strong correlations between jurors' demographic characteristics or general attitudes and their decisions. Moreover, although there is some evidence indicating that extralegal characteristics of the parties may bias juror decision making (Chin & Peterson, 1985; Dane & Wrightsman, 1982), the research consensus is that jurors are not ordinarily swayed, for instance, by racial prejudice (J. A. Tanford, 1993). (For research on evidence of other sorts of bias in decision making in accident cases, see chapter 4.)

Second, it is true that noncontent features of spoken communication are important to ethnographers and discourse analysts (Conley, O'Barr, & Lind, 1978; Sigal et al., 1985). Nonverbal features of the lawyer's presentation (e.g., posture, position in the courtroom, and physical appearance), as well as other elements of the performance (e.g., the use of visual aids, the spectators, and the courtroom itself), may very well be important to persuasion. Psychological research has associated persuasiveness with, for instance, the speaker's credibility, attractiveness, and power (Linz & Penrod, 1984). The greater the credibility of the communicator, the less counterarguing the listener will do, hence the more uncritically the message will be accepted. Attractiveness obviously cannot be gleaned from a transcript, and some of the determinants of perceived credibility, such as perceived expertise and trustworthiness, as well as such overt behaviors as pace of speech, usually cannot be either. The lawyers' words, however, remain significant. Most jurors try to attend carefully to message content (see also Footnote 2), and the words that comprise that content can persuade not only directly but also indirectly, because microlinguistic events such as the speaker's use of emotion words, verb tense, and the like may affect the speaker's perceived competence, dominance, and worth (Berry, Pennebaker, Mueller, & Hiller, 1997), which in turn affect the persuasiveness of the message. Furthermore, in many cases the persuasive effect of nonverbal factors may be roughly balanced between the two sides, while in other cases, a factor favoring one side may be canceled out by a different factor favoring the other; in both situations, the words the lawyers use may make the difference.

Third, advocates may begin persuading jurors during *voir dire*, but the closing argument, as noted in the text, is where the attorney explains the entire case to the jurors, in light of the evidence actually presented. My focus on closing arguments has, in addition, been guided by a practical concern. In the federal district courts in the state in which I teach (Connecticut), as a matter of practice rather than local rule, attorneys are usually not permitted to make opening arguments; therefore, only closing arguments are available. Because much of my data come from Connecticut, closing arguments thus provide the only basis for comparison of lawyer rhetoric across cases.

Fiedler, 1998), as well as their use of larger syntactic units such as explicit counterfactuals (Branscombe et al., 1996), can influence jurors' responsibility judgments. An exploration of the language of closing arguments, from their overall structure to their microlinguistic elements, should, therefore, illuminate jurors' conceptions of causation and responsibility for accidents.

FROM THINKING TO DISCOURSE: SOCIAL PSYCHOLOGY AND STRATEGIES OF LEGAL ARGUMENT

It would certainly make sense for lawyers in accident cases to appeal to the intuitive habits of thought and feeling explained in chapters 2 through 4.[2] As we will see, plaintiffs' and defendants' lawyers may be predicted to elicit those habits to different extents and in different ways. I would like to mention here three important aspects of juror cognition and trial advocacy: using stories to understand evidence; using melodramatic stories in particular to conceptualize the accident; and engaging the jurors as active rather than passive decision makers. These will provide additional context for understanding how norm theory, the fundamental attribution error, and other psychological dynamics are likely to manifest themselves in the discourse of argumentation at trial.

Stories as Knowledge Structures

Jurors in an accident case are asked to pass judgment on an event or series of events. One might, therefore, expect them to think in terms of prototypical scenarios or stories, as well as "person–situation" prototypes (Cantor & Kihlstrom, 1987; Cantor, Mischel, & Schwartz, 1982). That is, the schemas jurors use to make judgments about the reasonableness of the parties' behavior and their responsibility for the accident may include nar-

---

[2] According to the *elaboration likelihood model* of persuasion (Petty & Cacioppo, 1986; Petty & Wegener, 1999), people may process messages in a relatively effortful and systematic way or in a way that makes more use of heuristic thinking, depending on both their individual predilections and the situations in which they find themselves. Persuasion, then, may work through a "central" route featuring careful consideration of message content or a "peripheral" route featuring cues such as various characteristics of the message source or the message recipient's transitory affect (Petty & Cacioppo, 1986). To process information by the central route, people must be both motivated and able to scrutinize messages carefully. Jurors may in general be motivated to ponder message content carefully (it is debatable whether jurors should be considered "high involvement" or "high responsibility" listeners, as those terms are defined in the literature; Petty & Cacioppo, 1979, 1986), but they may lack the ability to do so, especially in factually or legally complex cases. The elaboration likelihood model, therefore, suggests that jurors may think heuristically using peripheral factors. Jurors also may be expected to think heuristically as they attend to the message presented by the advocates' arguments (see Schmid & Fiedler, 1998). For instance, even assuming that jurors are highly motivated to process trial information systematically and thus are likely to think about message content rather than peripheral cues, research shows that high motivation to perform difficult judgment tasks accurately can increase the (erroneous) reliance on heuristic thinking (Pelham & Neter, 1995). There is, therefore, good reason for trial advocates to expect even conscientious jurors to use intuitive habits of thought and feeling as they try to make sense of accident cases.

ratives about "how accidents (like this) typically occur," as well as category exemplars (e.g., "the careless driver is one who resembles my teenage son") and rulelike propositions (e.g., "the careless driver is one who poses unreasonable risks to others").

Organizing information and making sense of reality in terms of stories probably reflect a deep-seated, general human tendency (Bruner, 1990). Considerable research indicates that jurors typically organize complex evidence into narrative form, and that their judgments and the confidence with which they hold them depend in part on the ease with which they can generate acceptable stories from the data. The leading work is that of Pennington and Hastie (1991, 1992), who developed the *story model* to explain juror decision making.[3] According to the story model, jurors impose order on the evidence by constructing stories from it during the trial; learn the verdict categories (i.e., the elements of the tort claim or the criminal charge); and then reach a decision by matching the accepted story to the verdict categories and deciding if the fit is sufficient.

From the extensive literature on narrative and social judgment in the law, a few points are particularly relevant. First, Bennett and Feldman (1981) argued that it is the internal structure of the story that people find credible or not, rather than its correspondence to external evidence. Specifically, audiences find stories that vary from their expectations, that leave gaps or contradict their "stock scripts" or prototypes, to be dubious. The more a story departs from the prototype, the more ambiguities and gaps at crucial junctures, the less credible the story is.[4] Hence, one would expect

---

[3] The story model involves prototypical reasoning at the story construction stage, in that the choice of the best story involves, among other things, a judgment of coherence, which includes an intuitive comparison of the story with prior knowledge of how stories are supposed to go. It also involves prototypical reasoning at the last stage, in which the test is whether the accepted story fits well enough with the best-match verdict category. Obviously, legal rules, the elements of the crime, figure in both the second and third stages of this model. Moreover,

> The classification process [in the last stage of the model] is aided by relatively direct relations between the attributes of a verdict category (crime element) and components of the episode [or part of a story] schema. . . . The law has evolved so that the main attributes of the decision categories suggested by legal experts—identity, mental state, circumstances, and actions—correspond closely to the central features of human action sequences represented as episodes—initiating events, goals, actions, and states. This is not a coincidence; rather, it is a reflection of the fact that both stories and crimes are culturally determined generic descriptions of human action sequences. (Pennington & Hastie, 1991, pp. 530–531)

[4] To put this finding in a broader context, consider that, generally, people evaluate more critically arguments that are inconsistent with their prior beliefs, displaying a *disconfirmation bias* (Edwards & Smith, 1996; Lord, Ross, & Lepper, 1979). Similarly, people might be expected to view less favorably stories that depart from their prior beliefs about "how such things usually go." Research on mood effects on evaluative judgments shows that people evaluate a story more favorably the more it leaves them in the mood they expect from that kind of story (Martin, Abend, Sedikides, & Green, 1997). Thus, people who expect to hear an accident explained in, say, melodramatic terms and to feel the way they expect a melodrama to make them feel (anger at the malefactor, sympathy for the victim) may rate the melodramatic story to be a better account of the case than a competing account. (See also research on *affective expectancies*, discussed in chapter 4.)

to find advocates organizing information about the case and the world into stories that conform to the stock scripts they expect the jurors to bring with them to the courtroom (Lind & Ke, 1985; P. Meyer, 1994; Sherwin, 1994).

Second, the role of narratives in accident trials is not limited to matching events to prototypical scenarios; it also includes establishing differences between the two. Stories of accidents are likely to correspond to the stock scripts of everyday life, with one salient deviation: the accident itself. To explain the accident persuasively, the narrative must account for this deviation. Research in story comprehension indicates that readers will try to explain a deviation from a prototypical story (or script) by searching for another deviation and then by trying to make a causal connection linking the deviations (Black, Galambos, & Read, 1984). Hence, one might expect each attorney to construct a plausible "normal" or background scenario in which the accident does not occur, and which differs from the actual events by including something the *other party* did not do or by omitting something he or she did do. Each attorney would thereby emphasize that his or her client behaved normally, but that the other party acted "outside the script" in some respect. The attorneys would then play to the jurors' tendency to link the two deviations causally, thus attributing causal and legal responsibility for the accident to the other party. This process of attributing responsibility to the party whose conduct deviated from the relevant norm is, of course, exactly what norm theory describes. Consequently, one should look in the lawyers' arguments for discourse that reflects the dynamic of normalcy and deviance.

Third, and conversely, stories are also the ideal form for justifying deviant behavior within cultural norms, because stories allow people to understand intentions within contexts; they explain the actor's reasons for acting in a way that reconciles the aberrant with the normative (Bruner, 1990). One would, therefore, expect attorneys to craft stories to persuade jurors that their respective clients' apparently aberrant behavior actually conformed to social norms and thus was not culpable.

Thus far, there would be no reason to expect that plaintiffs' lawyers would differ generally from defendants' in their use of stories. And yet the uses of stories, and particular kinds of stories and story devices, do not seem to be evenly distributed between plaintiffs' and defendants' lawyers. My impression from reading trial transcripts and anecdotal evidence from trial lawyers suggests that plaintiffs' lawyers put more of their arguments in the form of stories (see Sanders, 1998). The next two subsections help explain why this might be so.

Melodrama as an Argumentative Strategy

In contemporary culture, people are inundated with dramatic stories, mostly through their viewing of television and movies (R. Williams, 1975), and are quite sophisticated in their appreciation of different story conventions (McKee, 1996). Melodrama is only one among many types of story or genre, but, as I suggested in chapter 4 in somewhat schematic fashion, it seems to capture a good deal of the social psychology of jurors' comprehension of accident cases.[5] I would like to explore here the implications of this melodramatic schema for how lawyers may be expected to argue accident cases. Specifically, I propose that the melodramatic conception of the accident is generally, but not exclusively, suited to the purposes of the plaintiff's attorney.

Most obvious in this regard is melodrama's focus on the plaintiff and his or her suffering. As explained in chapter 3, making the plaintiff's suffering salient for the jurors tends to elicit their sympathy, which may in itself lead them to view the case favorably to the plaintiff. Moreover, to depict the plaintiff as suffering is to depict the plaintiff in a *passive* position: "Passive" and "passion" are both derived from the Latin *passus*, the past participle of *pati*, "to suffer." This could serve the plaintiff's lawyer's purpose of describing only the defendant as someone who could have *acted* otherwise to avoid the accident, and as thus potentially blameworthy (recall that according to norm theory, acts are easier than omissions to imagine having been otherwise).

Another element of melodrama—the conception of accidents as due to the personal agency of the "bad" guy alone—could in theory be used by either the plaintiff's or the defendant's lawyer. One would expect the lawyers for either side to construct suitable personality profiles for the parties, to develop stock characters and scripts to represent reasonableness or its opposite, and to try to fit what the jurors know of the client (or the opposing party) into those characters and scripts. Indeed, currently popular attitudes toward law and legal culture would seem to support a defense lawyer's invocation of the fundamental attribution error: one that portrays the personal injury claimant as the bad guy (greedy, grasping, just hoping to hit the jackpot; Hans & Lofquist, 1992) and the corporate defendant as the good guy (providing the goods and services people enjoy—the modern way of life—which is unfortunately made more expensive by frivolous lawsuits). In practice, however, this feature of melodrama tends to be favored by plaintiffs' lawyers because, as noted in chapter 4, it *simplifies* causal explanation. The plaintiff would tend to prefer a simple explanation that jurors can grasp, because if jurors are sufficiently in doubt about causation

---

[5] Melodrama would seem even more obviously applicable to instances of intentional wrongdoing, in which the defendant is even more readily portrayed as a "bad guy." That intentional torts may lend themselves to melodramatic characterization does not undermine my thesis that lawyers, especially plaintiffs' lawyers, may encourage jurors to think melodramatically about accident cases; indeed, it becomes even more striking that jurors may comfortably adopt a way of thinking about mere negligence that seems better suited for describing intentional wrongdoing. (For research and analysis of common-sense views of responsibility for intentional [criminal] wrongdoing, see Finkel, 1995; P. Robinson & Darley, 1995.)

or responsibility, then the plaintiff will not have carried the burden of persuasion and will lose.

Melodrama's final element, that the case should end with a satisfying closure in which the good guy wins, is one that it shares with many popular story genres. Indeed, according to screenwriting expert Robert McKee (1996), closure and the protagonist's triumph describe *the* archetypal plot structure. Both plaintiffs' and defendants' lawyers would be expected to appeal to jurors' presumed preference for closure, but in very different ways. The typical defense lawyer in the accident case, like the typical prosecutor in a criminal case (as will be discussed shortly), wants the jurors to find closure in the facts of the case *as they are*. The plaintiff's lawyer's perspective differs. From the plaintiff's point of view, the real world has failed to conform to the archetypal, melodramatic plot structure, because the good guy has been injured without recompense. Whether the story will be satisfactorily completed is necessarily in doubt before trial; were it not, there would be no need for trial. It thus becomes the jury's job to *perform* the completion of the story by finding the defendant liable to the plaintiff. Let us see how that happens.

Engaging the Jurors as Active Decision Makers

In a landmark article, Amsterdam and Hertz (1992) explained how a prosecutor and a defense attorney in a criminal trial can use a range of linguistic devices to lead jurors to frame their role as passive or active decision makers, respectively, and how these "cognitive frames" are likely to shape the jurors' verdicts.[6] The issue in the case they examined was whether the assailant intended to kill the victim he shot at close range during an argument. That would determine the jurors' choice between second-degree murder and manslaughter. Amsterdam and Hertz observed that even in a relatively simple case, and within the constraints imposed by the evidence, the substantive and procedural law, and jurors' expectations about what closing arguments should sound like, advocates can construct very different stories about identical events.

The basic contrast between the prosecution and defense arguments in the case was between two distinct cognitive frames: history and dialogue. The prosecutor told a story about what happened on a New York City street on the date of the crime, inviting the jurors to accept those events as plain fact. She described events in the past tense and spoke to the jurors as if they needed only to register the objective evidence of what happened "out there" in the world of fact.

The defense attorney, of course, wanted to engender reasonable doubt

---

[6] By "cognitive frame," I mean to allude to but not to confuse the present discussion with the idea of *decision framing* (also known as *prospect theory*), discussed in chapter 2. Some research shows that message framing in the latter sense may also affect the persuasiveness of the message (S. Smith & Petty, 1996).

in the jurors' minds. He could not, however, do this explicitly; that would be contrary to the judge's instructions to the jury not to speculate. It would also have played into the stereotype of defense attorney as trickster and would have undercut his ability to take advantage of the strict formal burden of proof. So the defense counsel *implicitly* drew the jurors into an *imagined dialogue* in which they reconstructed the events of the crime, with the result that they implicitly understood those events not as givens, as facts, but as merely possible interpretations, open to reasonable doubt. The defense lawyer did this by speaking about the jurors' consideration of the evidence and their decision-making tasks using active verbs and metaphors rather than passive ones; by describing events in the present tense; by asking rhetorical questions; and by several other techniques. Thus the defense lawyer's closing argument told a story, not about what happened "out there" on the day of the crime, but about what was happening *at the trial itself*: how the jurors were reaching their decision.[7] Amsterdam and Hertz used this analysis of the advocates' closing arguments to contend that jurors frame the evidence differently when they conceive of themselves as actively constructing knowledge through engaging in dialogue than they do when they conceive of themselves as passive receptors for the "data" established at trial.

Advocates in accident trials, like those in criminal trials, might also try to exploit jurors' capacity to understand the case actively versus passively. I offer the following hypothesis: that plaintiffs' lawyers will tend to lead jurors to conceive of their decision-making role as active, so that the jurors will feel empowered to provide the closure that the accident case lacks. Specifically, plaintiffs' lawyers want the jurors to sense that they have the power to award defendants' money to their clients. This attitude, in turn, may shape jurors' attributions of responsibility. Research suggests that accident victims may first believe that they should be compensated, and only then attribute fault to justify that belief (Lloyd-Bostock, 1979). Similarly, jurors may be more inclined to find a defendant at fault the more they feel capable of awarding damages.[8] It has been shown, for instance, that although jurors hold defendants liable more often the more severely the plaintiff is injured because of the greater sympathy jurors feel for such plaintiffs (see chapter 3), this occurs only when the jurors are in a position to award damages to the plaintiff and not when, say, their decision could

---

[7]Specifically, Amsterdam and Hertz (1992) argued that the defense counsel's argument structure and microlinguistic uses cast the jurors in the role of the classical mythic hero whose efforts to decide the case comprise a quest. The defense lawyer's storyline is how "[t]he jurors, faithful to their oath, acquitted the defendant although he sorely tempted them to do otherwise by killing the victim in a dastardly fashion" (p. 67). This story of the trial also displaces the defendant's killing of the victim from center stage, subordinating it to the jurors' own task of deciding the case.

[8]More precisely, there is reason to believe that the *less* jurors feel capable of awarding damages, the more inclined they will be to blame the plaintiff (D. Miller et al., 1990), and the greater the fault attributed to the plaintiff, the less fault attributed to the defendant (Thomas & Parpal, 1987). The hypothesis offered in the text is the converse of this proposition.

result in a fine for the defendant but not directly in compensation to the plaintiff (Bornstein, 1998).

It is, therefore, important for plaintiffs' lawyers to imbue jurors with a sense of their ability and power to *participate* in the process of doing justice, and not to leave them thinking that their job is simply to apply the law the judge gives them to the facts the lawyers introduce as evidence at trial. One should test the hypothesis by seeing whether plaintiffs' lawyers engage the jurors as active decision makers to a greater extent than do defendants' lawyers.[9] One of the ways a lawyer may encourage jurors to participate in the construction of legal meaning and of justice is to exploit the characteristic *subjunctivity* of stories—"lexical and grammatical usages that highlight subjective states, attenuating circumstances, alternative possibilities" (Bruner, 1990, p. 53). One might also look for the particular involvement devices Amsterdam and Hertz (1992) identified: describing the events leading up to the accident and the jurors' own consideration of the evidence using active verbs and active metaphors, relating crucial aspects of the story in the present tense, drawing jurors into an imaginative dialogue through the strategic deployment of rhetorical questions, and so on (Parkinson, 1981).[10] In particular, lawyers can involve the jurors in the accident story by describing events using the second-person and first-person plural, which implicitly encourage jurors to participate in the story by adopting the perspective of whatever actor the lawyer is speaking about.

Although one may predict that plaintiffs' lawyers would more often use the second-person and first-person plural, especially at more crucial places in the story of the accident itself, to enhance jurors' involvement in the process of decision making, one can expect advocates on both sides to use these points of view to get jurors to *identify* with their respective clients. Identification is a way to reduce the client's perceived responsibility for the accident, and hence something to be sought by both lawyers. The research discussed in chapters 2 and 3 suggests several reasons why identification with the client would tend to counteract unfavorable attribution effects. Getting the observer (juror) to adopt the actor's perspective enhances the salience of circumstances (including other people's conduct), as opposed to that of the actor, in the observer's field of vision, thus making an attribution to someone or something other than the actor more likely (Nisbett & Ross, 1980). Furthermore, to the extent that jurors take a

---

[9]The number of cases analyzed in this book is, as I suggested in the introduction, too small to permit statistically significant generalizations about this or any other aspect of lawyers' rhetoric. One task for future research would be to accumulate enough case studies to test such generalizations.

[10]I am using rhetorical questions as a measure of the advocates' efforts to engage the jurors as active decision makers. Elaboration likelihood model research shows that rhetorical questions enhance message elaboration (as measured by the perceived difference between strong and weak messages) when the audience is not naturally devoting much effort to understanding or processing the message (as operationalized by low personal relevance of message), but reduce message elaboration when the audience is motivated to elaborate (Petty, Cacioppo, & Heesacker, 1981).

party's perspective on events, they are more likely to sympathize with the party, which makes them more likely to attribute to the party favorable characteristics they believe to be true of themselves (Davis et al., 1996).

Regardless of where melodrama or other story genres are found in the arguments of counsel in accident cases, one can expect that they would not be found in the same forms in which they appear in the dramatic arts. Lawyers are, of course, subject to situational constraints that guide the explicit form and content of their arguments. Rules and conventions of trial procedure provide some of these constraints (Feigenson, 1995). For instance, evidence and strategy partially limit the arguments lawyers can make about the kind of person a party is. Information about how a party has behaved in other, unrelated circumstances is often legally irrelevant to the party's responsibility for the incident at bar. The evidence in the trial may also not supply enough, or perhaps any, data from which jurors can formulate the prototype of due care in similar situations with which the parties will be compared. Rules of trial practice prohibit explicit appeals to sympathy (J. A. Tanford & Tanford, 1986). Jurors' expectations provide additional constraints (e.g., Hans & Sweigart, 1993). For instance, if the melodrama in a plaintiff's lawyer's argument is too blatant, jurors may simply refuse to accept it as a plausible depiction of reality. Too overt an appeal to sympathy may even have an effect opposite to what the advocate intends, because jurors may think: "If that's all the plaintiff has to go on, the legal case must be quite weak."

For all of these reasons, lawyers can go only so far in explicitly invoking melodramatic response patterns or engaging jurors as active decision makers (should they desire to do so). Therefore, if so motivated, lawyers must try to accomplish these ends *implicitly* (Schmid & Fiedler, 1998). It is, indeed, the mediation of melodramatic and other intuitive conceptions of accidents by the requirements and expectations of trial procedure that makes uncovering these conceptions in discourse such an interesting task. Let us turn to that task now.

NORMALCY AND DEVIANCE IN THE WORKPLACE: *BUTLER V. REVERE COPPER & BRASS, INC.*

The Facts

Our first case, *Butler v. Revere Copper & Brass, Inc.* (1990), is a fairly simple one. George Butler, a truck driver, was sent by his company to pick up a load of industrial machinery at Revere's plant and take it back to be fixed at his company's shop. Revere's employees loaded the machinery onto Butler's truck with a crane. Butler then tried to put a tarpaulin over the load; he fell, landed on his head, and was seriously injured. There was no evidence of how he fell. No one saw him fall, and he did not remember what happened.

The Plaintiff's Lawyer's Words

Butler's lawyer begins and ends his argument—in all, nearly two thirds of the argument-in-chief—by discussing his client's injuries and how the jurors should go about calculating damages. In between comes all he has to say about why the accident occurred and who should be held responsible for it:

> Now, let me tell you why they are legally responsible. On January 20, 1986, [Butler's] life changed and it didn't have to be changed this way. . . . Robert Brown [Butler's supervisor] told you . . . that the original order for the equipment to be picked up at Revere was . . . some kind of generator, some other kind of device. When George got up to the plant, somebody at Revere told him, "You got all these things to put on." Other things [in addition to the original order] to put on the truck. George said, "Let me call back and I'll see what happens." He calls up Bob Brown . . . . [who] says, "Look, they are a good customer. Do the best you can." And George is the type of person, I think we all know by now, he's going to give his best shot and he did, and he directed the crane operator at Revere and they managed to get all of the equipment on the truck. Revere wasn't satisfied with that, and you can look at the various changes in the invoices.
>
> Revere wants it tarped. Now, Bob Brown doesn't understand why they want it tarped and I don't understand why they want it tarped but they want it tarped. Bob Brown told you when those generators come in, they are steam washed so what difference does it make if they get wet on the way back? . . . But Bob Brown says, "Look, if they want them on the truck upside down, do whatever you can." And George, being the type of person he is, says, "I'm going to try to do it." George takes a . . . tarp that weighed two hundred pounds, approximately, and he starts tarping that load. And he's got a heavy load, equipment that weighs thousands of pounds, and he's climbing up on the equipment trying to pull that tarp all by himself, and at least three [Revere employees], and we had to read these depositions to you because those people weren't here, . . . said they saw him struggling with that tarp. He was having trouble—that equipment is not the nice square little packages or round packages. All sort of jagged edges, so it's getting caught on all the edges. Al Brockway [one of Revere's employees] talks to him for up to ten minutes while he's putting the tarp on, watching him struggling. . . .
>
> [L]et me just read two questions and answers [from Brockway's deposition] to you because I think they are the essence of what Revere did wrong.
>
> . . . .

My next question, "Is a part of your job to, say, take measures that will prevent people from being injured?"

Answer, "Yes, sir."

What did Mr. Brockway do? Mr. Brockway didn't lift a finger to help him with that canvas. Mr. Brockway, like everyone else . . . who was in the area, went on their 5:30 coffee break because they weren't going to do anything. It was coffee break time. "And we're going to have our coffee break and good luck, George, with the canvas. Goodbye. We're going to have our danish and our coffee and we don't care what you're doing.". . .

[L]ater on in his deposition, I said, "Mr. Brockway, tell me again how come you didn't help him?" He said, "Well, maybe, morally, I should have." Well, yeah, you should have. But he didn't. And I even went so far to ask him, "Mr. Brockway, did you think it was a one-man job?" No, sir. He knew it wasn't a one-man job, but he did nothing, absolutely nothing. What would it have taken to walk to the edge of the truck, straighten out the canvas a little bit, so that George could pull it a little easier? . . .

It's that kind of attitude, it's that kind of carelessness that resulted in this injury. Wouldn't have taken very much. Mr. Brockway told you it was his job. And he didn't do it. He didn't do it for the sake of a cup of coffee. (*Butler*, 24.4-27.24)[11]

In the remainder of the argument-in-chief, nearly a quarter of it, the plaintiff's lawyer speaks to the jurors about damages:

Now, when you go in and deliberate, the Judge will give you instructions on the law and I'm sure he'll talk about the testimony and the evidence. You're ultimately going to come down with the responsibility of trying to figure out how to evaluate this case.

. . .

How, how to award damages to Mr. Butler, and that's a very difficult chore and there is no formula. . . . I don't envy your task. It's a difficult, very difficult task.

Now, you hold his only chance. This is the last place, the only place he can come. You're the only people who can attempt to make him whole, as far as money can do it. Granted, money really can't do it. There is no amount of money that can do it, but the Judge will tell you so far as money can do it, that's your job, that's your duty. And society evaluates all sorts of things when they try to put dollars and cents on it. The only thing I can use as an illustration for you to give you some guidance is what price society puts on things, and we all know that [b]all players who play first season are paid four million dollars for six months or eight months. That's what society values that at. How can you compare, like baseball, football, basketball for half a year, three quarters of a year, to what Mr. Butler has gone through

[11] All references to the *Butler* trial transcript are to the page(s) and line(s) in the proceedings of April 27, 1990, unless otherwise indicated.

since 1986 and is going to have to continue to go through for the rest of his life? I don't know. But it's a job that you've been chosen to do and I have full confidence that you'll make your best effort to do. (27.25-28.6; 30.4-23)

Just what are we to make of this kind of talk? Much of it may sound perfectly unremarkable, even clichéd. I contend that the lawyer's words reflect some of the most important habits of thought and feeling that jurors can be expected to bring to an accident case. On the basis of the preceding discussions of how cognitive and emotional dynamics shape common-sense judgments of responsibility and compensation, we are in a position to see how the lawyer's words invoke those dynamics. We will be able to understand why a lawyer who knows that jurors will be instructed[12] to consider all elements of the prima facie case would spend only the few paragraphs quoted above on the highly contested issues of duty, breach, and causation, and the largest portion of his argument on the undisputed issue of damages; why characterizing George Butler as a "fighter" is at all relevant to how jurors may attribute responsibility; why drawing jurors' attention to their duty to decide affects *how* the lawyer wants them to decide; and several other features of this lawyer's discourse.

Moreover, the fact that some of the words may be clichés makes my claim stronger, not weaker. If traces of the habits of thought and feeling with which we are concerned were to be found only in the most original and eloquent summations, we might hesitate to infer that those words reflected the usual thinking of the audience. Where, however, we find those traces in language that seems ordinary—like the jurors' own—we may suppose that these common words are giving voice to what may also be the jurors' common sense.

The Emphasis on the Plaintiff's Injuries

Following a traditional introduction in which he praises the jurors for their time and attention, thus securing their goodwill by appealing to their worthy values and establishing his own good character (17.14-20), George Butler's lawyer describes his client's injuries (18.6-23.22). This is by far the most extensive part of the argument—especially when his advice regarding the calculation of damages for those injuries (27.25-30.5, 30.12-21) is included in the computation. Its placement at the beginning of the argument, moreover, may lead jurors to give it even more importance, owing to the

---

[12] The judge's instructions in *Butler* (40.3-71.11) are nearly half again as long as both closing arguments combined. The instructions on the elements of the prima facie case and comparative negligence occupy about 40% of the total (52.5-65.23). The judge then instructed the jurors on damages (60.9-65.23), how to complete the interrogatory or special verdict form (59.16-19; 65.24-69.3), and the deliberation process (69.4-71.11). An hour into deliberations, the jurors asked to hear the full definition of negligence again, and the judge repeated his charge on all items other than damages (74.21-82.4).

primacy effect (Linz & Penrod, 1984). The rhetorical significance of this emphasis is all the more striking in light of the fact that the defendant Revere's lawyer did not dispute any of the medical evidence (31.12-15).

Structuring the argument this way serves several purposes. The first is obvious: It takes advantage of the availability heuristic. By spending so much time on Butler's injuries and his struggles to overcome them during rehabilitation, his lawyer makes that suffering readily available to the jurors when they come to determine compensation. But not only that. The availability of the plaintiff's suffering is likely to engender sympathy (as we saw in chapter 3), which could in turn make the jurors more likely to hold the defendant responsible. This is the "straight" severity effect (explained in chapters 2 and 3). Indeed, the emphasis on injuries (as we saw in chapter 4) is a central element of thinking about the accident as a melodrama and may be calculated to trigger the other elements of that conception as well.

On the topic of injuries and damages, it is worth noting here how the plaintiff's lawyer concludes his argument by invoking the anchoring and adjustment heuristic. Having told the jurors that money cannot make the plaintiff whole (30.9), he mentions that professional athletes may be paid $4 million for less than a year's work (30.15-17). (This was in 1990, before the days of eight-figure annual contracts.) Perhaps the most striking thing about this anchor is its complete irrelevance to the judgmental task at hand. What the most talented professional athletes earn in a year ought to have as little to do with gauging the proper compensation for George Butler as a number picked at random ought to affect people's estimates of the percentage of African countries in the United Nations (recall the experiment from chapter 2). Yet randomly chosen numbers were shown to anchor those estimates, and Butler's lawyer was no doubt counting on a similar anchoring effect in his argument. (In point of fact, the jury determined the plaintiff's gross damages to be $2 million [82.25-83.2].)

Normalcy and Deviance in the Workplace

Narrative is crucial to the closing arguments in *Butler*, especially that of Butler's lawyer. To persuade the jurors that Revere should be held responsible for Butler's slip—remember, there was no direct evidence of how or why Butler fell—the lawyer tells a story that evokes a "normal" (and, by implication, accident-free) schema for the loading and covering of the machinery. He then emphasizes the conduct of Revere's employees, especially Brockway, as deviant, and hence presumptively to blame. Norm theory is crucial to understanding how jurors could plausibly assign responsibility to this untaken precaution, as opposed to anything else that preceded

Butler's fall—such as Butler simply not being careful enough and losing his footing while climbing around the truck.

But whence the particular norm or norms of workplace conduct on which Butler's lawyer's entire argument depends? The law does not provide it: Revere's attorney had (correctly) observed that it is the driver's duty to secure the load (32.12-33.2), but Butler's attorney had countered that this duty does not mean that the driver has to do the whole job himself (36.14-37.11), and the judge agreed (transcript of 4/25/90, 54.1-12, 58.26-59.8). The evidence does not provide it: The trial record specifies neither whether loads like Butler's were usually tarped or not[13] nor whether Revere employees typically helped drivers like Butler put tarps on their loads.[14] And the jurors cannot be expected to bring the norm with them to the case. They are not familiar with how machinery like this is usually loaded onto trucks like Butler's; hence, in Schank and Abelson's (1977) terms, they lack a *script* for the loading and tarping of machinery.

So Butler's attorney does not construct his normal scenario for the loading operation by using the law or evidence of the custom of the workplace. Nor does he rely on the jurors simply to "fill in the blanks." Instead, he *implies* a customary scenario by the way he describes what happened.

His story amounts to this: George Butler tries to do the job he is told to do and struggles to put the tarp on the machinery; Brockway and his men, having loaded the machinery and now seeing Butler struggle, go on their coffee break instead of helping. One norm implicit in this story is this: Working people are supposed to do their jobs, and *one who begins to help someone else with a difficult physical job at the workplace continues to help until the job is done*, if he or she can do so without significant inconvenience to himself or herself. That is the way things ought to happen. Butler behaves according to this scenario. His conduct is therefore "normal." We can understand why he would undertake the difficult tarping job alone—he always "gives his best shot" (24.22)—but we can also understand that normally (I use this word advisedly, to refer to the norm that the lawyer has implied), Revere's employees would help him.

Brockway's conduct, on the other hand, deviates from the normal story. Indeed, the coffee break is a prototypical image for not working at the workplace. It "[w]ouldn't have taken very much" to help (27.21-22) —by implication, just "lift[ing] a finger" (26.20-21)—but Brockway let

---

[13] Robert Brown, Butler's manager and supervisor, testified that loads picked up at Revere were sometimes tarped, sometimes not (transcript of 4/24/90, 30.14-23).

[14] Brockway testified that it was not his personal responsibility to help with the tarping (transcript of 4/24/90, 68.25-69.5, 78.24-79.2), but this does not establish whether he or others actually did so on other occasions. Another Revere employee, Jerry Stedman, testified that he had no knowledge of Revere employees helping drivers tarp their loads (transcript of 4/24/90, 108.10-17). A third Revere employee, Jerry Wall, testified that drivers pulled their own tarps on "all the time" but that "someone in the area" might help if asked (transcript of 4/26/90, 29.6-8,9). Butler didn't ask.

Butler struggle alone with the tarp "for the sake of a cup of coffee" (27.23-24). In contrast to the proffered normal scenario, the "cup of coffee"—the failure to help—becomes the salient, deviant behavior. Jurors striving to make sense of the accident by linking this deviation with the other (Butler's fall itself) are therefore likely to target it as the cause of the accident (Black, Galambos, & Read, 1984) and to hold Revere responsible. The perception that Brockway's failure to help is the cause of the harm is likely to be enhanced by observers' tendency to view as particularly reprehensible and to get especially angry at those who contribute to bad outcomes by not bothering to make an effort (Weiner, 1995).

Whether jurors will accept the norm that Butler's lawyer implies, and hence will make the judgments that conformance to or divergence from that norm suggest, depends on many factors, including their personal experiences. Someone who regards the workplace norm as not doing anything beyond the absolute minimum required to keep one's job, including not proceeding in the face of risk unless specifically ordered to do so, might find Butler's conduct less explicable and Brockway's more justifiable. The lawyer cannot, of course, be guaranteed that enough of the jurors will share and care deeply about the norm he or she tries to evoke. All the lawyer can do is to draw on her or his own experience and familiarity with society's common sense, as reflected in the popular entertainments people watch, the aphorisms people send to each other in greeting cards, the proverbs and other metaphors people use in everyday speech (Gibbs & Beitel, 1995; Lakoff & Johnson, 1980), and any number of other sources, in the hope that the important norm implicit in the story is one that jurors will find both credible and fundamental.

The lawyer can also hedge his or her bets by constructing an accident story that implies multiple norms, all of which serve the purpose of attributing blame to the other party. Here, for instance, Butler's lawyer's account of the accident implies the workplace (and broader cultural) norm of *reciprocity* (e.g., Ellickson, 1991; Gouldner, 1960). This norm is "the principle of getting something back for something given" (Macneil, 1983, p. 347). It could apply to *Butler* because there was a contract between Revere and Schultz Electric, Butler's employer (even though the contract did not, of course, prevent Butler for suing in negligence for personal injuries). If Butler was asked to do something different from what was agreed to under the contract (e.g., load other equipment and/or put a tarp on the load [24.12-25.14]), his doing it amounts to a favor to or accommodation of Revere; according to the norm of reciprocity, Revere's employees then owe a duty to help him, even if that, too, is outside the contract terms (i.e., under the contract they are not responsible for helping the driver put a tarp on the load). Once again, not helping—not lifting a finger—is the act that deviates from the norm, and is thus, according to norm theory, the most likely candidate for causal and moral responsibility for the accident. (We see another example of multiple norms in the next chapter.)

In targeting Brockway's and the other Revere employees' refusal to help Butler as the blameworthy behavior that caused the accident, Butler's lawyer takes advantage of two other robust findings in norm theory research. First, as we saw in chapter 2, people more readily mentally undo acts than omissions, and therefore, are more likely to select acts than omissions as the (culpable) cause of an outcome. Brockway's failure to help Butler may seem at first more like an omission than an act. But most omissions can be recharacterized as commissions, and this is just what Butler's lawyer does. He takes pains to emphasize that Brockway's not helping was a deliberate refusal to help—not heedlessness, but an affirmative choice to allow Butler to proceed in the face of a known risk. This characterization, of course, also makes sense in terms of culpable causation. "Goodbye. We're going to have our danish and our coffee and we don't care what you're doing" (remember that these words are the lawyer's invention, not a quotation from trial testimony) looks more morally blameworthy than mere inattentiveness, and is thus more likely to be selected as the cause of the accident.

Second, people tend to undo or mutate controllable antecedents more often than uncontrollable ones. In the *Butler* accident story, the Revere employees can control whether or not they help Butler tarp the load. Butler, by contrast, has no control over the situation; he has to finish the job.

Butler's lawyer draws on norm theory in three other ways as well. First, he explicitly prompts jurors to think counterfactually by introducing his story: "On January 20, 1986 [Butler's] life changed and it didn't have to be changed this way" (24.5-6). Second, he argues that Revere changed the work order detailing what machinery Butler was to load onto the truck (24.12-25.3, 37.12-38.3). It is unclear how this change, if indeed it occurred (35.12-24), could have made it any more likely that Butler would hurt himself; the lawyer's strategy, though, may help to prompt the jurors to think "what if" (as well as to trigger the implicit norm of reciprocity, as mentioned above). Third, the lawyer questions why Revere wanted the machinery covered with a tarp at all (25.4-12). By questioning the rationality of this demand, Butler's lawyer indicates that Revere's conduct was deviant and, of course, implicitly leads the jurors to infer that if Butler had not been required to cover the load, he would not have fallen and hurt himself.[15] Highlighting the customer's request to have its machinery tarped is a way of encouraging jurors to imagine how easily things could have been otherwise.

In sum, the plaintiff's lawyer tells the story he tells in order to facil-

---

[15] Requiring the load to be tarped does not appear to have been "unreasonable" in the legal sense that it unreasonably increased the risk of harm to Butler or others (Keeton et al., 1984).

itate jurors' habits of inferring blame on the basis of deviations from relevant norms. The more abnormal the defendant's behavior appears, the more likely jurors are to find that that behavior caused the plaintiff's injuries. What is more, the more abnormal the behavior, the angrier jurors are likely to get at the defendant and the more sympathy they are likely to feel for the plaintiff, both of which emotions should pull them in the direction of attributing blame and liability to the defendant. If the plaintiff's lawyer has successfully invoked the dynamic of normalcy and deviance, jurors' thoughts and feelings will work together in the direction he desires.

In contrast to all of this, the defendant Revere's lawyer organizes his argument between introduction and conclusion in rule-element fashion. He begins by reciting the elements of a *prima facie* negligence case (31.19-32.1) and repeats those elements later (35.2-5). Then, instead of telling a story of his own, he analyzes the accident in terms that emphasize the plaintiff's lack of proof of the required elements. First, he explains that Revere owed no duty of care to Butler: It was the driver's duty, not the defendant's, to secure the load (32.7-34.13). This is the longest portion of his summation. Second, he argues that there is no proof of causation (34.14-35.5). Finally, he emphasizes issues over chronology by going back to the beginning of the incident and refuting the plaintiff's argument that the defendant "switched the job" on the plaintiff (35.6-24).

Revere's lawyer tells but a single, brief story. The story is not about the accident itself; rather, it is an analogy intended to counter Butler's attorney's narrative of normalcy and deviance:

> Let's bring it down to something that all of us are familiar with. Let us assume that a piece of equipment in our own home, a combination ice box/deep freeze for example, breaks down. We call a repair person. They say, "We've got to take it to our shop." He can't fix it in your kitchen. It's heavy. I wouldn't expect one of you ladies to help him, but one of the gentlemen being at home might willingly assist that driver in putting the equipment, a refrigerator/ freezer on the driver's truck and then you walk away. You go back about your business. It isn't your job to secure or do anything further with respect to that load. And then while that truck is parked in your driveway, the driver, for some unknown reason, falls from the truck and is injured. Does that make you legally liable? Does that oblige you to pay compensation to this truck driver? Certainly not. It would be ridiculous. And that, on a larger scale, is exactly what the situation was in this case. (33.22-34.13)

This analogy seeks to reconcile Brockway's behavior with social norms. It does this by trying to persuade the jurors that Revere owed no duty to Butler to secure the load. The lawyer rhetorically asks the jurors whether they, having helped a repairman load a broken appliance onto his truck, should be held liable when the repairman, while the truck is still parked in the driveway, falls for an unknown reason and is injured. "Certainly not. It would be ridiculous." If jurors apply this prototypical scenario of reasonable behavior to Brockway, they should conclude that failing to help the struggling Butler is not, under the circumstances, deviant or blameworthy; Brockway simply had no obligation to help.

It is instructive to review the plaintiff's argument about responsibility for the accident in light of standard negligence doctrine and to compare it with other plausible accounts for why the accident happened. By persuading jurors that the norm is to help, the lawyer simultaneously persuades them that Brockway's failure to help is a breach of duty.[16] In terms of the Learned Hand test (chapter 1), the failure to help seems to represent a very small accident avoidance cost (i.e., it would have been inexpensive to take the precaution of helping), which makes it easier to establish that the cost of avoidance was less than the probability of harm times the severity of any harm that should occur (even though the likelihood of harm may have been small, its severity, we know now in hindsight, was very large), and consequently that the defendant was negligent.

The strength of the breach-of-duty argument, however, leaves Butler's lawyer with a rather weak connection between that breach and the plaintiff's injury (see M. Grady, 1989). To appreciate how problematic is the causal attribution that Butler's lawyer implies through norm theory, recall that there is no evidence at all of how Butler fell, and thus no way to determine whether Revere's employees' failure to help really had anything to do with the fall. For all we know, it is at least as likely that Butler fell because he simply lost his footing, without any carelessness on anyone's part. But such a slip does not stand out as a distinct event that can be contrasted to a no-accident normal scenario (which may be one reason why Revere's attorney does not use norm theory to argue that Butler caused the accident). To refer to the Kahneman and Tversky (1982) experiment used to illustrate norm theory in chapter 2, a misstep is like arriving at the intersection a few seconds earlier, rather than leaving the office at an unusual time or traveling by an unusual route. In contrast, the conduct of the defendant's employees, as Butler's attorney describes it, does stand out.[17]

---

[16] I thank my colleague Steve Gilles for suggesting this point to me.

[17] Steve Gilles has argued that there is no need to resort to the implication of cognitive bias to explain how the *Butler* jurors may have inferred causation from culpability. If jurors think that helping truck drivers with tarps is reasonable in part because it makes accidents like Butler's less likely to happen, then it makes sense to infer from the fact that Revere's employees did not help Butler (i.e., that they behaved unreasonably) that their unreasonable behavior may have caused the accident—that helping could have avoided the accident. This path from should to could makes sense to me, although it does not account for the rhetoric of moral culpability with which Butler's lawyer infuses his description of Revere's employees' behavior, and which itself (according to the notion of culpable causation) may have inclined the

Fundamental Attribution Error in a Lawyer's Argument

In addition to norm theory and culpable causation, the plaintiff's lawyer in *Butler* makes artful use of jurors' predilection for inferring conduct from character. He invokes the fundamental attribution error throughout his argument, both explicitly and implicitly. As an example of an explicit play to this habit of thought, consider the lawyer's statement that Butler "is the type of person, I think we all know now, he's going to give his best shot and he did" (24.21-22), and "being the type of person he is," tries to put the tarp on the load himself (25.14-15, 28.23-24). Butler is just that kind of guy. When the lawyer comes to describe Brockway, the Revere employee who did not help Butler tarp the load, he says that "that kind of attitude . . . resulted in this injury" (27.21-22). Brockway, too, is just that kind of guy.

More important and more interesting is Butler's lawyer's implicit, metaphoric argument that a guy like his client could not have caused this accident (and therefore, it is more likely that a guy like Brockway did). According to Butler's attorney, Butler is the *protagonist on a difficult journey*, with *the jury* (and its favorable judgment) *as his destination*.

This implicit argument consists of an interweaving of two metaphoric themes. The first is the *difficult journey*. The lawyer repeatedly says that Butler has "gone through" severe difficulties in overcoming the physical and mental effects of the accident (17.24, 20.2, 5, 21.7, 23.4, 5, 10, 29.6, 7, 18). "Gone through" sounds like a cliché, or even a figure of speech that has lost its metaphoric flavor entirely. When combined with other images the lawyer evokes, however, its significance emerges. The lawyer recalls Butler's own metaphor, from the direct examination, of striving "to reach a higher plateau" in his struggles during rehabilitation (17.25-18.2, 23.13). This introduces an explicitly spatial image to the idea of "going through," suggesting not merely physical movement but also movement toward a goal.[18] And in the conclusion of the summation, the lawyer addresses the jurors: "Now, you hold his only chance. This is the last place, the only place he can come" (30.6-7). Indeed, the jurors themselves have "come" to this same place[19] and now must calculate compensation for Butler, a "very difficult" task (30.5) that parallels Butler's own difficulties (18.13-15). The metaphor of the jurors' decision at the end of the trial as a spatial location neatly unifies Butler's metaphoric journey, through his

jurors (if they viewed the employees' behavior that way) to attribute causal significance to the failure to help.

[18] See also "he's gotten to the point" (21.5).

[19] The jurors' own metaphoric journey to their final decision is strongly suggested in one passage in which Butler's lawyer contrasts Butler's faulty memory since the accident with "our" ability to "remember about what happened to us and where our history is and where we come from as people" (20.9-11). I thank Richard Sherwin for the observation that the metaphor of journeying may be overdetermined, with many target domains.

impediments and frustrations, with the jurors' decision in his favor as the destination of the journey.

The second theme is Butler as a *fighter*. The lawyer says that Butler "continues to fight" (17.25) and describes him as a "fighter" (22.13, 23.15). The lawyer also notes that Butler will give a job "his best shot" (24.22). Also, "he's worked as hard as he can to get to this point," that is, the mental and physical skills he has partially recovered under rehabilitation since the accident (29.14-15). And, like an underdog pugilist, Butler has "beaten all the odds" (17.24).

Put together the fighter with the difficult journey and the result is *Rocky* (Avildsen, 1976): Sylvester Stallone running up the museum steps. One can almost hear the theme song from the movie in the background.[20] The implicit reasoning is that George Butler is an underdog hero who deserves to be compensated for his unfortunate injury because of the sort of person he is. And to the extent he deserves to be compensated, he cannot be to blame. Metaphor merges Butler with the prototype of the underdog hero, effacing the actual process of classification required for the implicit argument to succeed.[21]

I do not want to leave the topic of attribution error without mentioning how the plaintiff's lawyer modulates jurors' responsibility attributions by enticing jurors to identify with his client. Through his use of the second-person and the first-person plural, Butler's lawyer encourages jurors to put themselves in the plaintiff's shoes, which, as explained earlier, decreases the chance that they will blame the plaintiff for the accident. When the lawyer greets the jurors by saying, "George Frederick Butler, he should be an inspiration for all of us. . . . [His effort is] something we should all aspire to and . . . we hope we all do . . ." (17.14-24), he seeks to establish a general commonality among the jurors, Butler, and himself. When he describes Butler's headaches as "[n]ot the typical kind of headache where you and I can take two aspirins" (21.24-25), he again invites the jurors to identify with Butler in order to understand the severity of Butler's injuries. Butler's lawyer also, as noted above, equates the jurors' "difficult task" in

---

[20] Even such details as the lawyer's description of Butler's morning routine, explicitly relating how Butler's memory has been impaired by the accident (e.g., 20.7-24), implicitly recall the beginning of the same scene from *Rocky*, in which the hero wakes up before dawn and goes through his routine, drinks the raw eggs, and so on.

[21] Butler's lawyer uses many other metaphors, although none are as sustained or significant as the *Rocky* theme. For instance, Brockway, the defendant's employee, "didn't lift a finger" to help Butler with the canvas (26.20-21), a cliché that contrasts nicely with Butler's bodily struggle to manipulate the heavy tarpaulin.

Not all of the lawyer's metaphors are felicitous. One that rings hollow is his description of Butler as formerly a "free spirit" who had "white line fever" (22.21-22), in contrast to his present debilitated state. This doesn't work because we know that Butler didn't just drive his rig wherever he pleased but was always instructed to go "from Point A to Point B," as his lawyer now calls it (22.23); indeed, his lawyer elsewhere praises Butler for always following instructions and doing his job (e.g., 24.21-22). The reference to "free spirit" also seems to conflict with the lawyer's description of Butler as "the marrying kind" (29.24).

deciding the case with Butler's own difficulties in overcoming the effects of the accident, and just as Butler "give[s] his best shot" (24.22), so the lawyer tells the jurors that "I have full confidence you'll make your best effort" (30.23) to calculate damages. Jurors who accept these implicit invitations to identify themselves with the plaintiff will be more likely to interpret the case from the plaintiff's perspective and less likely to view the plaintiff as the bad guy who is responsible for the bad outcome, the accident.

By this point we can also see how norm theory, culpable causation, and the fundamental attribution error combine to generate a *melodramatic* conception of responsibility for George Butler's accident that jurors may find very compelling. Butler's lawyer draws on popular culture as a source of jurors' intuitive habits of thought and feeling, and does so implicitly enough to maintain his audience's belief and to avoid the censure of the court.

Engaging the Jurors as Active Decision Makers

Earlier I suggested that plaintiffs' lawyers would be more inclined than defendants' lawyers to lead jurors to conceive of their decision-making role as active, so that the jurors will feel empowered to award the defendants' money to the plaintiffs. The arguments of the advocates in *Butler* support this hypothesis. Butler's lawyer more often engages the jurors in active decision making through the use of the second-person and first-person plural, active verbs, and rhetorical questions. He uses the second-person and first-person plural at about double the rate of Revere's lawyer.[22] And when we go beyond this rather crude indicator to examine the sorts of verbs the advocates use in connection with the second- and first-person plural, we find that Butler's lawyer more often casts the jurors as actors.[23]

Moreover, while both lawyers conceive of the jurors as equally active and passive in their role as evaluators of the evidence,[24] a striking difference emerges when the lawyers address the jurors as decision makers. Butler's lawyer speaks to the jurors with active verbs that empower them. These jurors "hold [plaintiff's] only chance" (30.6); they will struggle in facing

---

[22] Considering the arguments in their entirety, Butler's and Revere's lawyers appear to use the second- and first-person plural at about the same rate (6.25 instances per 25-line transcript page for Butler's lawyer vs. 6.3 per page for Revere's lawyer). However, excluding the crucial analogy of the refrigerator repairman, during which Revere's lawyer uses the second-person plural at a rate of 19 per page (13 instances in 17 lines), he uses it at only 3.2 per page— about half as often as Butler's lawyer overall.

[23] Butler's lawyer, 62% of the time (60 out of 95 instances where second or inclusive first person is used with a verb); Revere's lawyer, only 47% of the time (14 out of 30, and only 27% outside of the refrigerator repairman story).

[24] Butler's lawyer: 23 active verbs out of 43 instances; Revere's lawyer: 5 out of 10. Both lawyers also treat the jurors as more active than passive when the lawyers are telling stories— Butler's lawyer: 14 active verbs out of 15 instances; Revere's lawyer: 6 out of 9.

the "difficult chore" (28.6, 29.5) of deciding, but "wi[ll] make [their] best effort" (30.22-23). When Revere's attorney addresses the jurors, by contrast, he tells them what to do, disempowering them. They "must . . . set aside all feelings of sympathy" (31.7); they "must not speculate" (31.8-9, 34.24); they "must bring in a verdict that is fair, just, and impartial" (31.9-10).[25] In all, Butler's lawyer portrays the jurors as active decision makers about six times as often as does Revere's lawyer.[26]

To sum up, a close reading of the lawyers' closing arguments in *Butler* reveals many of the habits of thought and feeling that jurors would be expected to use in determining responsibility and compensation for an accident. The lawyers' words offer lengthy examples of talk about the accident that jurors could accept as their own and are intended for that purpose. Whether the jurors actually thought about the case in the way that either lawyer seems to have wanted them to, we will never know; we know what they decided (defendant, 60% responsible; plaintiff, 40% responsible; full compensation [i.e., not adjusted for the plaintiff's fault], $2 million), but not why. Whatever the *Butler* summations tell us about the common sense of accidents, we can learn more by examining other cases. Let us study one more.

THE "REASONABLE PERSON" AS PROTOTYPE—AND METAPHOR: *GIULIETTI V. PROVIDENCE & WORCESTER CO.*

The closing arguments in a second workplace accident case, *Giulietti v. Providence & Worcester Co.* (1981), illustrate a number of additional aspects of common-sense discourse. We see how the defendant's lawyer tries, not entirely successfully, to invoke jurors' person–situation prototypes in a way that is favorable to the client and unfavorable to the opposing party. We also see how the plaintiff's lawyer (again, perhaps not with complete success) tries to involve the jurors in a vivid narrative of the accident. Neither advocate appears quite as gifted as the plaintiff's lawyer in *Butler*, who seamlessly constructed a credible and even compelling accident melodrama, starring his client. Yet ordinary as well as more inspired lawyering can provide valuable insights into how jurors think about accidents.

---

[25] The anaphora of these remarks in the introduction emphasizes the sense of obligation and command. In the argument on causation, Revere's lawyer again tells the jurors: "You cannot . . . speculate" (34.24-25). And in the conclusion, he says: "[A] verdict in [plaintiff's] favor in this case would be a breach of your oaths as jurors to bring in a verdict that is fair, just, and impartial" (36.4-6), and refers to "the law that you must follow" (36.8-9). Indeed, the only arguably nonpassive conception of the jurors in this respect is "[a]ll of us are sympathetic" to Butler (36.1), a weak copulative.

[26] Butler's lawyer portrays the jurors' decision making as active 68% of the time (15 instances out of 22 references to jurors as decision makers), whereas Revere's lawyer does this only 11% of the time (1 instance out of 9).

The Facts

John Giulietti, a young railroad worker, was assigned to conduct a three-man crew attempting a hook-up of cars in a rail yard at night. He was crushed to death when the rear of the car on which he was riding backed over an incorrectly aligned crossover switch and into a line of cars sitting on another track. Giulietti's estate sued the railroad. The plaintiff's lawyer charged that the railroad was negligent in numerous respects. For instance, the railroad did not properly train John Giulietti to be a conductor, yet compelled him to conduct a crew at night in an unfamiliar yard; Giulietti's fellow and senior crew member, Ed Hines, planned an unnecessarily dangerous hitching maneuver and did not comply with railroad rules when backing the train up; and the railroad yard had no flag marking the crucial crossover switch and lacked other safety devices. The railroad's attorney countered that Giulietti's own carelessness—for example, in allowing the train to back up too quickly and not looking where he was going—caused his death. As in *Butler*, most of the basic facts were not in dispute; ultimate responsibility for the accident and the amount of compensation due the decedent's estate very much were.

The Law

Giulietti is one of those instances mentioned in chapter 1 in which a statutory regime modifies the otherwise applicable common law. The lawsuit was brought under the Federal Employers' Liability Act (FELA, 1994). In FELA cases, the plaintiff must prove both that the defendant railroad was negligent and that the railroad's negligence was the sole proximate cause of the plaintiff's injuries (or the decedent's death) (§ 51). Any award to the plaintiff must be reduced by the percentage the plaintiff's (decedent's) own negligence contributed to the harm (§ 53). Thus far, the law sounds much like standard common law negligence, including a comparative negligence rule (typical today but not when the FELA was enacted). Courts have long interpreted the statute, however, in a manner favorable to plaintiffs. Jury verdicts are often allowed to stand on the basis of the most scant evidence of any lack of care by the defendant (Ehrenzweig, 1951/1966; *Wilkerson v. McCarthy*, 1949). The plaintiff's burden of proof on causation, moreover, is "low and liberal": The defendant railroad should be found liable if its negligence "played any part, even the slightest" in contributing to the plaintiff's injury (*Smith v. National R.R. Passenger Corp.*, 1988).

The Defendant's Lawyer's Words

The railroad's lawyer faced a daunting task, given the extensive evidence of his client's various failures to exercise due care and what he could safely assume would be the jurors' sympathy for Giulietti (not to mention, looking ahead to a possible appeal, the courts' traditionally liberal reading of the statute to accommodate plaintiffs' verdicts). Instead of concentrating his efforts on defending his client's conduct, he chose to spend almost all of his closing argument explaining why Giulietti's own carelessness superseded anything the railroad may have done, and thus proximately caused Giulietti's death:

> His Honor will instruct you that insofar as Mr. Giulietti's negligence was the sole proximate cause of his death, you must return a verdict for the Defendant. His Honor likewise will instruct you if you find that the railroad was negligent, you then have to find that the negligence caused the death of Mr. Giulietti. If you find that, nonetheless, you must still reduce any award which you might consider by the proportion of Mr. Giulietti's negligence. That is the framework you have to consider this case in.
>
> Let's consider this case. What did occur, ladies and gentlemen, I think can be set out by the first few words of testimony that you heard in this case. What was Mr. Giulietti saying during the day? "I have got an easy job in riding the engine." Ladies and gentlemen, you heard Mr. Lenahan testify for the Plaintiff that you must use extreme caution at all times. If he had the attitude that he had an easy job and was riding the engine and that is why he didn't bring his equipment that night, maybe that explains why he didn't see what he knew it was his duty to see.
>
> It is fine to say, well, he was looking the wrong way or maybe he wasn't familiar, but, ladies and gentlemen, he worked throughout the system of the Providence and Worcester Railroad. If he didn't know where the yard was or he didn't know what the characteristics of this yard were, it was negligent of him to proceed to act as a Conductor in that yard. No one twisted his arm and no one told him he had to act as Conductor. It was his decision. . . .
>
> . . .
>
> You people in your daily lives, if you go somewhere and someone says, well, what are we going to do tonight and says we will do this, if you don't think you are capable of doing it, you don't do it. If you do it, then I submit you would be negligent. That is the standard we have to give of John Giulietti. . . .
>
> What has to do with this case is the fact that John Giulietti said, "Okay to back up," climbed on the car. He never saw the switches. You know, people are talking about never seeing the switches like these switches are difficult to see or if that hadn't been the training. It is precisely his training and he knew it was his responsibility. Ladies and gentlemen, he not only missed switches, he missed the 41 cars dropped on the main line. You are talking about not seeing the switch. He didn't see 41 cars. What does that mean? . . . It says to me, logically, and I believe to you good ladies and gentlemen of good common sense, he wasn't paying attention to where he was going.

. . .

The key to this case, ladies and gentlemen, is not experience. The key simply is negligence. The most experienced of all of us make mistakes at times. We talk about driving a car, and maybe it is not a fair analogy to say, but we will say in driving a car, for instance, if you have ever driven a car, and you are right that you can't analogize an engine to a car. I am not trying to do that, but there are intersections that have lights and stop lights and there are intersections that have neither. Our caution is different at different intersections and is governed by what our experience is as drivers. That doesn't mean we have to qualify in physical characteristics every time we go to a strange place, but we have to exercise more caution. If we don't know where we are going, we have to stop and ask directions.

. . .

Now, John simply didn't pay attention to what he was doing and that is the bottom line of what this case is. . . . Had John Giulietti been paying attention and John been looking in the direction in which he was supposed to have looked and it was his responsibility to do it, John would be with us today. . . .

. . .

[Y]ou must consider the negligence of John Giulietti. If he, in the ultimate, by not paying attention caused his death, then everything washes, ladies and gentlemen. I submit to you under the facts of this case, either Mr. Giulietti was solely responsible for his death, because the ultimate was that he called the shots or he substantially contributed to his death. (*Giulietti*, 512.11-513.15, 515.8-13, 515.25-516.14, 517.10-25, 520.9-10, 522.4-8, 525.9-16)[27]

Perhaps this is not the most articulate summation ever delivered, yet the railroad's lawyer's analogies and clichés reveal a coherent approach to a difficult rhetorical problem. How can the jurors, who presumably are not intimately familiar with the norms and habits of railroad work, be guided to conclude that Giulietti behaved negligently, without offending their sense of sympathy for the unfortunate young man? The railroad's lawyer tries to accomplish this goal by constructing a *prototype* of reasonable behavior, and then *contrasting* Giulietti's behavior to the prototype.

Constructing Person–Situation Prototypes to Fit the Argument

As we saw in chapter 2, jurors are likely to use prototypes in making difficult social judgments, such as whether a person involved in an accident behaved reasonably or not. The law, indeed, encourages this way of thinking: The standard jury instruction asks jurors to determine whether the party in question acted as a *reasonable person* would have under the cir-

---

[27] All references to the *Giulietti* trial transcript are by page(s) and line(s).

cumstances (Devitt et al., 1987).[28] The first step in jurors' reasoning, then, is to formulate a person–situation prototype of how the reasonable person would behave under the circumstances (Cantor et al., 1982). Then, as explained in chapter 2, jurors must compare what the party did with the prototype and decide whether the conduct sufficiently fits the prototype to permit them to classify the party's behavior as "reasonable."[29]

One would expect lawyers on both sides of an accident case to evoke prototypes of the reasonable person and to characterize the evidence in ways that enhance the fit for the client and the lack of fit for the opposing party. The availability heuristic is plainly relevant here. Lawyers would be expected to make available for the jurors a prototype of reasonableness that favors the client (or disfavors the opposing party), because the more a category for classifying social information is activated, the more likely the perceiver is to use that category to classify new, ambiguous information (Srull & Wyer, 1979). Jurors tend to define reasonableness in terms of the way they like to think they would behave—an ideal, but based on their own experience as they perceive it.[30] Hence advocates would be expected to construct person–situation prototypes by telling stories and making analogies that match the jurors' ideas of their own experience, couched,

---

[28] The standard instruction defines *negligence* as

> the doing of some act which a reasonably prudent person would not do, or the failure to do something which a reasonably prudent person would do, when prompted by considerations which ordinarily regulate the conduct of human affairs. It is, in other words, the failure to use ordinary care under the circumstances in the management of one's person or property, or of agencies under one's control. (Devitt et al., 1987, pp. 133–134)

Ordinary care, in turn, is defined as "that care which reasonably prudent persons exercise in the management of their own affairs, in order to avoid injury to themselves or their property, or the persons or property of others" (p. 134). The instruction on contributory negligence similarly refers to the plaintiff's failure to use ordinary care.
Appellate opinions elaborate on the standard instruction's extremely abstract definition of reasonable care. For summaries of and variations on the reasonable person standard derived from appellate law, see, for example, Calabresi (1985); F. James (1951); Keeton et al. (1984); M. Wells (1992).

[29] I do not mean to imply that jurors proceed sequentially through these steps. The process of "fitting" data to prototypes, involving as it does the use of several mental shortcuts or heuristics, is probably not linear (Cantor & Kihlstrom, 1987). Indeed, the process is probably not fully conscious. Research on the activation and application of stereotypes, a kind of prototype, shows that activation of stereotypes is generally automatic (i.e., not conscious); the application of stereotypes in making person judgments may be automatic as well (Banaji, Hardin, & Rothman, 1993), although if people are aware of stereotypic influences on their judgments and both motivated and able to counteract those influences, they may do so (Blair & Banaji, 1996; for reviews, see Bargh, 1999; Devine & Monteith, 1999).

[30] This point is, of course, recognized by practitioners. In addition, research shows that "a large majority of the general public thinks that they are more intelligent, more fair-minded, less prejudiced, and more skilled behind the wheel of an automobile than the average person" (Gilovich, 1991, p. 77). The last observation receives some confirmation from a major survey conducted by the Institute for Civil Justice, which indicates that 91% of people involved in two-car automobile accidents believe that the other driver was mostly at fault (Hensler et al., 1991). Thus, when jurors are led to refer to their conception of their own behavior to derive the standard of "ordinary care," they may be induced to define a higher standard of conduct than their actual behavior would warrant.

if possible, in the sorts of familiar phrases that jurors are likely to find more persuasive (Howard, 1997). Indeed, as the railroad's lawyer tells the jurors, "[y]ou may not be railroad people or involved with freight trains or anything like that" (509.22-24), but that lack of knowledge needn't prevent them from correctly deciding where justice lies in this case; all they need to do, as we see below, is to use their own sensible, everyday judgment.

The excerpt above shows how the railroad's lawyer in *Giulietti* uses analogies and metaphors to build person–situation prototypes of reasonable behavior under the circumstances, and *contrasts* to them Giulietti's conduct on the night of the accident. The analogies are designed to appeal to the jurors' common experience. To help make the somewhat difficult argument that if Giulietti wasn't capable of acting as conductor, he was careless to accept the job and its attendant risks, the lawyer for the railroad argues: "You people in your daily lives, if you go somewhere and someone says, well, what are we going to do tonight and says we will do this, if you don't think you are capable of doing it, you don't do it. If you do it, then I submit you would be negligent" (515.8-13). Along the same lines, the lawyer tries to persuade the jury to infer from Giulietti's lack of familiarity with the yard, not that the railroad was negligent in assigning an inexperienced man to conduct the crew at night, but rather that Giulietti himself should have used greater caution in conducting the crew. He does this by means of the analogy to driving a car at an unregulated intersection (517.13-25).

Not every analogy is effective. The railroad's lawyer's analogies are flawed in two ways. First, neither seems obviously apt, as a good analogy must be. For instance, some jurors may imagine that conducting a train is like driving—but with one person on the floor controlling the brakes and the gas pedal, another steering blindfolded, and a third on the roof giving directions.[31] And second, the analogy to declining to participate in an activity the jurors feel incapable of doing is too abstract. It is not drawn at the more concrete "basic level" at which prototypes are most accessible (Lakoff, 1987).

The railroad's lawyer also uses metaphor to invoke a prototypical reasonable person, and he simultaneously argues that the *jurors themselves* fit the prototype but that Giulietti did *not*, and therefore acted unreasonably. It is an argument that assumes that jurors' habits of thought and feeling can be quite subtly tuned. To make it, the lawyer characterizes the jurors as "people of common sense" (509.22-25, 516.12-13) and seeks to distin-

---

[31] I owe this observation to the students in my jurisprudence course, fall semester, 1993. The relevance of the first analogy would also be limited for any juror who thought that Giulietti, as a junior employee of the railroad, was constrained to follow orders in a way that the juror, in selecting among possible leisure-time activities, would not be. By analogy to Bennett and Feldman's (1981) studies of the credibility of stories, jurors may find these analogies implausible because they do not conform unproblematically to jurors' background knowledge of how the "conducting a train" and "following orders at work" stories ought to proceed.

guish the exercise of common sense from "20/20 hindsight" (510.1-2) and "after-the-fact guesswork" (514.21-22) about what someone should have known or should have done. The lawyer's aim is at once to persuade the jurors not to engage in "after-the-fact guesswork" when they evaluate how *his* client, the railroad, behaved, yet to encourage them to evaluate John Giulietti's conduct "after the fact" and find that Giulietti was careless. This effort to distinguish the jurors' evaluation of Giulietti's conduct from their evaluation of the railroad's conduct depends on a metaphoric depiction of the person who uses common sense, which the jurors fit but which Giulietti does not.

First, the railroad's lawyer argues that when Giulietti was riding the train that night, he "wasn't paying attention" to where he was going (516.13, 518.6-7, 520.9, 522.5, 522.22, 525.11). This figure of speech understands thought as an object, and more particularly, as currency. *Attention* is something that can be *paid* (Lakoff & Johnson, 1980).

Next, the lawyer explains that Giulietti's failure to pay attention to what he was doing is "the bottom line of what this case is" (517.2, 520.8-10). The metaphor is: (complicated) trial as (simple) financial transaction. Here the lawyer metaphorically asks the jurors to think of the case as being like a balance sheet, with one feature—the *bottom line*—more important than any other. Again, the lawyer uses a fiscal metaphor; perhaps he thinks that people of "common sense" (i.e., the jurors) can understand a balance sheet, or at least imagine that they can balance a checkbook. And again, the jurors, who use common sense, are distinguished from the plaintiff, who did not.

Finally, the lawyer argues: "If [Giulietti], . . . by not paying attention caused his death, then *everything washes*, ladies and gentlemen" (525.10-12). The metaphor here, once again, is (complicated) trial as (simple) financial transaction. Although the popular understanding of "it's a wash" may not include the technical, financial meaning of the term (Rosenberg, 1978), the phrase is widely understood to mean a balanced exchange: "It's a wash" means one thing cancels out the other. The lawyer thus concludes by telling the jurors that if they give due weight to Giulietti's inattention, their understanding of the lengthy trial and complicated evidence will be balanced and in equipoise. More important, the trial (and the jurors' understanding of it) will be complete, with no loose ends ("everything washes"): Giulietti's negligence caused his own death. And the lawyer has used a sustained set of fiscal metaphors to distinguish the jury's task in evaluating Giulietti from its task in evaluating the railroad and its other employees. The latter involves "guesswork" or "judgment calls" that can go either way, but the former is a straightforward, simple matter of the "bottom line." [32]

---

[32] Of course, the metaphor "everything washes" is ambiguous; the source could be not financial

In addition, to get the jurors to identify with the prototype of reasonable care which, he argues, John Giulietti did not meet, the railroad's lawyer uses a rhetorical device we observed in the plaintiff's argument in *Butler*: the second-person and first-person plural. This takes two forms. First, the lawyer uses these points of view in his analogies aimed at helping jurors to understand the standard of care which Giulietti did not meet. He argues, as we have seen, that "[y]ou people in your daily lives" wouldn't go ahead and undertake something the jurors knew they weren't capable of doing, as John allegedly did (515.8-13). And he introduces his other major analogy by saying, "[w]e talk about driving a car" (517.11-25), to make the point that jurors know to exercise greater caution at uncontrolled intersections and in strange places.

The railroad's lawyer also uses the second-person plural to equate the jurors' present responsibility to decide the case with Giulietti's past responsibility to decide to be the conductor. "The responsibility is yours, ladies and gentlemen. In this country, the responsibility of people for their own negligent acts . . . lies with that person" (511.6-17). In this striking passage, echoed later in the argument (519.3-5, 521.21-22), the railroad's attorney does more than invoke the ethos of personal responsibility, which he hopes will be turned against the tort plaintiff (Engel, 1987). He explicitly empowers the jurors to decide the case (using "judgment" rather than "innuendo" and "hindsight" [511.17-18][33]), which, I might note, goes against the hypothesis I offered in an earlier section of this chapter, that plaintiffs' lawyers would be more likely to lead jurors to think of themselves as active decision makers (I take up this point again later). Most important, however, by using the same word, *responsibility*, to describe both the jurors' task and Giulietti's situation, the railroad's lawyer implicates the proposition: You jurors can decide, responsibly; therefore, so could have Giulietti (and he didn't).[34] The attorney thus implicitly encourages the jurors to

---

affairs, but liquids. The lawyer might be suggesting that the jurors, by understanding that Giulietti's negligence caused his own death, can award the plaintiff nothing and still feel clean, as if they have "washed their hands" of the trial. This also neatly responds to Giulietti's attorney's liquid metaphor for justice—the "full cup of justice" (discussed later)—and to his reference to "look[ing] anyone in the eye" as a metaphor for being satisfied with their decision.

[33] The defendant's lawyer thus conveys to the jurors a complete grasp of the hindsight bias. Indeed, because the hindsight bias is inherent in the lawsuit itself—the bad outcome has already happened, or there would be no claim for recovery—we might expect to see an awareness of the bias reflected in advocates' rhetoric only in attempts to debias, as here.

[34] The flip side of this strategy is that the railroad's lawyer uses the second- or first-person plural to equate the jurors' own imperfect conduct in everyday life with Ed Hines's imperfect performance on the fatal night. "Someone can say Ed should have done this, Ed should have done that. There are a lot of things *we* should have done" (514.20-22). This device builds on the lawyer's initial attribution of "common sense" to the jurors and his injunction that they use common sense as opposed to "20/20 hindsight" and the like (509.21-510.3), which occurs when one second-guesses "judgment calls" (518.18-19, 23-25, 522.25-523.7).

But this is a risky rhetorical strategy. The railroad's lawyer is trying to persuade the jury that when they analyze the defendant's conduct, they're "second-guessing," using "20/20 hindsight"; that when the decision could have gone either way, that's a "judgment call," not negligence (523.7). Yet at the same time, as we've seen, the lawyer wants the jury to do precisely this

attribute fault and responsibility for the accident by identifying themselves with a standard of behavior and contrasting to themselves (and hence, to the standard) the behavior of the decedent, John Giulietti.

For at least two reasons, the metaphoric construction of the "economic man" prototype of reasonableness, on which so much of the railroad's lawyer's argument seems to depend, may not be persuasive. First, the prototype may be drawn too abstractly. Second, the cues for the prototype are relatively obscure. As noted above, the accessibility of a schema for making social judgments (like how to evaluate a party) increases with the number of behavioral concepts relating to that schema that have been activated but decreases with the length of time between activation and judgment (Srull & Wyer, 1979). By failing to activate the schema early, late, and often, the lawyer may not adequately "prime" the jurors to use his "economic man" prototype. In sum, although the strategy of priming jurors to define the reasonable person in a way that includes themselves but excludes Giulietti through *assimilation and contrast effects* is psychologically sound (Schwarz & Bless, 1992), the lawyer's execution of that strategy seems flawed.[35]

Successful or not, the lawyer's rhetoric gives us a basis for inferring how jurors *might* have thought about responsibility for an accident like Giulietti's—how they would have to have thought in order for the lawyer's words to make sense, even if those words did not convince. It is also worth pointing out the intersection of the common sense of responsibility and the formal law of negligence. For instance, the proposition for which the lawyer offers his analogies—that Giulietti, not the railroad, is to blame if Giulietti went ahead with the job knowing he was not qualified to do it —is derived from textbook tort law: "[a] person may be found negligent in proceeding in the face of known ignorance" (Keeton et al., 1984, pp. 184–185). And, as we saw, the law's definition of negligence invites reasoning by prototypes. So the law exerts a pull on how jurors think about accidents, but their habits of thought and feeling—elicited by the lawyers or summoned from other sources—do the rest of the work of judgment.

The Plaintiff's Lawyer's Words

In *Giulietti*, neither the defendant's lawyer nor the plaintiff's builds his respective arguments around sustained stories of the accident (unlike the plaintiff's lawyer in *Butler*). The bulk of Giulietti's lawyer's summation consists of 10 different contentions as to why the defendant railroad was

---

with respect to Giulietti's behavior. It is unclear whether he avoids this apparent contradiction through his attempted metaphoric distinction.

[35] In particular, by failing to describe the reasonable person prototype sufficiently *distinctly* and in a way that allowed jurors to see the *relevance* of the description to their evaluation of Giulietti, the defendant's lawyer made it less likely that the desired contrast effect would occur (Stapel & Winkielman, 1998).

negligent. These are listed in roughly chronological order, from the rail-road's failure to train Giulietti adequately to be a conductor to its failure to mark the fatal crossover switch with lights or targets, but the overall conception is what Jerome Bruner calls *paradigmatic* rather than narrative thinking (Bruner, 1986). Only toward the very end of his argument, pressed for time by the judge, does Giulietti's lawyer try to tell an uninterrupted story of the young man's last evening:

> Now, we also believe that when you [are] perched on top of a rail car and are looking to see if there is a switch ahead of you. . . . As you are traveling down, you know that track two eventually comes into the lead. So you know there is a switch up there, and you know that track one eventually comes to the lead, and you know there is a switch up there. Cross-over switches, there is no break in the iron. You have to know that cross-over switch is there. You can't see any track alongside you that would give you any warning.
>
> . . . If you are on top of a boxcar ten or fifteen feet high, it is even more difficult [to ascertain an unmarked switch in the middle of the night], and you would have to know where you are looking as you are coming down that track. If you had some lights there, that would benefit the switching crew, because they would be able to see the area and would not be in the dark of night.
>
> . . .
>
> Now, what happened on July 28, 1980, was that John was perched on top of the lead car trying to ascertain a position of the switch, which he never even knew existed. He has a lantern and we are not saying with a lantern you can't tell the position of the switch. Of course you can, but it is a difficult thing to do. You have to know where the switches are, and you have to know exactly where to point the lantern.
>
> When John was coming down that lead track, he knows that track one switch is going to be in front of him and he will put on the switch at the point of the track one switch, but what he did not expect was right behind that track one switch, there was a cross-over switch. John was on the side ladder . . . and he began to make this cross-over move towards the main line. The clearance between his car as it was on track one and the cars on the main line is very close. He does not have room to ride between the cars. . . . Once you begin that cross-over move, that gap begins to narrow on you.
>
> If you look at the autopsy report, it will clearly show that John died from a crush injury of his lower abdomen and chest, but also will indicate that as far as his lower extremities were concerned, that he had a compound fracture and dislocation of his left ankle.
>
> . . . When the car that he was riding . . . side-scraped the car ahead, he was actually crushed into the—he side-scraped it for about thirty feet, and this is possibly what they heard with the transmission of scraping and scratching noise. As John was trying to cross over, he had to know that his life was over, unless Ed, hearing the scratching

and scraping noise on the radio, applied the emergency brake and stopped the train instantly. He scraped that car for approximately thirty feet. . . . The car was actually derailed and pushed off the rail, and you will see that eventually he came into the next car. (501.20-502.8, 502.20-503.2, 504.11-506.11)

To the extent this account of the accident helps jurors to think and feel that John Giulietti's estate deserves to receive compensation for his death, how does it do this? As explained earlier in the chapter, the very fact that this account is a *story* should appeal to jurors' preferred method for understanding how and why events occur. Certain aspects of the telling, though, should lead jurors to decide favorably to the plaintiff; other aspects may not serve the lawyer's purposes as well. The social psychology of jurors' common sense allows us to identify each.

Involving the Jurors in the Accident Story

Two features of the plaintiff's lawyer's account of the accident are worth noting: the way in which he encourages jurors to *identify* with Giulietti and the way in which he makes the events and the injuries *vivid*. Both would be predicted to guide jurors' intuitions toward a favorable verdict for Giulietti.

Giulietti's lawyer uses the second- and first-person plural, verb tense, and metaphor to lead the jurors to identify with John Giulietti as the passive victim of the railroad. On more than a third of the occasions in his summation on which he addresses the jurors as "you" (or includes himself and the jurors as "we"),[36] including the most sustained instances (multiple instances in consecutive lines of transcript), he places the jury in John Giulietti's shoes as the events unfold.[37] And in all of these instances, the lawyer uses the present tense with the second- or first-person plural point of view, heightening jurors' sense of participation in the events. (It is noteworthy that aside from these uses of the present tense, Giulietti's lawyer uses the past tense almost exclusively in the rest of his argument.) The lawyer then combines the second-person plural and present tense with metaphoric reconstructions of the events. The railroad, Giulietti's attorney argues, "will put you behind the seat" without adequate training (501.15).

---

[36] These constitute 36 of 94 total instances, or about 38%. This is the lawyer's most common use of the second-person and first-person plural.

[37] Like the railroad's lawyer, Giulietti's lawyer also uses the second- and first-person plural to invite jurors to identify with particular standards of reasonable care that the opposing party (Hines, Giulietti's fellow employee, and the railroad) did *not* meet (487.23; 489.2-7; 497.7-10; 498.11-13; 500.21; 503.7-11). For instance, arguing that the railroad did not train Giulietti adequately to assume the conductor's job that night, the plaintiff's lawyer contends that "you don't throw men out to learn for themselves in the middle of the night. You should instruct a conductor . . ." (489.2-7). Or, arguing that Ed Hines and hence the railroad imprudently planned the move of the cars, he says: "[I]f you have two cars, you can stop a two-car train a lot quicker than an eleven-car train" (498.11-13).

The gap between track one and the main line "begins to narrow on you" (505.10-11). Here the attorney attributes agency to an inanimate, fixed physical fact, the space between the two tracks.

These devices do more than put the jurors in Giulietti's place, increasing their identification with him and encouraging consequent favorable attributions of responsibility. They also emphasize that Giulietti was *victimized by forces beyond his control*. In other words, Giulietti is a prototypical melodramatic protagonist, the passive victim of others' agency. By contrast, when Giulietti's lawyer describes the defendant railroad's conduct, he stresses not only agency but impulsive action: The trainmaster "thr[e]w" the men onto the job (489.2); Ed Hines "shove[d]" the train (500.1, 3). Such choices of language have been proven to affect audiences' memory and judgment. Experimental participants who were shown a film of an automobile collision and asked how fast the cars were going when they "hit" each other gave lower estimates of speed than did participants asked how fast the cars were going when they "smashed into" each other (Loftus & Palmer, 1974). Here, we might predict that jurors who conceive of the train accident in terms of a passive Giulietti and an active railroad would be more likely, for a host of the reasons explained in chapters 2 through 4, to hold the railroad, not Giulietti, responsible for the accident.

Giulietti's lawyer also uses much more concrete language to describe the victim and the accident than does the railroad's lawyer. The plaintiff's lawyer refers to the decedent as "Johnny" or "John" throughout the argument. He says that Giulietti was "killed" (490.3, 495.22, 24). He observes that just before the accident, Giulietti had been "perched" on top of the train car (501.21; 504.14). Then Ed Hines heard "scratching and scraping noises" over the radio (500.5, 7, 13, 505.25-506.5), and Giulietti was "crushed" (505.23; 508.1). "John died from a crush injury of his lower abdomen and chest" (505.12-14). The railroad's lawyer, by contrast, eschews concrete description. He refers to decedent as "John Giulietti" or "Mr. Giulietti," occasionally as "John," but never as "Johnny." And he mentions "death" only once—to say that it was instantaneous and therefore that no pain and suffering damages should be awarded (523.24).

The plaintiff's lawyer's relatively vivid language should make both his version of the accident and Giulietti's suffering more available to the jurors (Loftus & Palmer, 1974; Nisbett & Ross, 1980). This greater availability, in turn, should incline jurors' judgments of responsibility and compensation in the plaintiff's favor. In particular, it may trigger the severity effect, whereby an increased sense of the severity of the plaintiff's injuries leads jurors to attribute greater responsibility for that suffering to the injurer, the railroad.

Yet Giulietti's lawyer does not take full advantage of what we are presuming to have been the jurors' habits of thought and feeling. By waiting until nearly the end of his summation to pull the accident together for the jurors in story form, he reduces the chance that jurors will use the story as a cognitive frame for the entire case. And despite its generally concrete imagery, his story occasionally neglects to describe events vividly; for instance, "as far as his lower extremities were concerned" (505.15-16) sounds clinically detached.

Finally, and curiously, it is the railroad's lawyer, much more so than Giulietti's, who actively involves the jury in the decision-making process. The railroad's lawyer uses the second- and first-person plural almost $2\frac{1}{2}$ times as often as does Giulietti's,[38] and almost four times as often (as a percentage of each lawyer's overall uses) to engage the jurors in their decision-making function.[39] Moreover, the railroad's lawyer asks rhetorical questions no less than 17 times as often as does Giulietti's.[40] Perhaps the evidence of the defendant railroad's negligence was so strong that its lawyer, atypically, wanted jurors to conceive of their role as active, so that they might more readily challenge the "default" interpretation of the case.

Or perhaps Giulietti's lawyer, concluding his argument in his seemingly less-than-eloquent fashion, understood quite well how jurors were likely to think and feel about the case:

> The family does not want any sympathy. They have received buckets and buckets of sympathy. Today being Johnny's twenty-first birthday, they have received more sympathy than anyone could imagine. What they are here today in court for is to vindicate Johnny. In order to vindicate Johnny, I think you would be proud to return a verdict between one and a half and two million dollars. I think if you return a verdict in that range, that you would be proud to look anyone in the eye and tell them that you gave a full cup of justice to the Plaintiff in this action. (508.6-17)

We hear the lawyer disclaiming an appeal to sympathy while hoping for the "ironic effect" of *increased* sympathy in response to the disclaimer (Edwards & Bryan, 1997). We hear him speaking of "Johnny's twenty-first birthday" and thus prompting jurors to think "if only . . . ," which should move them to regret the accident even more (Kahneman & Tversky, 1982). We hear him offering an anchor for the jurors' damage award. All of this is to be expected.

---

[38] Railroad's lawyer: 10.2 instances per 25-line page (179 instances, or 4.3%, of an estimated 5,100 total words, given an average of 9.4 words per line, 25 lines per page, and 17.6 pages); Giulietti's lawyer: 4.3 instances per 25-line page (94 instances, or 1.8%, of an estimated 4,136 words [21.7 pages]).

[39] Railroad's lawyer: 60 of 179, or 34%; Giulietti's lawyer: 8 of 94, or 9%. About the same proportion of each counsel's overall uses are to describe the jurors' understanding of the evidence (railroad's lawyer: 63 of 179, or 35%; Giulietti's lawyer: 32 of 94, or 34%). And both equally use the second- or first-person plural to get the jurors to identify with a prototype of due care which the other party did not meet (railroad's lawyer: 38 of 179, or 21%; Giulietti's lawyer: 17 of 94, or 18%).

[40] Giulietti's lawyer uses two rhetorical questions in almost 22 pages of transcript, or .09 instances per page; whereas the railroad's lawyer uses 27 rhetorical questions in under 18 pages, or 1.53 per page.

Somewhat less expected is the juxtaposition of liquid metaphors for sympathy ("buckets and buckets") and justice (the "full cup"). Here Giulietti's lawyer ingeniously connects with three aspects of jurors' sense of total justice. First, total justice encompasses both thought and feeling, cognition and emotion. Hence, sympathy and justice are represented by the *same state of matter* (liquid). Second, however, jurors know that they are supposed to *distinguish* emotion from reason, sympathy from justice; the judge will so instruct them. Giulietti's lawyer encourages them to believe that they can do what the law asks them to do: He *contrasts* sloshy sympathy to self-contained justice. Finally, jurors' justice is inadequate unless it is exact, complete, total: a *full* cup, no more, no less. Of such mundane, even unartful talk is our common sense of justice constructed.[41]

---

[41] The plaintiffs in *Giulietti* received a verdict in the amount of approximately $500,000, which was reduced by 1% for Giulietti's contributory negligence (according to Bill Nelson, who provided me with the trial transcript). The trial verdict was affirmed by the Second Circuit Court of Appeals.

6

ACCIDENTS AS MELODRAMA: LAWYERS' ARGUMENTS AND JURORS' RESPONSES

This chapter examines more of what trial lawyers say to jurors to help them think about accidents. We are, however, no longer required merely to speculate about what the jurors think, because the jurors tell us in their own words. By unpacking the social psychological dynamics of the lawyers' arguments *and* the jurors' responses, we see how the jurors' ways of determining responsibility for the accident correspond at least in part to what the plaintiff's lawyer argues.

The ideal way to learn how laypeople think and talk about blame and compensation when they are serving as jurors would be to listen to them deliberate. For the most part, however, observing or recording actual jury deliberations is prohibited (Kassin & Wrightsman, 1988; Ruprecht, 1997). So if we want to listen to common sense about accident cases, our best sources are mock jury deliberations (which are examined in the next chapter) and postverdict interviews with actual jurors.

The strengths of juror interviews as a database for common-sense views of blame and compensation in accident cases are obvious. The interviews are from people who have served as jurors in actual cases, not laboratory experiments. This means not only that their judgments are responses to the most realistic of stimuli (the evidence and arguments presented in a real trial), but also that they knew when they were deciding that the fate of real litigants depended on their decisions (Kaplan & Krupa, 1986; D. Wilson & Donnerstein, 1977). Thus, jurors' postverdict remarks are not prone to some of the major external validity concerns raised by much experimental research (see Diamond, 1997).

Although the jurors' words promise to add to our understanding of how the jurors thought about the case, postverdict interviews are not by any means a clear window into the jurors' mental processes during deliberations. Assuming that the interviewees are trying their best to report honestly what they remember, at least three caveats remain. First is a self-presentational bias (Aronson, Wilson, & Brewer, 1998; Leary, 1995). Jurors are likely to want to present themselves in what they believe the interviewer (and sometimes, especially in high-profile cases, other audiences, such as family, friends, or neighbors) will consider to be a favorable light. At the very least, jurors would be predicted not to confess to racial or other invidious biases in reaching their decisions. Second, introspection provides no privileged access to one's own higher-order cognitive processes. What a juror reports about *why* he or she decided as he or she did is as likely to be due to the juror's *a priori* theories about what influences such decisions as it is to any reliable empirical insight (Nisbett & Wilson, 1977). Third, where, as here, the jurors' words are mediated by a reporter and his or her publication, what is provided is a version of the jurors' remarks that has been edited to serve the reporter's and publisher's purposes (Marder, 1997). Given these caveats, how actual jurors talk about accidents may provide additional insight into how they think about accidents, especially when their words converge with other evidence of common sense decision making in this context.

The case I have chosen to present, *Faverty v. McDonald's Restaurants of Oregon, Inc.* (1991, 1995), is a fascinating and controversial one. Frederic Faverty was driving his pickup truck to work one morning when Matt Theurer, a teenage McDonald's employee who was driving home after working a midnight shift, fell asleep at the wheel and crashed into Faverty, seriously hurting Faverty and killing himself. Faverty sued McDonald's, arguing that by allowing the teenager to work until he was sleep-deprived, McDonald's unreasonably increased the risk of harm to other drivers on the road. The jurors, by a vote of nine to three, found McDonald's responsible for Faverty's injuries and awarded the plaintiff $400,000 damages. The verdict was upheld on appeal.[1]

Blaming McDonald's for this accident certainly seems anomalous, at least at first glance. McDonald's had no power or duty to control its em-

---

[1] The case was also argued before the Oregon Supreme Court but was settled before that court rendered a decision. I refer throughout simply to *Faverty*, regardless of the stage of proceedings; where not specified, it should be clear from the context (in this chapter and in chapter 8) whether the 1991 trial or the 1995 appellate opinion is meant.

ployees' behavior off the job, and it is not at all clear how McDonald's could have taken cost-effective precautions against this sort of accident. Perhaps the jurors were simply seeking a deep pocket in which to find compensation for the unfortunate Faverty (see chapter 4 for research on the deep pocket bias). Perhaps it was just a "crazy" verdict, as Stuart Taylor, Jr., subtitled his *American Lawyer* article about the case, from which the juror interviews are drawn (Taylor, 1991).

A close study of the lawyers' and the jurors' words may give us reason to reconsider those first impressions. I hope to show how the plaintiff's lawyer's summation and the jurors' postverdict remarks reflect a common method of attributing responsibility for accidents. It is a method we have seen in the *Butler* and *Giulietti* cases analyzed in chapter 5: to identify relevant norms of behavior and then to infer blame from perceived violations of those norms. More specifically, both Faverty's lawyer and many of the jurors talk as if they conceive of the accident as a *melodrama*, which, as explained in chapter 4, provides a cognitive and emotional framework for assigning liability to the defendant. In chapter 8, I return to the case and discuss the extent to which the decision can be reconciled with relevant tort doctrine and the leading expert justifications for it.

THE FACTS

Matt Theurer was an 18-year-old high school student who worked at McDonald's to make money to pay for his car. As he had done occasionally in the past, he volunteered to work a midnight shift cleaning deep-fat fryers. The previous day he had worked at McDonald's after school from 3:30 p.m. to 7:30 p.m., then gone out with friends, then returned to work at midnight. McDonald's' own policy barred "split shifts" or more than one shift in a day; technically Theurer's schedule did not violate this policy because the midnight shift was on a different calendar day than the preceding shift, but it was his second shift within 24 hours.[2] A little past 8:00 the next morning, very tired, Theurer left work to drive home. He never got there. Minutes after leaving, he fell asleep at the wheel, and his car drifted into the oncoming lane, striking a small truck driven by Frederic Faverty. Faverty was seriously hurt. Theurer was killed. Faverty settled with Theurer's estate, then sued McDonald's.

THE ISSUE

The central facts, as in the *Butler* and *Giulietti* cases discussed in chapter 5, were not really in dispute. No one, for instance, thought Faverty was

---

[2] McDonald's' policy also barred teenagers from working past midnight more than once per week. Theurer had worked past 11:00 p.m. on three of the five nights which he worked during the week preceding his death (Taylor, 1991).

contributorily negligent (Taylor, 1991), although McDonald's' attorney raised the possibility. Instead the case turned on a stark opposition between two conceptions of responsibility. The basic question was (a) whether McDonald's should be held responsible in any way for allowing an 18-year-old high school student to work midnight shifts and put himself into a sleep-deprived state, then allowing him to drive home on the highway, creating a foreseeable risk that he would fall asleep and endanger other drivers and himself, or (b) whether Theurer, an adult, should be held fully responsible for his choice to work late, not to get adequate sleep when he wasn't working or in school, and then drive home from work, knowing how tired he was. In sum, what sense would it make to divert responsibility for the accident from Theurer, the driver, and place it on McDonald's, especially considering that the accident occurred after working hours when McDonald's had no right or ability to control Theurer's behavior?

THE PLAINTIFF'S LAWYER'S WORDS

Toward the beginning of his closing argument, Frederic Faverty's lawyer makes one explicit legal argument as to how McDonald's could be responsible when it was Theurer who fell asleep at the wheel, after work hours and off work premises. He analogizes McDonald's to a bar that serves liquor to an intoxicated person who then gets into an accident (*Faverty*, 575.1-19).[3] Under common law, the bar is typically liable for injuries to third parties caused by the drunken driver in these circumstances.[4] This is the traditional technique of argument by analogy, a straightforward request to apply established law to a new situation. If the argument is successful, then the fact that Theurer was the immediate cause of the accident does not excuse McDonald's; rather, Theurer's foreseeable dangerous driving is the very reason McDonald's should be held responsible. The argument was indeed effective enough to be recognized by the appellate court,[5] but only one of the jurors referred to it when explaining her decision (Taylor, 1991).

A more promising clue to how most of the jurors thought about the case may be found in a set of arguments *implicit* in the plaintiff's lawyer's summation. Consider this brief excerpt:

> This kid is set up. He is ripe to fall asleep and like all kids that age, if they don't get enough sleep, they're tired; they're nodding off in school. Okay. Then that's not McDonald's' fault necessarily. They may

---

[3] The lawyer also claims that "this case—is about a business that caused a young man's impairment, a sleep impairment, no different than if they'd handed him sleeping pills until the point he was ready to fall asleep" (575.13-17) (all references to the *Faverty* trial transcript are to the page[s] and line[s] in the proceedings of March 29, 1991, unless otherwise indicated).
[4] See, for example, *Campbell v. Carpenter* (1977); *Vesely v. Sager* (1971).
[5] *Faverty* (1995, p. 710).

contribute a little bit too, but the point of it is that's the background we start with. We don't start with a kid who's fresh and awake.

. . .

And when you take somebody who has a cumulative loss of sleep over a period of time, it brings down that period between being awake and the danger of falling asleep dramatically. And it's worse in the earlier morning hours. And then if you miss an entire night's sleep—and that's exactly what happened. This kid should have been home and in bed by 11 o'clock. And that is where McDonald's blew it, because they should have known and they're the ones that kept him up. He's doing work for them; they're going to make money because they're going to have clean deep fat fryers, and they pushed Matt Theurer over the edge.

. . .

The evidence is that McDonald's is the only one that does that, and what's crazy is they didn't have to do it. They didn't have to make this kid work on an all-night shift on a school night. Common sense tells—should have told them that. Common decency should have told them that. . . .

Was McDonald's thinking about safety? Was safety job one at McDonald's? Is this sad event something that could have been easily prevented: to have a couple of high school kids clean out the deep fat fryers for 4 bucks an hour, stay up all night on a school night. . . . And that's why McDonald's is responsible for Matt Theurer's death and Fred Faverty's injuries.

Take Matt Theurer off that shift, you put him home, you put him in bed, by 8:30 in the morning he's not on the road with heavy eyelids, with impaired judgment, with poor concentration, all the other things that Dr. Rich told you go along with sleep deprivation. That's why McDonald's is responsible. (584.25-585.6; 585.15-25; 589.17-21; 589.25-590.17)

MELODRAMA AND BLAME FOR ACCIDENTS

This is a melodramatic argument. It is melodramatic because it conceives of the accident in simplified, personalized, moralized, and dichotomized terms. As explained in chapter 4, these features of melodrama map onto specific habits of thought that social psychology elucidates. The habit of thought most crucial to this argument is norm theory, although I will note many others as well.

Faverty's lawyer takes advantage of norm theory in several ways to pin responsibility on McDonald's. First, the argument emphasizes that what made the difference between accident and no accident was what McDonald's did (or failed to do), not what Theurer did (or failed to do). It was McDonald's' acts or omissions that caused Faverty's injuries, not

Theurer's acts or omissions. The climactic last paragraph of the excerpt above focuses on what McDonald's could and therefore should have done differently. And the lawyer's use of the second-person plural in this crucial paragraph to encourage jurors to (imaginatively) avoid the accident and thus correct McDonald's' error puts them in the active role of *performing* the closure that the melodramatic plot requires, a closure that is consistent with corrective justice.[6]

Now look at the particular norms that Faverty's lawyer makes salient for the jurors, in contrast to which McDonald's' untaken precautions appear deviant. First, the repeated references to Theurer as "the kid" (582.23-24, 583.2, 584.19-20, 22, 25, 585.5, 20, 589.19) invoke a schema or prototype of *Theurer as a child and McDonald's as his parent.* The operative norms, deeply embedded in our culture, are *parents have responsibility for their children,* and, relatedly, *parents are supposed to know better.* Accordingly, it is no excuse that Theurer volunteered for the late shift and chose to drive home; common-sense norms dictate that McDonald's still should have done more to keep Theurer from putting himself and others at risk.

Second, consider the lawyer's assertions that McDonald's "ha[s] a couple of high school kids clean out the deep fat fryers for 4 bucks an hour" (590.2-3) and that McDonald's is "going to make money because they're going to have clean deep fat fryers" (585.23-24). This invokes a schema or prototype of *McDonald's as a (greedy) corporate profiteer,* which triggers the following cultural norms: *Corporations should not be allowed to cut corners on safety for profit,* and perhaps also: *Corporations should not get away with exploiting low-paid employees.*[7]

How does Faverty's lawyer call the jurors' attention to McDonald's' deviance from these norms? One crucial technique is to exploit the active versus passive distinction. As noted in chapter 2, jurors are more likely to mentally "undo" acts—that is, to complete their "if only . . ." counterfactual thinking with an act ("If only McDonald's had not done x") rather than an omission ("If only McDonald's had done x")—and thus they are more likely to target acts as the cause(s) of the accident. Faverty's lawyer, therefore, tries to cast McDonald's as the active party and its failure to keep Theurer off the road as an affirmative mistake, while describing Theurer as passive.

Of course, just about any behavior can be characterized as either an act or an omission. Here, McDonald's could be said to have failed to keep Theurer from working late (omission) or to have created a system that

---

[6] I thank Tony Sebok for this observation.

[7] I am less certain about the status of this second proposed norm, because it is so routinely violated in policy and practice, and because it conflicts with perhaps more deeply entrenched beliefs in individualism and free-market capitalism. Nevertheless, it seems consistent with a broad egalitarian attitude toward justice in accident cases (Polisar & Wildavsky, 1989) and with the "relational" idea of justice, which views the courts as agents for rectifying broad social inequalities (J. Conley & O'Barr, 1990).

invited him to work late and then refused to prevent him from working (which sounds more like an act). Faverty's lawyer uses the microlinguistic techniques of verb choice and sentence structure to identify McDonald's as the agent of harm. He talks about what McDonald's "did," "was doing," or "does." He says that McDonald's "kept [Theurer] up" (585.22-23) and that they "ma[d]e this kid work on an all-night shift on a school night" (589.19-20).[8]

At the same time, the lawyer casts Theurer as a passive victim. It would have been implausible to argue explicitly that Theurer was not a human being who made choices, so the lawyer does it implicitly, through the use of metaphor. Matt is "ripe" to fall asleep (584.25), like a fruit about to fall off the tree.[9] Matt is "set up" (584.25), the passive victim of what, impliedly, is a sort of entrapment by McDonald's.

The depictions of McDonald's as the agent of harm and Theurer as passive came together most (melo)dramatically in the assertion that McDonald's "pushed Matt Theurer over the edge" (590.24-25). Certainly this is a cliché, but in context it is disturbingly graphic: the image of a person falling off a cliff and striking the ground evoking the terrible force of the fatal car crash. The phrase encapsulates the complex chain of events leading up to the accident as a compact, monocausal account: McDonald's did it, Theurer did not.[10] Moreover, it evokes popular cultural stereotypes of the "bad guy"—who but a cad would push someone off a cliff?

In sum, the rhetorical techniques that allow the lawyer to invoke norm theory simultaneously construct the accident as melodrama. And this is so in yet one more respect: the elicitation of emotional response. I observed in chapter 4 that accident cases tend to lack those sudden plot developments on which melodramas rely to exploit their audience's emotions. As psychologists of the emotions explain, plot twists and reversals would tend to have this effect because the more unexpected an event, the more intense the emotional reaction to it (Ortony et al., 1988). Prior

---

[8] The lawyer uses similar locutions in his opening argument as well: "McDonald's had had Mr. Theurer go to work" (9.7); "they had him work until 11:30 that night" (9.14); "The issue in this case is whether or not someone who makes a young person—makes any worker work those kind of hours ought to be responsible" (11. 17-19); "that's what McDonald's did to this young man" (13.3-4) (all references to transcript of 3/25/91).

[9] Elsewhere the lawyer analogizes Theurer to "narcoleptics [who] fall asleep almost at the drop of a hat" (587.22-23), again imagining Theurer as an inanimate object without will.

[10] In one sense, of course, this accident is *not* monocausal—it took *both* Theurer's falling asleep at the wheel and McDonald's bringing him to that state. The plaintiff's lawyer admits as much: "Mr. Theurer[,] let's face it, folks, he was on the wrong side of the road; and that in our society, you're responsible" (576.10-12), and "[i]t wasn't all [Theurer's] fault" (599.3). But the Oregon comparative negligence statute in effect at the time of the case prohibited any nonparty's responsibility from being taken into account (*Oregon Revised Statutes*, 1975). So in the context of the litigation, given Faverty's lack of fault, the decision came down to Faverty's fault (none) versus McDonald's' (576.17-20). Oregon later revised its comparative negligence statutes to require the percentage fault of any person with whom the claimant has settled to be taken into account when computing each defendant's percentage fault (*Oregon Revised Statutes*, 1995).

events create expectations that the plot twists upset. Norm theory works in precisely the same way, but here the salient norms (rather than prior events) establish the expectations that the defendant's behavior, portrayed as deviating from those norms, upsets. The result, norm theory research predicts, is that the more deviant McDonald's' conduct appears, the more likely jurors are to respond with more intense emotions, to blame the defendant more, and to award the plaintiff greater compensation—all without any need for the plaintiff's lawyer to make too overt an emotional appeal.

Culpable causation underscores this interpretation of the accident as melodrama. Deviations from the norm of responsible parent are, of course, morally blameworthy in our culture. Deviations from the norm of decent corporation are also morally blameworthy (although perhaps less so). In both instances, the moral stigma that jurors may attach to McDonald's' behavior reinforces the jurors' tendency to see what McDonald's did or failed to do, and not what Theurer or anyone else did or failed to do, as the cause of the accident.

The role of fundamental attribution error in Faverty's lawyer's argument—attributing the parties' actions to the sort of people they are—is a little more complicated. As suggested in chapter 5, plaintiffs' lawyers in civil cases may be reluctant to depict defendants, especially familiar corporate defendants like McDonald's, as purely "bad guys" who do bad things, because jurors can be expected to depend on businesses like McDonald's for the satisfaction of their own consumerist desires and, to some extent, to trust those businesses. Thus, notwithstanding the implications of the prototype of the exploitative, profit-seeking corporation and the entity that shoved Matt Theurer off a cliff, the plaintiff's lawyer also acknowledges that "[t]he issue in this case is not whether it's okay for McDonald's to make money. There's no challenge that they're a business and that's okay" (transcript of 3/25/91, 11.24-12.1).

Faverty's lawyer, however, does not forgo the opportunity to present his client as a good guy (e.g., 594.10-17). More important, he takes every opportunity to present *Theurer* as a good guy. Matt "was a good kid. Everybody liked him. All the terrible things that kids can get involved in and exposed to, he'd done a good job of avoiding most of them" (transcript of 3/25/91, 8.25-9.3). What possible relevance to the case can these assertions have? None, except to frame the case for the jurors as an opposition between a good guy and a (somewhat) bad guy.

Indeed, throughout the argument Faverty's lawyer puts Theurer, not his client, on center stage. This is, of course, not inadvertent. "Today . . . you'll judge the life of Matt Theurer" (574.13–14), he begins his summation, and he closes it by telling the jurors, "you write the epitaph that goes on Matt Theurer's tombstone" (598.23–24). By doing this, the lawyer not only seeks to bootstrap jurors' sympathy for his client onto their sympathy for the dead young man, but also puts the several relational norms identified earlier (parent–child, corporation–employee) at the center of the case. The focus on Theurer rather than the plaintiff is not, therefore, a violation of the element of melodrama that highlights the plaintiff and his suffering; rather, it is a strategic elaboration of that element. And there is no question that Faverty's lawyer seeks to emphasize the plaintiff and his suffering. He devotes nearly two-fifths of his opening statement[11] and a third of his closing[12] to the essentially uncontested issue of Faverty's injuries and the argument for damages. So, despite the obligatory disclaimer that he is not seeking jurors' sympathy for his client (578.17-25), Faverty's lawyer makes salient for the jurors his client's suffering, one of the most important factors in the arousal of sympathy and, of course, a key element in the melodramatic conception of accidents.[13]

THE DEFENDANT'S LAWYER'S WORDS

McDonald's' lawyer presents a "somewhat scattershot" closing argument (Taylor, 1991, p. 89). In the middle of his various efforts to suggest other causes for the accident (including blaming Faverty), to question whether Theurer was in fact sleep-deprived, and to counter Faverty's damages claims, the lawyer for McDonald's briefly makes a coherent effort to assign full responsibility for the accident to Theurer[14]:

> And the other liability issue that we've presented in good faith is that Matt chose not to nap not McDonald's. McDonald's understood that he was going to take a nap. We're not so naive to know that working at night on a cleanup shift isn't tiresome work. It is tiresome work. The supervisor said to Matt, I don't want you to do this unless you agree to take a nap. Are you going to take a nap? Yes.
>
> Matt arranged to take a rest. He called George VanDeCoevering [a friend], and this place was two or three blocks from the restaurant.

---

[11] One hundred eight out of 274 lines (39.1%).

[12] Two hundred four lines out of 618 (33.0%).

[13] As a final flourish that could be described as melodramatic in the sense of using excessive (Brooks, 1976) and gothic detail, Faverty's lawyer tells jurors: "You judge not only Faverty today, you write the epitaph that goes on Matt Theurer's tombstone. You decide should the stonemaker write, here lies a young man who died at his own hands or here lies the body of a young man who died because of a mistake, a series of mistakes that could have been avoided" (598.23-599.3).

[14] Other things that Theurer did or could have done but did not that McDonald's' lawyer states explicitly or intimates could have avoided the accident include: Theurer choosing to work as many hours as he did in the weeks and months before the accident (613.24-614.1); Theurer (perhaps) choosing not to rest sufficiently during his spring break a few weeks before the accident (608.21-609.13); Theurer (perhaps) choosing not to sleep enough during the days preceding the accident (613.16-20); Theurer volunteering for the particular shift on the fatal morning (615.2-23) (this last one also makes a brief appearance in the excerpt discussed in the text, at 611.21-22). None, however, forms the basis of an argument as sustained as the one discussed in the text.

George was expecting him. Matt came by; he had Vicki [another friend] with him. He didn't do it.

Now, we're getting again into a situation of what is the responsibility of an eighteen year old? Was McDonald's reasonable in assuming that Matt would follow through? I think you have to judge McDonald's in this case and the manager involved on this basis: We had a right to assume that Matt would take a nap. Assuming that, are we wrong in having him or allowing him to volunteer for a late shift? That I think is the question, and that's why we brought Dr. Graeber [expert witness] in to tell you how beneficial a nap would be.

Had he taken it, I don't think we'd be here today. I don't think there would be the heart break that's existed because of this accident. I don't think Mr. Faverty would be injured. I think we'd be in an entirely different situation. Because Matt elected as an eighteen year old adult not to do what he said he was going to do, that caused us to be here. (611.5-612.5)

Holding out Theurer's failure to nap (and, somewhat secondarily, his choice to work late) as the blameworthy cause(s) of the accident makes a certain amount of sense as a strategy to deflect responsibility from McDonald's.[15] Norm theory illuminates one reason why the argument might be persuasive. As discussed earlier, decision makers are biased toward choosing acts over omissions as causes. Theurer's choice to work is plainly an act. His not napping, on the other hand, could be construed as either an omission or an act, so McDonald's' lawyer bolsters his case by describing it as an act: Theurer "*chose* not to nap" (611.6). Elsewhere the lawyer emphasizes Theurer's agency, reiterating that "[h]e's a decision-making adult person. He makes his own decisions; he's legally entitled to make his own decisions" (609.4-6).

Culpable causation helps us to understand another feature of this argument. McDonald's' lawyer strengthens his position by implicitly characterizing Theurer's failure to take a nap as *morally* deviant, in that Theurer said he was going to nap but did not. The lawyer first reenacts

---

[15] It is questionable whether Theurer's failure to nap, even if the jurors accept the lawyer's invitation to view it as the *sine qua non* of this accident story, should negate McDonald's' responsibility entirely. Under standard tort doctrine, intervening acts of negligence do not relieve the original wrongdoer from liability if that negligence was a foreseeable result of the original negligence (American Law Institute, 1965; see chapter 1). If one of the things that arguably makes McDonald's' scheduling practices negligent is that they put immature persons in a position to get more tired than is good for them, impairing their judgment, then Theurer's choices, even if negligent, do not let McDonald's off the hook. Even worse for McDonald's, it could be argued that it is McDonald's' act in letting Theurer work late and not keeping him from driving that is most proximate to the accident; that is, that Theurer's negligence did not *intervene* between McDonald's' negligence and the accident.

McDonald's' argument would be much stronger if Theurer's estate were the plaintiff. Then the untaken precaution looks more like implied contributory fault or assumption of risk. Oregon abolished implied assumption of risk in 1975 (*Oregon Revised Statutes*, 1975). But Theurer, for failing to take the precaution, could very well be attributed more than half of the total fault for the accident, in which case he would still be barred completely from recovery under Oregon's limited comparative negligence rule (*Oregon Revised Statutes*, 1995).

the *promise*: "I [the supervisor] don't want you to do this unless you agree to take a nap. Are you going to take a nap? Yes" (611.10-11). He then stresses how Theurer *broke* that promise: Theurer "elected . . . not to do what he said he was going to do" (612.4-5). Breaking a promise is morally suspect behavior and therefore, by the logic of culpable causation, causally and legally blameworthy as well.

But social psychology also offers interrelated reasons why jurors are less likely to target Theurer's failure to nap than McDonald's' failure to keep him from working as the behavior that deviates most from relevant norms, and therefore as the blameworthy cause of the accident. Theurer's decision to work late may appear less deviant than McDonald's' decision to let him work late because Theurer's decision is merely the poor judgment of an 18-year-old, whereas McDonald's' decision is corporate policy. Poor judgment is typical enough for young people that the law, for instance, prohibits them from drinking, and insurance companies issue policies on their driving only at higher rates. McDonald's' lawyer himself says that Theurer was "burning the candle at both ends" (613.11-12), also typical enough for an 18-year-old. Thus Theurer's conduct conforms to prototypical behavior; he is not a deviant. McDonald's' conduct, on the other hand, especially on the level of company-, region-, or storewide policy, represents a corporation's deliberate, profit-seeking choice. (Recall that Faverty's lawyer emphasizes that McDonald's was "going to make money because they're [Theurer and others] going to have to clean deep fat fryers" and how McDonald's "ha[d] a couple of high school kids clean out the deep fat fryers for 4 bucks an hour, stay up all night on a school night" [585.23-24, 590.2-4].) Moreover, as we saw in chapter 2, observers reasoning counterfactually are more likely to undo deliberate failures to avoid risk than mere inattention, and thus to choose the former as the cause of harm. To the extent that McDonald's' conduct is understood as corporate policy and Theurer's as mere lack of prudence, jurors are more likely to blame McDonald's.

A different theme, which would resonate with at least some of the jurors, is that to hold McDonald's responsible for what Theurer did after work would be to imply that an employer had a right of control or surveillance over its employees after work, which would constitute an unwarranted infringement on the personal liberty and autonomy of employees. McDonald's' lawyer invokes these values on several occasions (609.8-20, 612.23-613.3, 615.2-616.15, 618.2-5, 620.16-18), but does not begin to do so until nearly halfway into his summation, and all in all this theme occupies less than an eighth of his speech.[16] We cannot be sure, but perhaps if the lawyer had emphasized these ideas more, they would have played a larger role in the jurors' evaluation of the case.

---

[16] Sixty-four transcript lines out of a total of 536 (11.9%).

THE JURORS' WORDS

We know *what* the jurors decided: a 9–3 verdict for Frederic Faverty in the amount of $400,000. But *why* did they decide as they did? How did they think about responsibility for this accident? Let us listen to some of their postverdict remarks, as reported in the media (Taylor, 1991, pp. 88–91)[17]:

Thomas Berguin (30 years old, manager):

(1) [McDonald's] could have used a little better judgment. . . . [But] I asked myself, where is this kid's mother? . . . Why is it up to McDonald's? . . . I've done that kind of thing at work, come in at eight in the morning and stay until eight-thirty in the evening, and I don't expect my employer to be checking on me. . . . And now am I going to have my employer telling me I can't work overtime? Where is it going to stop?

(2) The way [the judge's instruction] was worded, it was really hard to say no. . . . Were they [McDonald's] at fault at all, any little bit? . . . Yeah, they should have known this kid's schedule, they should have told him, "No thanks, Matt, don't work."

Irma Wilson (64 years old, factory worker):

(1) Somebody should have asked, "Are you too tired to drive your car?"

(2) I just don't think McDonald's should be able to get away with that kind of crap. . . . They're just absolutely using these high school kids for all they can get out of them.

Verna Misenhimer (49 years old, teacher's aide):

(1) My first feeling . . . was, "Well, here's an 18-year-old boy, why should McDonald's be responsible for him?" . . . But by the end I thought, "Well, why not?" . . . It was important that he was a student. Perhaps because I am a mother, I thought that if he was my son I would appreciate it if they'd said he shouldn't work this shift. Somebody's got to take responsibility.

(2) You'd have to be a robot not to feel some emotion about the situation. . . . [The case was] almost like letting a drunk go out on the road . . . [and] these companies should not let a person out to drive an automobile home with that lack of sleep.

Claudia Dockter (40 years old, executive secretary):

They kept saying that [because] he was eighteen, he was an adult, but that just wasn't true. . . . He did volunteer to work that shift, from

---

[17]Material in brackets includes quotations from Taylor (as opposed to the exact words he attributes to jurors) or my own paraphrases of Taylor's words.

what we understood. But they knew he was a high school student, they knew he was going right from there to school—I just don't think that absolves them.

Pat Weiler (52 years old, electronics technician):

[T]he whole thing was bordering on the ridiculous. [There's nothing unusual about an employee working long hours and driving home] barely on the edge of consciousness. . . . I know I've done it. I'm sure you have too.

John Lorett (foreperson) (51 years old):

I thought at first that there was no way McDonald's could be liable. . . . [But the evidence convinced Lorett that] there was no doubt that McDonald's was working him more hours than they should have, especially on a school night.

Teri Killaby (27 years old, registered nurse):

(1) McDonald's [was] responsible in some way for breaking their own scheduling policies, so we all felt that yes, McDonald's shouldn't have done that, and they were negligent in that respect. And [that] yes, they had some part in causing the deceased to fall asleep at the wheel. . . . [McDonald's needed to] hold some responsibility in their scheduling practices . . . and not schedule [students] on a school night all night and expect them to function.
(2) I was divided in my own mind. . . . A lot of us didn't like the idea that an employer could be liable for getting his employees to and from work. . . . [But t]he way the judge gave us the questions, it was like we didn't really have a choice.

Perhaps the first thing these excerpts reveal is that the jurors did not have an easy time reaching what they felt would be a just result in this case. Not only did they disagree with one another, but several were also, as juror Killaby put it, "divided in [their] own mind[s]." On the fundamental values implicated by this lawsuit, such as individual versus corporate responsibility, there may be as many viewpoints as jurors.

The jurors' words also suggest that emotion—sympathy for the plaintiff or anger toward the defendant—played some part in their judgment, although it is unclear how much. Juror Wilson expressed anger at McDonald's; juror Berguin acknowledged sympathy for Faverty but implied that he was able to put it aside in determining responsibility for the accident. Aside from what may be read into Wilson's remarks, the jurors did not attribute their own decisions to emotion or to deep pocket bias, although some jurors, interestingly, said that *other jurors* were so motivated.[18] Even jurors striving to be honest and accurate in their postverdict assessments, however, would be predicted to understate somewhat the extent of emotion in *their own* decision making, because of both self-presentation bias (they want others to believe, and they want to believe themselves, that they complied with the judge's instructions not to be influenced by emotion) and an inability to identify the real causes of their judgments (Nisbett & Wilson, 1977).

It does not seem, then, that these jurors simply gave in to what I have described as the melodramatic conception proffered by Faverty's lawyer. Yet, as I argue below, we can find in many of these jurors' remarks the basic structure of the melodramatic conception of accidents. The majority of the jurors thought about responsibility in a personalized and moralized way. They reasoned by identifying relevant norms of behavior—mostly the ones Faverty's lawyer wanted them to identify—and then inferring blame from perceived violations of those norms. Their words indicate that they used norm theory and other heuristics to reach their decision. I also argue that jurors Berguin, Killaby, and others, who claimed in effect that "the law made them do it," as journalist Stuart Taylor (1991, p. 86) put it in the title of his article, were in one sense more correct than Taylor acknowledged, and the ways in which their common-sense habits of thought intersect with the substantive tort law offer a nice illustration of the analytic framework introduced in the introduction.

THE JURORS' SENSE OF RESPONSIBILITY FOR ACCIDENTS

In chapter 5 I observed how the plaintiff's lawyer in *Butler* told the story of his client's accident in a way that drew on more than one schema of "how things ought to go" in that workplace situation. Individual jurors could decide in the plaintiff's favor without necessarily agreeing on the particular norm from which the defendant deviated. Indeed, it has been argued that one virtue of the concept of "reasonableness" as the linchpin of the negligence claim is that it allows for a single justification of the decision (i.e., the defendant behaved unreasonably) without requiring everyone to agree on the specific values subsumed within the general concept (S. Smith, 1984).

The *Faverty* case offers an even better example of how the meaning of responsibility for accidents can be negotiated within the scope of the

---

[18] For instance, juror Diana Debray (28 years old, bookkeeper), said of juror Wilson that "I wanted to gag her. . . . She would interrupt you every time you started to say something, and I wanted to bonk her head. She was one of the little people who works for a big company who [thinks] that big companies are responsible for you totally, and big companies have a lot of money, so why shouldn't you take some?" (Taylor, 1991, p. 91). Juror Berguin also attributed sympathy and anti-corporate defendant sentiment to his fellow jurors.

substantive law of negligence. Faverty's lawyer gave jurors *several* options as to how the defendant, McDonald's, could have acted otherwise to avoid the accident, thereby allowing different jurors to blame McDonald's on the basis of different violations of common-sense justice norms. Thus, the jurors' decision reflects a confluence of various cultural norms but a common pattern of inferring blame from the transgression of those norms.[19]

At one end of the continuum are the jurors such as Wilson, Misenhimer, and Dockter, who focused on the belief that McDonald's should not have worked teenage students so hard and especially should not have taken advantage of them by having them work midnight shifts on school nights. Culpable causation makes this convincing as the target of blame because, as we have seen, exploiting kids—making them slave over deep-fat fryers in the middle of the night for minimum wage, at the same time depriving them of opportunities for healthful sleep and possibly undermining their ability to do their schoolwork—seems morally deviant.[20] This behavior also conflicts with the norm that corporations should not be allowed to cut corners on safety for profit. Justice is then served by blaming McDonald's for harms traceable to its corporate policies, not because McDonald's is the deep pocket (see MacCoun, 1996), but because such a standard of care, even if it entails greater responsibility for the well-being of others than an individual defendant would have to bear, is appropriate given corporations' superior ability to foresee risks and marshal resources to address them (Bornstein, 1994; Hans, 1994, 1998).

A narrower conception of what McDonald's did wrong is expressed by jurors like Killaby, who thought that "McDonald's [was] responsible in some way for breaking their own scheduling policies (barring split shifts or multiple late shifts in a single week), so we all felt that yes, McDonald's shouldn't have done that, and they were negligent in that respect" (Taylor, 1991, p. 90). According to norm theory, jurors would be likely to blame McDonald's for deviating from its own scheduling policies, which limited workers' hours for their own safety. Indeed, this may have been prima facie evidence of negligence according to modern tort doctrine.[21]

---

[19] I do not mean to claim that each juror who found McDonald's responsible identified only one thing that McDonald's did or failed to do, justifiable in terms of only one conception of negligence. No doubt at least some jurors (perhaps without realizing it) entertained multiple grounds for believing McDonald's to be at fault.

[20] Jurors could also find that McDonald's' employment practices were abnormal in the sense that other fast-food restaurants did not conduct themselves as McDonald's did (589.9-18). It is, however, unclear from the transcript of his closing argument just what Faverty's lawyer was referring to when he contrasted McDonald's' conduct with that of other fast-food restaurants: for example, allowing teenagers to work late at night, allowing them to work shifts beginning at midnight, or not monitoring them more carefully for sleepiness.

[21] See, for example, *Lucy Webb Hayes National Training School v. Perotti*, 1969. Moreover, culpable causation could lead jurors to solidify the somewhat problematic causal status of this conduct (see discussion of *Butler* in chapter 5). Violation of its own scheduling policies supports a stronger doctrinal argument that McDonald's breached its duty of reasonable care but makes for a less convincing case for causation. Allowing Theurer to work that last shift

Again, however, in the words of Killaby and other jurors (e.g., Dockter, Lorett), McDonald's' mistake was to break its scheduling policies by allowing Theurer to work the late shift *on a school night*. In terms of the causal connection between the alleged negligence and the fatal accident, whether Theurer was leaving work to drive to school rather than home, or whether he would have been able to "function" adequately at school the next day (juror Killaby), seems irrelevant. The only relevant causal connection ought to be between McDonald's conduct and Theurer's ability to drive safely, whatever his destination. Again, culpable causation seems to describe how the jurors are taking a plausible legal basis for negligence and moralizing it.

Finally, there were the jurors who seem to have focused blameworthiness most narrowly. These jurors imagined a counterfactual world in which McDonald's avoided the accident by asking Theurer, "[A]re you too tired to drive your car?" (juror Wilson) or: "[T]hey should have known this kid's schedule, they should have told him, 'No thanks, Matt, don't work'" (juror Berguin; Taylor, 1991, p. 90). On this view, therefore, McDonald's was responsible because it failed to perceive that Matt Theurer was tired on the early morning of April 5, 1988 and/or to do anything about it. McDonald's' negligence consisted of its failure to act carefully *on this particular occasion* to avoid a foreseeable risk of harm to Theurer and any driver unfortunate enough to be in his way that morning.[22]

Norm theory makes this lapse by McDonald's very convincing as the act which, had it been taken, would have avoided the accident, because so little effort would (seemingly) have been required to act otherwise. It was thus easy for jurors to imagine a world in which McDonald's did pay more attention to Theurer's condition. But why was this norm salient to jurors in the first place? Why should it have been relevant that McDonald's *could* have asked (or told) Theurer not to work? Faverty's lawyer's closing argument provides an answer. By repeatedly referring to Theurer as a "kid,"

---

may indeed have led to his being more tired (and having to drive while tired) than he otherwise would have been. But even in compliance with company policies, someone like Theurer could still work a midnight shift after a sufficiently long period without sleep (for reasons other than working prior shifts) and be tired enough to be at risk of falling asleep at the wheel. Other possible precautions—prohibiting all midnight shifts or scrutinizing all employees for tiredness (and keeping the overly tired from driving)—seem much more likely to reduce the risk of the sort of harm that occurred in this case (and, therefore, would support stronger causation arguments).

[22]Perhaps jurors combined this conduct with the first, broader one as follows: It may not be negligent for McDonald's to allow teenagers to work midnight shifts, but given that it does, creating a significant safety risk, McDonald's has a duty to take reasonable precautions to prevent overly sleepy teenagers from driving home. Allowing Theurer to work that last shift or allowing him to drive himself home right after that shift breached that duty. (I thank Steve Gilles for suggesting this to me.) This construction of duty and breach avoids the argument that holding McDonald's liable for the broader untaken precaution by itself is not cost-effective (see discussion in chapter 8). It still faces, however, the argument that it is not cost-effective (or even practicable) to impose on employers a duty to scrutinize employees for sleepiness and then do something about it.

the lawyer invoked the social norm that parents are responsible for their children, especially when the parent knows or should know that the child may harm him- or herself or others. And we know from the jurors' own words that they took up this implication: Note how juror Berguin, in offering his counterfactual explanation of why McDonald's was responsible, speaks of Theurer as "the kid." Once jurors have identified this norm as one that governs this situation, they can readily infer McDonald's responsibility from its "abnormal" behavior. Thus it is the dynamic of normalcy and deviance, central to the idea of melodrama at the accident trial, that best explains how the majority of the *Faverty* jurors thought about this case.

Plainly the paternalistic norms that Faverty's lawyer sought to have the jurors adopt and that a majority of them seem to have accepted were not the only common-sense values that this accident story engendered. Jurors Weiler and Berguin (as well as another juror not quoted above, Edra Nohr) refer to the competing value of individual liberty and autonomy. Berguin believes that holding McDonald's responsible for its employees' off-work behavior raises the specter of Big Brother. Against this background conception, McDonald's did not behave deviantly by not inquiring into Theurer's degree of wakefulness or his activities once he left the workplace.

Weiler and Berguin also remark that it is the way of the world that people sometimes work too hard and sometimes drive home tired. Compared with this norm, *no one* in this accident case behaved deviantly (except, presumably, Theurer at the point he lost control of his car); the collision between Theurer's car and Faverty's truck was just one of those things.

These common-sense beliefs about the way the world works are no less intuitively compelling than the ones favoring the plaintiff. As I have observed throughout the book, common sense is complex and contradictory, whether one is talking about the preconceptions and habits of mind of a single individual, a group, or society at large. Author Stuart Taylor asked juror Killaby how the jurors would have decided had the judge simply told them "to do what they thought right"; Killaby responded that they might still be deliberating (Taylor, 1991, p. 90). The jurors, of course, were not so instructed; they were given legal rules to frame their decision, and several of the jurors—Berguin, Killaby, and foreperson Lorett—claimed that these instructions made the difference, breaking the logjam among competing common-sense tenets. Such claims, to be sure, could be the product of self-presentational bias; that is, jurors know they are supposed to be following the law and would likely be inclined to present themselves to the interviewer (and to the public, and themselves) as having done so. Let us see what else there may be to these jurors' contentions that "the law made them do it."

Two of the judge's instructions were most important. First, the jurors had to decide: "was the defendant, McDonald's, negligent in working Matt Theurer more hours than was reasonable under the circumstances existing when the defendant knew or in the exercise of reasonable care should have known that Matt Theurer would operate a motor vehicle and be a hazard to himself and others?" (Taylor, 1991, p. 89).[23] Second, they had to decide whether McDonald's negligence, if any, was a "substantially contributing factor" in bringing about Faverty's injuries. Breach and causation: textbook tort law, as we saw in chapter 1.

As juror Berguin (who appears to have been one of the three jurors who voted for McDonald's) said, "[t]he way [the judge's instruction] was worded, it was really hard to say no. . . . Were they [McDonald's] at fault at all, any little bit?" (Taylor, 1991, p. 90). Berguin indeed correctly understood that if McDonald's was at all to blame, it would have to be held liable for the entire damage award, because given Faverty's lack of fault (a point with which everyone agreed), McDonald's was the only other entity whose responsibility could be taken into account. Under relevant law, that is, the jurors needed to determine only that McDonald's was *more at fault* than the plaintiff, Faverty, in order to hold McDonald's liable for all of Faverty's damages.[24] The law *did* make the jurors reach *that* conclusion— assuming they had decided that Faverty was not at fault and that McDonald's was, to at least some extent.

But why did jurors think that the judge's instructions pulled them toward blaming McDonald's? A clue may be found in the remarks of John Lorett, the foreperson, who said both "there was no doubt that McDonald's was working him [Theurer] more hours than they should have, especially on a school night," and that this act, in the interviewer's paraphrase, "fit right into the judge's definition of negligence" (Taylor, 1991, p. 90). This conception of McDonald's blameworthiness "fit[s] right into the judge's definition," however, only if McDonald's conduct was *unreasonable*. And what makes that conduct unreasonable is that it *deviates from a norm the juror himself has supplied*. Lorett's comment that McDonald's "work[ed] him more hours than they should have" is based on an implicit ideal of how McDonald's "should have" behaved, not (as we have seen) on any clear evidence of industry custom or (as we see in chapter 8) on any clear notion of what might constitute cost-effective accident avoidance. The tag "especially on a school night" suggests the true nature of the ideal; as explained above, it combines norms of parental solicitude for "kids" and corporate obligations not to exploit them. And Lorett's contention that

---

[23] Note that the wording of this instruction practically requires jurors to *assume* that McDonald's was working Theurer "more hours than was reasonable" and that (McDonald's knew or should have known that) Theurer would "be a hazard to himself and others." A better instruction would have been something along these lines: "Did McDonald's use less than reasonable care in allowing Matt Theurer to work the hours he did and then drive home?" (I thank Linda Meyer for this observation.)

[24] See discussion of relevant Oregon statutes in Footnote 10.

"McDonald's was *working him*" shows that he is thinking of McDonald's as the active party in this accident story, which facilitates the use of norm theory to blame McDonald's.

This is melodramatic thinking—simplifying, personalizing, and moralizing accidents by attributing responsibility to the party who deviates from accepted cultural norms. Melodrama may not be sufficient to explain the outcome in *Faverty*. Had the law permitted jurors to take Theurer's or other nonparties' responsibility into account, it seems likely that the verdict would have reflected a more complicated pattern of blaming. But without the melodramatic conception of the accident, the jurors may not have held McDonald's responsible at all.

7

PRIOR BELIEFS AND COMMON-SENSE JUDGMENT: MOCK JURORS DELIBERATE A MEDICAL MALPRACTICE CASE

As mentioned in chapter 6, actual jury deliberations have rarely been recorded, and never in an accident case (Levin & Herzberg, 1986; Manzo, 1993, 1994; Mason & Klein, 1997). An alternative approach that many social scientists have taken to learn about how jurors think and talk is to simulate actual jury decision making by presenting mock jurors with the facts of an accident case, and then to observe how the mock jurors deliberate and decide.

This chapter analyzes three such sets of deliberations in a case of delayed diagnosis of breast cancer, a common type of medical malpractice claim. "The failure of a physician to diagnose breast cancer is the second most common medicolegal allegation filed against physicians, [and] it accounts for the greatest liability costs in settling medical malpractice suits" (Kern, 1992, p. 542). The facts of the case are also relatively typical. A 42-year-old woman, mother of two teenagers, went to see her family doctor, a general practitioner, for her annual check-up, at which the doctor palpated a large lump in one breast. The doctor ordered a mammogram and told the woman to return in one week for a follow-up visit, at which time

171

he would have discussed with her the need for a biopsy. The woman had the mammogram, but instead of returning for the second visit, she called in for the mammogram results and was told by the receptionist that they were negative. The doctor did not attempt to contact the woman to find out why she did not return for the follow-up visit, and the woman did not see the doctor again for another year. By this time the woman had developed an open sore at the site of the lump; the doctor biopsied it and diagnosed Stage IV breast cancer, with metastasis to the spine. The woman died two years later.

The woman's estate claimed that the doctor did not diagnose the cancer in a timely fashion, and that by not doing so, he deprived her of a significant chance of survival or cure. The doctor argued in response that the patient herself was to blame for not returning to his office for the scheduled follow-up visit, which prevented him from ordering the biopsy that would have yielded a definitive diagnosis. The doctor also argued that the woman's chances of surviving were already far less than even when she first presented with the breast lump, so that any negligence on his part did not cause her death or even deprive her of any substantial chance of survival.

How might people, using their prior knowledge and their common sense, attribute responsibility for an unfortunate outcome in a case like this? The mock jury deliberations reveal, in addition to some of the habits of thought and feeling explained in earlier chapters, various *case-specific prior beliefs* about medical care in general and breast cancer in particular. Mock jurors' thoughts and decisions are influenced by these common-sense preconceptions, as well as by a confusion specific to certain medical malpractice cases and by the process of deliberation itself. These influences do not sum to any simple anti-defendant (physician) or anti-plaintiff (patient) bias; jurors do not appear to think about this case melodramatically. Rather, the combined effects of the habits of thought the deliberations reveal are ambivalent, complex, and dependent on the particular facts of the case.

The first prior belief is a prototype of the doctor as someone who cares personally and deeply about his or her patients. The second equates the seriousness of the woman's breast cancer with the size of the breast lump. These beliefs derive both from jurors' personal experience and from the culture at large. And both beliefs are at least partially grounded in medicolegal reality. People's ideas about medical care in general and breast cancer in particular are relatively well-informed. Yet precisely because many people think they know a lot about these subjects, they may be prone to rely on their preconceptions too much (see Nisbett & Ross, 1980). Mock jurors who compare the doctor in this case to the *caring-physician prototype* may be more inclined to find him negligent than the legal standard of ordinarily prudent medical care would warrant. Mock jurors who rely too much on the *size-of-the-lump heuristic* may downplay the difficulties of breast cancer diagnosis and may too readily hold the doctor or the patient responsible for not managing the condition more aggressively.

The confusion concerns the *loss of chance* doctrine, the rule in many jurisdictions that a doctor may be liable for negligently depriving the patient of a loss of chance of survival, even if the patient probably would not have survived anyway (see chapter 1). When asked to determine the respective parties' responsibility for the bad outcome, some mock jurors rely exclusively on loss of chance information, a *causation* rule, ignoring the parties' legally relevant perceived *fault*; others rely on perceived fault, seemingly ignoring loss of chance. The result of this confusion and conflation of legally distinct elements of the case is that jurors may blame the patient too little by downplaying either the patient's negligence after the initial visit or the patient's poor prognosis when she first saw the doctor.

Finally, in a case such as this in which both parties are arguably at fault, a jury in a comparative negligence jurisdiction must decide how to apportion fault, and hence liability, between the parties. In this chapter, we see how the deliberation process, beginning with the use of the *split the difference* rule of thumb, leads mock jurors toward a roughly even division of fault—which on the facts of this case probably results in too much blaming of the patient, as measured by medicolegal expert judgment. Yet we also see how a limited comparative negligence rule can lead mock jurors to *reduce* the percentage of fault they attribute to the patient to a figure that allows her estate to recover something.

The deliberations I analyze in this chapter differ somewhat from those of most experimental juries reported in the literature, offering both more and less insight into the thinking and decision making of ordinary people. Unlike most such mock jury experiments, the conditions under which these deliberations were produced did not aim to simulate those of an actual trial. The participants, whose age and gender (but not race) are fairly representative of the jury-eligible population,[1] did not first observe a real or simulated trial, receive actual (or condensed but accurate) instructions on the relevant law, and then retire to deliberate. Instead, in two of the three instances, the lawyers conducting each session told the participants the important facts of the case, interspersed with questions about certain of these facts as well as more general questions about the jurors' experiences with and attitudes toward doctors, medical treatment, and other relevant topics. In response to the questions, participants voiced their opinions and asked questions of their own. Participants were then told, either orally or by means of a special verdict form, to decide whether the

---

[1] The 27 participants on the three mock juries studied consist of 16 women and 11 men. Two of the women on the second mock jury are Black and one is Asian; all other participants are White. The precise ages of the participants were not ascertained, but on the basis of their appearance and personal histories (where solicited), 6 are classified as young (under 30 years of age), 13 as middle-aged (between 30 and 60), and 8 as older (over 60).

doctor was negligent and if so, whether that negligence caused the patient harm; whether the patient was also negligent; and if both, to apportion fault between the parties. Participants then deliberated and reached a decision.[2]

The differences between these conditions and those of an actual trial, as well as the failure to control for slight variations in the facts presented to the different mock juries, would make tentative at best any inferences from the participants' words to conclusions about how real jurors would be likely to decide a malpractice case similar to this. That is not my main purpose here. Instead, these deliberations offer a glimpse of what the participants' common sense about a delayed diagnosis case looks like when it is not being pulled by the full force of the substantive and procedural law and the decision-making context of an actual case (summarized in chapter 1). Indeed, these deliberations may yield even more information about the mock jurors' thinking than does the typical experiment, because we have the participants' responses to focused questions about specific aspects of the case, as well as their own inquiries, which help to indicate what information they deem most important to making their decisions. By studying their words, we learn much about the ways they reason to their ultimate judgments of responsibility for the delayed diagnosis of breast cancer. And we also see the extent to which, in the course of persuading and being persuaded by one another as they work toward their verdict, they adopt a common language for expressing their thinking (see Ruscher et al., 1996).

THE LAW AND THE MEDICAL FACTS

As in any negligence case (see chapter 1), the plaintiff in a medical malpractice case must prove that the doctor, or other defendant(s), owed the patient a duty of reasonable care, that the doctor breached that duty by acting negligently, and that that negligence caused the patient's injuries. In the present case, as in most other medical malpractice claims, the parties dispute neither that the doctor owed the patient a duty to provide reasonable medical care nor that the patient suffered damages. What is at issue is whether the doctor acted carelessly and whether the patient's damages were a result of that carelessness, if any. Evidence as to both negligence and causation must be established by expert testimony (Keeton et al., 1984).

---

[2] Two of the mock jury deliberations I analyze were staged and recorded for instructional purposes by the Association of Trial Lawyers of America's National College of Advocacy. The third was created by private lawyers for use in preparing litigation strategy in a particular case.

Breach of Duty

A doctor is held to the standard of the ordinarily prudent medical practitioner; a specialist, to the standard of the ordinarily prudent practitioner in that specialty. Evidence of customary medical practice thus provides the measure by which the doctor's conduct is to be judged. Depending on the law of the jurisdiction, reasonable care may be based on a national standard or on the standard of care customary in the locality in which the doctor practices. In this failure to diagnose case, the doctor's alleged negligence consists of not referring the patient to a general surgeon for a biopsy, which would have permitted a definitive diagnosis, in a timely fashion. This would be negligent (a) if reasonable care would have required the doctor to advise the woman at the initial visit that a biopsy would be needed even if the mammogram were negative or (b) if reasonable care would have required the doctor to attempt to contact the patient after she missed the follow-up visit he recommended (at which visit, he says, he would have stressed the importance of biopsy), so that he could refer her for biopsy within a reasonable period of time.

Proper evaluation of a breast mass depends on the size, firmness, contours, and movability of the lump—the larger, harder, more irregular, and more fixed the lump is, the greater the chance of malignancy (Balon & Wehrwein, 1997; Quinlan & Ernst, 1982). Proper care also requires knowing the patient's age and her family's relevant medical history to assess factors associated with increased risk of breast cancer. The risk increases with age, with previous breast cancer, with incidence of breast cancer in close female relatives, and with nulliparity (if the patient has never given birth; American College of Obstetricians and Gynecologists, 1996). Diagnosis is neither simple nor certain. Half or more of physicians fail to detect masses as large as 1.5 cm on clinical examination (Reintgen et al., 1993; but cf. U.S. Preventive Services Task Force, 1989); studies document a wide range of false-negative rates for mammograms, reaching as high as about one-third, depending on the patients' age and other factors (Mann et al., 1983; U.S. Preventive Services Task Force, 1989); and masses detected by palpation may not be detected by mammogram and vice versa (Reintgen et al., 1993).

Recommendations regarding the initial evaluation of a breast mass vary, and as medical technology progresses, making available new diagnostic methods in addition to mammograms (for instance, ultrasound and needle biopsy), the standard of reasonable care in diagnosis also varies. Experts do recommend prompt biopsy of any suspicious mass (Balon & Wehrwein, 1997; Quinlan & Ernst, 1982). The biopsy need not be done immediately but should be done within a reasonable period of time.

The doctor in this case, as noted, argues that it is the patient's fault that a biopsy was not done promptly because the patient did not return to his office after the initial visit as he had recommended. If, however, the doctor was at least partly responsible for the patient's failure to return, then he would still be negligent for the delay in diagnosis. With regard to communications with a patient after the initial visit, many experts strongly recommend that the doctor's office notify a patient who does not return for recommended follow-up visit (Cohn, 1991; Dewar & Love, 1992; Osuch & Bonham, 1994). It is unclear whether most physicians conform to this standard, however, and the spate of recommendations that doctors do so may even indicate that some substantial number do not.[3] Thus, although the standard of the ideal practitioner is clear, that of the ordinary one is less so. In addition, there do not appear to be any formal rules of medical practice that conclusively establish notification as a component of ordinarily reasonable medical care.[4]

Causation

For the medical malpractice plaintiff to recover damages, the doctor's negligence, if any, must also have been a legal cause of the patient's injuries. Like the question of negligence in most medical malpractice cases, whether any delay in diagnosis attributable to the doctor actually caused the patient's injuries would be a matter of controverted expert testimony. In most other contexts, the defendant would not be liable unless the plaintiff can prove that the defendant's negligence was a "but for" cause of the plaintiff's injuries; that is, that had it not been for the negligence, the plaintiff probably would have avoided those injuries. In the context of medical care, however, another rule has been adopted in one version or another in many jurisdictions: the *loss of chance* rule (*Herskovits v. Group Health Cooperative*, 1983). One version of the loss of chance rule allows the estate of a victim of medical malpractice to recover full damages resulting from the premature death if the physician's negligence decreased the victim's chance of survival by a "substantial" amount, even if the victim more likely than not would not have survived anyway (the *full-damages* approach). In a second version of the loss of chance rule, the victim recovers only that proportion of damages represented by the percentage decrease in chance of recovery attributable to the doctor's negligence. Thus, the estate of a patient whose chance of survival was reduced from 30% to 10% as a result of the doctor's

---

[3] One study indicates that patients attribute delay in breast cancer diagnosis to themselves instead of or in addition to the health care provider in about 40% of cases (Caplan, Helzlsouer, Shapiro, Wesley, & Edwards, 1996), but it is not clear how many of these delays between initial visit and diagnosis are due to missed appointments (nor in how many of those the doctor's office made some attempt to contact the patient) as opposed to appointments postponed or simply not scheduled until later.

[4] There is, however, some suggestion that failing to follow up after the patient fails to keep appointments is a departure from accepted medical practice in this context (*Lyons v. McCauley*, 1998).

negligence could recover 20% of the total wrongful death damages (the *proportional valuation* approach; Aagard, 1998; King, 1981).[5]

In the typical delay in diagnosis of breast cancer case, the plaintiff argues that had the physician diagnosed the cancer in a timely fashion, the patient could have begun treatment at an earlier stage of the disease, at which the patient would have had a greater chance of surviving the illness. The standard method for staging or classifying breast cancers is the TNM system, which takes into account characteristics of the tumor (T), lymph node involvement (N), and metastases to other parts of the body (M). Patients diagnosed with Stage I breast cancer have a 5-year survival rate of 90% and a 10-year survival rate of 76%; Stage II, 68% and 58%; Stage III, 52% and 37%; and Stage IV, 10% and 5% (Balon & Wehrwein, 1997).

There is considerable medical evidence that early diagnosis of breast cancer in general increases the chance of disease-free survival (measured as survival without symptoms for 5 or 10 years) among certain age groups (U.S. Preventive Services Task Force, 1989) and that delay in diagnosis may be correlated with survival rate (E. Robinson, Mohilever, Zidan, & Sapir, 1984). Others have reported no such correlation (Dennis, Gardner, & Lim, 1975; Kern, 1992).[6]

The defendant physician often argues that any delay in diagnosis made no difference to the patient's medical outcome. On average, cancer is not detectable until about 8 years after the first cancer cell appears in the woman's breast (Plotkin & Blankenberg, 1991). Given the rate at which cancer cells proliferate, known as *doubling time* (the estimated number of days it takes for the number of cancer cells to double), and extrapolating backward from the size of the tumor at diagnosis, the doctor argues that the cancer had already metastasized by the time it was first clinically detectable (Stone, 1998). There was, that is, a "negative cancer control window" (Steyskal, 1996): The disease could not have been detected in time to do anything about it, so any delay in diagnosis is irrelevant (Plotkin & Blankenberg, 1991; Reintgen et al., 1993; Spratt, von Fournier, Spratt, & Weber, 1993). In general, it is the predetermined biology of the tumor —"the natural history and biologic variability" (Reintgen et al., 1993, p. 105) of the disease—rather than the diagnosis or care given that is the most important determinant of chance of survival.

The doubling time defense, however, is based on assumptions about the constancy of the rate of cancer growth and the composition of the

---

[5] A third approach, *discretionary valuation*, simply leaves the damage award to the discretion of the trier of fact (Aagard, 1998).
[6] Various biases may enter into the evaluation of data purporting to show the benefits of early diagnosis. One such bias is the *lead time bias*: Periodic screening detects some cancers that have already metastasized at an earlier stage of disease; the patient survives longer *from the point of diagnosis* (hence, researchers may report increased survival rates) but eventually dies from systemic breast cancer at the same time as a patient diagnosed later (Watts, 1990).

tumor through time that may not be accurate (Citron, 1991). Indeed, tumor growth rates are not constant through the course of the disease and vary greatly from one individual to another (Spratt et al., 1993). In sum, whether any delay in diagnosis attributable to the doctor actually caused the patient to lose a legally compensable chance of survival is often a hotly contested question.

JURORS' PRIOR BELIEFS ABOUT PHYSICIAN RESPONSIBILITY

Jurors, as we have seen in previous chapters, bring to the accident case many diverse habits of thought and feeling that they will use to assign blame. They also bring with them particular beliefs about the world that they deem relevant to the subject matter of the case at hand. Manzo (1994) showed how actual jurors rely on their everyday experience to support the positions they take during deliberations. The mock jurors studied in this chapter also draw extensively on their knowledge of how things are supposed to go and how people are supposed to behave. In the first mock jury, for instance, participants devote nearly one quarter of their utterances during deliberations to their "world knowledge" as opposed to, say, the facts in evidence.[7] Learning what jurors think they know about medical care in general and breast cancer in particular is thus crucial to understanding how they determine the responsibility of the doctor and the patient in this case.

The mock jurors studied in this chapter are fairly knowledgeable about some aspects of breast cancer and its treatment. They know, for instance, that the doctor should take a medical history, including how long the woman has had any palpable breast lump and whether other close relatives have had breast cancer, because the answers are relevant to the likelihood that the patient's lump is malignant and hence to the choice of the appropriate initial workup and treatment (2.28.8-14 [D, middle-aged White man][8]; 2.44.11-17 [Li, young White woman, college student]). They

_____

[7] One hundred out of a total of 408 utterances, or 24.5%. The next largest categories of utterances in this mock jury consist of discussions of whether the parties were negligent (20.1%), assertions of verdict preferences (i.e., statements that a party was negligent or apportionments of fault; 14.7%), and statements about the evidence (13.2%). (The 408 utterances are those made during the course of the mock jury's "unguided" deliberations, the phase of the simulation that most resembles the deliberations of actual juries, as opposed to the earlier, question-and-discussion phase.) The relatively small percentage of utterances about the facts of the case (compared with, say, Hastie et al., 1983, whose mock juries devoted more than half of their utterances to the trial evidence) may be due to the highly simplified presentation of the facts and to the participants' opportunity to ask questions about the facts before the unguided deliberations commenced.

[8] Citations to transcripts of the mock jury deliberations are as follows: case number.page(s).line(s) (juror). So "2.28.8-14 (D)" refers to the second (of three) mock jury transcripts studied, transcript portion beginning on page 28, line 8 and continuing to page 28, line 14, juror identified as "D." Each juror is identified only by first initial (or, where necessary to distinguish between jurors, first initial and next letter of first name) to ensure confidentiality. Where the juror is identified in the text immediately preceding or where the

know that mammography is a standard diagnostic procedure but that a negative mammogram does not necessarily mean a clean bill of health, and that a suspicious mass should be biopsied (e.g., 1.9.4-12 [B, older White woman, homemaker]; 1.11.17-21 [Ma, older White woman, homemaker]).[9] They also know, as we see later, something about the symptoms and course of the disease.

Jurors also bring to their consideration of the breast cancer case at least two case-specific prior beliefs that are grounded in or at least partly conform to medicolegal fact, and yet which, if relied on too heavily, may lead their judgments to diverge from those of medicolegal experts. One is a prototype of the doctor as someone who cares personally, and not just professionally, about his or her patients. The second is what I call the *size-of-the-lump heuristic*: the belief that the size of a patient's breast mass is correlated with the seriousness of the disease, and thus should guide judgments about both the physician's responsibility to diagnose and treat the disease appropriately and the patient's responsibility to look out for her own well-being. Both of these preconceptions are sensible, and each will often guide jurors to decisions that medicolegal experts would regard as correct. Like other common-sense beliefs, however, they may also lead jurors astray—all the more so to the extent that jurors believe that they are pretty knowledgeable about breast cancer and its proper treatment. Specifically, these two beliefs, together with some of the intuitive habits of thought discussed in earlier chapters, make jurors readier to find fault with the doctor than medical and legal experts would find appropriate, and readier to downplay the requirement of causation and to hold the blameworthy doctor responsible for the patient's bad outcome.

"Doctors Should Care Personally About Their Patients"

What do people think in general about doctors, and in particular, about those engaged in general family practice? Unsurprisingly, people expect general practitioners to be qualified, competent (1.6.24-7.3 [S, middle-aged White man, accountant]), and knowledgeable (1.5.8-9 [J, middle-aged White woman, bookkeeper and part-time college student]). People also expect them to be honest (1.5.8 [JJ]; 1.5.25 [K, middle-aged White man, works for county services for the aged, graduate student]).[10]

---

reference is to the remarks of the lawyers or others managing the mock jury deliberations, no initial is specified. Demographic information about the mock juror, where available, is provided the first time that juror is mentioned.

[9] One juror also knows that "the older you get, probably, there are more chances of problems" (1.9.1–2 [B]), which is true in general, although underestimating younger women's breast cancer risk is a documented mistake of some physicians (e.g., Kern, 1992).

[10] Mock jurors' questions about the doctor in this case suggest other beliefs that may or may not be legally relevant to their decision. For instance, they want to know how long the doctor has been in practice (1.28.25, 29.16 [Mi]; 3.26.16 [Je]), the scope of his practice (1.30.23-31.6 [K]), and specifically, his past experience with breast cancer and breast tumors (1.30.12-13 [JJ]).

Most important, people expect doctors *to care personally* about their patients (1.5.14-15 [J]). There are a number of ways in which doctors show that they care about their patients. One is that "[t]hey take time with you, listen to what you have to say; [you] ask questions, your doctor answers; he asks questions, you answer to the best of you[r] ability" (1.7.6-8 [Ma]). Patients expect their doctors to pay attention to them: "I want him to listen to me" (1.6.18-23 [A, older White woman, helped recently deceased husband in business, volunteer elementary school teacher]). They also expect their doctors to empathize with them, to understand their fear about the prospect of a diagnosis of cancer (1.12.2-5 [J]).[11] Conversely, if a doctor has too many patients, that suggests that his basic interest is not with the patients and that he is not attending to them as he should (1.49.17-19 [J]; 3.28.1-14 [Jo, older White man, retired air traffic controller]). If the doctor has so many patients that, according to the doctor, he must depend on the patients to be responsible in following up, "[t]hen maybe he better cut his load back . . . where he can care about each patient" (1.38.3-8 [J]; see also 3.27.9-28.21 [Jo]).

This prototype of the doctor as attentive companion is indicated still more explicitly by the juror who says that a general practitioner should "be your friend as well as a physician" (1.7.8-9 [Ma]). As in an ideal friendship, it is a good thing when the patient feels comfortable with her doctor (1.7.15-19 [Be, older White woman, homemaker]); mistrust of doctors, by contrast, may lead patients to forgo needed treatment (1.27.5-16 [J]). And just as one might expect a friend to go out of his or her way, even to his or her own disadvantage, to provide help, so some jurors believe that a caring physician should help a patient whose concerns about expenses lead the patient not to seek recommended treatment to get in touch with providers of free medical treatment (1.49.12-18 [A]), or even that the caring doctor should provide services for free, on a *pro bono* basis, if the patient cannot afford treatment (1.59.4-5 [J], 1.59.6, 62.8-9 [K]).

In the image of the doctor as caring is grounded another set of expectations: that the doctor should communicate to the patient everything the patient needs to know. For example, the doctor can show that he cares by *personally following up* with the patient (2.3.14-18 [E, young White man, college student]), including calling the patient with test results himself instead of having his receptionist do it (1.22.16-20, 38.12-17 [J]; 1.22,

---

Presumably these jurors are prepared to reason that the less experience he has had in general and with breast cancer in particular, the more readily he should have sought outside help in this case. Some participants want to know where the doctor went to medical school and where he did his residency (3.29.12-22 [S]), facts which would seem to be of questionable legal relevance, although laypeople might take them as diagnostic of whether the doctor exercised reasonable care in this case. Then one juror remarks that "if his father was a doctor it gave him more incentive to become one, you know, and possibly of being better than his father" (1.30.8-10 [Mi]), a speculation whose significance is obscure.

[11] This preference for empathy has been confirmed in quantitative research (Roberts, Cox, Reintgen, Baile, & Gibertini, 1994).

7-11 [A]; 2.3.24-4.2, 2.48.12-14, 16-18 [Le, older Black woman]). "It would be preferred to have your doctor sit with you," especially if the test results indicate a serious concern (3.10.8-9 [De, middle-aged White woman, corporate meeting planner]). The doctor should also put the patient's mind at ease by obtaining test results as quickly as possible (1.12.1-13 [JJ]).

The expectation that the doctor will give the patient "full and accurate information" (2.2.19-20 [Li]) may not be entirely consistent with the prototype of doctor-as-friend. First, friends are presumptively equals (at least in their friendship), whereas the expectation that the doctor will communicate fully is also grounded in the perception that the doctor's superior knowledge and professional expertise obligates the doctor to communicate what she or he knows and justifies the patient in depending on the doctor for that knowledge. "We put our lives in their . . . care" (3.83.6-7 [De]). "I depend on [the doctor] to look out for me" (1.9.19-25 [A]; 3.83.1-3 [An, older White woman, teacher's assistant]).[12] And if the doctor, by talking to the patient and listening attentively as he or she should, realizes that the patient does not know much about her health, then "he should help her and guide her, that's what he's for" (1.52.14-20 [A]). Moreover, the doctor's otherwise laudable concern for the patient's emotional state is no excuse not to communicate needed information (2.27.20-25, 28.5-7, 84.18-20 [Li]; 2.86.8-13 [Jo]; 2.86.21-87.6 [O, older White woman]).

Jurors also believe that a doctor who cares should accept personal responsibility if he or she does not manage the patient's condition as she or he should have. Many are outraged when a doctor whom they believe to have been at least partly responsible for a delay in diagnosis attempts to shift the blame to the patient (3.82.15 [R, older White woman, accountant]); 3.82.17 [K, middle-aged White man, sales supervisor for state lottery]; 3.82.19 [Jo]). "[I]t's unconscionable . . . just unheard of" (3.82.20, 83.8 [De]).[13] One juror links the expectation that the doctor will accept responsibility to the ethic of caring: "Does he feel any responsibility that he didn't urge her to come back? Or give her a call personally?" (1.32.4-5 [A]).

Jurors are, however, well aware that real medical care does not always match their ideal. "[D]octors aren't perfect" (1.6.1 [K]; 1.7.24, 8.7 [Mi, young White man, account manager for credit card company]). And doc-

---

[12] Turning this thinking around, one mock juror (who initially attributed 65% of the fault to the patient) in the second group reasons: "Like if you say [that fault should be divided between the patient and doctor] 50–50, you're sort of saying she is not her own person anymore . . . she's sort of like running her life according on the word of God-slash-doctor. And you know she's not that. She's a human being who is—who is an adult, at middle age, so I think she should be more responsible for herself" (2.52.23-54.6 [Ji, young Asian woman]).
[13] On the other hand, one juror believes that a doctor who tries to shift the blame to the patient in these circumstances is probably just following his lawyer's advice, and would not hold it against him (3.84.11-85.12 [Sh, middle-aged White woman]).

tors are busy (1.56.17-18 [Ma]). "They get so wrapped up they go boom boom boom, see everybody, tell them this, that, and the other thing ... boom, out the door. And I mean it's not the way it should be but that's the way it is" (2.17.21-24 [O]).[14] So while "physicians should really make every effort to communicate explicitly what patients need to do" (2.43.4-5 [Jo]), the norm is that most of them sometimes do not (2.43.7-12 [Jo]). Indeed, because the patient ought to realize that doctors are busy, it is also the patient's responsibility to see to it that she obtains any test results (1.56.16-23 [Ma]).

This expectation that doctors should care deeply about their patients derives from at least two sources. One, of course, are the jurors' own experiences, as they construe them (e.g., 1.7.14-15 [Be]; 1.9.15-19 [A]; 1.38.11-17 [JJ]).[15] Manzo (1993, 1994) showed how jurors in actual deliberations bring narratives of their personal experience to bear in forming judgments about the parties' behavior. Another source may very well be the image of doctors portrayed on prime-time television. The doctor on the popular televised melodrama is someone who takes a deep personal interest in the patient and spends all the time necessary to see the patient through his or her troubles, personal as well as medical (Turow, 1989; Wober & Gunter, 1988).[16] Although empirical research on this specific point is lacking, it is certainly conceivable that televised depictions of doctors as intimately concerned with and caring for their patients' personal as well as medical problems provide viewers with *personal scripts* that define their expectations about how medical care "ought to go" (Janis, 1980).

The Size-of-the-Lump Heuristic

Mock jurors believe that the size of a breast mass dictates the appropriate level of concern and action. They recognize that the size of this patient's lump on initial presentation to the doctor—10 cm by 2 cm—is

---

[14] Interestingly, some jurors contrast their perceptions of the state of medical care in general, and their dissatisfaction with HMOs in particular, with their personal satisfaction with their own doctors (1.10.4-5 [A]; 1.38.11-17 [JJ]) ("I think I just must be very, very lucky"). This may be comparable with the effect of media on risk judgments: Media coverage of an issue affects people's judgments about the societal importance of the risk ("crime is a major public problem") but less so their judgments about their personal susceptibility to that same risk ("I don't feel any less safe"; Tyler & Cook, 1984).
[15] A recent survey of patients' levels of satisfaction with hospital care indicated that patients rate hospitals on such bases as how adequately the hospitals address their emotional needs and whether care was coordinated and continuous, in contrast with other studies that rank hospitals on the basis of "objective" criteria such as rates of mortality or other outcomes for the treatment of particular ailments (see Kassirer, 1999).
[16] For instance, in the epitome of the televised doctor program, *Marcus Welby, M.D.*, "[doctors'] attendance to medical problems included spending much time counseling [patients] and their family, driving them to the hospital, adjusting their oxygen, sitting with them through the night, and standing by in the operating room while the surgeon did his thing. Beyond these duties, the doctors found time to take patients to ball games, serve them elaborate dinners, stop by their workplaces, and attend their weddings" (Turow, 1989, p. 129).

"pretty big" and a "pretty serious" matter (1.14.2—15.3 [J, A, K, S]). "Rush her to the hospital for the tests" (1.14.18 [S]). They think that a lump of that size is sufficiently suspicious that even after the blood tests and mammogram come back negative, the patient should not be satisfied, and should go for a second opinion (1.18.4-9 [S], 1.19.18-19 [Ma]), biopsy (1.19.1-4 [Be]), or even a lumpectomy (1.18.20-25 [J]).

Later in their deliberations, the first mock jury tries to grasp the significance of the size of the patient's lump:

> Mi: Size is an issue, though.
> A: A lump that size—
> S: Ten centimeters is about that much, two centimeters is almost an inch, about like that—
> J: OK, so it was two this way and wide—
> A: You would, you would feel that—
> Mi: It's about the size of a kosher pickle.
> K: It is, it is like a kosher pickle, I don't know how you can miss a pickle, I mean—
> A: Especially when you take a shower and you're washing you would feel it—
> . . .
> J: Well, it depends how big her breast is.
> B: Well, that's another thing, we don't know what size of woman she was.
> A: I mean we don't miss something that large no matter how large your breast is. (1.47.1-13, 20-24)

The mock jurors then continue to stress the size of the lump as an important factor in judging whether the doctor breached his duty of care by not doing more to impress on the patient the need for biopsy. One juror's (J) remarks capture the group's sense:

> I think that should have been a major concern with that size of a lump, and, you know, I think if biopsy is something he does when they come back, if she called the receptionist, . . . when the receptionist told him that she had called in he should have called her and said, you know, my normal practice is to have a biopsy, I think you should have this done. I think he should have communicated to her about a biopsy.
> . . .
> We're all saying, hey, something that size is something to worry about. Why wasn't he saying that? We are not doctors, we are not educated like doctors, and yet we would, every one of us in this room be concerned about a lump that size. . . . With a lump that big, why didn't he call and say, hey you know, I would still—I would still, you know, suggest you have a biopsy.
> . . . .
> I would have, as the doctor, said, "Oh my gosh, this is huge," you

know, "let's get some help," you know. (1.36.2-9; 1.48.13-16, 20-22; 1.59.13-14)[17]

Jurors are correct to recognize the seriousness of a breast lump of this size. A tumor that large indicates that cancer has progressed to at least Stage IIB regardless of other symptoms (Balon & Wehrwein, 1997). The jurors' belief that the size of the lump in itself was sufficient to demand more aggressive action by the doctor is consistent with sound medical practice. Yet the importance that jurors place on the size of the lump *oversimplifies* the nature of breast cancer and its proper diagnosis. Lymph node status, not tumor size, is the most important predictor of 5-year survival rate (Reintgen et al., 1993). Indeed, sufficient lymph node involvement indicates Stage III cancer *regardless* of tumor size, and any distant metastasis indicates Stage IV cancer regardless of any other features, including tumor size (Balon & Wehrwein, 1997). Considerable research shows no correlation among diagnostic delay, increase in tumor size, and chance of survival (Dennis et al., 1975; Kern, 1992; Reintgen et al., 1993).

True, these jurors appreciate that the size of the lump is not the only factor relevant to diagnosis and prognosis. Their inquiries into whether the patient or others in her family had a history of breast cancer (1.20.9–16 [Mi]) show some awareness of the fact that a positive family history is one of the most significant breast cancer risk factors (Quinlan & Ernst, 1982).[18] And at least one of the jurors concerned to know how long the woman had had the lump before the initial visit—"If she's known about [the lump] for a while and kind of hesitated, it could be further along that anything could be done to treat it" (1.13.3-5 [K])—may understand that the persistence of the lump is relevant to diagnosis (Quinlan & Ernst, 1982).

[17] See also 1.60.20-22 (J): "[H]e knows how serious a lump that size is, and it wasn't an open sore when she first went in to him." Another juror says: "[H]e'd know, he'd know that she didn't come in and he would know that there is a large lump there that he's dealing with and I, I think he should have followed up on her no matter what. . . . 'Cause I think if I was a doctor and I saw a lump that big I'd, I'd want to do what I could for her no matter what the situation was rather than just say 'come back in a week, and we'll see what happens with your test'" (1.37.20-23; 1.59.6-9 [K]). Still another remarks: "[B]ut if it is that big, then now, the question is the doctor, you know, I would think the doctor would think that is very serious. You know, that size" (1.48.3-5 [S]). And another, on the second mock jury: "She has a sizable lump at this point with an inconclusive test at that initial point. And that's something that neither side can get around or should try to get around, I don't think. But the reality is that he didn't really push the issue at that point" (2.27.11-15 [D]).

[18] Several mock jurors believe that if the patient had a family history of breast cancer, then *both* the patient and the doctor should have acted more aggressively (1.20.9-23 [Mi, others]). In the second mock jury in particular, several participants believe that the doctor should have been more concerned and proactive given the family history (2.28.8-14 [D]; 2.44.11-17 [Li]), although a few jurors put the onus on the patient to follow through because she may have had a family history of breast cancer (2.43.22-44.2, 21-23 [T]; 2.47.3-4 [D]).

Jurors also ask other questions about the patient's personal health history but do so for what seem to be medicolegally irrelevant reasons. For instance, one mock juror asks whether the patient "drinks or takes drugs" (1.15.17 [A]), but apparently not because the juror knows that drinking significant amounts of alcohol increases the risk of breast cancer (Longnecker, Berlin, Orza, & Chalmers, 1988).

There are, however, some medically relevant facts about the lump that the mock jurors do not seem to care about. For example, concerning the doctor's palpating the lump at the initial visit, jurors are not told, and do not ask, how firm the lump was, whether it was movable or fixed, or whether its contours were distinct or not, all of which are relevant diagnostic factors (Quinlan & Ernst, 1982). Indeed, the striking image of the lump as a "kosher pickle," offered by one mock juror and seized on by others, may lead jurors to think that the lump, like a pickle in a jar, was relatively firm, with distinct contours—characteristics associated with a worse diagnosis.[19] In sum, these jurors may fail to appreciate the difficulties of correctly diagnosing breast cancer in some cases.[20]

This simplification of breast cancer symptomatology to tumor size derives from a common cultural model of breast cancer as signified by palpable lumps and/or discoloration of the breast (Benyamini, Leventhal, & Leventhal, 1997). Certainly a lump may be more salient than other symptoms, such as lymph node involvement, that are actually better predictors of the patient's chances of survival. The vivid imagery of the kosher pickle makes an impression on jurors' common-sense reasoning in a way that diagrams of lymph nodes and graphs representing tumor doubling times are unlikely to match.

Jurors then combine this size-of-the-lump notion with the representativeness heuristic (see chapter 2). Reasoning by representativeness probably accounts for the widespread overestimate of the likelihood that a lump is malignant: If cancer is signified by a lump, then a lump means cancer. In fact, only 10%–15% of breast masses are malignant (S. Schwartz, 1994). Representativeness also explains the next step in the reasoning of the mock jurors observed here: If a lump equals cancer, then the larger the lump, the worse the cancer.

REASONING FROM PRIOR BELIEFS TO JUDGMENTS OF THE PHYSICIAN'S RESPONSIBILITY

Let us explore how these prior beliefs about medical care and breast cancer, together with some of the more general habits of thought discussed in chapter 2, may make jurors somewhat readier to find fault with the doctor than medicolegal expertise would dictate—and, having found fault, some-

---

[19] The vivid image of the lump as a pickle may thus provide not only a "psychological anchor" (Vinson, 1982) for individual jurors' thinking about the case, but also a kind of "deliberative anchor," a common ground on which different jurors can reason toward consensus (cf. Ruscher et al., 1996).

[20] This may be due in part to expectations derived from the depiction of medical care on prime-time television, in which diagnoses are "usually quick and easy" (Wober & Gunter, 1988, p. 187), as well as to simplifying heuristics such as the size of the lump.

what readier to elide the causation requirement and blame the doctor for the patient's bad outcome.

Finding the Doctor Negligent

> S (foreperson): Now I think from the feeling I get in here is, and I personally do feel like [the doctor] didn't do all that he should have. OK? Um, so do we feel as a group that the doctor was negligent at least to some degree?
> Be (and others): Yes, I think so.
> K: I think he should have referred her the first day—
> (Several): Yes, right.
> K: And not wait . . .
> J: Especially not something like that.
> (Several): I agree with that, too (1.51.6-15).[21]

All of the participants in all three mock juries agreed that the doctor was negligent. But why? In the excerpt above, several mock jurors in the first group focus on the doctor's failure to refer the patient for biopsy at the initial visit. Presumably, although it is not clear from their remarks, they do not expect the doctor to have done this before the mammogram results were received from the radiologist. More important, this supposedly negligent omission ought not to be viewed in isolation from the doctor's failure to attempt to contact the patient to urge her to return promptly for a second visit. If the doctor's version of the facts is believed, it was his standard practice to recommend biopsy at the return visit, and he would have done so here (1.36.21-37.2); hence, his failure to do so earlier ("the first day") would have been responsible at most for a medically insignificant delay of one week.[22]

It is at this point in the story that the prototype of the doctor as caring may have affected the jurors' judgments. How caring the patient perceives the doctor to be ought in itself to be legally irrelevant to whether the doctor has conformed to the standard of the reasonably careful practitioner. This expectation may, however, lead jurors to find the doctor at fault in at least two ways that may be inconsistent with the relevant law. First, if jurors perceive the doctor to have deviated from the norm of caring, they may be more willing to blame him for any bad outcome, even if his conduct actually conformed to the operative legal standard of the ordinarily prudent practitioner. Second, jurors who believe that the ideal of caring requires the doctor to communicate to the patient every bit of information

---

[21] See also 1.59.10-18, 1.60.16-24 (J): The doctor should have referred the woman to a specialist.
[22] The plaintiff could argue, however, that the doctor should have foreseen that some percentage of patients would not return as recommended unless he told them at the initial visit that a biopsy would be necessary even if the mammogram were negative. (I thank my colleague Sheila Taub for this observation.)

that, in hindsight, turns out to have been relevant, may hold the doctor to a higher standard than that of the ordinarily prudent practitioner. (The latter inference may be tempered or offset, as we see later, to the extent that jurors believe that the patient herself is responsible for seeking out information that the doctor does not provide on his own.)

I cannot prove that mock jurors' prototype of the caring doctor affected their decision making in this case. And even if it did, it may have led to judgments about the doctor's responsibilities that are largely congruent with the law of medical malpractice. Caring or not, a physician certainly has an obligation to provide the patient with sufficient information about the risks and benefits of possible treatment so that the patient can give her *informed consent* to a course of treatment (Keeton et al., 1984).[23] And, as described earlier, most experts recommend that physicians contact a patient who does not show up for a scheduled follow-up visit. Some of the mock jurors who find the doctor careless for not doing this do not refer to or even imply the prototype of the caring doctor.[24]

The deliberations do, however, suggest that the prototype of the deeply caring physician may have influenced some mock jurors to conclude that the doctor in this case was negligent. Three mock jurors find the doctor to blame for not *personally* calling her back with the test results (1.21.23-22.17 [J, A]; 2.3.15-19 [E]), even though this does not appear to be required by the standard of ordinarily prudent medical care. "He should have called her himself and spoke with her, and not left it to the receptionist or nurse or whoever" (2.4.1-2 [Le]).[25] One mock juror explicitly grounds this in the ethic of caring, not in purely professional obligation: "It shows the caring, I mean when the doctor takes the time to call and tell you . . . , that's—that caring, that professional friendship caring, to take the time to call and give you your results" (1.22.13-16 [J]). Had the doctor personally called or answered the patient's inquiry about the test results, he could in that same phone call have made clearer to the patient the need to biopsy the lump (1.32.10-12, 36.6-9 [J]). Another juror couches the doctor's omission in the context of companionate conversation: "I would want to know why he didn't have her come back. . . . 'Come in and let's talk about it'" (1.31.14-17 [A]). For these people, the doctor's legal

---

[23] For instance, several participants on the second mock jury, presented with slightly different facts than were the first group of mock jurors, fault the doctor for communicating to the patient (through the receptionist) that her test results were "normal" or "negative," when those results, given the size of the woman's breast and her family history, should have been reported as "inconclusive" (2.10.15-14.6 [several jurors]; 2.21.5-14 [Li, O, Le]).

[24] One thinks that the doctor "probably should have followed up on her anyway, saying why didn't you come back?" (1.21.18-22 [K]), especially given the size of the lump (1.37.21-23, 39.5-8 [K]). Another believes that "there should have been some second response" but not necessarily by the doctor himself (1.39.9-18 [S]); and yet another mentions that her doctor's office always calls her if she misses an appointment (2.16.14-20 [T, young Black woman]).

[25] The same mock juror adds: "I think he should have been talking to her individually, himself, . . . not in the beginning, I mean after the, the test he should have spoken to her himself, and said, this is serious and I want you to follow it up" (2.48.12-18 [Le]).

obligations seem to be bound up with the expectation, in itself legally immaterial, that the doctor take a personal interest in the patient.[26]

The size-of-the-lump heuristic may also have helped the mock jurors to find the doctor negligent. Although most women who have breast cancer have breast masses, only a small fraction of those with breast masses have cancer (Quinlan & Ernst, 1982).[27] Yet, as noted above, because laypeople perceive a breast lump to be the "signature" of cancer, they may misread the latter, relevant probability (what is the likelihood that a woman presenting with a lump has cancer?) as the former (what is the likelihood that a woman with breast cancer has a lump?), and thereby overestimate the probability that a woman with a lump has cancer (S. Schwartz, 1994).[28] And the larger the lump, the more representative of the disease the woman's symptoms are perceived to be. The last step in the chain of reasoning is a straightforward application of the Learned Hand calculus of risk (see chapter 1): The greater the perceived likelihood of cancer, the more careless the doctor was for not evaluating and managing the patient's condition more aggressively.

Even to the extent that these case-specific beliefs lead the mock jurors to judgments that conform to medicolegal expertise, two other habits of thought suggest that mock jurors may be too ready to find the doctor negligent. The foreperson of the first mock jury asks about the doctor: "Did he do all that he could have done?" (1.52.12 [S]). Inadvertently, this juror thus conflates *should* have with *could* have: If the doctor could have acted otherwise, then he should have. This, as we recall from chapter 2, exemplifies norm theory at work. Having identified some behavior that could have been otherwise, observers are ready to find that the actor should have done otherwise, and that he is legally responsible for not doing so.

The foreperson also asks: "[D]id [the doctor] do enough to prove himself not negligent, you know, at all? . . . [Did he do all that he] should have done professionally to warrant not being negligent . . . ?" (1.48.9-10, 52.12-13 [S]). Again inadvertently, he seems to *shift the burden of proof* on the issue of the defendant's negligence from the patient to the doctor. This way of thinking, too, makes it easier for jurors to find the doctor legally responsible for the patient's bad outcome.

---

[26] Still another mock juror posits that if the doctor "was always so concerned about every little facet of her emotional well being, I think he would have given her a call" (2.28.5-7 [Li]). The juror says this to support her refusal to credit the doctor's rationalization for not disclosing more information to the patient (that the doctor was trying to be sensitive to the patient's fear), but she might also draw from the proposition that "a caring doctor calls" the inference that "a doctor who doesn't call doesn't care (enough)," which might make her readier to find the doctor's conduct deviant and hence to find the doctor responsible for the delay in diagnosis.

[27] Quinlan and Ernst (1982) reported a malignancy rate of 20% to 30% of masses diagnosed as cystosarcoma and 5% to 10% of masses associated with fibrocystic disease.

[28] S. Schwartz (1994) noted that physicians as well as laypeople make this error.

Assuming That the Doctor's Negligence Caused Harm

Mock jurors, like real ones, are instructed to consider causation as a distinct element of the case (e.g., 1.42.13-19; 2.7.22-25, 2.24.5-7 [special verdict question given to second mock jury, specifying recovery for loss of substantial chance of survival]). Yet it is quite striking how participants in the first mock jury whisk through the causation requirement:

> J: . . . I mean, his expert says, she would have died anyway. Her expert says she might not have. But my opinion is you don't know whether she would have lived or not, but he took her chances away by not acting on that lump, the size that it was, and finding out for sure, he took any chance she did have of living to five years, ten years, whatever, he took that away from her.
> Be: That's true.
> K: Yeah.
> . . .
> S: . . . The second part of that question was, is, did it cause damage to her?
> (Several jurors): Yes.
> (Someone): It cut her chances down.
> S: It cut her chances down.
> . . .
> S: But do we all feel that there was some damage done. That whatever his failure to act or do more did cause her, like, some, maybe take her chance away?
> J: Take away from the children . . . (1.49.3-11, 51.16-20, 52.1-4)

This constitutes almost the entirety of the first group's talk about whether the doctor's negligence caused the patient harm. The brevity of their discussion is one indication that they do not seriously consider the possibility that any delay in diagnosis for which the doctor is responsible may not have harmed the patient. Perhaps these mock jurors deliberated as they did because they were not provided with enough information to feed a more thorough discussion. They were not given detailed simulations of expert testimony, for example, a doubling time defense and plaintiff's response to that defense (Citron, 1991), but were merely told that experts with equivalent credentials had testified, respectively, that the patient more likely than not would or would not have survived with timely diagnosis and treatment (1.40.21-41.17).[29]

---

[29] Some research indicates that more realistically complex causation testimony may not have increased jurors' comprehension of the issue. Sanders (1998) reported that jurors in Bendectin cases, faced with an array of complicated causation evidence, tended to resort to simple judgmental heuristics such as "an equal number of experts on each side means the evidence is balanced," which was plainly incorrect as a matter of science—the overwhelming scientific view is that Bendectin did not cause the birth defects claimed by the plaintiffs in these cases. Cooper, Bennett, and Sukel (1996) showed experimentally that the more complex the expert

But in that case, why does the first group of mock jurors opt for the conclusion that the doctor's negligence *did* cause harm? One possibility is that their judgments are being driven by *norm theory*. One belief about breast cancer often commented on in the medicolegal literature is the popular assumption that "early diagnosis equals, at least, a possible cure" (Mueller, 1994; Ryan, 1998) and, therefore, that any delay in diagnosis followed by a bad outcome means that the patient has been deprived of cure or at least a chance of survival.[30] If jurors believe that breast cancer can be cured if it is detected soon enough, then the outcome that disappoints expectations (patient dies) may be traced to the antecedent event that stands out as deviant—the failure to detect the disease soon enough. Thus, "if only the doctor had done more to identify the disease, the patient would have survived." *Culpable causation* points toward the same act or omission as the cause (as it does in some of the case studies discussed in earlier chapters). The more strongly jurors believe that a caring doctor would have spoken personally to the patient a week after the initial visit, the more likely they are to find that *not* calling was deviant and therefore blameworthy, and thus the more likely they are to attribute greater causal significance to the doctor's failure to urge the patient to return to his office. In any event, it appears that these mock jurors, like real jurors in the Bendectin cases (Sanders, 1998) and certain other tort cases, may be "commingling" the issues of fault and causation in such a way that a stronger plaintiff's case on the former issue may compensate for a weaker case on the latter (Nagareda, 1998).

There is yet another explanation for the mock jurors' judgments. The words excerpted above indicate that the participants in the first mock jury find sufficient causation where the delayed diagnosis resulted in the patient's losing some chance of survival. Yet these mock jurors, unlike those in the second group (to be discussed below), were *not* instructed that loss of chance would suffice; indeed, they were told the contrary: "[the doctor's] negligence has to actually cause some injury, in this case, would have prevented her death" (1.42.15-17). These jurors, in effect, are legislating a rule permitting recovery for loss of chance where the relevant law of causation does not provide for it.

Additional insight is offered by the last remark excerpted above. When the foreperson asks, "But do we all feel that . . . whatever his failure to act or do more did cause her, like, some, maybe take her chance away?,"

---

testimony on causation in a toxic tort case, the more mock jurors rely on the expert's credentials rather than the content of the testimony to determine causation. (Jurors' recourse to peripheral cues in the face of their inability to process a complex message is predicted by the elaboration likelihood model of persuasion [Petty & Cacioppo, 1986], briefly discussed in chapter 5.)

[30] Similarly, and contrary to the medical research summarized earlier, "[t]he public assumes that if, at the time of diagnosis, a tumor has metastasized to lymph nodes or systematically, a diagnostic error must have resulted in a delayed diagnosis" (Osuch & Bonham, 1994).

one juror responds: "Take away from the children ..." (1.52.1-4 [S, J]). That offhand comment suggests thinking in terms of *total justice*. The speaker seems to be taking into account the entire context of the malpractice claim, and specifically the impact of the mother's death on her children, in determining whether the defendant should be liable (cf. Goodman et al., 1989).

Whatever their reasoning processes, the decision of these mock jurors (and those of the other two groups studied) to hold the doctor responsible for a delay of 12 months or more in diagnosing the patient's breast cancer cannot be considered atypical. The average delay in lawsuits alleging delayed diagnosis of breast cancer is 10 months (median) to 15 months (mean; Kern, 1994). Plaintiffs win only about 10% of cases alleging delay in diagnosis of all kinds of cancer when the delay is 3 months or less, whereas defendants win over 60% and the remainder settle; from 4 to 6 months, plaintiffs win about 30%, defendants about 40%; beyond that point, the plaintiff win rate stays about the same whereas defendants' verdicts decrease to the 20%–35% range and settlements increase (Kern, 1994). Thus, across a variety of situations, lengthy delays in diagnosis often lead to findings of physician liability.

BLAMING THE PATIENT

In deciding legal responsibility for delay in diagnosis of breast cancer, jurors must, of course, consider not only the doctor's fault but also the patient's. Almost all of the mock jurors in the three groups studied find that the patient was careless in some respect. They think she should have done more to "follow through" (2.1.24-2.4 [M]) or "follow up" (2.4.3-5 [Le]) because "it was her body" (1.56.3 [Mi]; 2.4.20, 25 [O]; 2.42.2 [Le]), although it is not entirely clear what more she was supposed to have done: see the doctor sooner about the lump (1.15.4-9 [Mi]; 1.17.18 [A]), go for a second opinion (1.52.23-24 [Mi]),[31] return for the recommended one-week follow-up visit instead of calling in for the test results (1.21.17 [J]), or, not having done so, return sooner than she did thereafter, especially when she noticed the sore (1.24.29-20, 1.25.9 [J], 1.25.1-8 [S]).[32]

Most if not all of these perceptions of negligence on the part of the patient are consistent with what medicolegal experts might conclude. As we have seen, jurors know something about breast cancer and medical care

---

[31] Some mock jurors think that the patient should have gone for a second opinion, even though the tests were normal, because of the lump (1.18.6-14 [S]; 1.19.21-22 [Ma]; 2.4.12-16, 8.21-23, 51.23-25 [O]). On the other hand, "the majority of people are not going to seek a second opinion when you get the first opinion that ... there is nothing wrong to go forward with" (2.54.9-11 [D]).

[32] Note that, unless required to do so by special verdict or otherwise, jurors do not have to agree on the precise act of negligence, as mentioned in chapter 6.

in general, and their expectations about patient behavior, consequently, are fairly realistic. Their thinking is confused, however, in two respects. Some of them blame the patient for not going to see her doctor sooner in the first place, even though any carelessness on her part at that point in time is legally irrelevant to her loss of chance claim against the doctor for delay in diagnosis. And they ignore the extent to which the fault they assign her for not returning sooner once she noticed the sore at the site of the tumor may be *causally* irrelevant. In both respects, some of the same habits of thought that lead jurors to blame the physician too much also incline them to blame the *patient* more than they would if they fully understood the legal rules governing causation, given their own judgments of blameworthiness.

The Patient's Negligence

Mock jurors conceive their task in terms resembling the law's: to determine whether "the plaintiff has also some negligence in this because they just didn't do what you think a normal person would do under the circumstances" (1.55.15-19 [S, others]).[33] How do jurors decide what a "normal person" in this woman's position would have done? First, and unsurprisingly, they draw on what they consider to be their own relevant experiences in forming a standard by which to judge the patient's behavior:

> Mi: Which I've had a fatty cell on my body and I had to get that cut off, you know, it wasn't bad, it was just irritating once in a while. You know, I take, I got that taken care of. If I had something like a lump on my breast, which I guess guys can get too, I would get it taken care of. If I had one doctor telling me it's okay, I would follow up on that in a couple of months. (1.56.8-14)
> Ma: Well, I had an experience not too long ago with a possible cancer. And boy, I followed up on that right on top of it, because I realize that the doctor is busy, well what doctor isn't busy that's, you know, in practice and doing well? And I wanted to know. And I made an appointment to go in and get the results. From him. And that's what I did. (1.56.15-20)[34]

---

[33] None of the mock juries were provided with detailed definitions of negligence like those that would be provided to a real jury.

[34] Another juror says: "I would have had [a breast lump] removed. Benign or whatever, I would have had it removed. . . . I know that my daughter had a lump . . . at one time when she was twelve. . . . [T]hey told me my daughter's was okay too, I had it removed. There is no chance it will become cancerous if it is no longer there" (1.11.6-7, 18.20-25 [J]). And consider this exchange:

> Be: I was going to say, I have a mammogram every year, and the nurse talks to you, and you wait for the technician and they give you all this information, and it lists, and they go over it with you, the list, the sore, the lump, it tells you what to watch for, and uh—
> A: Well they probably did that to her too don't you think. (1.54.22-55.3)

The jurors also hold the patient to a certain level of knowledge about breast cancer; ignorance is no excuse. For instance:

> S: Why didn't she do something sooner? Um, with all, you know, even in the media there's things about breast cancer and going to get a mammogram, that, that is seen on TV, seen all sorts of places, there's more awareness about that type of thing now maybe than there's ever been. And, uh, I can't help but feel that she was exposed to some of this, somewhere, you know, didn't have an awareness, and to have an open sore, you thought she'd have went sooner than fourteen months. (1.25.1-8)[35]

These assumptions that public health campaigns and the mass media have made people more aware of the risk of breast cancer seem correct. Indeed, the result of this deluge of information is that women tend to *overestimate* breast cancer risks (D. Grady, 1999; B. Smith et al., 1996).[36] In any event, these jurors' beliefs that the woman could have been expected to do more about the lump, and later the sore, on her breast are grounded in fact.[37]

Several jurors, focusing on the size of the lump, are very concerned to know why the patient didn't first go to see the doctor sooner:

> S: [I]t might be something quite serious if the lump was that large, so—
> Lawyer: So is a ten centimeter by two centimeter mass, is that something that in your mind says, "this is serious"?
> (Several): Yes.
> Mi: I wonder why she hadn't gone in earlier. . . . I know I would be curious on why she didn't go in earlier.
> . . .
> Lawyer: [T]he patient actually had felt a lump for some time . . . and she was kind of worried about going to a doctor. . . .
> A: But she still should have gone. (1.14.22-15.5, 17.13-14, 17.18)[38]

---

[35] Another mock juror says: "But for her to not know seems way out of hand because of all the —I mean people to me, not to be against somebody, but I think a lot of uneducated people stay home and watch TV a lot. So you're going to have a lot of exposure on TV—I mean, you have all this free literature that's out, you have billboards on—on breast cancer" (1.45.21-46.1 [Mi]). And another: "[S]he's forty-six and she's had a history of maternal breast cancer. . . . Someone along the line must have told her at some point that she had, like, some sort of risk, so that's why I gave [the doctor] a little less liability" (2.43.22-44.1 [T]).

[36] Breast cancer risk perceptions may vary by race (Royak-Schaler, Stanton, & Danoff-Burg, 1997).

[37] One juror seems to hold the woman to a higher standard of behavior than he otherwise might because it matters to him whether the patient is a *single mother* (1.10.17-24 [K])— perhaps he is thinking that if she knows she is the sole supporter of the children, she should be more vigilant about her health situation.

[38] See also 2.6.16-19 (Ka, older White woman) ("I think she should [have] actually gone to the doctor earlier then she had, because she knew the lump was there and supposedly in January, and she didn't go in until July").

The jurors also wonder about how long before her first visit the woman knew about the lump:

K: .... And even before [the first visit], she goes in with a big old lump, and it kinda makes me question her, you know, and how up she is on things.

. . .

J: Well, if she didn't do regular breast check, you could have a lump for a while and not know it, depending on where that lump is located.
K: A lump that size, though, you think?
J: Oh yeah. Maybe not like that big, but I think there are, you could have a lump—
B: You could have a smaller lump. . . . Maybe it grew rapidly.

. . .

Mi: Size is an issue, though.
[Here follows the discussion of the size of the lump and the comparison to the "kosher pickle" excerpted on page 183.] (1.45.8-10, 46.2-14, 47.1-13, 20-24)[39]

Consider how the size-of-the-lump heuristic, and in particular the image of the kosher pickle, may influence these jurors' reasoning. As explained earlier, this habit of thought inclines people to think that the bigger the lump, the worse the cancer. And pickles don't grow—at least, not after they are put into the jar. Thus, jurors who conceive of the lump as a pickle may at some level mistakenly believe that the mass was *always* the size it was when the patient initially presented to the doctor. To focus on the size of the lump, and to do so by thinking of the lump as a pickle, may prompt these jurors to blame the woman more than they otherwise might.[40]

Now let us turn to the patient's delay in *returning* to the doctor's office, either one week after the initial visit or at least sooner than she eventually did. A number of mock jurors specify that the patient should have returned to the office one week after the initial visit instead of merely calling for her test results (1.21.17 [J]; 1.37.2-10 [Mi]; 2.52.7-9 [O]). And many of

---

[39] Similar thinking is evident on the second mock jury: "Um, I think this [responsibility] falls on both sides, but I think she should [have] actually gone to the doctor earlier then she had, because she knew the lump was there . . ." (2.6.16-18 [Ka]); "It comes back to the patient again. I mean, if someone told me I had a lump, I would not walk, I would run and I would get more than one opinion" (2.8.21-23 [O]); 2.42.1-8 [Le]; 2.43.1 [Ka]). Later in the deliberations these and other mock jurors speculate about how long the woman must have known about her lump before she went to see the doctor for the first time (2.44.25-46.21 [several]).

[40] It is true that at least one juror does not appear to be guided by a simple size-of-the-lump formula; she points out to the others that even though the lump was large by the time the woman first visited the doctor, it may have grown rapidly, or that the woman may have been so large that she might not have felt it for some time, especially if she did not perform regular breast self-examinations (1.46.2-25, 47.25-48.1 [JJ]). But the pickle, and with it the size-of-the-lump heuristic, evidently makes an impact on the deliberations. It leads at least one juror (K) to shift from agreement (1.46.19) to disagreement (1.47.10-11) with the ostensibly more knowledgeable juror (J), and inspires a more reticent female juror to one of her few vocal assertions (1.47.23-24 [A]).

them fault the woman for not going to see the doctor sooner than one year after the visit:

> Be: She should have gone sooner than a year. . . . [E]specially if she'd noticed [the lump] getting bigger, or changing, then she should have called back.
> Lawyer: But the doctor said it was normal. Uh, I mean, he said everything was OK.
> J: Well, it might have been OK at that time but that doesn't mean it's going to be OK for a year. . . . So she should monitor it, you know. (1.23.16-24.4)
> M: But I'm surprised also, too, where she had that lump, and she waited so long in between to go back to the doctors and all, I mean, didn't she notice that that lump was getting larger and larger and—?
> Le: She should have, and she should have been in discomfort. . . . That's why I say, I think most of it is her fault.
> O: Sometimes they don't have discomfort but the fact that the lump is there she should have been alarmed. (2.18.11-20)

In particular, several mock jurors in the first group believe that she should have returned at least after the sore appeared:

> K: I wonder about that, because the year later thing, where she had the open sore, I mean that kind of tells me negligence on her part to a point too . . .
> J: And he told her she was OK, now once the sore was there she should have gone back whenever it appeared, but—
> A: On the account that it was open, she should have herself realized that she needed to do something. (1.40.2-12)[41]

The mock jurors also speculate about factors that might mitigate the woman's blameworthiness for not returning to the doctor's office sooner than she did. One such reason would be fear or denial (1.26.25-27.3 [S]; 2.2.17 [Li]). Another would be the patient's financial constraints (1.25.24, 1.27.18-23 [K]; 1.45.12-20 [J, K, Be]; 1.54.15-19, 1.57.16-58.9 [JJ]).[42] These are two of the three leading reasons why cancer patients in general delay seeking care (Love, 1991); as for the third, lack of information, jurors are

---

[41] And:

> J: Well she should have gone in the minute she had the open sore appear. For sure. It wasn't just there that day.
> S: Why didn't she do something sooner? Um, with all, you know, even in the media there's things about breast cancer and going to get a mammogram, that, that is seen on TV, seen all sorts of places, there's more awareness about that type of thing now maybe than there's ever been. And, uh, I can't help but feel that she was exposed to some of this, somewhere, you know, didn't have an awareness, and to have an open sore, you thought she'd have went sooner than fourteen months.
> J: Especially at the site of the tumor. (1.24.19-20, 25.1-8)

[42] One juror also mentions financial constraints as a reason not to pursue a second opinion (1.54.4-5 [A]).

unwilling to excuse the patient, and in fact, as noted above, they suppose that she ought to be knowledgeable about the warning signs of breast cancer. Jurors also explore other possible excuses for the patient's delay, including her fear of doctors (1.17.16, 27.5-14 [J]; 1.26.18-27.2 [Mi]).[43] Mock jurors who take these kinds of reasons into account when judging the reasonableness of the patient's conduct display a fairly good understanding of how the ordinary woman behaves in these difficult circumstances.[44]

From Negligence to Legal Responsibility: Confusion About Causation

It is in drawing inferences from the patient's lapses in prudence to her legal responsibility for those lapses that the mock jurors' judgments diverge from those that medicolegal experts might make. As we have seen, the common-sense judgment that the woman should have gone to see her doctor sooner in the first place seems reasonable and justifiable. The interesting question is why so many mock jurors think that any negligence by the patient *before* her first visit to the doctor is legally relevant to her malpractice suit.[45]

Had the woman's cancer been diagnosed before that first visit, it is certainly possible that treatment could have begun sooner and that the

---

[43] Some of the jurors also surmise that the patient's delay might have arisen from her (understandable) reluctance to tell her husband, who otherwise could have prodded her to go to the doctor (1.26.2-7 [Be]). Some of the speculations get pretty far afield: speculations about whether the husband did not notice the sore (and hence did not encourage her to go back to the doctor) because the patient and here husband were having marital problems (1.25.23 [K]) or even that their relationship was abusive, which excuses her failure to go in for the visit for some jurors (1.62.16-19 [Mi]) but not for others (1.63.4-7 [K]).

[44] According to one study of why women who are eventually diagnosed with breast cancer contribute to delays between initial medical consultation and diagnosis, almost 40% of the women surveyed reported delays of 4 weeks or more, and almost 25% delays of 8 weeks or more; and 40% of those who gave reasons for delaying between their first and second visit to the physician attributed the delay to themselves (Caplan et al., 1996). Thus, the "ordinary" (although not necessarily the "ordinarily prudent") woman with breast cancer symptoms may be responsible for at least some delay in diagnosis. Delays of more than a year are unusual in the breast cancer population as a whole, though not, as noted earlier, in that subset of patients who sue for malpractice. As for the particular reasons cited, more than a third of women who attribute delay in part or in whole to themselves said that they felt the problem was not urgent or important enough; two-fifths identified competing obligations of one kind or another; and 1 in 8 mentioned fear (Caplan et al., 1996). Other studies indicate that women may delay seeking help for self-discovered breast symptoms for a host of personal, social, and other reasons (Facione, Dodd, Holzemer, & Meleis, 1997).

[45] I cannot prove from an analysis of the deliberations that the mock jurors who remarked on the woman's delay in seeing the doctor in the first place counted that behavior against her when apportioning fault. Perhaps, as my colleague Sheila Taub has suggested, these jurors were just venting their opinions about that behavior, aware that those opinions were not legally relevant. On the other hand, the jurors never indicate that they were *not* taking these views into account in apportioning fault. (At least one mock juror, the foreperson of the second jury, may recognize that the patient's behavior before she first saw the doctor is not relevant (2.20.15-19 [Jo]), although this should be read in context; he says this in order to confine the group's discussion to the specific question at hand, the doctor's negligence.) I assume that the jurors, unless they state otherwise, draw on all of their expressed opinions about matters relevant to the subject matter of the case in forming their ultimate judgments of legal fault (an assumption that is supported by the idea of total justice, explained in chapter 4).

woman's chances of survival may have been greater. But the doctor in this case cannot possibly be held responsible for any reduction in her chance of survival before he first saw the patient. Whatever her medical condition at that point, he may be liable if he thereafter deprived her of a significant chance of survival by negligently delaying biopsy and hence diagnosis (and then treatment). And if the patient was negligent *after* that point, the doctor's liability would be reduced by the percentage which the patient's negligence contributed to her loss of chance. *Before* the first visit, however, there is no negligence by the doctor toward this patient against which her lack of regard (if any) for her own well-being can be set. There is conflicting expert testimony as to what the patient's chances of survival would have been given a timely diagnosis, but whatever they were, only the patient's negligence after the point at which diagnosis could reasonably have been made would reduce her recovery. Her negligence before that point is simply irrelevant.

Why do these jurors apparently think that it is relevant? Very possibly they are using the size-of-the-lump heuristic in tandem with a habit of thought we have seen in all of the other cases analyzed in this book: norm theory. Focusing on the size of the lump leads jurors to believe that the woman could have noticed the lump sooner and could have done something about it. Then jurors may reason counterfactually: "If only the woman had first gone to the doctor sooner, she would not have died (so quickly)." And (as explained in chapter 2) the more strongly people believe that things *could* have been otherwise, the likelier they are to think that things *should* have been otherwise and to hold legally responsible the party who committed the act or omission. The counterfactual supposition itself is plausible, but the structure of the malpractice claim makes legally irrelevant any patient fault before the first visit to the doctor.

Finding the woman at fault for not returning to the doctor *after* the initial visit, as the doctor had recommended, seems perfectly reasonable.[46] The later the point at which the patient's inaction is targeted as negligent, however, the less such negligence could have affected her medical outcome. Although the medical evidence is not altogether clear from the simplified versions of the facts given to these mock jurors, by the time the sore appeared, if not sooner, the woman's cancer had progressed quite far— perhaps as far as it had by the time the doctor ultimately made his diagnosis. Thus, it may have been careless for the woman not to return promptly once she noticed the sore, but that negligence was probably causally irrelevant. Once again, it appears that the mock jurors, having found fault, are not especially scrupulous in demanding that that fault be causally

---

[46] As would finding her not at fault for not returning; both fall within the broad range of judgments the legal system generally yields to the jury (see chapter 1).

connected to the harm suffered. The result in this instance is that they may blame the plaintiff more than they should.[47]

CONFUSION ABOUT LOSS OF CHANCE AND ULTIMATE RESPONSIBILITY

Another factor influencing mock jurors' reasoning about responsibility in a case of delayed diagnosis of breast cancer arises not from prior beliefs specific to medical care or breast cancer, but from conceptual confusion about a crucial aspect of medical malpractice law in many jurisdictions: the loss of chance rule. As discussed earlier, this rule allows a patient who had a less than even likelihood of surviving his or her disease to recover from a health care provider whose negligence caused the patient to lose a substantial chance of surviving.

The second mock jury is explicitly instructed in the loss of chance rule (2.24.6-7 [Jo]). After some discussion, they all agree that decreasing a patient's chance of survival from 30% or 40% to "almost no chance" is substantial (2.24.9-32.3), although one does so for what appears to be the wrong reason—"I guess, well, I blamed [the doctor] in the beginning, I guess I'll have to say yes [i.e., his negligence caused the patient to lose a substantial chance of survival]" (2.24.9-10 [M])—and another initially says "no, because it's 30 to 40% which is less than 50" (2.24.24-25 [Ji]), which mistakes loss of chance for the traditional but-for causation rule.[48]

When asked later to apportion responsibility for the patient's untimely death (2.37.16-18), however, some mock jurors reduce this question to that of loss of chance:

> Jo (foreperson): Forty-sixty, that's almost an even split but [the patient]'s a little more responsible, you think?
> T: Yeah, because by the time she got there she had like a 30 to 40% chance to live anyway, and I figure, he pretty much destroyed that 40% and she screwed up the other 60 by not coming in early. (2.40.9-14)

Others think the same way:

> Li: If I think of it in [the doctor's] role in causing the death, he, it's true that he only came in at this 40% mark, I guess? Um, but I—I

---

[47] That conclusion, of course, must not be pressed too far, because we lack any benchmark for the "correct" amount of blaming in this case. Controlled experimentation has detected anti-plaintiff biases (see chapters 3 and 4), but these mock jury decisions cannot be calibrated in the same way. The final section of this analysis, on how the mock jurors deliberate toward the apportionment of fault, revisits this question.

[48] Indeed, some mock jurors seem inclined to consider *any* loss of chance, for instance, 5% (2.29.19-22 [Li]) or even 1% (2.30.2-8 [D, T, Jo]), to be "substantial."

think that he was definitely responsible for pretty much close to every-thing that happened after she got into the 40% mark, so I'll go, I'll go to 40-60.

. . .

D: I mean I would like to think of his 40% or 50% of being 100%. I mean, it's every bit of that percentage. So, what I think that, I kind of wish, summarily what she said, is that—

O: He's 100% liable—?

D: No, no, no, no, no, he's 100% within the 40% or whatever per-centage—

T: Right, within the 30 to 40%, yeah.

D: And I think that is the point we are trying to say, from that point—

T: I think that's what the 30 to 35 people are trying to say also.

D: From that point of her best, most optimistic survivability.

T: Yeah.

D: Was at best 40%, and both sides have said so.

E: So, she is responsible for 60% of her life.

T: 60 to 70%, yeah. (2.61.2-62.6)[49]

This reasoning appears to conflate what ought to be distinct questions of causation, as defined by the loss of chance doctrine, and fault.[50] The out-come of this reasoning may very well be "correct" by these jurors' own lights, *if* the jurisdiction follows the second version of the loss of chance rule, which provides that the victim of malpractice recovers that proportion of his or her damages represented by the percentage decrease in chance of recovery attributable to the doctor's negligence.[51] Some of these jurors (T, Li, D) seem to believe that the doctor is entirely responsible for the delay in diagnosis from the point of the patient's initial visit onward. In that event, awarding the patient's estate 30% to 40% of the wrongful death damages seems right. And if these mock jurors, like some of those in the first group, find the patient to have been *negligent* in not seeing the doctor sooner in the first place—"she screwed up the other 60 [percent]" (2.40.13 [T]; see also 2.43.14-44.2 [T])—then even though that negligence is legally irrelevant (as explained in the preceding section), the net result, discount-ing her recovery by 60% to 70%, is the same as that produced by (properly)

---

[49] This same mock juror elsewhere confuses fault and causation when she says, responding to the foreperson's argument about the percentage fault that should be allocated to the doctor based on his failure to communicate adequately, "[b]ut by the time she got there she had at most only 40% chance to live anyway" (2.57.3-4 [T]).

[50] Arguably the mock jury moderator's "instruction" asked for this conflation by requesting participants to assign percentages of "responsibility" (2.37.17-18). On the other hand, the jurors had just explicitly confronted loss of chance as the second question on the special verdict form (2.24.5-32.6), so they might very well have thought that the distinct (fourth) question about "percent[ages] of responsibility" was soliciting something other than a recapitulation of their views on loss of chance.

[51] At least one of the mock jurors grasps the meaning of this rule: "the percentage of chance ought to somehow equate the percentage of award" (2.35.4-5 [D]).

reducing her recovery on the basis of her *reduced chance of survival* at the time of the first visit. These jurors, then, could well be "right for the wrong reasons"—they decide *holistically* (see chapter 4), folding the legally distinct elements of fault and causation into a single conclusion about just desserts.

For other mock jurors, however, who are more disposed to blame the patient for not returning to the doctor's office (Le, O, Ka, Ji), the result of confusing fault and causation may be to blame the patient *less* than they otherwise would. Each of these jurors offers a single apportionment of responsibility to the parties that adds up to 100% of the damages (2.37.16-42.16). But unlike the mock jurors quoted above, these jurors cannot justifiably equate the reduction in the plaintiff's recovery with her initially reduced chance of survival; on the basis of *their own views* about the patient's negligence *after* the initial visit, they ought to discount her recovery by her initially reduced chance of survival *and* by her negligence after that point. Because these mock jurors do not appear to do this, the percentages of responsibility they initially assign to the patient, which range from 60% to 75%, would result in too *large* an award of damages. Their allocations of responsibility may strike them as "correct enough" on the whole, but their failure to appreciate the upshot of the loss of chance doctrine biases their ultimate judgments against the doctor.[52]

APPORTIONING FAULT DURING DELIBERATIONS

Jurors who believe that both the patient and the doctor are to blame face a difficult task in apportioning fault between the parties, as the law of comparative negligence requires them to do (see chapter 1). The law provides next to nothing in the way of guidance (Feigenson, et al., 1997). As the foreperson of one mock jury says, "I'm not sure exactly how to determine that" (1.57.2 [S]). The lack of guidance leaves jurors free to rely on their intuitive inferential habits—their common sense.

We could try to examine how individual mock jurors attempt to justify the apportionments they reach, but an individual's words do not necessarily tell us why that person divides the blame precisely as he or she does. Consider one participant (J) on the first mock jury. Juxtaposing the patient's negligence in not returning when recommended to the doctor's negligence in not being more aggressive, this juror remarks that "I can't really think she's at fault for not going back in to the office [when she was supposed to have returned, one week after the initial visit]. I mean—she

---

[52] The same is true of those participants in the first mock jury (such as Mi) who appear to blame the patient for her conduct both before and after the first visit.

called" (1.54.11-12). Had the doctor even "hinted" that the problem was serious, the woman "probably would have" come back in (1.54.16-17, 58.4-9); after all, she had done the other tests he told her to have (1.39.18-20). In addition, the doctor, not the patient, should bear the bulk of the responsibility because he didn't give her the options for less expensive follow-up treatment (1.58.22-59.5). The doctor is "more educated, he knows the options that are available to her, he knows how serious a lump that size is, and it wasn't an open sore when she first went into him. Um, he has learned about breast cancer, things in his training, he knows how fast it can grow, he knows how serious it is" (1.60.20-61.1). All of this might suggest that this mock juror is ready to apportion almost all of the fault to the doctor—and yet she assigns 40% of the fault to the patient on the ground that the patient herself should also have been more aggressive in dealing with her symptoms.

We may be able to make more sense of apportionment of fault by studying how mock jurors *as a group* deliberate toward consensus. Jury deliberations have been much studied, most often in the context of criminal cases. Controlled experiments using mock juries have examined how the size of the jury, the decision rule, juror gender, choice and role of foreperson, jurors' initial verdict preferences, the size of the majority faction, the length of the deliberations, and other factors affect the content and outcome of deliberations (Hastie et al., 1983; for a survey, see Stasser et al., 1982). It is not my intention to add to this extensive literature; as already noted, the mock jury deliberations examined here do not reflect a controlled experimental test of specific hypotheses about jury decision making. However, I draw on prior research where appropriate to inform my observations about the ways in which these mock jurors apportioned fault between the patient and the doctor.

I describe significant moments in the apportionment deliberations of the mock juries, allowing us to see some of the dynamics of group decision making. I then identify three habits of thought that work together to lead these mock juries to divide the fault roughly evenly between the doctor and the patient. First, jurors may adopt *split the difference* or something close to it as a *focal point* solution to the difficult task of quantifying relative fault. Second, as jurors try to compromise during deliberations, more extreme views are drawn toward the group average. And finally, the second group of mock jurors, when instructed that limited comparative negligence in the jurisdiction means that the plaintiff gets nothing if the patient was 50% or more at fault, caps the patient's fault at just under 50%, so that her estate may recover something.

To describe how these mock jurors deliberate apportionment, I borrow a simple schema applicable to group problem-solving processes generally: orientation, conflict, resolution, and reconciliation (Kassin & Wrightsman,

1988; Stasser et al., 1982). Here is the opening stage of the first mock jury's discussion of apportionment of fault:

K: I think, yeah, I agree with you I think they are both negligent—
A: Both of them negligent.
Ma: I think so too.
Be: I think that they both are.
[Discussion of both parties' negligence.]
S: OK. So, like, I say we have determined, then, am I safe in saying that we've determined that the doctor does have some negligence, involved in this, OK, is that—?
(Several): Uh-huh.
S: Number two, also we agree that the, uh, that the plaintiff has also some negligence in this because they just didn't do what you think a normal person would do under the circumstances.
(Several): Uh-huh.
S: Um, I guess now the point is, is who, what percentage of, who's more negligent than the other—
(Someone): That's tough.
S: Weighing everything that we're given. Anybody want to throw one out, to start?
M: He was negligent, but I don't think he was as negligent as she was.
Ma: I agree.
[Discussion of patient's negligence.]
S: So I think the thing we need to do is determine between all of this that—what percentage negligence falls to each party. I'm not sure exactly how to determine that.
[More discussion of both parties' negligence.]
S: So it still boils down to negligence, and how much—
[More discussion of doctor's negligence.]
S: OK. As I say, still the issue is, is we need to determine, I guess, percentage negligence, how much is the doctor at fault, how much the plaintiff is at fault, and after that we get to determine damages, whatever—. (1.50.23-60.19)

We notice three things about the first phase of apportionment discussions in this mock jury: The jurors begin by acknowledging that both parties are at fault; the foreperson admits that the task of quantifying fault is difficult; and then the group repeatedly wanders away from that task into discussions of why one party or the other was careless. The foreperson tries three times to bring the group back to the task of numerical apportionment before the others, finally, begin to take up the job:

J: Well, you may not agree with me, I would say he's sixty percent at fault, she's forty percent at fault. He's more educated, he knows the options that are available to her, he knows how serious a lump that size is, and it wasn't an open sore when she first went in to him. Um, he has learned about breast cancer, things in his training, he knows how fast it can grow, he knows how serious it is. That would be my—

S: OK. Anyone else now? How do you feel about it?

A: Well I think he's more negligent than she is.

S: OK, would you like to—

Be: I tend to agree with that.

S: Put a number on it, or percentage, or—?

A: How about twenty-five, seventy-five?

S: The doctor seventy-five?

A: Um-hum.

S: The plaintiff twenty-five. And who's next, who would like to—?

J: Well, he's more educated than she is. He's got the education to know—

Mi: Fifty-fifty—

S: Fifty-fifty?

Mi: I'm debating on that right now.

K: I would lean more towards the physician being at fault, but I, I don't know how much more—

Ma: I feel that same way but I don't know how much more.

Mi, K: [Discussion of patient's negligence.]

(All except Be): [Discussion of whether patient had set appointment to return to the office after initial visit.]

K: Well, anyway, I mean she had the choice, she chose not to. But I mean, I still think he's very negligent, but yet she is too.

J (and others): They both are.

(Someone): Oh gosh.

S: So it makes it tough, where do you draw the line. He is more, or is it fifty-fifty, or what.

(Someone): Gee.

K: I would probably say fifty-fifty. They want us to prove it.

Mi: I would have to go more toward the patient, or towards the—as far as the patient being at fault, so sixty—sixty-forty.

S: Sixty-forty for the patient?

Mi: As being in the wrong.

S: OK.

Ma: I think I'll go along with that.

A: I'll go along with that.

S: Sixty-forty? Personally, it's so close to even, but, I think the doctor is just maybe a little bit more, I'd say fifty-five forty-five.

(Several): OK [laughter]. (1.60.20-64.15)

We see from just these few minutes of deliberation (which in many ways are representative of this group's deliberations as a whole) that, as prior studies have shown, individual jurors vary in persuasiveness (Shestowsky et al., 1998): Some jurors talk much more than others; some offer more arguments in support of their outcome preferences than others. Consistently with mock jurors studied previously (Hastie et al., 1983; R. James,

1959), the three older women (A, Be, Ma), none of whom have significant higher education, speak the least frequently.[53] And when they do speak they agree with the previous speaker more often, and disagree or challenge the previous speaker less often, than do the other participants.[54] (Juror A shows a striking malleability in appearing to accede to apportioning 60% of the fault to the patient, having just moments before volunteered to apportion 75% of the fault to the doctor.) The male jurors in general speak more[55]; the anomaly, if it may be called that, is that the most talkative of all jurors throughout the deliberations (not just this portion) is J, who as a woman without prior jury experience would not have been predicted to take such an active role.[56]

The end stage follows, and is quickly concluded:

> S: I think we all recognize that there is negligence on both sides, I think it's both severe enough on both sides, it's relatively close.
> (Someone): I agree.
> S: OK, there's sixty-forty, the first number I mentioned is the doctor, the plaintiff second: sixty-forty against the doctor, seventy-five twenty-five against the doctor, fifty-five forty-five, then there's two forty-sixties against the complainant, OK, the plaintiff, that she didn't do enough to take care of herself, there's one at fifty-fifty and another fifty-five forty-five. . . . I think we all agree—we all say there's negligence on both sides. What do we feel comfortable as a group, as a whole, percentage?
> J: I would feel comfortable with fifty-five forty-five against the doctor.
> Be, A, Ma: OK, uh-huh.
> K: Yeah, I would go along with that.
> Mi: I'd go more for the patient.

---

[53] Jurors Ma and A each contribute 24 of 408 utterances during this seven-person mock jury's unguided deliberations, or 6% of the total; juror Be makes 21 utterances, or 5% of the total. Women like Ma and A may, however, be participating in the deliberations more than these quantitative observations suggest. A comparison of the deliberation videotape and the transcript made from it indicates that these women (perhaps more so than other jurors) sometimes appear to speak in asides to other jurors, rather than to the group as a whole. Asides are less likely than utterances to the group to be sufficiently intelligible to be transcribed and thus included in the quantitative analysis.

[54] For the group as a whole, 53 of 408 utterances, or 13%, express agreement with the preceding speaker; for these women, the figures are: Ma, 21%; A, 38%; and Be, 38%. For the group as a whole, only 13 utterances, or about 3%, express challenges to or disagreements with the preceding speaker; neither Ma nor Be overtly challenges or disagrees with anyone, and A does it once. To look at these data another way, utterances expressly challenging or disagreeing with the previous speaker are just under one-quarter as frequent as agreements; these women agree with the previous speaker on 22 occasions and disagree or challenge just once, or less than 5% as often.

[55] The three men account for half of the utterances; their *pro rata* share would be about 43% (three of seven speakers). Also consistent with prior research (Stasser et al., 1982), the foreperson speaks often in the deliberations as a whole (although not that much in this excerpt). Here he contributes the second greatest number of utterances (86), of which 53, or about 62%, concern the process of deliberation (e.g., posing questions to the group, recording individual jurors' apportionments of fault, and otherwise attempting to move the deliberations along).

[56] This juror contributes 134 of 408 utterances, or nearly one-third.

S: Fifty-five forty-five towards the doctor? And, fifty-five for the doctor, forty-five for the plaintiff?

K: 'Cause she did go in to see him and—

S: OK.

K: He did, he could of—. (1.64.15-65.16)

The foreperson begins the resolution of the apportionment discussion by reminding the group of how far they agree and then by recapitulating the individual apportionments. The juror who has been most talkative throughout (J) then suggests a compromise apportionment of 55% to the doctor, 45% to the patient, which reflects a small (5%) concession from her initial position. Everyone readily agrees, with the exception of Mi, who still wants to blame the patient more.[57]

The second mock jury's deliberations on apportionment resemble those of the first in some respects. The group begins by polling individual jurors (2.37.16-39.18), with markedly less hesitation in delving into the task of quantifying comparative fault, and then discusses reasons for various apportionments of fault. Once again, different jurors contributed unequally to this discussion (D, a middle-aged man, speaks at by far the greatest length).

This group's deliberations, however, differ noticeably from those of the first group in a few respects. I discuss one below, regarding the impact of the limited comparative negligence rule.[58] The difference I want to mention here is that the second group of mock jurors begins by attributing more blame to the patient (58% vs. 46% in the first jury). Perhaps this is merely an instance of the wide range within which juries' determinations of comparative negligence may vary (V. Schwartz, 1986) or it may be due to differences in the manner in which the facts of the case were presented to the respective mock juries.[59] Certainly the kinds of reasons the second group of mock jurors offer for blaming the patient do not seem to differ much from those heard from the first group of mock jurors: "She should not have ignored her condition" (2.40.6 [Li, who assigned 50% of the fault to each party]); "it was her body" (2.40.22 [E, who apportioned 70% of the fault to the patient]; 2.42.2-5 [Le, 60%]); "if she had this lump she

---

[57] Note that this rapid compromise represents quite a concession by at least one of the other jurors (15% more blame to the doctor by Ma), which may be explained by her amenability to being persuaded, as noted earlier, or perhaps by her desire (not unlike that of some actual jurors) to compromise in order to conclude the session.

[58] A second difference is that this mock jury deliberated the issue for much longer than did the first—935 transcript lines (second mock jury) versus (at most) 370 lines (first mock jury)—and without ever reaching consensus. This may have been due to the larger size of the second mock jury (10, vs. 7 in first group); research has shown that larger juries deliberate longer (see Hastie et al., 1983).

[59] The second mock jury heard the facts in the form of a presentation by persons playing the roles of the lawyers for the respective parties. From comments elicited by the moderator of the session, it is not clear that participants found the defendant's lawyer to have been especially persuasive, although they were also somewhat critical of some of the plaintiff's lawyer's tactics (2.76.12-87.18).

should have really gone after it so she got a satisfied answer" (2.42.14-16 [O, 75%]).[60]

Let us now observe and try to explain the three deliberative habits that seem to incline mock jurors to apportion the fault roughly evenly between the parties. All of the mock juries approach this task by first eliciting the jurors' individual allocations of percentages and then deliberating to a consensus. We might expect this process to follow the *anchoring and adjustment* heuristic that people often use to estimate quantities (see chapter 2). Either the first juror's apportionment, or some rough average of all of the individual apportionments, would create the anchor (indeed, the first juror to speak to the issue may create an anchor for subsequent jurors' initial estimates); further discussion would then adjust those figures to reach the final judgment. But how is the anchor selected—how do jurors arrive at their initial estimates?

The anchors in these deliberations (and the ultimate apportionments) tend to cluster around an even split of responsibility between doctor and patient. In the first mock jury, the first juror to speak on this issue volunteers a split of 60% responsibility to the doctor, 40% to the patient; in the second mock jury, the first speaker reverses these figures.[61] "[T]hat's almost an even split," comments the foreperson in the second group (2.40.9 [Jo]). And the mean of the individual jurors' initial apportionments is 54% (doctor)–46% (patient) in the first group, 42% (doctor)–58% (patient) in the second. I suggest that these estimates are guided by a *split-the-difference* heuristic: Believing that both parties are blameworthy, but without any algorithm to follow in apportioning fault, jurors divide the fault more or less equally.

This split-the-difference rule of thumb is frequently used as a *focal point* solution in negotiations (Schelling, 1960). "[T]here seems to be a strong magnetism in mathematical simplicity," evidenced in "the tendency for the outcomes to be expressed in 'round numbers,'" of which split-the-difference is a prototypical instance (Schelling, 1960, p. 67). We may think of the extent of each party's negligence as pulling the outcome, apportionment, toward that party. The percentages allocated to the respective parties ought, of course, to be precisely in proportion to the contribution that each party's fault made to the accident (see chapter 1). But just as groups

---

[60] Also, as discussed earlier in this chapter, at least some of the participants in the second mock jury may attribute to the patient the percentages of negligence that they do because they understand their task as assessing the patient's *responsibility* as reflected by her initially reduced chance of survival. That is, they are really speaking of the portion of *causal* responsibility— 60% to 70% on the facts provided—that cannot be attributed to the doctor, and hence must be borne by the patient.

[61] Similarly, in the third mock jury, which, presented with somewhat different facts, was asked to apportion fault among four actors (two doctors at the clinic, the radiologist, and the patient), the first two jurors to speak to the issue divided the fault evenly among the four (3.79.9-11 [Jo]; 3.79.24-25 [Sh, middle-aged White woman, worked in vocational rehabilitation]).

of people dining together often decide to split the check evenly rather than determine what each person owes based on what each ordered (see Ellickson, 1991), so jurors may decide to forgo the attempt at precise distributive justice in favor of a more pragmatic solution. Indeed, the task confronting jurors in a comparative negligence case is even more difficult, because unlike the diners, jurors have no data from which they could reliably calculate exact percentages of fault even if they wanted to. Accordingly, as the second mock juror to speak to the issue in the second group says, "I split it in half" (2.38.14 [M, middle-aged White woman]).

Mock jurors begin their discussion of apportionment, then, with figures that are not too far removed from a 50-50 split. But there is intragroup disagreement: Apportionments of fault to the doctor range from 75% to 40% in the first mock jury, and 65% to 25% in the second. One would expect that the deliberations would involve adjustments to these individual anchors, as jurors attempt to justify their initial positions and sometimes to question others'. The overall trend of this adjustment process in the mock juries observed here is that apportionments furthest removed from the group mean are drawn toward it as jurors try to compromise to reach closure. We see this most clearly in the deliberations of the first mock jury: The group mean is 54% fault to the doctor, with a range from 40% to 75%; the compromise position is 55% to the doctor.[62]

The movement, at least in the first mock jury, toward the group's mean initial division of responsibility may seem to conflict with the often-observed *group polarization* phenomenon: that "the average postgroup response will tend to be more extreme in the same direction as the average of the pregroup responses" (Myers & Lamm, 1976, p. 603; see Levine & Moreland, 1998; Moscovici & Doise, 1994; Schkade et al., 1999). The reason for the discrepancy may be that this medical malpractice case did not produce a dominant *predeliberation* tendency in one direction or the other, which group polarization would be predicted to enhance. In contrast to the stimulus materials that yielded polarization effects in prior jury research, which presented either decidedly strong or weak evidence of the criminal defendant's guilt, and hence generated the dominant predeliberation tendencies, the facts of this case struck most jurors as evenly balanced (predeliberation group means of 54% and 42% defendant fault, respectively[63]), so there was not enough of a dominant tendency for group discussion to polarize.[64]

---

[62] This is less true of the second mock jury. There, the only juror initially to allocate more blame to the doctor (65%) than the patient (35%) is willing to move to 49%–51% (2.56.17-18 [Jo, foreperson]), approaching the initial mean of 42%–58%; in response to the foreperson's suggestion, another juror contemplates moving from an initial 40%–60% split to something closer to even (2.51.19-20 [T]), and a third juror indicates a willingness to adjust her initial figures in either direction (2.57.24-58.1 [Li]). Yet two jurors remain fixed in extreme positions (2.51.3 [O, 25%–75%]; 2.58.7-8 [E, 30%–70%]).

[63] As for the individual mock jurors' initial apportionments, 13 of 17 do not vary from 50%–50% by more than 10%. This is a slightly but not significantly greater percentage of individual

Finally, the second mock jury displays a very interesting phenomenon that ultimately pushes the group toward a nearly even division of fault. This jury, as noted earlier, initially assigns on average nearly 60% of the fault to the *patient*. Lengthy deliberations result in some reduction of that figure, but the group remains undecided—until this belated instruction from the judge:

> Judge: Actually I would like to give you a more complete instruction and I apologize ladies and gentlemen, and I don't know if it would affect your deliberations or not. . . . But the law in this state, uh, there is such as a thing as what we call comparative negligence. . . . The other thing I need to tell you is that the law in this jurisdiction is that if [the patient] was 50% negligent or greater, her estate recovers nothing.
> (Several): Hmmm.
> Judge: And I don't know if that is of any significance to you or not. I wanted to make sure you understood the law. . . . I just want you to be aware the law in this jurisdiction is, if [the patient] was 50% negligent or more, the estate gets zero. All right? (2.64.19-24, 65.4-9, 66.16-18)

The jurors indeed find this rule—the law of *limited* comparative negligence (see chapter 1)—to be significant. In fact, it is a bombshell:

> Jo (foreperson, responding to judge's previous statement): Zero.
> T: I'm changing my—
> (Several): [Laughter.]
> T: I'm changing my percentage—
> Li: Yeah.
> T: I'll change it to, 49 for [the patient] and 51 for [the doctor], 'cause I think she gets some money. . . . That sucks, but—
> Li: I really think that it was negligent enough that she deserves some money.
> Jo: I—I agree, that's what I'm going to do. I'm going to split, I'll tell you what, let's—let's go around and do a third vote.
> T: If that's the only way that she can get money, I—I really don't feel that, I feel she was more liable, but I feel that—
> D (middle-aged White man): I got a question for our bailiff. Is it—is it normal that our instructions get changed, I mean we really look— I mean, we really look pretty foolish here . . . having debated this and —
>
> Jo: Well, I'll tell you what. If we are going to—if we all want to— obviously want to award [the patient] something. So we're going to have to give her it—it, this is my opinion, you can. . . . We're going to have to give her more—it has to be 51% or greater to get anything. . . . Why don't we, I, well, let's just take a vote, then.

---

predeliberation apportionments within 10% of the midpoint than one would expect by mere chance.
[64] In any event, the sample of mock juries studied here is, of course, too small to offer a statistically significant test of the group polarization hypothesis.

M: I guess I'll go 51-49.
Jo: 51 [doctor], 49 [patient], OK?
D: It's the only way to be sure. . . .
Jo: Yeah, I agree. Um—
Li: I'll give 55, um, to [the doctor].
Jo: OK. And, uh—
T: 51-49. (2.66.19-68.24)

Before learning of the limited comparative negligence rule, all but 1 of the 10 mock jurors in this group allocated a majority of the fault to the patient. Afterward, all but 2 of those 9 switch to apportion just under 50% to the patient, so that her estate may recover something. This plainly demonstrates the ceiling effect that the limited comparative negligence rule places on the plaintiff's percentage fault where the evidence of that fault is strong but does not overwhelm evidence of the defendant's.[65] This mock jury was not set up as a controlled experiment, yet one could scarcely ask for a better within-subjects design to confirm widespread anecdotal reports of the effect of the limited comparative negligence rule on apportionment decisions.

These mock jurors are *not* just ignoring the law to do what they think is right, as a recent poll (Aronson, Rovella, & Van Voris, 1998) indicated most prospective jurors are wont to do. Instead, they seem quite willing and able to adjust their common-sense apportionments to the legal rule in order to reach a decision they regard as just. They submit to the law's authority, but without sacrificing what they think is right.

CONCLUSION

The most in-depth analysis of jury decision making in medical malpractice cases concludes that "there is no empirical support for the propositions that juries are biased against doctors or that they are prone to ignore legal and medical standards in order to decide in favor of plaintiffs with severe injuries" (Vidmar, 1995, p. 182). The preceding discussion of mock jury deliberations offers a small step from the *what* toward the *how* of common-sense judgments about medical accidents. We find, at least in the single context of a delayed diagnosis of breast cancer case and with a limited sample of data, that laypeople's decisions may indeed fall within a

---

[65] It also demonstrates the wisdom of the author of the leading treatise on comparative negligence, who wrote, weighing in on the conflict between jurisdictions that do and those that do not inform the jury of the consequences of apportionment: "When the jury is not aware that a plaintiff who is 50% negligent recovers nothing [as was the case in the majority of limited comparative negligence states when the treatise was written], it may casually return a 50–50 verdict as a compromise. The jury does not realize the very devastating impact of its decision. Further, it will have devoted unnecessary time computing plaintiff's damages. These factors persuade this author that the jury should be informed of the legal effect of the apportionment of fault" (V. Schwartz, 1986, pp. 312–313).

range deemed acceptable by the legal system and medicolegal experts, even when that decision making is not as disciplined by legal rules and processes as it would be in an actual trial. The path to these common-sense decisions, however, is complicated: a mixture of partially accurate prior beliefs and expectations, sound judgment, inferential bias, and conceptual confusion. Common-sense judgments about medical malpractice, as about other things, may often be right enough, even if not always for the right reasons.

8

SOME IMPLICATIONS OF LEGAL BLAMING

It is time to step back and consider the broader social and cultural significance of legal blaming practices. We have seen in *Butler*, *Giulietti*, and *Faverty* a conception of accidents as *melodrama*. I argue in the first part of this chapter that, by personalizing responsibility, melodramatic blaming in both law and popular culture often occludes the systemic causes of accidents. It thereby tends to protect the corporate industrial status quo and to shift public attention from society's implicit choice to endure significant and largely random injury as a price of modern life. We have also seen throughout the book, however, that there is more to legal blaming than melodrama. Juror decision making in accident cases is complex, inconsistent, and imperfect. Some observers have sharply criticized the jury's role in the legal system. I argue in the second part of this chapter that understanding juror decision making in terms of *total justice* will help us to maintain a more accurate and constructive view of how laypeople try to do justice in accident cases.

CULTURAL AND LEGAL IMPLICATIONS OF MELODRAMATIC BLAMING

Most accidents do not result in claims for compensation (Hensler et al., 1991), and most claims are resolved without jury trial (Galanter, 1996;

Gross & Syverud, 1996). But when jurors decide, they often blame someone for the accident, and when jurors conceive of accidents as melodrama,
they implement a particular, culturally significant way of blaming. By simplifying and personalizing responsibility, melodrama in accident cases, as
in popular culture generally, tends to divert attention from the more systemic causes of many unintended harms, and thus to preserve the status
quo of corporate industrial society. Often melodramatic blaming is perfectly
consistent with legal norms, which invite this way of assigning responsibility for accidents. Sometimes, however, thinking about accidents as melodrama extends tort liability beyond legal norms, and in some of those
cases, the language of melodrama may actually be the means for attending
to systemic causes of accidents.

The Culture of Melodramatic Blaming

Melodrama is a way of implementing a culturally significant *blaming
practice*. Douglas's (1992) anthropological analysis explains the cultural–
political, that is, the *forensic*, purposes of various ways of attributing responsibility for misfortune. In certain tribal societies, Douglas observed,
personal calamity is attributed to the victim's own sin, the violation of
taboo; in others, it is attributed to enemies outside the community. Still
another type of society tends to attribute such misfortune to individual
adversaries within the community (Douglas, 1992).

In the United States, a heterogeneous society of 270 million people
is bound to display various attitudes toward misfortune. On the whole, and
contrary to much popular wisdom, Americans are reluctant to blame others
for accidents (Saks, 1992). We attribute only a third of our own accidents
purely to human acts, and of those accidents believed to have been caused
in part or in whole by human agency, victims blame themselves nearly two
thirds of the time (Hensler et al., 1991). Some Americans profess a sense
of individualism that emphasizes rugged self-sufficiency, according to which
the victim of accidental injury is supposed to take misfortune in stride
(Engel, 1987). Others are fatalistic, believing simply that "stuff happens"
(Cusimano, 1998).

Still, many accidents do result in claims for compensation, including
lawsuits, and some of these claims proceed to trial. And although those
that do comprise a small minority of all accidents, their significance extends beyond their numbers—in their influence on the filing and settlement of other claims, and on popular images of the litigation system (Daniels & Martin, 1995). From these accident claims and trials, it is clear that
blaming individual others for misfortune is a culturally important practice.

Douglas (1992) wrote that this kind of blaming "is partly a public
backlash against the great corporations" (p. 15). The globalization of the
marketplace has led to an increasing sense of personal vulnerability and,

in return, increasing demands for protection against that vulnerability as a basic matter of fairness. The more the normative foundations of our lives are threatened, especially the belief that our fate can be controlled (if not by ourselves, then by some identifiable other), the more forcibly we articulate and seek to implement those very norms. Thus, as Douglas (1992) somewhat hyperbolically wrote, "the [blaming system] we are now in is almost ready to treat every death as chargeable to someone's account, every accident as caused by someone's criminal negligence, every sickness a threatened prosecution. Whose fault? is the first question. Then, what action? Which means, what damages? what compensation?" (pp. 15–16).

Yet Douglas (1992) also contended that blaming others for misfortune (her focus is the contemporary rhetoric of "risk") is perfectly suited "to the task of building a culture that supports a modern industrialized society" (p. 15). How can the blaming of "bad guy" corporate defendants *support* a largely corporation-driven industrialized society? The answer, I believe, derives mainly from the way in which *melodramatized* blaming *simplifies* and *personalizes* responsibility. This tends to divert attention from the social and systemic causes for accidents and thus to protect the underlying corporate industrial power structure from critical reassessment.

Attributing responsibility in melodramatized fashion is pervasive in American society. Let me begin to explore the connections between melodramatized blaming and the blocking out of systemic responsibility by turning to theorists of melodrama in film and other media. According to Elsaesser (1987):

> The persistence of the melodrama might indicate the ways in which popular culture ... has ... resolutely refused to understand social change in other than private contexts and emotional terms. In this, there is obviously a healthy distrust of intellectualisation and abstract social theory—insisting that other structures of experience (those of suffering, for instance) are more in keeping with reality. But it has also meant ignorance of the properly social and political dimensions of these changes and their causality. (p. 47)

If one substitutes "the injuries resulting from modern technology and industry" for "social change," one begins to get an idea of the effect of melodramatic thinking on judgments of legal responsibility for accidents.[1] Dorfman's (1983) analysis of superhero melodrama makes even plainer the analogy between melodrama's personalization and simplification of conflict and the occlusion of systemic responsibility for accidents:

---

[1] Similarly, Nowell-Smith (1987) wrote that melodrama "supposes a world without the exercise of social power," in which "[t]he characters are neither the rulers nor the ruled" (p. 71); rather, power in the melodrama is local and personal, the universe that of the family or the small town. If the *form* of such melodrama, as it has developed since the late 18th century, connotes a similar background of power relations even when transposed to the very different world of the modern industrial (or highway) accident, then perhaps the result will similarly be the masking of underlying social forces (see Rapping, 1997).

[A given episode of *The Lone Ranger* presents] a typical situation, a real dilemma, which the reader should be able to recognize. A man is fired. Reasons: laziness, drunkenness, bad company, an unlawful past. People have been fired, it is true, for that sort of conduct. But this is only part of the truth. There is nothing to remind the reader that people are fired primarily due to other pressures: mechanization, competition for lowering costs, etc. So the crisis that the reader witnesses (and often suffers) in the real world is only apparently, externally, similar to the one that fiction presents. It is, however, similar enough to allow the reader to automatically correlate and substitute the one for the other, so that the solution given in the comic can be translated by the reader into the kind of solution that will work for his own genuine, ongoing troubles. (pp. 92–93)

Kleinhans's (1991) analysis of melodrama and ideology situates the analogy between melodrama in the arts and in accident trials in its historical context. The emergence of melodrama coincided roughly with the Industrial Revolution and the rise of capitalism. Industrial culture divided work from family, putting unprecedented and ultimately unbearable demands on the private family to satisfy the sense of meaning in life that was now absent from the public sphere of work. The bourgeois domestic melodrama arose and continues to thrive because it expresses this basic contradiction in people's everyday lives,[2] while generally avoiding explicit mention of the conditions of capitalism (e.g., layoffs, unemployment) that often give rise to family tensions. By analogy, in a world of increasing privatization (i.e., corporate control of formerly public functions) and decreasing faith in elected government, legal cases and especially jury trials bear an ever-growing and perhaps ultimately unbearable burden of providing the sense of justice that is otherwise absent from the public sphere.[3] In the face of such

---

[2] Kleinhans (1991) added:

> The more the family loses its possibilities for material production, the more it becomes a prime site of consumption. Mass consumption, the domestic side of imperialist market expansion, contains an ideology of pleasure and self-gratification which is defined largely in individual rather than social terms. With consumption detached from production (the fetishism of commodities Marx describes in the first chapter of Capital), a full life is thwarted. Rather than life, one has a succession of lifestyles.
>
>   The family becomes a center of subjectivity, cut off from the world of action and decisions. Home is for passion, suffering, sympathy, sacrifice, self-attainment. Work is for action, doing, for the money which pays for the home. Yet home is also shaped by the ideology of individualism, especially as shaped by the Puritan-Protestant heritage of U.S. life. The family is supposed to achieve the personal fulfillment denied in the workplace for adults and denied in school for children. At home everyone becomes a consumer trying to get a bigger slice of the emotional pie. (pp. 199–200)

[3] Of course, as observed in the introduction, other institutions besides juries address the vast majority of claims of accidental injury, seeking to accomplish the goals of deterrence (e.g., through governmental regulation), compensation (e.g., through settlement, with or without insurance, before or after the filing of a lawsuit), or both. But insofar as accidents are seen as

circumstances and the very real difficulties of understanding the often complex causes of accidents, the temptation to resort to simplified, personalized, and moralized justice—accidents as melodramas—may be great.

When one moves from the dramatic arts to the world of "facts," one continues to find evidence that American culture conceives of accidents as melodrama. For instance, many studies show that media reporting on hazards and accidents tends to adopt a melodramatic structure. The media tend to report harms, not risks; that is, they individualize danger (Singer & Endreny, 1987). The media tend to prefer monocausal accounts of hazards (Spencer & Triche, 1994) and to identify individuals rather than physical or social forces as causes (Stallings, 1990). Thus, "news of disaster tends to be portrayed as melodrama—a form of communication that relies heavily on plot predictability and stereotype" (Wilkins & Patterson, 1987, p. 81).[4] In all of this, media coverage of accidents and hazards is consistent with their coverage of news in general (Ewen, 1988; Hallin, 1986).

The social construction of people's knowledge about accidents as matters of purely individual responsibility extends beyond the mass media to government and private industry sources of information—indeed, to the entire cultural and institutional apparatus by which people identify certain kinds of recurring events but not others as worthy of attention. As Gusfield (1981) explained so brilliantly, from the collecting of relevant information to its analysis, dissemination, and use in subsequent debate, Americans have tended to approach automobile accidents, and in particular, those involving the use of alcohol by one or more drivers, as a matter of individual morality. In research reports and Congressional hearings, the focus becomes not drinking and driving, but the *drunk driver*: the sinner against society, the deviant "problem drinker" as opposed to the "normal" user of alcohol, *the* cause of half of all traffic deaths. From a complex reality, the drunk driver is constructed as the villain in a cultural melodrama, the sower of disorder in an otherwise orderly world. Thus, through the familiar techniques of monocausality, norm theory, culpable causation, and fundamental attribution error, responsibility for these accidents is simplified, personalized, dichotomized, and moralized—individual responsibility (the "unsafe driver") rather than corporate (the "unsafe car") or collective (the "unsafe road" or "unsafe transportation system") responsibility.

Personalized blaming is indeed everywhere. Social psychologist Daniel Gilbert, quoting and discussing the ideas of Gustav Icheiser, who wrote in the 1940s, gets to the heart of its ideological function:

---

occasions for *doing justice*, jury decision making carries significance far out of proportion to the number of cases in which it takes place.

[4] The authors added that "[b]ecause news is based on the concept of novelty rather than situational analysis . . . [and because of] the professional demands to 'humanize' individual stories, . . . news reports of risk make . . . the fundamental attribution error" (Wilkins & Patterson, 1987, pp. 82–83; see also Fischhoff, 1985).

[Icheiser] believed that the fundamental [attribution] error was not a rationalizing maneuver designed to pamper a frail ego, but a stubborn cultural myth:

> These misinterpretations [i.e., overattributing behavior to dispositions] are not personal errors committed by ignorant individuals. They are, rather, a consistent and inevitable consequence of the social system and of the ideology of the nineteenth century, which led us to believe that our fate in social space depended exclusively, or at least predominantly, on our individual qualities—that we, as individuals, and not the prevailing social conditions, shape our lives. [Citation omitted.]

> . . . . In a society that rewarded some with wealth and others with hardship, the tendency to attribute people's outcomes to dispositions served to justify the status quo. Classist society could only perpetuate itself by brainwashing its members to think of people as the authors of their actions, and thereby deserving of their fates. (Gilbert, 1998, p. 128)

Thus, melodramatic blaming supports a culture of individualism. It offers us a world in which human agency is responsible for bad outcomes, and in which responsibility for those outcomes is assigned to the people (the bad guys) who deviate from accepted behavioral norms. In this way the norms are reinforced, the wrongs done to the good guys are rectified—and the systemic causes of those bad outcomes are ignored.

In all of this, to claim that melodramatic blaming blocks awareness of the systemic causes of accidental injuries is *not* to argue that people would necessarily prefer to avoid those injuries at any cost. It is not to contend that people would (or should) give up the convenience of private automobile driving to eliminate auto accidents, the pleasure of certain affordable consumer goods to avoid the environmental hazards incident to their production, or the benefits of corporate capitalism to reduce unemployment and income inequality. The point is that melodramatic blaming tends to impede people's recognition that in their everyday lives they trade off vast, "accidental" human suffering for these benefits, and that the tradeoffs are ones they *might not* want to make, or make on the same terms, if they fully confronted the choice (cf. Calabresi, 1985). Conceiving of accidents as melodrama diverts people's focus from *systemic alternatives* to the mixes of benefit and harm they tacitly accept under the status quo.

To put it another way: Melodramatic thinking leads people to believe that they know what unduly risky behavior looks like. Sometimes, however, undue risk does not wear a black cape and speak with a deep voice. Sometimes it is practically invisible because it is just part of the background of people's daily lives. The melodramatic conception makes it harder for people to put in the foreground causes of accidental harm they might be better off recognizing.

Melodramatic Blaming and the Law

Common sense is inclined to simplify and personalize responsibility for accidents, and when common sense sits in the jury box, it works within a tort law regime that largely encourages exactly those habits of judgment. When an accident victim decides not to "lump" his or her injury and insurance does not suffice, he or she must seek compensation from identifiable defendants, not from the corporate economy or society as a whole. At trial, judge and jury are ordinarily constrained by rules of evidence to focus on the causation of particular harms rather than the creation of more general risks. The requirement of proximate cause, despite its reformulations throughout the 20th century, still tends to discourage assigning responsibility too far beyond the immediate injurer. And the instruction in negligence cases to gauge the parties' culpability by comparing their behavior to that of the "reasonable person" further encourages jurors to personalize responsibility. In sum, the substance and procedure of tort law display important features of the melodramatic conception of accidents.

Nowhere is the occlusion of systemic responsibility for accidental harm clearer than in the very use of the jury as an institution for allocating accident losses. Calabresi and Bobbitt (1978) argued 20 years ago that our society makes a de facto "tragic choice" to let a certain large number of ourselves be maimed and killed in (standard industrial and transportation) accidents, because some such large number of injuries and deaths is, as a statistical matter, inevitable, given contemporary methods of manufacture and transportation. To avoid confronting this choice collectively and explicitly, American society (*inter alia*) assigns to juries the task of allocating the costs of, and thus responsibility for, these accidents. Because different groups of citizens sit on different juries, each (ordinarily) deciding responsibility for a single accident, the allocation is decentralized and discontinuous; and because the legal system does not (ordinarily) require juries to give reasons for their decisions, the allocation is made aresponsibly. The decentralization, discontinuity, and aresponsibility allow us not to consider the cumulative tragedy as collectively chosen.

It can be seen that melodrama, which focuses on individual rather than social forces and does so in a moralizing way, is an appropriate mindset for jurors deciding responsibility for accidents, especially when they are deciding a negligence case, in which liability is based on fault, that is, individual blameworthiness.[5] And the sense of closure, the squaring

---

[5] The fault standard for gauging liability facilitates the avoidance of the tragic choice because it makes the award of compensation hinge on an "absolute standard of worthiness" instead of a comparative judgment across cases (Calabresi & Bobbitt, 1978, pp. 62–63, 72–79). Victims recover only if they can show that defendants' conduct (but not their own, to an extent depending on the comparative negligence law of the jurisdiction) falls short of the standard. The victim deserves compensation only because the defendant acted wrongfully—not because

of accounts, which people seek in melodrama, exactly matches the self-contained nature of discontinuous decision making by juries. Thus, jurors whose thinking and decisions fail to address the systemic causes of accidents are to a great extent behaving just as the situation demands, implementing the norms inherent in tort litigation.

For the distinct contribution that jurors' melodramatic blaming makes to blocking awareness of systemic responsibility for accidents, we must look to cases in which jurors' decision making appears to diverge from legal norms. That is, in many cases jurors' melodramatic thinking probably leads them to the same conclusions that nonmelodramatic thinking would have, in which event we cannot attribute any independent causal significance to the former, even if the use of melodramatic thinking in such cases remains an interesting ethnological fact.

One possible source of divergence, as observed in chapter 4, is jurors' tendency to conflate elements of liability that the law keeps separate into a single, holistic judgment of responsibility. The judge in a negligence case ascertains whether the defendant is responsible for the accident by focusing on what the plaintiff identifies as one or more "untaken precautions" by the defendant (M. Grady, 1989). The judge decides, first, whether the untaken precaution would have avoided the harm, and second, whether the precaution was worth taking. That is, causation and fault remain separate, albeit interrelated, elements of the case.

Jurors, by contrast, tend to conflate causal with legal responsibility. Thinking in the way that norm theory describes, jurors who determine that the party in question *could* have acted otherwise may infer as well that the party *should* have acted otherwise. Thinking in terms of culpable causation, jurors may draw the converse inference from blameworthiness to causation (see Nagareda, 1998). In either event, jurors may hold liable a defendant who either did not cause the accident or whose behavior was not legally wrongful.

An example of blame without much proof of causation is *Butler*, as we saw in chapter 5. Recall that there was no evidence at all as to why Butler fell off his truck. His attorney, however, took advantage of the tools of melodrama, especially norm theory and fundamental attribution error, to encourage jurors to blame the defendant's employees, whose untaken precaution was that they could have helped the plaintiff with the tarpaulin but did not.

To understand the larger significance of melodramatic blaming in such

---

industry and transportation systems are designed, quite beyond the control of the individual parties, in a way that is bound to cause some great number of injuries. The fault standard is a "perfectible" standard—in each individual case, its application allows us to believe that if only no one had been at fault, no one would have been hurt; it is individual fault that brings about injuries, not the fact that society collectively has set up the game to injure large numbers, however carefully they act (Calabresi, 1985). As Gusfield (1981, p. 173) said, "the science and law of drinking-driving create an orderly account of danger in the contemporary world."

a case, consider that slips and falls—at home, at the workplace, or else-where—account for nearly 40% of reported accidental injuries (Hensler et al., 1991). These kinds of things often just happen: Although slip-and-fall victims more often blame others for their accidents when they slip at work, they also chalk up their injuries partly or entirely to chance two-thirds of the time. So Butler's accident was typical—endemic to work and life. In situations like this, in which the limits of effective deterrence are quickly reached, the more important causes of accidents are systemic: the sheer number of people engaged in the activities in question, the extent to which they engage in them, and the physical and technological environment in which they find themselves (see Weiler, 1991). The analogy is to auto-mobile accidents: Whatever incentives people create to deter unusually risky driving, as long as there are enough millions of cars on the road being driven enough billions of miles by ordinary people with ordinary levels of attentiveness and degrees of coordination, there will also be tens of thousands of automobile fatalities every year (Gusfield, 1981).

In *Butler*, therefore, to blame the defendant's employees because of their supposed individual failings on this one occasion (they did not help) is to divert attention from all of the ways in which the configuration of the workplace (e.g., the loading dock, availability of adequate machinery for loading the equipment), standard work practices (e.g., Butler's own employer's implicit expectation that he could do the job alone), and work-place safety rules—none of which were at issue—may have increased the risk of slip-and-fall injuries, including serious ones like Butler's. Individu-alized blaming here tends to block awareness of the importance of back-ground causes, just as focusing blame for automobile accidents on the un-safe driver tends to block awareness of the importance of unsafe cars, unsafe roads, and inadequate transportation alternatives.[6] *Not* blaming in *Butler* and similar cases, on the other hand, could very well increase the pressure (on legislators and regulators) to reevaluate the background level of risk.[7]

An example of blaming the defendant despite a weak case on fault

---

[6] For a similar argument concerning iatrogenic medical injuries and liability rules, see Weiler (1991).

[7] The risk perception literature provides a useful analogy (Margolis, 1996). People's "visceral reactions" to risk, which influence how much they are inclined to avoid those risks, may depend on any number of features of the risk, including unfavorable moral associations. Thus, laypeople are much more bothered about dioxin than aflatoxin, even though the latter is a greater cancer risk owing to people's wider exposure to it (in peanut butter), in part because of the unfavorable associations between dioxin and the napalm used during the Vietnam war. So people's attitude toward dioxin is "better safe than sorry," which means, spend billions to eliminate trace amounts (e.g., at Times Beach, Missouri); people's attitude toward the more pervasive risk posed by aflatoxin is pretty much "who cares?" The consequence of this diversion of attention from what is in fact the more pervasive risk is *not* necessarily that people would want to eliminate aflatoxin in the same way they have tried to eliminate dioxin, but simply that people's disproportionate attention keeps them from performing a rational cost–benefit analysis with respect to either; indeed, according to Margolis, it keeps people from even seeing that there is a tradeoff to be made (in the case of dioxin or other feared contaminants, no risk-avoidance cost is too great).

is *Faverty*. What McDonald's did or failed to do may very well have contributed to the accident, but unless McDonald's behaved unreasonably, it should not have been held responsible. And whether one understands negligence in terms of social utility (defined either by public policy or by optimal care, i.e., the Learned Hand test) or fairness, there are good reasons to think that any act or omission by McDonald's was not unreasonable.

First, whether McDonald's' conduct unreasonably created a risk of the type of harm that befell the plaintiff "involve[s] considerations of public policy" (*Faverty*, p. 718), and public policy in this case is almost certainly on McDonald's' side. A plaintiff's verdict could "make all employers potentially liable for their employees' off-premises negligence when an employee becomes tired as a result of working" (p. 714), a rather broad but plausible extension of the majority's decision.[8] Second, it does not seem that McDonald's behaved unreasonably under the standard optimal care definition of negligence, because not letting teenagers work late shifts or effectively scrutinizing all departing employees for sufficient signs of drowsiness would very likely be inefficient.[9] Third, in terms of fairness, there is

---

[8] Among other things, the dissenters on the appellate court wondered how employers, at the time they scheduled employees for work assignments as much as 30 days in advance, could possibly anticipate those employees' mental and physical states at the end of those assignments, as the majority's holding made them responsible for doing (*Faverty*, p. 719.) The enormity of the potential consequences is suggested by the fact that some 20 million Americans work on rotating or night shifts and are particularly susceptible to increased accident risk from drowsiness (Moor-Ede, 1995). Representatives of employer groups naturally agreed with this assessment of the policy implications of the *Faverty* verdict. One (incidentally underscoring the analysis of the case I present in chapter 6) said that "[i]t's like putting someone's boss in the position of being their parents and deciding when they should go home to bed" (Taylor, 1991, p. 86, quoting Mona Zeiberg, senior labor counsel for the U.S. Chamber of Commerce).

[9] The cost of not scheduling (willing) high school students to work midnight shifts may very well have been paying extra to others to induce them to work those shifts (a cost that would eventually be passed on to customers), delaying the opening of business each morning waiting for the cleanup that could not be completed overnight (perhaps resulting in lost business), or reducing work opportunities for willing, able teenagers (with consequent effects on the local economy; for instance, the Matt Theurers of the world might not be able to purchase cars). Against these costs could be set the arguable social benefits of not allowing teenagers to work midnight shifts (e.g., interfering with their ability to study and engage in extracurricular activities, depriving older adults of work). (I thank Steve Gilles for pointing out to me the social benefits of a rule barring teenagers from working late shifts.) Moreover, the cost of enforcing a don't-let-tired-employees-work (-and-then-drive-home) policy would be enormous, as supervisors, fearful of liability, would have to spend time and effort scrutinizing every employee for signs of sleepiness. Thus James M. Coleman, counsel to the National Council of Chain Restaurants, a restaurant owners' association: "What are you supposed to do, sit there and run a monitoring device at the door as your employees leave and make a decision as to who looks too tired to drive home and start taking people's key? Then you're liable for false imprisonment" (quoted in Lafayette, 1992, p. 30). Presumably supervisors would be held to a standard of "reasonable" accuracy in detecting problematic levels of sleepiness, but it is unclear how any such standard would be applied.

My colleague Steve Gilles has argued to me that there is a plausible Hand formula case against McDonald's, based on its failure to prevent obviously tired teenage employees from working a second shift. Consider the analogy to the dram shop cases (such as *Vesely v. Sager*, 1971). It may be very costly for bartenders and waitpersons to decide whether each customer has had too much to drink, but a rule that tells bartenders and waitpersons not to serve people who are *obviously* intoxicated will prevent some accidents at much lower cost. It would,

another compelling reason not to hold McDonald's liable: It was *Theurer* who caused the accident, and his responsibility dwarfs that of McDonald's, if any. As the dissenting judges on the appellate court believed:

> That question [whether McDonald's created an unreasonable risk] must be answered in light of the uncontroverted facts that Theurer was an adult employee, that defendant did not require him to work the shift, that Theurer assured defendant's manager that he would rest between shifts and that he would be able to handle the shift physically, that Theurer never asked to be relieved from the shift, and that the harm to plaintiff occurred off defendant's work premises as a result of an activity over which defendant had no right of control. (*Faverty*, p. 717)

Arguably, then, *Faverty* is another case in which jurors stretched the bounds of negligence law, although the appellate court's affirmance suggests that the decision is at least defensible.

And yet imposing liability on McDonald's, albeit in terms of a personalized, melodramatized conception of responsibility, could lead to a questioning of at least one of the underlying, systemic causes of such accidents. Faverty's lawsuit may not—could not—have challenged the entire status quo in which 18-year-olds want and need cars so badly that they would drive 20 miles to and from midnight shifts to work at minimum wage to pay for them. Indeed, the lawyer explicitly disclaims any such intent: "This is not a case about whether high school kids should work or

---

however, seem less efficient to give employers the incentive to take the recommended precaution (check departing employees for obvious tiredness) than it is to give liquor providers an incentive not to serve the obviously intoxicated. Tiredness of the sort that is likely to lead a person to fall asleep at the wheel seems to me to be much more difficult to discern than intoxication of the sort that is likely to lead a person to drive unsafely. As Janet Bachman, vice president for claims administration for the American Insurance Association, said: "They're [the trial court] expecting an employer to be responsible for a circumstance he cannot control or predict. How can you tell how tired someone is unless they fall asleep while you're talking to them?" (quoted in Shalowitz, 1991, p. 73). Therefore, a liability rule pegged to "obvious" tiredness will be far more underinclusive (of the class of employees at risk for unsafe driving because of tiredness) than a rule pegged to obvious intoxication; to be effective, the precaution would have to be implemented across the board, leading to costly reassignments and overtime.

And the benefits to be gained from taking such precautions (the other side of the Hand optimal care formula) might very well be less than in the dram shop context, although this is a close question. Automobile accidents can be very costly. But given the driver's presumably superior ability to gauge his or her own level of wakefulness and competence to drive and his or her incentive to do something about it, it could certainly be argued that the probability of an accident, *ex ante*, was small. McDonald's could reasonably anticipate that employees who were so tired at the end of their shifts as to pose a driving risk would rest first, find alternative transportation, or pull over rather than chance falling asleep at the wheel. To put this same observation (that the employee/driver is in the superior position to gauge his or her ability to drive) in another light, it could be argued not only that McDonald's did not fail to use *optimal* care in these circumstances, but that McDonald's was not the *cheapest cost-avoider* with respect to this kind of risk; the employee/driver was. So holding McDonald's liable is probably inconsistent with the leading economic rationale even for strict liability. (On the other hand, evidence that at least two other employees had recently fallen asleep while driving home after late shifts and gotten into accidents, though contested [e.g., 603.18-21 (McDonald's' lawyer calls Dennis Dowrey's story about driving home drowsily after a late shift and crashing "completely false")] loomed large at trial and in the appellate court's reasoning.)

shouldn't work" (transcript of 3/25/91, 11.14-15). But the lawsuit did ask whether accidents such as this need be inherent in a world in which employees drive to and from round-the-clock businesses. Holding McDonald's liable could have prompted it (and other similarly situated organizations) to consider alternative ways of doing business—for instance, by implementing an "alertness assurance plan" including worker training and task forces as well as alternatives to driving home from work (Coburn, 1996). If this reading of the case is correct, then perhaps the plaintiff's lawyer really was inviting jurors to question the underlying conditions that increased the risk of accidents like Theurer's and Faverty's.[10] If it is true, however, that "people can only speak through the stories they understand" (Ferguson, 1994, p. 73), then we should not be surprised to find this awareness of a systemic cause of highway accidents couched in the language of melodramatized responsibility.

It is unclear what common factors, if any, distinguish the cases in which melodramatic thinking broaches the issue of systemic causes of accidents from those in which it typically inhibits people from considering such causes. Perhaps the first group is especially likely to include cases in which the plaintiff argues that while the defendant is not the direct cause of the harm, the defendant created a dangerous condition of which some other party took advantage to harm the plaintiff. *Faverty* is such a case. So too are lawsuits against tobacco companies for harm to smokers, although there it is the plaintiff who harms himself or herself (Nagareda, 1998). One upshot of this stretching of tort doctrine is to make people think about whether they should continue to accept the background condition—for instance, the availability of cigarettes—that allows so many millions of people to risk lung cancer and other diseases as the price of relaxation and stimulation. Lawsuits against gun manufacturers for injuries caused by the use of nondefective guns may prove to be a third prominent example (e.g., *Hamilton v. Accu-Tek*, 1999).

---

[10] Think about the plaintiff's litigation strategy in the following way. In looking beyond the other driver's estate for a deep pocket from which to seek compensation for his client's injuries, Faverty's lawyer could not sue the government (for designing, building, and maintaining the roads, which in all relevant respects were adequate) or the manufacturer of Faverty's truck (which met all standards of crashworthiness). That left Theurer's employer, McDonald's. To make McDonald's a plausible responsible party, Faverty's lawyer had to reconceive a highway collision case as a kind of workplace (or employment-related) injury case, and in so doing gestured at one of the systemic conditions for highway accidents. Many people in society have to drive to and from work; and given this, it is a statistical certainty that some of them will sometimes do so in a dangerously sleepy state. Faverty's lawyer could not, however, sue society at large for creating the patterns of residence, work, and transportation that required Theurer and Faverty to be driving between home and work; "society at large" is not an identifiable defendant. Instead, he personalized systemic risk creation in the form of a discrete party—the employer—and then argued that the employer behaved in a deviant way that caused the accident. Only by using the language of personalized, moralized (i.e., melodramatic) responsibility, therefore, could such an argument for systemic responsibility succeed. (I thank my colleague Linda Meyer for showing me the force of this interpretation of melodramatic blaming.)

Then again, the reasons why melodramatic thinking sometimes points society toward rather than away from the systemic causes of accidents may be extrinsic to tort litigation itself. It may be that only where the tradeoff of safety for pleasure and convenience becomes sufficiently prominent in the mass media and other aspects of popular culture does personalized responsibility become a vehicle for considering systemic responsibility. This is certainly more true of the tobacco cases than of *Faverty*; the danger posed by overtired drivers has generally failed to capture public attention. Even so, the *Faverty* trial does suggest the ambivalence of the melodramatic conception. Melodramatized blaming typically leaves the systemic causes of accidents unscathed, but occasionally it may be a kind of Trojan horse, a way not to reconcile ourselves to the status quo but to challenge it.

The Illusion of Control

Ever since the theatrical melodramas of the mid-19th century, Americans have reveled in stories in which the rich and powerful are the bad guys, and the humble are virtuous (Grimsted, 1994). This traditional American populism, of course, has persisted into the 20th century and today through innumerable movies and television programs. Media content analyses consistently find that prime-time television dramas depict business people as villains (Lichter, Lichter, & Amundson, 1997; Theberge, 1981). Business people lie, cheat, and, most often, kill; they are often, as in the title of a 1981 study, "crooks, con men, and clowns" (Theberge, 1981). And the heads of big businesses—that is, the characters most readily taken to represent the stereotype of "the corporation"—are the worst of all. Their villainy consists of easily recognizable, discrete criminal acts for which they are brought to justice by the end of the show (Theberge, 1981). Thus melodrama encourages people to believe that they can do something about the harms that corporate capitalism causes. By contrast, when corporate conduct that actually hurts real people—for instance, when General Motors closes a major plant and displaces thousands of workers—goes on screen, it is not the stuff of fictionalized melodrama, but of fact, and major news media frame the story to imply that workers and local communities have no alternative but to accept the plant closure and consequent misery as a business necessity (C. Martin & Oshagan, 1997).[11]

As in popular melodrama, melodramatized blaming in the accident case allows people to think and feel that they are doing something about misfortune, while diverting attention from the underlying causes of injuries in industrialized society and people's real lack of control over the riskiness

---

[11] See also Dreier (1987, p. 77): "The national press may criticize or expose *particular* corporate or government practices or *particular* corporations or elected officials who violate the public trust. Thus, a scandal like Watergate . . . or a Pentagon weapons boondoggle lends credence to the view that these violations are *exceptions* to an otherwise smoothly running system."

of their lives. In the melodrama of the accident case, as in popular culture, the plaintiff is the little guy, the innocent sufferer, the good guy who deserves to win from the bad guy defendant (and can do so with the jury's help). Empirical research confirms that jurors sometimes do take up the invitation to blame the corporate defendant; one of the more robust findings in the literature on juror decision making in accident cases, as we saw in chapter 4, is an anti-corporate defendant effect. But these individual instances of liability, even under products liability, have not on the whole been detrimental to corporate well-being (Dewees et al., 1996). Perhaps this is because the baseline response to accidental injury remains simply to lump it, for whatever reasons, and thus tacitly to accept the status quo; or perhaps it is because melodramatized blaming tends not to question the systemic ways in which life under corporate capitalism subjects people to risks of accidental injury. And yet melodramatized blaming in individual accident cases gives people the *sense* that they are addressing those risks, those feelings of vulnerability, just as the anti-corporate melodrama in popular culture allows people to indulge in fantasies of individual control and self-realization—in the belief that they can do something about corporate conduct that harms them—while in fact control over the conditions of economic life increasingly rests in the hands of fewer and larger corporations.[12]

If anything, people's urge to understand accidents as melodrama is becoming greater the more technologically advanced society becomes. As Friedman (1985) wrote, advances in technology lead people to expect that the riskiness in their lives can be controlled—if not by themselves, then surely by someone (e.g., most people have no personal control over airplane safety, but the manufacturers, airline maintenance crews, and pilots pre-

---

[12] My analysis is thus consistent with leftist critiques of popular media, which "interpret these results [the fictionalized portrayals of businessmen as bad guys] as a form of Marcusean 'repressive tolerance,' in which television neutralizes resistance against a repressive capitalist system by providing a fantasy outlet for the expression of mass resentment" (Lichter et al., 1997, pp. 79–80). Thus Todd Gitlin (1987, p. 258): "Television, like much popular culture through the ages, embodies fantasy images that speak to real aspirations.... The hegemonic image is an active shaping of what actually exists, but it would not take hold if it did not correspond, one way or another, to strong popular desires—as well as to defenses against them [citation omitted]. 'False consciousness' always contains its truth: the truth of wish, the truth of illusion that is embraced with a quiet passion made possible, even necessary, by actual frustration and subordination."

The Lichters themselves disagree with this interpretation, preferring to understand television's negative portrayals of businessmen as representing the opposition of Hollywood's relatively progressive creative community toward more conservative business interests (Lichter et al., 1997; Lichter, Lichter, & Rothman, 1994). The greater the consolidation of entertainment and other industries into fewer and fewer hands, the weaker the Lichters argument becomes, but I acknowledge their criticism of hegemony theory as essentially unfalsifiable (i.e., according to that theory, positive portrayals of business people reinforce the dominant capitalist structure, whereas negative portrayals also reinforce the dominant capitalist structure through repressive tolerance). Moreover, the fact that corporate interests and their right-wing advocates appear to attack with great vigor and sincerity negative portrayals of business people in the media (Dreier, 1987) indicates that they do not think those portrayals support capitalism, although the attackers could, of course, be wrong. Indeed, I suspect that both explanations are partly correct.

sumably do). People thus expect those others to exercise that control. The greater one's expectation of absolute security, the more a catastrophic accident stands out as senseless, shocking, something that *should not be*. The need to *make sense* of accidental harm becomes even greater, and melodrama is one of the primary ways people do this.[13] In any event, there is good reason to believe that the absolute *amount* of drama of all sorts, including melodrama, to which people in the last 40 years have been exposed (primarily through television) is very much greater than that to which people in previous generations were exposed (R. Williams, 1975). This suggests that the influence of melodramatic sensibility on people's judgments may very well be increasing as well.

Interestingly, a standard critique of juror decision making in accident trials also serves to personalize society's conceptions of responsibility for accidents. The popular stereotype of personal injury lawyers as melodramatic and jury verdicts in personal injury cases as driven by emotion can itself be understood as a forensic maneuver that preserves the status quo. As I hope to have shown, jurors may indeed think about accidents in terms of melodrama, but for the most part it is melodrama in the structural sense: responsibility simplified, personalized, dichotomized, and moralized. The usual critique of juror decision making in accident cases, by contrast, focuses on the emotional aspect of melodrama (e.g., Daniels & Martin, 1995). This critique allows for selective criticism of plantiffs' verdicts perceived to be too frequent and/or too large as driven by irresponsible sympathy for the plaintiff or anti-corporate defendant animus. At the same time, the critique leaves unquestioned and thus intact the structural components of thinking and blaming that support the status quo in modern industrial society.

In sum, accident trials are people's opportunity to reaffirm sense and meaning in the wake of accidental destruction, just as through popular melodramas people seek to reaffirm moral order in a confusing world. And just as melodrama offers a kind of fantasy that tends "to deny the always morally messy realities of life" (Grimsted, 1994, p. 202), at least some aspects of common-sense thinking about accidents also display a reassuring

---

[13] A similar argument may be found in M. Grady (1988), who posed the question of how medical malpractice claims and verdicts can be increasing at the same time that medical technology has been advancing (and, presumably, making people safer and healthier). He answered that advancing technology makes available more "durable precautions" (e.g., dialysis machines) to avoid harms that formerly would have been chalked up simply to misfortune (i.e., there's nothing we can do about this case of kidney disease). The presence of those precautions, however, increases the need for accompanying "nondurable" precautions—having sufficient machines, operating them properly, and so on—and thus multiplies the opportunities for failing to take those nondurable precautions, which may be negligence (see also Weiler, 1991). Once again, advancing technology enhances the controllability of what had been thought of as fate, and this, in turn, generates expectations that fate *will* be controlled, and hence increases the urge to blame for not controlling it. Hence, increased technology leads to a greater need to find individualized justice in the wake of an accident, which, somewhat ironically, can divert attention from the systemic causes of technology-based accidents.

fantasy of justice that denies some of the causally messy realities of life—a fantasy that usually reinforces the economic status quo, even while appearing to challenge it.

TOTAL JUSTICE AND PEOPLE'S ATTITUDES TOWARD JURIES

Criticism of juries is nothing new (Hans & Vidmar, 1986), and the attacks are as prevalent now as ever. Adler (1994), reviewing half a dozen jury trials, wrote that "[w]hile some American juries perform admirably, a shockingly large number do not" and that "[a] jury system that works as badly as this book shows it does shouldn't, and won't, survive" (pp. xv–xvi). Strier (1994) wrote that "the jury's ignorance, bias, and susceptibility to influence by expert witnesses and attorneys" has led to "the unpredictability of civil damage awards" and to "extremely high awards" (p. 115). The civil justice system—by which critics usually mean that part of it represented by jury verdicts—is lambasted as "seriously flawed" and "out of control" (see Galanter, 1996, 1998).[14]

Social scientists (Daniels & Martin, 1995; Galanter, 1996, 1998; Saks, 1992; Vidmar, 1995, 1998) have presented statistical analyses of jury verdicts and the results of controlled experiments that show the criticisms to be generally unfounded or overstated. I summarized some of this research in chapters 1 and 4. Here I would like to make a different kind of claim. I argue that understanding jury decision making in accident cases as *total justice* gives us another reason to pause before accepting prevalent criticisms of the civil jury.

How Just Is Total Justice?

In chapters 5 through 7, I examined in detail the efforts of jurors to do justice in a variety of mostly routine cases (routine except insofar as they are among the fewer than 5% that go to trial).[15] When discussing these cases, I compared the jurors' judgments with those that the law's rules and rationales indicated, noting both congruence and divergence.

---

[14] Even the deliberative process is assailed. In a recent case in which jurors rendered an unprecedented verdict against gun manufacturers, holding some of them liable for contributing to shooting injuries by negligent marketing practices that promoted illegal gun trafficking (Fried, 1999; *Hamilton v. Accu-Tek*, 1999), the *Wall Street Journal* referred to the jurors as "squabbling and haggling" (O'Connell & Barrett, 1999, p. 1). One could describe the deliberations more charitably. It is hardly surprising that the question of gun manufacturer liability would be deeply contested, because it pits deeply held intuitions about risk and responsibility (Margolis, 1996) against each other.

[15] *Butler* and *Giulietti* are routine workplace accident cases; the medical malpractice scenario about which the mock jurors in chapter 7 deliberated is not an actual case but is based on a typical case. Only *Faverty* is unusual in that a verdict for the plaintiff "made law" by extending liability in a novel fashion.

Now I would like to pull together those observations into a general evaluation of the jurors' efforts to do total justice.

First, it should be clear that total justice does *not* mean that jurors simply ignore the law in order to do what they think is right—in sharp contrast to recent poll results in which three quarters of respondents said that jurors should do just that (Aronson et al., 1998).[16] The jury instructions in *Faverty* appear to have led several of the jurors to decide as they did, contrary to what initially struck them as the "right" thing to do. And most of the jurors on the second mock jury in the case of delayed diagnosis of breast cancer quite dramatically adjusted their apportionments of fault to comply with the judge's instruction on the effects of limited comparative negligence. Juror decision making is multidimensional, and one of the dimensions which certainly influences jurors is the law as the judge presents it to them.

Second, the particular features of total justice are to a considerable extent consistent with the rules and rationales of tort law; and even if, on balance, jurors' total justice seems more at odds with legal rules or expert rationales than some alternative way of deciding tort cases would be, it may still be desirable, for political reasons, as part of the process for doing justice in the wake of accidents. Let us begin by considering each of the first four features of total justice (those that affect outcomes rather than mainly the deliberative process) in turn.

The first sense of total justice, the squaring or balancing of accounts, is, as noted in chapter 4, corrective (and distributive) justice in a nutshell, reflecting values deeply rooted in the doctrines and philosophy of tort law. With the exception of instances in which jurors exceed legal bounds to make things come out right (e.g., with regard to compensatory damages, see Goodman et al., 1989), this sense of total justice seems to implement an entirely defensible conception of fairness.

The second sense of total justice, jurors' desire for all the information they deem relevant to their decision, is somewhat more problematic. The rules of evidence generally aim to give jurors what they want, and jurors' persistent disregard of certain limiting instructions may be reduced some-

---

[16] These poll results do not, for a number of reasons, support the claim that jurors are "independent" in the sense claimed by the title of the article (Aronson et al., 1998). To agree with the statement, "whatever a judge says the law is, jurors should do what they believe is the right thing," is not to imply that the respondents, *as jurors*, would disregard the law. First, the law and the jurors' sense of the "right thing" may coincide. Second, respondents' answers to a very general question like the one posed by the poll—"whatever a judge says the law is"—may differ from their responses to questions soliciting their views on the propriety of disregarding specific instructions on particular legal issues. For instance, it is well established that public support for the death penalty drops when polls move from general inquiries ("do you support the death penalty?") to more specific ones ("do you support the death penalty for rapists?" or "do you support the death penalty for those guilty of felony murder?") (Finkel, 1995). Third, people's responses in the polling situation are unlikely to predict reliably how they would themselves behave *as jurors*, in the context of the trial, constrained by the powerful symbolism of the legal process.

what by rewriting the instructions to make them more comprehensible and by explaining to jurors the policies behind the instructions (Diamond & Casper, 1992; Lieberman & Sales, 1997). Still, jurors' inclination to use admissible evidence in ways that do not conform to the law—for instance, determining causal and hence legal responsibility in part on the basis of information about a party's character, a habit of thought using culpable causation and the fundamental attribution error—does suggest a (melo)-dramatic blaming practice at odds with the formal law and with the leading rationales for how the costs of accidental misfortune ought to be allocated.

The third feature of total justice, jurors' tendency to decide holistically by "commingling" what ought to be distinct steps or elements in the decision making process, sometimes leads to decisions that do not seem legally justified (Nagareda, 1998), but, as we saw in *Butler* and the medical malpractice scenario (if not also in other cases), also produces decisions that seem correct enough, although not arrived at in the legally prescribed manner. Moreover, even if one would like to increase the proportion of "correct enough" decisions by discouraging holistic decision making, it is not clear that efforts to reduce jurors' blurring of discrete elements will yield decisions that on the whole are less flawed. Special verdicts, or general verdicts accompanied by jury interrogatories, may focus jurors' decisions on particular aspects of the case and thus reduce commingling. Bifurcating the trial to separate liability and damage phases may result in fewer plaintiffs' verdicts than standard unitary trials (Horowitz & Bordens, 1990); if, however, the current blurring of liability and damages leads to an anti-plaintiff bias to begin with (Feigenson et al., 1997), bifurcation would exacerbate rather than correct the problem.

The fourth aspect of total justice, jurors' striving for a kind of justice that is total in its incorporation of their emotions as well as their "reason," presents another characteristic that is not easily reconciled with the formal law's dictates (Feigenson, 1997). Yet would it be preferable for jurors to exclude emotion from their decision making, even if that were possible? As I have written elsewhere about sympathy, but in words that apply to the use of emotion generally: "[t]o conceive of justice as non-emotional implies a model of decision making in which the decision maker acts without body or soul. It seems reasonable to suppose that many people would find such a model of decision making not only impossible to approximate, but also not worth striving for" (Feigenson, 1997, pp. 37–38). If the goal is to enhance justice, perhaps the law should stop its futile efforts to exclude emotions from decision making, but instead try to educate decision makers so that they use their emotions in a more prudent and well-informed fashion (Pillsbury, 1989; but cf. Feigenson, 1997).

When one evaluates the decisions that total justice produces, one should remember that the practical question is not whether juries' decisions are "right" in some absolute sense, but whether the likeliest alternative decision makers, judges, would do better—and according to what standard of measurement. Most of the time, the outcomes would be the same (Kalven & Zeisel, 1966; Saks, 1992). Experimental studies, moreover, tend to show that judges are susceptible to some of the same biases and imperfections as lay decision makers (Howe & Loftus, 1992; Landsman & Rakos, 1994; Vidmar, 1998; but cf. Hastie & Viscusi, 1998). In any event, the question of whether the judge's or the jury's decision is preferable in cases of divergence is unanswerable until criteria for evaluating outcomes, and their relative importance, are specified: fairness, efficiency, compensation, or some combination thereof.

Critics of tort juries are probably on their strongest footing when using the criterion of efficiency to evaluate jury decision making. As we have seen, total justice, as displayed by the lawyers' and jurors' talk in cases like *Butler*, *Giulietti*, and *Faverty*, may lead to results that are questionable in terms of efficient accident avoidance, although in each case the issue is certainly debatable.[17] And there are several other reasons, in addition to their inclination toward total justice, why civil juries may not be especially well suited to regulate the major risks of accidents that arise in a mass industrial society. The jury is a discontinuous decision maker (a different jury decides each case) and is neither asked nor presented with the information necessary to make comparative cost-allocation judgments across cases (does this plaintiff deserve compensation more than that one?) (Calabresi & Bobbitt, 1978). Lay jurors may be particularly ill equipped to perform the kind of quantitative analyses required in risk management (Hastie & Viscusi, 1998). The few accident cases to reach trial are unlikely to be representative in important respects relevant to societal risk management of the far greater number of accident-causing incidents as a whole, and each case tried offers at least partly idiosyncratic facts. And the presentation of those facts, and thus the jury's decision, may be affected by the vagaries of skill and resources the respective lawyers possess (Strier, 1994). All of these points argue in favor of giving other decision makers, legislative or administrative, the primary authority to make these kinds of decisions (Calabresi, 1970; Calabresi & Hirschoff, 1972; Rose-Ackerman, 1991).

---

[17] On a related topic, research shows that claims that the current tort liability system substantially impairs the innovativeness and economic competitiveness of American business are overstated. Litan (1991) wrote that "at most the 'liability tax' has imposed direct social costs of as much as 2 percent of GNP; that the liability tax probably harms innovation; but that considerable uncertainty remains about the size of any net social—and thus 'competitive' loss—resulting from that tax, if indeed a net loss exists at all" (p. 149). Viscusi and Moore (1991) seemed generally to agree: "Although . . . product liability places relatively high burdens on the more innovative firms, these costs are not a dominant component of firms' product costs. No economic catastrophe is imminent, but the costs of product liability may have a marginal influence on a variety of product decisions" (p. 125). According to Dewees et al. (1996), the limited empirical evidence on these questions is simply inconclusive.

Even so, one may want juries, seeking total justice, to make some decisions about how the losses from accidents should be allocated. Society should consider community participation in the process of doing justice to be worthwhile as an important democratic value in itself (for a critical discussion of this point, see Priest, 1993). One may also value the jury as a relief valve in just those most difficult cases that are likeliest to go to trial (Gertner, 1995), and within those cases, with regard to those issues, like apportioning fault or deciding damages, that "involve a complex value judgment as well as a literal determination of fact" (Kalven, 1958, p. 161). And society may want juries to bring the community's sense of total justice to decide liability particularly in those situations in which legislatures and administrative agencies are prone to make poor cost–benefit decisions because the people most likely to be victimized are inadequately represented in the legislative and administrative processes. In these situations, jury decision making may prompt those better suited to make societal risk management decisions to do so wisely (Zacharias, 1986).

Ultimately, people's views about the proper role of jury decision making in the civil justice system are political judgments, not scientific ones. Yet it seems reasonable to suppose that people's political judgments will be better if they are informed by what social science can tell us about what and how civil juries decide. It has been one of my aims in writing this book to contribute to this body of knowledge.

Thinking Better of Ourselves and the Justice We Create

Juries, as noted earlier, do not have very good press these days. Some of the prevailing negative view of tort juries in the media can be traced to the efforts of business interests that have publicized and lobbied for tort reform (Daniels & Martin, 1995; Galanter, 1998). Some of it can be traced to the exigencies of media coverage generally, with its emphasis on anecdotal rather than statistical information and its attraction to the atypical case (both of which tend to feature the "horror story" of the extreme plaintiff's verdict); its predilection for the simple soundbite ("tort damage awards have skyrocketed") rather than complex, variable, and incomplete data; and its efforts to frame both particular cases and aggregate trends as narratives which, to be compelling to the audience, must largely correspond to the audience's "common knowledge" about the subject matter (Haltom, 1998; Haltom & McCann, 1998). All of this tends to lead the public to think that juries in accident cases decide in favor of plaintiffs more often than they actually do, to think that those juries give higher awards than, on average, they actually do (Bailis & MacCoun, 1996; Galanter, 1998; Garber & Bower, 1999)—and to think that those accident juries, when they decide as they appear to have done, are deciding wrongly.

These perceptions of jury bias and incompetence are likely to be exacerbated the more that the justice system is captured on, and by, commercial television. While the regular trial coverage to be found on *CourtTV*, not to mention the exceptional coverage of sensational trials like that of O.J. Simpson, tends to focus on criminal rather than civil cases (Sherwin, 2000), the attitudes the public forms from watching these trials may generalize to their attitudes about *all* juries, including those in more routine accident cases. What attitudes about juries does the current televising of major trials foster?

First, watching television coverage empowers viewers to feel that they can knowledgeably criticize jurors. People who watch *CourtTV* or who regularly followed the continuous Simpson coverage think that they are seeing everything that the actual jurors see, and so they each become the "thirteenth juror" whose judgment about the case is just as good as that of the jurors. In fact, viewers are likely to believe that their judgment is *more* informed than that of the jurors. Viewers get to see and hear information that is excluded from the actual jurors' consideration; viewers, unlike actual jurors, get the benefit of expert commentary on the case in the form of the "talking heads" who speak during recesses and after the day's close of business; and viewers, unlike actual jurors, get the opportunity to discuss and reinforce their beliefs with others, either in person or through call-in television and radio programs (Sherwin, 2000).

In all of these respects, viewers are prone to be misled about their competence to evaluate the case, and hence, the actual jurors' performance. Information excluded at trial is not subject to cross-examination, so viewers may have a mistaken impression of its relevance or probative value. Many viewers, however much they watch televised trial coverage, do not in fact attend continuously to the coverage, and so may miss important information. Commentators may be biased or uninformed, and on a long-running show like *CourtTV*, some of them play ongoing roles (e.g., the "street-smart prosecutor") that make the substance of their remarks more significant as self-reference than as assertions about the reality outside the show. Moreover, viewers do not take the oath to which jurors swear, nor do they think and talk about the case within the solemn surroundings of the trial process, and as a result, their talk may very well lack the seriousness and continuity of actual jury deliberations.

Second, the kind of television that is increasingly absorbing law— *CourtTV*, consciously conceived as a combination of *C-SPAN* and soap operas (Sherwin, 2000), and talk shows—have often been characterized as "low culture." Soap operas and talk shows have traditionally been denigrated through their association with women and the working class. Those who denigrate the vehicles that increasingly provide knowledge about juries and the justice system (primarily members of the cultural elites, though some of them, too, may watch soap operas and talk shows) thereby reflect a distrust of "low" forms of knowledge traditionally associated with women

(Huyssen, 1986). At the same time, as more women and racial minorities serve on juries, legal elites have been calling for greater controls on jury discretion (e.g., through the increased use of summary judgment, in which the judge decides the case before a jury gets to hear it at trial) based on descriptions of juries as "irrational" and "emotional," language traditionally used to devalue the judgment of women and racial minorities (Dooley, 1995).

Both of these aspects of the mass mediation of popular knowledge about juries tend to undermine the sense of community. The false sense of superior knowledge and judgment offered by viewing televised trials and commentary tends to validate the individual viewer's opinions over reflective judgment reached after deliberation with others—in one of the few remaining fora in society in which the collective deliberation of laypeople carries political weight. Perhaps more important, the denigration of juries along demographic lines threatens to truncate one's understanding of the justice system by substituting for reflection the most invidious of stereotypes. This can be seen in the popular criticism of the predominantly Black female jury in the O.J. Simpson case for their supposed irrationality and emotionalism (Alexander & Cornell, 1997; Lipsitz, 1997; Marder, 1999); it is also seen in Taylor's (1991) article about *Faverty*, when he introduced his discussion of pro-plaintiff jurors' views with the subtitle, "Mothers Get on McDonald's' Case," as if those views were somehow less worthy because women with children provided them. This attitude toward jurors and juries is especially ironic in light of the research that shows that jurors' demographic characteristics have little to do with their verdicts in civil cases.

The social psychological conception of legal blaming that I have explained and illustrated in this book may help to counteract some of these tendencies and to foster a more appreciative, as well as more accurate, view of the role of juries in the civil justice system. The multidimensional nature of legal blaming reminds us of the importance of the situation in legal, as in other, social judgments. Close attention to the contextual influences on juror decision making—the law, the evidence, and the facts of the case as presented at trial—may help us to avoid simplistic attributions of jury decisions with which we may happen to disagree to "the (different) kind of people those jurors are." Social psychology teaches us that people tend to be "naive realists" who underestimate the extent to which their own subjectivity affects their impressions of the behavior of others (and everything else), who believe instead that their knowledge of the world reflects simple "read-offs" of an objective reality, and who thus attribute any differences between others' views and their own to those others' self-interest, bias, or perversity (R. Robinson et al., 1995). If we keep in mind these upshots of naive realism, we will more readily trace any differences between a given jury's decision and the one we think we would have reached to different construals of reality by people (we and the jurors) sharing fundamental habits of thought and feeling, rather than to unbridgeable differences between we the observers and they the observed that somehow lead *them* to get the plain facts wrong (see Marder, 1999).

The notion of total justice, moreover, allows us to see both the decisions we regard as correct enough and those we think mistaken as derived from the same habits of thought and feeling, habits that in any event most of us routinely apply in our everyday lives, and generally to good effect. We may thus be less prone to attribute (at least not without very good cause) what we identify as incorrect decisions to bad motives or deviant thinking—to incompetence, bias, or willful disregard of the law.

Finally, by providing a way to understand how even those jurors whose decisions we regard as incorrect may have honestly thought they were doing justice, we may be better able to accept the decision makers as members of a common community with ourselves. *We* are, indeed, the jury; and before we too hastily treat juries in accident cases as scapegoats onto which we can displace our own misgivings about our uncertain grasp of contemporary life, perhaps we should try to understand them as people essentially like ourselves, trying their best to do justice—just as we, too, would in their situation.

APPENDIX
A NOTE ON EMOTIONS AND
SOCIAL JUDGMENT

In chapter 3 I discuss research on the effects of specific emotions on legal judgment. Because emotions may sometimes be indistinguishable from more general moods (Clore, Schwarz, & Conway, 1994) and may influence judgments in similar ways, and because considerably more research has been conducted on the effects of moods on social judgments, some discussion of the larger body of research on mood effects may be helpful.

First, a comment about terminology. The most general category is *affect*; within affect, *moods*, which tend to be less intense, more diffuse, and relatively enduring, and to lack a readily identifiable source, may be distinguished from *emotions*, which tend to be more intense and short-lived, and to have an identifiable cause (e.g., a person is angry at or about something; Davidson, 1994; Forgas, 1992; Isen, 1984). One might then add a distinction between affective *states* (emotions or moods) and affective *traits* (enduring dispositions of the person; Goldsmith, 1994). Although the following survey of research on affect and social judgment primarily concerns mood effects, when the distinctions do not matter, I use *mood, emotion,* and *affect* interchangeably. In any event, my focus (in both this Appendix and in chapter 3) is on states, not traits; as in chapters 2 and 3, I am not primarily concerned with individual differences among people's habits of thought and feeling.

IN GENERAL

Two theories dominated the first decade or so of research (roughly the early 1980s to the early 1990s) on how affect influences social judgments. The first, known as *affect priming*, is that moods *indirectly* influence judgments by priming mood-congruent perceptions and memories on which the judgments are based. Affect priming is explained by Bower's (1991) *associative network model*. It posits that emotions function as nodes in a cognitive network, linking similarly valenced ideas and life events, as well as corresponding bodily and expressive activity. Mood directs attention to and facilitates learning and memory of congruent phenomena, and it biases interpretation of ambiguous stimuli in a mood-congruent direction (Bower, 1981, 1991). Mood congruence in memory (discussed further below) operates similarly: Present mood primes recall of congruent memories because they are associated with matching emotion nodes. All of these effects make mood-congruent data more available to the person making a social judgment, and thus, through the availability heuristic (Tversky & Kahneman, 1982a, 1982b), those data play a larger role in shaping the judgment (Bower, 1991; Forgas, 1991).

Thus, in a classic experiment, people who are asked whether they are generally satisfied with their lives give more negative answers on rainy days (when they are temporarily in a negative mood) than on sunny days (when they are temporarily in a positive mood; Schwarz & Clore, 1988). Affect priming explains this effect as follows: Participants in a negative mood more readily recall negative events and are more likely to classify ambiguous events as negative, and then base their overall judgment of life satisfaction on that skewed sampling.

The second theory is that moods more *directly* influence social judgments. This is the *feelings-* (or mood- or affect-) *as-information* theory of Schwarz and Clore (Clore et al., 1994; Schwarz, 1990; Schwarz & Clore, 1988). According to this view, people faced with a complex judgmental task "frequently use their affective state at the time of judgment as a piece of information that may bear on the judgmental task, according to a 'How do I feel about it?' heuristic" (Schwarz & Clore, 1988, p. 527). Thus, participants in the sunny day/rainy day experiment above did not evaluate their lives negatively (or positively) because their mood triggered congruent memories and guided them to congruent interpretations of past events. Instead, they gauged their life satisfaction as if their current mood itself told them something about the answer to that question. Schwarz and Clore established that mood influenced judgment in this way, rather than through affect priming, because participants contacted on rainy days whose attention was casually drawn to the weather (and who were still in a relatively negative mood) evaluated their lives as positively as did those contacted on sunny days. That is, their mood influenced their judgment only when they did not attribute it to a judgment-irrelevant source (the weather). The researchers concluded that it is the mood itself that people take as informative about the judgment at hand, and not the mood's propensity to trigger congruent memories (Schwarz & Clore, 1983). Other research shows that mood-as-information, rather than affective priming, accounts for various phenomena, although the two theories are not mutually exclusive and may even "be describing different ends of the same elephant" (Clore & Parrott, 1991, p. 118). A substantial amount of other research confirms that people use their transient moods as diagnostic information in making difficult judgments (L. Martin, et al., 1997; Schwarz & Clore, 1988), especially when their processing capacity has been reduced by time pressure or competing task demands (Siemer & Reisenzein, 1998). On the other hand, there does seem to be some disagreement in the literature as to whether the complexity of the judgment task increases (Bodenhausen & Lichtenstein, 1987) or decreases (Branscombe & Cohen, 1991) the heuristic use of affect.

Each of these theories, however, fails to account for some of the evidence. For example, the associative network model is unable to explain why affect sometimes motivates people in sad moods to "repair" their mood by avoiding, rather than seeking, congruent (i.e., sad) thoughts (Fiedler, 1991; Isen, 1984). The mood-as-information theory cannot account for the impact of mood at the time of encoding on a later judgment not made in that same mood (see Bower, 1991), nor for findings that, given the opportunity, participants in a happy mood may choose to process information more deliberately (Mackie & Worth, 1991).

In response to these and other conflicts and inconsistencies, some psychologists have argued that other factors moderate the effects of mood on cognition and have attempted to synthesize the competing theories. Two such syntheses are Fiedler's (1991) *dual-force model* and Forgas's (1992, 1994) *multiprocess* or *affect infusion model*. Fiedler argued that affect in general has a greater impact on cognition when the task at hand requires relatively more active generation of new information than when it involves the passive conservation of given information. It has also been shown that people reduce their heuristic use of moods (i.e., what affect-as-information theory describes) when personal involvement in or accountability for the judgment motivates them to think through the decision more carefully. Legal decision making would appear to require precisely the sort of active information processing and construction of new information that, according to the dual-force model, makes affect important.

Largely consistent with these views, Forgas's (1992, 1994) affect infusion model of emotion and cognition categorizes four different ways in which affect may influence social judgment, depending on features of the target of judgment, the person making the evaluation, and the situation. Forgas argued, for instance, that when people make social judgments about familiar targets, they directly access evaluations stored in memory; affect plays little role in generating the judgment. In other situations, mood may motivate people to process information in a certain direction, for example, to maintain positive moods or repair negative ones.

More relevant to most legal judgments are the third and fourth types of process. Where the target is unfamiliar, the person making the judgment is not strongly motivated toward a particular outcome, and the judgment task is relatively simple, Forgas (1994) predicted the heuristic use of affect, that is, mood-as-information. Good moods, moreover, tend to induce simplified, heuristic information processing styles (as is discussed below). Where, however, the judgment task is complex or unusual, and especially when the situation demands accuracy or accountability, people are more likely to engage in the "substantive" use of affective processing, that is, affect priming (Forgas, 1994). The affect infusion model of the role of emotion in social judgment is to some extent consistent with the *elaboration likelihood model* of persuasion (for a comparison of the two, see Petty & Wegener, 1999).

We can infer that both affect-as-information and affect priming would be relevant to how jurors think about responsibility for accidents, although it is unclear which would be more important. The typical legal judgment involves an unfamiliar target, a complex judgment, and the motivation to judge accurately, all of which suggest that the decision maker's mood will influence his or her judgment by priming mood-congruent perceptions, memories, and interpretations. However, the decision maker is typically not motivated toward a particular outcome, a factor more likely to trigger the use of mood as a judgmental heuristic.

SPECIFIC INFLUENCES OF AFFECT ON SOCIAL JUDGMENT

Both general moods and more specific emotions have been shown to influence how people perceive, remember, and evaluate information, as well as their styles of processing information in general. I give brief summaries of each of these cognitive operations, mentioning mood effects first, then emotion effects.

Perception

In general, people prefer to be exposed to mood-congruent stimuli (Bower, 1991). For instance, in studies of how people perceive others, participants in a positive mood spent more time examining positive aspects of the target person, whereas participants in a negative mood dwelt on negative aspects (Forgas & Bower, 1987). On the other hand, people who want to temper their mood in order to achieve composure before an anticipated meeting with a stranger may seek out mood-incongruent stimuli (Erber, Wegner, & Therriault, 1996). People also more readily identify faces (Niedenthal, 1992) and recognize words (Niedenthal, Halberstadt, & Setterlund, 1997; Niedenthal, Setterlund, & Jones, 1994) that express a mood congruent with their own.

Memory

Mood congruence in memory has been identified in at least two forms: state-dependent and mood-congruent recall. State-dependent recall exists when people in a given mood more readily remember information that they learned while in the same mood (i.e., happy people more readily remember information they encoded while in a happy mood). Mood-congruent recall, by contrast, refers to the match between mood at the time of remembering and the valence of the remembered material. For instance, people in a positive mood more easily recall positive material (Clore et al., 1994). It should be noted that some research has failed to confirm state-dependent recall, and reviewers have described mood-congruent recall as "a rather fragile phenomenon" (Clore et al., 1994, p. 380; Mayer & Salovey, 1988). Both Clore et al. (1994) and Mayer and Salovey (1988) also noted that it is sometimes difficult to distinguish mood-congruent recall from state-dependent recall, in part because it is hard to distinguish the valence of the target material itself from the valence of the participant's mood when he or she learned the material.

Emotion-congruent perception and memory have also been observed, although the research is limited. People tend to remember more information when their particular emotion at recall matches their emotion when they learned the information (Bower, 1981). In one experiment, participants in whom anger had been induced and who then read a restaurant review containing statements designed to elicit a customer's anger or disgust remembered more of the information designed to provoke anger; disgusted participants remembered more of the disgust-provoking information (Bower, 1991).

Evaluation

One of the most reliable findings in the research on affect and cognition is the mood congruence of evaluative judgments. People's social judgments tend to be biased toward their prevailing mood. "Judgment effects due to mood are unquestionably the most robust, replicable, and general effects in the domain of cognition and affect" (Mayer & Salovey, 1988, p. 93). "[C]heerful people like just about everything better" (Fiske & Taylor, 1991, pp. 446–447). This has been shown for a variety of judgments, ranging from satisfaction with consumer goods to satisfaction with one's own life as a whole (Clore et al., 1994; Mayer & Salovey, 1988). Evidence for the converse proposition—that people in a negative mood tend to dislike whatever it is they are judging—is more equivocal, but not insubstantial (Fiske & Taylor, 1991). In addition, longitudinal studies show that moods covary with judgments over time; that is, the same person will make more positive judgments when in a positive mood and more negative judgments when in a negative mood (Mayer & Hanson, 1995).

More specifically, people's moods shape the ways in which they categorize objects and events (Halberstadt & Niedenthal, 1997), including social situations and other people (Cantor & Kihlstrom, 1987), and these categorizations, in turn, can shape legal judgments concerning the conduct of those other people (Feigenson, 1995). For instance, given various members of a category, people tend to classify as prototypical the member whose evaluative tone is closest to their current mood, apparently an example of mood congruency. Thus, when asked to pick the most prototypical "type of physical contact," sad participants will choose "hit," whereas happy participants choose "kiss" (Mayer & Salovey, 1988).

The effects on evaluative judgments of the specific emotions (as opposed to moods) most relevant to decision making in accident cases (sympathy, anger, and anxiety or fear) are discussed in chapter 3.

Information Processing

A very robust finding in the research is that people in a (moderately) positive mood tend to think more creatively and to be better at drawing associations and inductive reasoning than people in a neutral mood, whereas people in a (moderately) negative mood tend to be somewhat better at analytic and deductive reasoning (Estrada, Isen, & Young, 1994; Fiedler, 1988; Palfai & Salovey, 1994; Schwarz & Bless, 1991; Sinclair & Mark, 1992). More generally, people in happy moods tend to engage in "looser," less systematic, less detailed, and less effortful thinking strategies than do people in negative moods, whose cognitive style, by contrast, is characterized by "tightening" (Fiedler, 1988; Mackie & Worth, 1991; Sinclair & Mark, 1995). Thus, people in sad moods are less likely than those in neutral moods, and people in happy moods more likely than those in neutral moods, to commit the fundamental attribution error (Forgas, 1998).

Affect-as-information theory, discussed above, offers one explanation for why affect shapes cognitive style. Positive affect signals that a person's world is generally safe and secure, reducing the motivation to engage in cognitive effort unless required by the person's other goals. Negative affect, by contrast, motivates the person to change something about his or her world, which inspires a more careful assessment of present conditions and their causal links and a more deliberate consideration of ways to change those conditions (Bless et al., 1996; Forgas, 1991; Schwarz & Bless, 1991).

TABLE OF AUTHORITY

An n following a page number indicates location in a footnote.

REFERENCES

Aagard, T. (1998). Identifying and valuing the injury in lost chance cases. *Michigan Law Review, 96*, 1335–1361.

Abel, R. (1995). A critique of torts. In R. Rabin (Ed.), *Perspectives on tort law* (4th ed., pp. 322–342). Boston: Little, Brown.

Adler, S. (1994). *The jury.* New York: Doubleday.

Affron, C. (1991). Identifications. In M. Landy (Ed.), *Imitations of life* (pp. 98–117). Detroit, MI: Wayne State University Press.

Ajzen, I., & Fishbein, M. (1983). Relevance and availability in the attribution process. In J. Jaspars, F. Fincham, & M. Hewstone (Eds.), *Attribution theory and research* (pp. 63–89). London: Academic Press.

Alexander, N., & Cornell, D. (1997). Dismissed or banished? A testament to the reasonableness of the Simpson jury. In T. Morrison & C. Lacour (Eds.), *Birth of a nation'hood* (pp. 57–96). New York: Pantheon Books.

Alicke, M. (1992). Culpable causation. *Journal of Personality and Social Psychology, 63*, 368–378.

American College of Obstetricians and Gynecologists (1996). *Guidelines for women's health care.* Washington, DC: Author.

American Law Institute. (1965). *Restatement of the law (2nd): Torts.* Philadelphia: American Law Institute.

American Law Institute. (1997). *Restatement of the Law (3rd): Torts: Products liability.* Philadelphia: American Law Institute.

Amsterdam, A., & Hertz, R. (1992). An analysis of closing arguments to a jury. *New York Law School Law Review, 37*, 55–122.

Anderson, M., & MacCoun, R. (1999). Goal conflict in juror assessments of compensatory and punitive damages. *Law and Human Behavior, 23*, 313–330.

Aristotle. (1926). *Rhetoric.* Cambridge, MA: Harvard University Press.

Aristotle. (1934). *Nicomachean ethics.* Cambridge, MA: Harvard University Press.

Aristotle. (1942). *Poetics.* Cambridge, MA: Harvard University Press.

Arkes, H. (1989). Principles in judgment/decision making research pertinent to legal proceedings. *Behavioral Sciences and the Law, 7*, 429–456.

Aronson, E., Wilson, T., & Brewer, M. (1998). Experimentation in social psychology. In D. Gilbert, S. Fiske, & G. Lindzey (Eds.), *Handbook of social psychology* (Vol. 1, pp. 99–142). Boston: McGraw-Hill.

Aronson, P., Rovella, D., & Van Voris, B. (1998, November 2). Jurors: A biased, independent lot. *National Law Journal,* p. 1, col. 2.

Averill, J. (1982). *Anger and aggression: An essay on emotion.* New York: Springer-Verlag.

Averill, J. (1983). Studies on anger and aggression: Implications for theories of emotion. *American Psychologist, 38*, 1145–1160.

Averill, J. (1994). Emotions unbecoming and becoming. In P. Ekman & R. Davidson (Eds.), *The nature of emotion* (pp. 265–269). London: Oxford University Press.

Avildsen, J. (1976). *Rocky* [Film]. Los Angeles: United Artists.

Azevedo, D. (1990). Destroying the sympathy element in a malpractice trial. *Medical Economics, 67,* 102–108.

Bailis, D., & MacCoun, R. (1996). Estimating liability risks with the media as your guide: A content analysis of media coverage of tort litigation. *Law and Human Behavior, 20,* 419–430.

Balon, J., & Wehrwein, T. (1997). Cancer of the breast. In G. Moore (Ed.), *Women and cancer: A gynecologic oncology nursing perspective* (pp. 348–383). Sudbury, MA: Jones & Bartlett.

Banaji, M., Hardin, C., & Rothman, A. (1993). Implicit stereotyping in person judgment. *Journal of Personality and Social Psychology, 65,* 272–281.

Bandura, A. (1997). *Self-efficacy.* New York: Freeman.

Bargh, J. (1999). The cognitive monster: The case against the controllability of automatic stereotype effects. In S. Chaiken & Y. Trope (Eds.), *Dual-process theories in social psychology* (pp. 361–382). New York: Guilford Press.

Baron, J., & Ritov, I. (1993). Intuitions about penalties and compensation in the context of tort law. *Journal of Risk and Uncertainty, 7,* 17–33.

Baron, R., & Kenny, D. (1986). The moderator–mediator variable distinction in social psychological research: Conceptual, strategic, and statistical considerations. *Journal of Personality and Social Psychology, 51,* 1173–1182.

Batson, C. D. (1991). *The altruism question.* Hillsdale, NJ: Erlbaum.

Batson, C. D. (1998). Altruism and prosocial behavior. In D. Gilbert, S. Fiske, & G. Lindzey (Eds.), *Handbook of social psychology* (Vol. 2, pp. 282–316). Boston: McGraw-Hill.

Batson, C. D., Early, S., & Salvarani, G. (1997). Perspective taking: Imagining how another feels versus imagining how you would feel. *Personality and Social Psychology Bulletin, 23,* 751–758.

Batson, C. D., Polycarpou, M., Harmon-Jones, E., Imhoff, H., Mitchener, E., Bednar, L., Klein, T., & Highberger, L. (1997). Empathy and attitudes: Can feeling for a member of a stigmatized group improve feelings toward the group? *Journal of Personality and Social Psychology, 72,* 105–118.

Batson, C. D., Turk, C., Shaw, L., & Klein, T. (1995). Information function of empathic emotion: Learning why we value the other's welfare. *Journal of Personality and Social Psychology, 68,* 300–313.

Baumeister, R. (1982). A self-presentational view of social phenomena. *Psychological Bulletin, 91,* 3–26.

Bell, P., & O'Connell, J. (1997). *Accidental justice.* New Haven, CT: Yale University Press.

Bennett, W. L., & Feldman, M. (1981). *Reconstructing reality in the courtroom.* New Brunswick, NJ: Rutgers University Press.

Benyamini, Y., Leventhal, E., & Leventhal, H. (1997). Attributions and health. In A. Baum, S. Newman, J. Weinman, R. West, & C. McManus (Eds.),

Cambridge handbook of psychology, health and medicine (pp. 72–77). Cambridge, England: Cambridge University Press.

Berry, D., Pennebaker, J., Mueller, J., & Hiller, W. (1997). Linguistic bases of social perception. *Personality and Social Psychology Bulletin, 23,* 526–537.

Biek, M., Wood, W., & Chaiken, S. (1996). Working knowledge, cognitive processing, and attitudes: On the determinants of bias. *Personality and Social Psychology Bulletin, 22,* 547–556.

Bix, B. (1996). *Jurisprudence: Theory and context.* London: Sweet & Maxwell.

Black, J., Galambos, J., & Read, S. (1984). Comprehending stories and social situations. In R. Wyer & T. Srull (Eds.), *Handbook of social cognition* (Vol. 3, pp. 45–86). Hillsdale, NJ: Erlbaum.

Blair, I., & Banaji, M. (1996). Automatic and controlled processes in stereotype priming. *Journal of Personality and Social Psychology, 70,* 1142–1163.

Blanck, P., Rosenthal, R., & Cordell, L. (1985). The appearance of justice: Judges' verbal and nonverbal behavior in criminal jury trials. *Stanford Law Review, 38,* 89–164.

Bless, H., Schwarz, N., Clore, G., Golisano, V., Rabe, C., & Wölk, M. (1996). Mood and the use of scripts: Does a happy mood really lead to mindlessness? *Journal of Personality and Social Psychology, 71,* 665–679.

Bodenhausen, G. (1993). Emotions, arousal, and stereotypic judgments: A heuristic model of affect and stereotyping. In D. Mackie & D. Hamilton (Eds.), *Affect, cognition, and stereotyping* (pp. 13–37). San Diego, CA: Academic Press.

Bodenhausen, G., & Lichtenstein, M. (1987). Social stereotypes and information-processing strategies: The impact of task complexity. *Journal of Personality and Social Psychology, 52,* 871–880.

Bodenhausen, G., Sheppard, L., & Kramer, G. (1994). Negative affect and social judgment: The differential impact of anger and sadness. *European Journal of Social Psychology, 24,* 45–62.

Bonazzoli, J. (1998). Jury selection and bias: Debunking invidious stereotypes through science. *Quinnipiac Law Review, 18,* 237–295.

Booth, W. (1983). *The rhetoric of fiction.* Chicago: University of Chicago Press.

Bornstein, B. (1991). *The effect of sympathy on attributions of liability: Legal and Bayesian perspectives.* Unpublished doctoral dissertation, University of Pennsylvania.

Bornstein, B. (1994). David, Goliath, and Reverend Bayes: Prior beliefs about defendants' status in personal injury cases. *Applied Cognitive Psychology, 8,* 233–258.

Bornstein, B. (1998). From compassion to compensation: The effect of injury severity on mock jurors' liability judgments. *Journal of Applied Social Psychology, 28,* 1477–1502.

Bornstein, B. (1999). The ecological validity of jury simulations: Is the jury still out? *Law and Human Behavior, 23,* 75–91.

Bornstein, B., & Rajki, M. (1994). Extra-legal factors and product liability: The influence of mock jurors' demographic characteristics and intuitions about the cause of an injury. *Behavioral Sciences and the Law, 12,* 127–147.

Bovbjerg, R., Sloan, F., Dor, A., & Hsieh, C. R. (1991). Juries and justice: Are malpractice and other personal injuries created equal? *Law and Contemporary Problems, 54,* 5–42.

Bower, G. (1981). Mood and memory. *American Psychologist, 36,* 129–148.

Bower, G. (1991). Mood congruity of social judgments. In J. Forgas (Ed.), *Emotion and social judgments* (pp. 31–53). Oxford, England: Pergamon Press.

Branscombe, N., & Cohen, B. (1991). Motivation and complexity levels as determinants of heuristic use in social judgment. In J. Forgas (Ed.), *Emotion and social judgments* (pp. 145–160). Oxford, England: Pergamon Press.

Branscombe, N., Owen, S., Garstka, T., & Coleman, J. (1996). Rape and accident counterfactuals: Who might have done otherwise and would it have changed the outcome? *Journal of Applied Social Psychology, 26,* 1042–1067.

Bray, R., & Kerr, N. (1982). Methodological considerations in the study of the psychology of the courtroom. In N. Kerr & R. Bray (Eds.), *The psychology of the courtroom* (pp. 287–323). San Diego, CA: Academic Press.

Brill, S. (1982, November). Inside the jury room at the *Washington Post* libel trial. *The American Lawyer, 1,* 89–94.

Brooks, P. (1976). *The melodramatic imagination.* New Haven, CT: Yale University Press.

Brown, R., & Fish, D. (1983). The psychological causality implicit in language. *Cognition, 14,* 237–273.

Bruce, C. (1984). The deterrent effects of automobile insurance and tort law: A survey of the empirical literature. *Law and Policy, 6,* 67–100.

Bruner, J. (1973). *Beyond the information given.* New York: Norton.

Bruner, J. (1986). *Actual minds, possible worlds.* Cambridge, MA: Harvard University Press.

Bruner, J. (1990). *Acts of meaning.* Cambridge, MA: Harvard University Press.

Buck, M., & Miller, D. (1994). Reactions to incongruous negative life events. *Social Justice Research, 7,* 29–46.

Burger, J. (1981). Motivational biases in the attribution of responsibility for an accident: A meta-analysis of the defensive-attribution hypothesis. *Psychological Bulletin, 90,* 496–512.

Butler v. Revere Copper & Brass, Inc., No. Civ. N-87-476 (WWE) (D. Conn. 1990).

Byrne v. Boadle, 159 Eng. Rep. 209 (Ex. 1863)

Cacioppo, J., Petty, R., Feinstein, J., & Jarvis, W. (1996). Dispositional differences in cognitive motivation: The life and times of individuals varying in need for cognition. *Psychological Bulletin, 119,* 197–253.

Calabresi, G. (1970). *The costs of accidents.* New Haven, CT: Yale University Press.

Calabresi, G. (1985). *Ideals, beliefs, attitudes, and the law.* Syracuse, NY: Syracuse University Press.

Calabresi, G., & Bobbitt, P. (1978). *Tragic choices*. New York: Norton.

Calabresi, G., & Hirschoff, J. (1972). Toward a test for strict liability in torts. *Yale Law Journal, 81*, 1055–1085.

Campbell v. Carpenter, 566 P.2d 893 (Or. 1977).

Cantor, N., & Kihlstrom, J. (1987). *Personality and social intelligence*. Englewood Cliffs, NJ: Prentice Hall.

Cantor, N., Mischel, W., & Schwartz, J. (1982). A prototype analysis of psychological situations. *Cognitive Psychology, 14*, 45–77.

Caplan, L., Helzlsouer, K., Shapiro, S., Wesley, M., & Edwards, B. (1996). Reasons for delay in breast cancer diagnosis. *Preventive Medicine, 25*, 218–224.

Carroll, J., & Russell, J. (1996). Do facial expressions signal specific emotions? Judging emotion from the face in context. *Journal of Personality and Social Psychology, 70*, 205–218.

Casper, J., Benedict, K., & Perry, J. (1989). Juror decision making, attitudes, and the hindsight bias. *Law and Human Behavior, 13*, 291–310.

Cather, C., Greene, E., & Durham, R. (1996). Plaintiff injury and defendant reprehensibility: Implications for compensatory and punitive damage awards. *Law and Human Behavior, 20*, 189–205.

Cecil, J., Hans, V., & Wiggins, E. (1991). Citizen comprehension of difficult issues: Lessons from civil jury trials. *American University Law Review, 40*, 727–774.

Chapman, G., & Bornstein, B. (1996). The more you ask for, the more you get: Anchoring in personal injury verdicts. *Applied Cognitive Psychology, 10*, 519–540.

Charrow, R., & Charrow, V. (1979). Making legal language understandable: A psycholinguistic study of jury instructions. *Columbia Law Review, 79*, 1306–1374.

Chin, A., & Peterson, M. (1985). *Deep pockets, empty pockets: Who wins in Cook County jury trials*. Santa Monica, CA: RAND Institute for Civil Justice.

Choi, I., & Nisbett, R. (1998). Situational salience and cultural differences in the correspondence bias and the actor–observer bias. *Personality and Social Psychology Bulletin, 24*, 949–960.

Christianson, S., Säisä, J., & Silfvenius, H. (1995). The right hemisphere recognizes the bad guys. *Cognition and Emotion, 9*, 309–324.

Cialdini, R. (1994). *Influence: The psychology of persuasion* (Rev. ed.). New York: William Morrow.

Cialdini, R., Braver, S., & Lewis, S. (1974). Attributional bias and the easily persuaded other. *Journal of Personality and Social Psychology, 30*, 631–637.

Citron, R. (1991). Faulty reasoning guides doubling-time defense. *Medical Malpractice Law and Strategy, 9*(1), 1, 4–5.

Clermont, K., & Eisenberg, T. (1992). Trial by jury or judge: Transcending empiricism. *Cornell Law Review, 77*, 1124–1177.

Clermont, K., & Eisenberg, T. (1998). Do case outcomes really reveal anything about the legal system? Win rates and removal jurisdiction. *Cornell Law Review, 83*, 581–607.

Clore, G. (1994). Why emotions require cognition. In P. Ekman & R. Davidson (Eds.), *The nature of emotion* (pp. 181–191). New York: Oxford University Press.

Clore, G., & Parrott, G. (1991). Moods and their vicissitudes: Thoughts and feelings as information. In J. Forgas (Ed.), *Emotion and social judgments* (pp. 107–123). Oxford, England: Pergamon Press.

Clore, G., Schwarz, N., & Conway, M. (1994). Affective causes and consequences of social information processing. In R. Wyer & T. Srull (Eds.), *Handbook of social cognition* (2nd ed., Vol. 1, pp. 323–417). Hillsdale, NJ: Erlbaum.

Coburn, E. (1996, August 5). Fatigue can spawn perils at round-the-clock cos. *National Underwriter*, pp. 9–10.

Cohen, R. (1982). Perceiving justice: An attributional perspective. In J. Greenberg & R. Cohen (Eds.), *Equity and justice in social behavior* (pp. 119–160). New York: Academic Press.

Cohn, S. (1991). Delay in diagnosis of breast cancer. *Journal of Nurse-Midwifery*, 36(1), 74–79.

Coleman, J., & Ripstein, A. (1995). Mischief and misfortune. *McGill Law Journal*, 41, 91–130.

Conley, J., & O'Barr, W. (1990). *Rules versus relationships*. Chicago: University of Chicago Press.

Conley, J., O'Barr, W., & Lind, E.A. (1978). The power of language: Presentational style in the courtroom. *Duke Law Journal*, 1978, 1375–1399.

Conley, T. (1990). *Rhetoric in the European tradition*. Chicago: University of Chicago Press.

Cooper, J., Bennett, E., & Sukel, H. (1996). Complex scientific testimony: How do jurors make decisions? *Law and Human Behavior*, 20, 379–394.

Cover, R. (1975). *Justice accused*. New Haven, CT: Yale University Press.

Cusimano, G. (1998, March). *Understanding how and why jurors decide issues and using that information to your advantage*. Paper presented at Association of Trial Lawyers of America, National College of Advocacy, Overcoming Juror Bias seminar. Salt Lake City, UT.

Damasio, A. (1994). *Descartes' error: Emotion, reason, and the human brain*. New York: Grosset/Putnam.

Dane, F., & Wrightsman, L. (1982). Effects of defendants' and victims' characteristics on jurors' verdicts. In N. Kerr & R. Bray (Eds.), *The psychology of the courtroom* (pp. 83–115). San Diego, CA: Academic Press.

Daniels, S., & Martin, J. (1995). *Civil juries and the politics of reform*. Chicago: Northwestern University Press/American Bar Foundation.

Danzon, P. (1985). *Medical malpractice*. Cambridge, MA: Harvard University Press.

Darden, W., DeConinck, J., Babin, B., & Griffin, M. (1991). The role of consumer sympathy in product liability suits: An experimental investigation of loose coupling. *Journal of Business Research*, 22, 65–89.

Davidson, R. (1994). On emotion, mood, and related affective constructs. In P.

Ekman & R. Davidson (Eds.), *The nature of emotion* (pp. 51–55). New York: Oxford University Press.

Davies, M., Stankov, L., & Roberts, R. (1998). Emotional intelligence: In search of an elusive construct. *Journal of Personality and Social Psychology, 75*, 989–1015.

Davis, M. (1994). *Empathy: A social psychological approach.* Boulder, CO: Westview Press.

Davis, M., Conklin, L., Smith, A., & Luce, C. (1996). Effect of perspective taking on the cognitive representation of persons: A merging of self and other. *Journal of Personality and Social Psychology, 70*, 713–726.

Dawes, R. (1998). Behavioral decision-making and judgment. In D. Gilbert, S. Fiske, & G. Lindzey (Eds.), *Handbook of social psychology* (Vol. 1, pp. 497–548). Boston: McGraw-Hill.

Dennis, C., Gardner, B., & Lim, B. (1975). Analysis of survival and recurrence vs. patient and doctor delay in treatment of breast cancer. *Cancer, 35*, 714–720.

Denove, C., & Imwinkelried, I. (1995). Jury selection: An empirical investigation of demographic bias. *American Journal of Trial Advocacy, 19*, 285–341.

de Sousa, R. (1987). *The rationality of emotion.* Cambridge, MA: MIT Press.

Deutsch, M. (1985). *Distributive justice: A social–psychological perspective.* New Haven, CT: Yale University Press.

Devine, P., & Monteith, M. (1999). Automaticity and control in stereotyping. In S. Chaiken & Y. Trope (Eds.), *Dual-process theories in social psychology* (pp. 339–360). New York: Guilford Press.

Devitt, E., Blackmar, C., & Wolff, M. (1987). *Federal jury practice and instructions: Civil.* St. Paul, MN: West.

Dewar, M., & Love, N. (1992). Legal issues in managing breast disease. *Postgraduate Medicine, 92*, 137–151, 154.

Dewees, D., Duff, D., & Trebilcock, M. (1996). *Exploring the domain of accident law.* New York: Oxford University Press.

Diamond, S. (1997). Illuminations and shadows from jury simulations. *Law and Human Behavior, 21*, 561–571.

Diamond, S., & Casper, J. (1992). Blindfolding the jury to verdict consequences: Damages, experts, and the civil jury. *Law and Society Review, 26*, 513–563.

Diamond, S., Saks, M., & Landsman, S. (1998). Juror judgments about liability and damages: Sources of variability and ways to increase consistency. *DePaul Law Review, 48*, 301–325.

Dijksterhuis, A., van Knippenberg, A., Kruglanski, A., & Schaper, C. (1996). Motivated social cognition: Need for closure effects on memory and judgment. *Journal of Experimental Social Psychology, 32*, 254–270.

Dooley, L. (1995). Our juries, our selves: The power, perception, and politics of the civil jury. *Cornell Law Review, 80*, 325–361.

Dorfman, A. (1983). *The empire's old clothes.* New York: Pantheon.

Douglas, M. (1992). *Risk and blame: Essays in cultural theory.* London: Routledge.

Dreier, P. (1987). The corporate complaint against the media. In D. Lazere (Ed.), *American media and mass culture* (pp. 64–80). Berkeley: University of California Press.

Edmonson v. Leesville Concrete Co., 500 U.S. 614 (1991).

Edwards, K., & Bryan, T. (1997). Judgmental biases produced by instructions to disregard: The (paradoxical) case of emotional information. *Personality and Social Psychology Bulletin, 23*, 849–864.

Edwards, K., & Smith, E. (1996). A disconfirmation bias in the evaluation of arguments. *Journal of Personality and Social Psychology, 71*, 5–24.

Ehrenzweig, A. (1951/1966). Negligence without fault. *California Law Review, 54*, 1422–1477.

Eisenberg, N., & Fabes, R. (1990). Empathy: Conceptualization, measurement, and relation to prosocial behavior. *Motivation and Emotion, 14*, 131–149.

Eisenberg, N., Fabes, R., Murphy, B., Karbon, M., Maszk, P., Smith, M., O'Boyle, C., & Suh, K. (1994). The relations of emotionality and regulation to dispositional and situational empathy-related responding. *Journal of Personality and Social Psychology, 66*, 776–797.

Eisenberg, N., Fabes, R., Schaller, M., Miller, P., Carlo, G., Poulin, R., Shea, C., & Shell, R. (1991). Personality and socialization correlates of vicarious emotional responding. *Journal of Personality and Social Psychology, 61*, 459–470.

Eisenberg, N., & Lennon, R. (1983). Sex differences in empathy and related capacities. *Psychological Bulletin, 94*, 100–131.

Ekman, P. (1973). Cross-cultural studies of facial expression. In P. Ekman (Ed.), *Darwin and facial expression: A century of research in review* (pp. 169–222). New York: Academic Press.

Ekman, P. (1992). An argument for basic emotions. *Cognition and Emotion, 6*, 169–200.

Ekman, P. (1994a). All emotions are basic. In P. Ekman & R. Davidson (Eds.), *The nature of emotion* (pp. 15–19). New York: Oxford University Press.

Ekman, P. (1994b). Strong evidence for universals in facial expressions: A reply to Russell's mistaken critique. *Psychological Bulletin, 115*, 268–287.

Ellickson, R. (1991). *Order without law.* Cambridge, MA: Harvard University Press.

Ellsworth, P. (1989). Are twelve heads better than one? *Law and Contemporary Problems, 52*, 205–224.

Ellsworth, P. (1993). Some steps between attitudes and verdicts. In R. Hastie (Ed.), *Inside the juror* (pp. 42–64). Cambridge, England: Cambridge University Press.

Ellsworth, P. (1994). Some reasons to expect universal antecedents of emotion. In P. Ekman & R. Davidson (Eds.), *The nature of emotion* (pp. 150–154). New York: Oxford University Press.

Elsaesser, T. (1987). Tales of sound and fury: Observations on the family melodrama. In C. Gledhill (Ed.), *Home is where the heart is* (pp. 43–69). London: British Film Institute.

Elwork, A., Sales, B., & Alfini, J. (1982). *Making jury instructions understandable.* Charlottesville, VA: Michie.

Emmons, R., King, L., & Sheldon, K. (1993). Goal conflict and the self-regulation of action. In D. Wegner & J. Pennebaker (Eds.), *Handbook of mental control* (pp. 528–551). Englewood Cliffs, NJ: Prentice Hall.

Engel, D. (1987). The oven bird's song: Insiders, outsiders, and personal injuries in an American community. *Law and Society Review, 18,* 551–582.

English, P., & Sales, B. (1997). A ceiling or consistency effect for the comprehension of jury instructions. *Psychology, Public Policy, and Law, 3,* 381–401.

Epstein, R. (1973). A theory of strict liability. *Journal of Legal Studies, 2,* 151–204.

Epstein, R. (1995). *Cases and materials on torts.* Boston: Little, Brown.

Epstein, R. (1999). *Torts.* Boston: Aspen Law and Business.

Erber, R., & Tesser, A. (1992). Task effort and the regulation of mood: The absorption hypothesis. *Journal of Experimental Social Psychology, 28,* 339–359.

Erber, R., Wegner, D., & Therriault, N. (1996). On being cool and collected: Mood regulation in anticipation of social interaction. *Journal of Personality and Social Psychology, 70,* 757–766.

Eriksen, C. (1966). Cognitive responses to internally cued anxiety. In C. Spielberger (Ed.), *Anxiety and behavior* (pp. 327–360). New York: Academic Press.

Estrada, C., Isen, A., & Young, M. (1994). Positive affect improves creative problem solving and influences reported source of practice satisfaction in physicians. *Motivation and Emotion, 14,* 285–299.

Ewen, S. (1988). *All consuming images.* New York: Basic Books.

Facione, N., Dodd, M., Holzemer, W., & Meleis, A. (1997). Helpseeking for self-discovered breast symptoms. *Cancer Practice, 5,* 220–227.

Faverty v. McDonald's Restaurants of Oregon, Inc., No. A90001–00394 (Oregon Circuit Court, Multnomah County, March 29, 1991), aff'd 892 P.2d 703 (Or. Ct. App. 1995).

Federal Employers' Liability Act, 45 U.S.C. § 51–60 (1994).

Feigenson, N. (1995). The rhetoric of torts: How advocates help jurors think about causation, reasonableness, and responsibility. *Hastings Law Journal, 47,* 61–165.

Feigenson, N. (1997). Sympathy and legal judgment: A psychological analysis. *Tennessee Law Review, 65,* 1–78.

Feigenson, N., Park, J., & Salovey, P. (1997). Effect of victim blameworthiness and outcome severity on attributions of responsibility and damage awards in comparative negligence cases. *Law and Human Behavior, 21,* 597–617.

Feigenson, N., Park, J., & Salovey, P. (in press). The role of emotions in comparative negligence judgments. *Journal of Applied Social Psychology.*

Fein, S., McCloskey, A., & Tomlinson, T. (1997). Can the jury disregard that information? The use of suspicion to reduce the prejudicial effects of pretrial publicity and inadmissible testimony. *Personality and Social Psychology Bulletin, 23,* 1215–1226.

Felstiner, W., Abel, R., & Sarat, A. (1981). The emergence and transformation of disputes: Naming, blaming, claiming . . . *Law and Society Review, 15,* 631–654.

Ferguson, R. (1994). Story and transcription in the trial of John Brown. *Yale Journal of Law and the Humanities, 6*, 37–73.

Festinger, L. (1957). *A theory of cognitive dissonance*. Evanston, IL: Row, Peterson.

Fiedler, K. (1988). Emotional mood, cognitive style, and behavior regulation. In K. Fiedler & J. Forgas (Eds.), *Affect, cognition, and social behavior* (pp. 100–119). Toronto, Ontario, Canada: Hogrefe.

Fiedler, K. (1991). On the task, the measures, and the mood in research on affect and social cognition. In J. Forgas (Ed.), *Emotion and social judgments* (pp. 83–140). Oxford, England: Pergamon Press.

Fincham, F., & Jaspars, J. (1979). Attribution of responsibility to the self and other in children and adults. *Journal of Personality and Social Psychology, 37*, 1589–1602.

Fincham, F., & Jaspars, J. (1980). Attribution of responsibility: From man the scientist to man as lawyer. In L. Berkowitz (Ed.), *Advances in experimental social psychology* (Vol. 13, pp. 81–138). New York: Academic Press.

Finkel, N. (1995). *Commonsense justice*. Cambridge, MA: Harvard University Press.

Fischhoff, B. (1975). Hindsight ≠ foresight: The effect of outcome knowledge on judgment under uncertainty. *Journal of Experimental Psychology: Human Perception and Performance, 1*, 288–299.

Fischhoff, B. (1982a). Debiasing. In D. Kahneman, P. Slovic, & A. Tversky (Eds.), *Judgment under uncertainty: Heuristics and biases* (pp. 422–444). Cambridge, England: Cambridge University Press.

Fischhoff, B. (1982b). For those condemned to study the past: Heuristics and biases in hindsight. In D. Kahneman, P. Slovic, & A. Tversky (Eds.), *Judgment under uncertainty: Heuristics and biases* (pp. 335–351). Cambridge, England: Cambridge University Press.

Fischhoff, B. (1985). Managing risk perceptions. *Issues In Science and Technology, 2*(2), 83–96.

Fischhoff, B., & Beyth, R. (1975). "I knew it would happen": Remembered probabilities of once-future things. *Organizational Behavior and Human Performance, 13*, 1–16.

Fiske, S. (1982). Schema-triggered affect: Applications to social perception. In M. S. Clark & S. Fiske (Eds.), *Affect and cognition: The 17th Annual Carnegie Symposium on Cognition* (pp. 55–78). Hillsdale, NJ: Erlbaum.

Fiske, S., & Taylor, S. (1991). *Social cognition* (2nd ed.). New York: McGraw-Hill.

Fletcher, G. (1994, February 17). Convicting the victim. *New York Times*, A-17, col. 2.

Ford, M. (1986). The role of extralegal factors in jury verdicts. *Justice System Journal, 11*, 16–39.

Forgas, J. (1991). Affect and social judgments: An introductory review. In J. Forgas (Ed.), *Emotion and social judgments* (pp. 3–29). Oxford, England: Pergamon Press.

Forgas, J. (1992). Affect in social judgments: A multiprocess model. In M. Zanna

(Ed.), *Advances in experimental social psychology* (Vol. 25, pp. 227–275). San Diego, CA: Academic Press.

Forgas, J. (1994). The role of emotion in social judgments: An introductory review and an Affect Infusion Model (AIM). *European Journal of Social Psychology, 24,* 1–24.

Forgas, J. (1998). On being happy and mistaken: Mood effects on the fundamental attribution error. *Journal of Personality and Social Psychology, 75,* 318–331.

Forgas, J., & Bower, G. (1987). Mood effects on person-perception judgments, *Journal of Personality and Social Psychology, 53,* 53–60.

Fried, J. (1999, February 12). 9 gun makers called liable for shootings. *New York Times,* A-1, col. 1.

Friedman, L. (1985). *Total justice.* New York: Russell Sage Foundation.

Frijda, N. (1986). *The emotions.* Cambridge, England: Cambridge University Press.

Funder, D. (1987). Errors and mistakes: Evaluating the accuracy of social judgment. *Psychological Bulletin, 101,* 75–90.

Galanter, M. (1993). The regulatory function of the civil jury. In R. Litan (Ed.), *Verdict: Assessing the civil jury system* (pp. 61–102). Washington, DC: Brookings Institution.

Galanter, M. (1996). Real world torts: An antidote to anecdote. *Maryland Law Review, 55,* 1093–1160.

Galanter, M. (1998). Oil strike in hell: Contemporary legends about the civil justice system. *Arizona Law Review, 40,* 717–752.

Gallagher, D., & Clore, G. (1985, May). *Effects of fear and anger on judgments of risk and evaluations of blame.* Paper presented at Midwestern Psychological Association annual meeting, Chicago.

Garber, S., & Bower, A. (1999). Newspaper coverage of automotive product liability verdicts. *Law and Society Review, 33,* 93–122.

Geertz, C. (1983). *Local knowledge.* New York: Basic Books.

Gerould, D. (1991). Russian formalist theories of melodrama. In M. Landy (Ed.), *Imitations of life* (pp. 118–134). Detroit, MI: Wayne State University Press.

Gertner, N. (1995). Is the jury worth saving? [Review of S. Adler, *The jury*]. *Boston University Law Review, 75,* 923–939.

Gibbs, R., & Beitel, D. (1995). What proverb understanding reveals about how people think. *Psychological Bulletin, 118,* 133–154.

Gilbert, D. (1998). Ordinary personology. In D. Gilbert, S. Fiske, & G. Lindzey (Eds.), *Handbook of social psychology* (Vol. 2, pp. 89–150). Boston: McGraw-Hill.

Gilbert, D., & Malone, P. (1995). The correspondence bias. *Psychological Bulletin, 117,* 21–38.

Gilles, S. (1992). Negligence, strict liability, and the cheapest cost-avoider. *Virginia Law Review, 78,* 1291–1375.

Gilles, S. (1994a). Inevitable accident in classical English tort law. *Emory Law Journal, 43,* 575–646.

Gilles, S. (1994b). The invisible hand formula. *Virginia Law Review, 80,* 1015–1054.

Gilovich, T. (1991). *How we know what isn't so.* New York: Free Press.

Gitlin, T. (1987). Television's screens: Hegemony in transition. In D. Lazere (Ed.), *American media and mass culture* (pp. 240–265). Berkeley: University of California Press.

Giulietti v. Providence & Worcester Co., Civ. Nos. 81–7453 & 81–7625 (D. Conn. 1981), aff'd without opinion, 688 F.2d 815 (2d Cir. 1982).

Gledhill, C. (1987). The melodramatic field: An investigation. In C. Gledhill (Ed.), *Home is where the heart is* (pp. 5–39). London: British Film Institute.

Golding, J., Fowler, S., Long, D., & Latta, H. (1990). Instructions to disregard potentially useful information: The effects of pragmatics on evaluative judgments and recall. *Journal of Memory and Language, 29,* 212–227.

Goldsmith, H. H. (1994). Parsing the emotional domain from a developmental perspective. In P. Ekman & R. Davidson (Eds.), *The nature of emotion* (pp. 68–73). New York: Oxford University Press.

Goleman, D. (1995). *Emotional intelligence.* New York: Bantam Books.

Goodman, J., Greene, E., & Loftus, E. (1989). Runaway verdicts or reasoned determinations: Mock juror strategies in awarding damages. *Jurimetrics Journal, 29,* 285–309.

Gouldner, A. (1960). The norm of reciprocity: A preliminary statement. *American Sociological Review, 25,* 161–178.

Grady, D. (1999, January 26). In breast cancer data, hope, fear, and confusion. *The New York Times,* F-1, col. 4.

Grady, M. (1988). Why are people negligent? Technology, nondurable precautions, and the medical malpractice explosion. *Northwestern University Law Review, 82,* 293–334.

Grady, M. (1989). Untaken precautions. *Journal of Legal Studies, 18,* 139–156.

Graham, S., Weiner, B., & Zucker, G. (1997). An attributional analysis of punishment goals and public reactions to O. J. Simpson. *Personality and Social Psychology Bulletin, 23,* 331–346.

Graziano, S., Panter, A., & Tanaka, J. (1990). Individual differences in information processing strategies and their role in juror decision making and selection. *Forensic Reports, 3,* 279–301.

Green, E. (1968). The reasonable man: Legal fiction or psychosocial reality? *Law and Society Review, 1,* 241–257.

Green, W. (1990, April 18). Attorneys try to defuse sympathy in injury cases. *The Wall Street Journal,* B-1, col. 5.

Greene, E. (1989). On juries and damage awards: The process of decisionmaking. *Law and Contemporary Problems, 52,* 225–246.

Greene, E. (1990). Media effects on jurors. *Law and Human Behavior, 14,* 439–450.

Greene, E., Downey, C., & Goodman-Delahunty, J. (1999). Juror decisions about damages in employment discrimination cases. *Behavioral Sciences and the Law*, *17*, 107–121.

Greene, E., Goodman, J., & Loftus, E. (1991). Jurors' attitudes about civil litigation and the size of damage awards. *American University Law Review, 40*, 805–820.

Greene, E., & Loftus, E. (1985). When crimes are joined at trial. *Law and Human Behavior, 9*, 193–207.

Greenspan, P. (1988). *Emotions and reasons*. New York: Routledge.

Grice, P. (1989). *Studies in the way of words*. Cambridge, MA: Harvard University Press.

Grimsted, D. (1994). Vigilante chronicle: The politics of melodrama brought to life. In J. Bratton, J. Cook, & C. Gledhill (Eds.), *Melodrama: Stage, picture, screen* (pp. 199–213). London: British Film Institute.

Gross, S., & Syverud, K. (1996). Don't try: Civil jury verdicts in a system geared to settlement. *U.C.L.A. Law Review, 44*, 1–64.

Gusfield, J. (1981). *The culture of public problems*. Chicago: University of Chicago Press.

Halberstadt, J., & Niedenthal, P. (1997). Emotional state and the use of stimulus dimensions in judgment. *Journal of Personality and Social Psychology, 72*, 1017–1033.

Hallin, D. (1986). We keep America on top of the world. In T. Gitlin (Ed.), *Watching television* (pp. 9–41). New York: Pantheon.

Haltom, W. (1998). *Reporting on the courts*. Chicago: Nelson-Hall.

Haltom, W., & McCann, M. (1998, August). *Law and lore: Media, common knowledge, and the politics of civil justice*. Paper presented at the 1998 meeting of the American Political Science Association, Boston.

Hamilton et al. v. Accu-tek et al., No. CV-95-0049, 1999 U.S. Dist. LEXIS 8264 (E.D.N.Y. June 3, 1999).

Hamilton, V. L. (1980). Intuitive psychologist or intuitive lawyer? Alternative models of the attribution process. *Journal of Personality and Social Psychology, 39*, 767–772.

Hamilton, V. L., & Sanders, J. (1992). *Everyday justice*. New Haven, CT: Yale University Press.

Hammitt, J., Carroll, S., & Relles, D. (1985). Tort standards and jury decisions. *Journal of Legal Studies, 14*, 751–765.

Hans, V. (1994, June 18). *Lay reactions to corporate defendants*. Paper presented at Law and Society Association annual meeting, Phoenix, AZ.

Hans, V. (1998). The illusions and realities of jurors' treatment of corporate defendants. *DePaul Law Review, 48*, 327–353.

Hans, V., Hannaford, P., & Munsterman, T. (1999). The Arizona jury reform permitting civil jury trial discussions: The views of trial participants, judges, and jurors. *University of Michigan Journal of Law Reform, 32*, 349–377.

Hans, V., & Lofquist, W. (1992). Jurors' judgments of business liability in tort cases: Implications for the litigation explosion debate. *Law and Society Review, 26*, 85–115.

Hans, V., Mott, N., & Simpson, L. (1998, June 5). *"How do you know what half a lung is worth?" Civil jurors' accounts of their award decision-making.* Paper presented at Law and Society Association annual meeting, Aspen, CO.

Hans, V., & Sweigart, K. (1993). Jurors' views of civil lawyers: Implications for courtroom communication. *Indiana Law Journal, 68,* 1297–1332.

Hans, V., & Vidmar, N. (1986). *Judging the jury.* New York: Plenum Press.

Harré, R. (1986). An outline of the social constructionist viewpoint. In R. Harré (Ed.), *The social construction of emotions* (pp. 2–31). London: Basil Blackwell.

Hart, A., Evans, D., Wissler, R., Feehan, J., & Saks, M. (1997). Injuries, prior beliefs, and damage awards. *Behavioral Sciences and the Law, 15,* 63–82.

Harvey, J., & McGlynn, R. (1982). Matching words to phenomena: The case of the fundamental attribution error. *Journal of Personality and Social Psychology, 43,* 345–346.

Harvey, J., Town, J., & Yarkin, K. (1981). How fundamental is "the fundamental attribution error"? *Journal of Personality and Social Psychology, 40,* 346–349.

Hastie, R. (1999). The role of "stories" in civil jury judgments. *University of Michigan Journal of Law Reform, 32,* 227–239.

Hastie, R., Penrod, S., & Pennington, N. (1983). *Inside the jury.* Cambridge, MA: Harvard University Press.

Hastie, R., Schkade, D., & Payne, J. (1998). A study of juror and jury judgments in civil cases: Deciding liability for punitive damages. *Law and Human Behavior, 22,* 287–314.

Hastie, R., Schkade, D., & Payne, J. (1999). Juror judgments in civil cases: Effects of plaintiff's requests and plaintiff's identity on punitive damage awards. *Law and Human Behavior, 23,* 445–470.

Hastie, R., & Viscusi, W. K. (1998). What juries can't do well: The jury's performance as a risk manager. *Arizona Law Review, 40,* 901–921.

Hawkins, S., & Hastie, R. (1990). Hindsight: Biased judgments of past events after the outcomes are known. *Psychological Bulletin, 107,* 311–327.

Hays, M., & Nikolopolou, A. (1996). Introduction. In M. Hays & A. Nikolopolou (Eds.), *Melodrama: The cultural emergence of a genre* (pp. vii–xv). New York: St. Martin's Press.

Heider, F. (1958). *The psychology of interpersonal relations.* New York: Wiley.

Henderson, J., & Eisenberg, T. (1990). The quiet revolution in products liability: An empirical study of legal change. *U.C.L.A. Law Review, 37,* 479–553.

Hensler, D., Marquis, M. S., Abrahamse, A., Berry, S., Ebener, P., Lewis, E., Lind, E. A., MacCoun, R., Manning, W., Rogowski, J., & Vaiana, M. (1991). *Compensation for accidental injuries in the United States.* Santa Monica, CA: RAND Institute for Civil Justice.

Herskovits v. Group Health Cooperative, 664 P.2d 474 (Wash. 1983).

Hilton, D. (1990). Conversational processes and causal explanations. *Psychological Bulletin, 107,* 65–81.

Hinsz, V., & Indahl, K. (1995). Assimilation to anchors for damage awards in a mock civil trial. *Journal of Applied Social Psychology, 25,* 991–1026.

Hoffman, M. (1990). Empathy and justice motivation. *Motivation and Emotion, 14*, 151–171.

Holmes, O. (1963). *The common law*. Boston: Little, Brown. (Original work published 1881).

Holstein, J. (1985). Jurors' interpretations and jury decision making. *Law and Human Behavior, 9*, 83–100.

Holyoak, K., & Gordon, P. (1984). Information processing and social cognition. In R. Wyer & T. Srull (Eds.), *Handbook of social cognition* (Vol. 1, pp. 39–70). Hillsdale, NJ: Erlbaum.

Horowitz, I., & Bordens, K. (1990). An experimental investigation of procedural issues in complex tort trials. *Law and Human Behavior, 14*, 269–285.

Howard, D. (1997). Familiar phrases as peripheral persuasion cues. *Journal of Experimental Social Psychology, 33*, 231–243.

Howe, E., & Loftus, T. (1992). Integration of intention and outcome information by students and circuit court judges: Design economy and individual differences. *Journal of Applied Social Psychology, 22*, 102–116.

Huyssen, A. (1986). *After the great divide*. Bloomington: Indiana University Press.

In re Polemis & Furness, Withy & Co., [1921] 1 A. C. 617 (P.C. Aust).

Isen, A. (1984). Toward understanding the role of affect in cognition. In R. Wyer & T. Srull (Eds.), *Handbook of social cognition* (Vol. 1, pp. 179–236). Hillsdale, NJ: Erlbaum.

Jacowitz, K., & Kahneman, D. (1995). Measures of anchoring in estimation tasks. *Personality and Social Psychology Bulletin, 21*, 1161–1166.

James, F. (1951). The qualities of the reasonable man in negligence cases. *Missouri Law Review, 16*, 1–26.

James, F., Hazard, G., & Leubsdorf, J. (1992). *Civil procedure* (4th ed.). Boston: Little, Brown.

James, R. (1959). Status and competence of jurors. *American Journal of Sociology, 64*, 563–570.

Janis, I. (1980). The influence of television on personal decision-making. In S. Withey & R. Abeles (Eds.), *Television and social behavior: Beyond violence and children* (pp. 161–189). Hillsdale, NJ: Erlbaum.

Johnson, E., & Tversky, A. (1983). Affect, generalization, and the perception of risk. *Journal of Personality and Social Psychology, 45*, 20–31.

Jones, E. E. (1998). Major developments in five decades of social psychology. In D. Gilbert, S. Fiske, & G. Lindzey (Eds.), *Handbook of social psychology* (Vol. 1, pp. 3–57). Boston: McGraw-Hill.

Josephson, B., Singer, J., & Salovey, P. (1996). Mood regulation and memory: Repairing sad moods with happy memories. *Cognition and Emotion, 10*, 437–444.

Kahan, D., & Nussbaum, M. (1996). Two conceptions of emotion in criminal law. *Columbia Law Review, 96*, 269–374.

Kahneman, D. (1994). New challenges to the rationality assumption. *Journal of Institutional and Theoretical Economics, 150*, 18–36.

Kahneman, D., Knetsch, J., & Thaler, R. (1991). Anomalies: The endowment effect, loss aversion, and status quo bias. *Journal of Economic Perspectives, 5,* 193–206.

Kahneman, D., & Miller, D. (1986). Norm theory: Comparing reality to its alternatives. *Psychological Review, 93,* 136–153.

Kahneman, D., & Tversky, A. (1973). On the psychology of prediction. *Psychological Review, 80,* 237–251.

Kahneman, D., & Tversky, A. (1982). The simulation heuristic. In D. Kahneman, P. Slovic, & A. Tversky (Eds.), *Judgment under uncertainty: Heuristics and biases* (pp. 201–208). Cambridge, England: Cambridge University Press.

Kahneman, D., & Tversky, A. (1984). Choices, values, and frames. *American Psychologist, 39,* 341–350.

Kakalik, J., King, E., Traynor, M., Ebener, P., & Picus, L. (1988). *Costs and compensation paid in aviation accident litigation.* Santa Monica, CA: RAND Institute for Civil Justice.

Kalven, H. (1958). The jury, the law, and the personal injury damage award. *Ohio State Law Journal, 19,* 158–178.

Kalven, H., & Zeisel, H. (1966). *The American jury.* Boston: Little, Brown.

Kamin, K., & Rachlinski, J. (1995). Ex post ≠ ex ante: Determining liability in hindsight. *Law and Human Behavior, 19,* 89–104.

Kanouse, D. (1972). Language, labeling, and attribution. In E. E. Jones, D. Kanouse, H. Kelley, R. Nisbett, S. Valins, & B. Weiner (Eds.), *Attribution: Perceiving the causes of behavior* (pp. 121–135). Morristown, NJ: General Learning Press.

Kaplan, M. (1991). The joint effects of cognition and affect on social judgment. In J. Forgas (Ed.), *Emotion and social judgments* (pp. 73–82). Oxford, England: Pergamon Press.

Kaplan, M., & Krupa, S. (1986). Severe penalties under the control of others can reduce guilt verdicts. *Law and Psychology Review, 10,* 1–18.

Karlovac, M., & Darley, J. (1988). Attribution of responsibility for accidents: A negligence law analogy. *Social Cognition, 6,* 287–318.

Kassin, S., & Sommers, S. (1997). Inadmissible testimony, instructions to disregard, and the jury: Substantive versus procedural considerations. *Personality and Social Psychology Bulletin, 23,* 1046–1054.

Kassin, S., & Studebaker, C. (1998). Instructions to disregard and the jury: Curative and paradoxical effects. In J. Golding & C. MacLeod (Eds.), *Intentional forgetting: Interdisciplinary approaches* (pp. 413–434). Hillsdale, NJ: Erlbaum.

Kassin, S., & Wrightsman, L. (1983). The construction and validation of a juror bias scale. *Journal of Research in Personality, 17,* 423–442.

Kassin, S., & Wrightsman, L. (1988). *The American jury on trial: Psychological perspectives.* Bristol, PA: Taylor & Francis.

Kassirer, J. (1999). Hospitals, heal yourselves. *New England Journal of Medicine, 340,* 309–310.

Kaye, D. (1979). Probability theory meets res ipsa loquitur. *Michigan Law Review, 77*, 1456–1484.

Keating, G. (1996). Reasonableness and rationality in negligence theory. *Stanford Law Review, 48*, 311–384.

Keeton, W., Dobbs, D., Keeton, R., & Owen, D. (1984). *Prosser and Keeton on torts.* St. Paul, MN: West.

Kelley, H. (1973). The processes of causal attribution. *American Psychologist, 28*, 107–128.

Keltner, D., Ellsworth, P., & Edwards, K. (1993). Beyond simple pessimism: Effects of sadness and anger on social perception. *Journal of Personality and Social Psychology, 64*, 740–752.

Kern, K. (1992). Causes of breast cancer malpractice litigation. *Archives of Surgery, 127*, 542–547.

Kern, K. (1994). Medicolegal analysis of the delayed diagnosis of cancer in 338 cases in the United States. *Archives of Surgery, 129*, 397–404.

Kerr, N., MacCoun, R., & Kramer, G. (1996). Bias in judgment: Comparing individuals and groups. *Psychological Review, 103*, 687–719.

Kerr, N., & Sawyers, G. (1979). Independence of multiple verdicts within a trial by mock jurors. *Representative Research in Social Psychology, 10*, 16–27.

King, J. (1981). Causation, valuation, and chance in personal injury torts involving preexisting conditions and future consequences. *Yale Law Journal, 90*, 1353–1397.

Kingston v. Chicago & N.W.Ry., 211 N.W. 913 (Wis. 1927).

Kleinhans, C. (1991). Melodrama and the family under capitalism. In M. Landy (Ed.), *Imitations of life* (pp. 197–204). Detroit, MI: Wayne State University Press.

Kline v. 1500 Massachusetts Avenue Apartment Corp., 439 F.2d 477 (D.C. Cir. 1970).

Kramer, G., Kerr, N., & Carroll, J. (1990). Pretrial publicity, judicial remedies, and jury bias. *Law and Human Behavior, 14*, 409–438.

Krauss, R., Curran, N., & Ferleger, N. (1983). Expressive conventions and the cross-cultural perception of emotion. *Basic and Applied Social Psychology, 4*, 295–305.

Kruglanski, A. (1989). *Lay epistemics and human knowledge.* New York: Plenum.

Kruglanski, A., & Mayseless, O. (1988). Contextual effects in hypothesis testing: The role of competing alternatives and epistemic motivations. *Social Cognition, 6*, 1–20.

Kruglanski, A., & Webster, D. (1996). Motivated closing of the mind: "Seizing" and "freezing." *Psychological Review, 103*, 263–293.

Kruglanski, A., Webster, D., & Klem, A. (1993). Motivated resistance and openness to persuasion in the presence or absence of prior information. *Journal of Personality and Social Psychology, 65*, 861–876.

Kuhn, D., Weinstock, M., & Flaton, R. (1994). How well do jurors reason? Competence dimensions of individual variation in a juror reasoning task. *Psychological Science, 5,* 289–296.

Kulka, R., & Kessler, J. (1978). Is justice really blind? The influence of litigant physical attractiveness on juridical judgment. *Journal of Applied Social Psychology, 8,* 366–381.

LaBine, S., & LaBine, G. (1996). Determinations of negligence and the hindsight bias. *Law and Human Behavior, 20,* 501–516.

Lafayette, J. (1992, July 20). The case of the off-duty employee. *Restaurant Business, 91,* 30.

Lakoff, G. (1987). *Women, fire, and dangerous things.* Chicago: University of Chicago Press.

Lakoff, G., & Johnson, M. (1980). *Metaphors we live by.* Chicago: University of Chicago Press.

Landsman, S., & Rakos, R. (1994). A preliminary inquiry into the effect of potentially biasing information on judges and jurors in civil litigation. *Behavioral Sciences and the Law, 12,* 113–126.

Landy, M. (1991). Introduction. In M. Landy (Ed.), *Imitations of life* (pp. 13–30). Detroit, MI: Wayne State University Press.

Lazarus, R. (1991a). *Emotion and adaptation.* New York: Oxford University Press.

Lazarus, R. (1991b). Progress on a cognitive–motivational–relational theory of emotion. *American Psychologist, 46,* 813–834.

Lazarus, R. (1994). Universal antecedents of the emotions. In P. Ekman & R. Davidson (Eds.), *The nature of emotion* (pp. 163–171). London: Oxford University Press.

Lazarus, R., & Averill, J. (1972). Emotion and cognition: With special reference to anxiety. In C. Spielberger (Ed.), *Anxiety: Current trends in theory and research* (Vol. 2, pp. 241–283). New York: Academic Press.

Leary, M. (1995). *Self-presentation.* Madison, WI: Brown & Benchmark.

LeDoux, J. (1996). *The emotional brain.* New York: Simon & Schuster.

Lempert, R. (1993). Civil juries and complex cases: Taking stock after twelve years. In R. Litan (Ed.), *Verdict: Assessing the civil jury system* (pp. 181–247). Washington, DC: Brookings Institution.

Lerner, J., Goldberg, J., & Tetlock, P. (1998). Sober second thought: The effects of accountability, anger, and authoritarianism of attributions of responsibility. *Personality and Social Psychology Bulletin, 24,* 563–574.

Lerner, M. (1980). *The belief in a just world.* New York: Plenum Press.

Levin, A., & Herzberg, S. (1986, April 8). *Inside the jury room* [Television broadcast]. Washington, DC: Public Broadcasting System.

Levine, J., & Moreland, R. (1998). Small groups. In D. Gilbert, S. Fiske, & G. Lindzey (Eds.), *Handbook of social psychology* (Vol. 2, pp. 415–469). Boston: McGraw-Hill.

Levy, S., & Dweck, C. (1998). Trait- versus process-focused social judgment. *Social Cognition, 16,* 151–172.

Levy, S., Plaks, J., & Dweck, C. (1999). Modes of social thought: Implicit theories and social understanding. In S. Chaiken & Y. Trope (Eds.), *Dual-process theories in social psychology* (pp. 179–202). New York: Guilford Press.

Leyens, J.-P., Yzerbyt, V., & Corneille, O. (1996). The role of applicability in the emergence of the overattribution bias. *Journal of Personality and Social Psychology, 70*, 219–229.

Lichter, S. R., Lichter, L., & Amundson, D. (1997). Does Hollywood hate business or money? *Journal of Communication, 47*, 68–84.

Lichter, S. R., Lichter, L., & Rothman, S. (1994). *Prime time: How TV portrays American culture.* Washington, DC: Regnery.

Lieberman, J., & Sales, B. (1997). What social science teaches us about the jury instruction process. *Psychology, Public Policy, and Law, 3*, 589–644.

Lind, E. A., & Ke, G. (1985). Opening and closing statements. In S. Kassin & L. Wrightsman (Eds.), *The psychology of evidence and trial procedure* (pp. 232–252). Beverly Hills, CA: Sage.

Linz, D., & Penrod, S. (1984). Increasing attorney persuasiveness in the courtroom. *Law and Psychology Review, 8*, 1–47.

Lipsitz, G. (1997). The greatest story ever sold: Marketing and the O.J. Simpson trial. In T. Morrison & C. Lacour (Eds.), *Birth of a nation'hood* (pp. 3–29). New York: Pantheon Books.

Litan, R. (1991). The liability explosion and American trade performance: Myths and realities. In P. Schuck (Ed.), *Tort law and the public interest* (pp. 127–149). New York: Norton.

Li v. Yellow Cab Co. of California, 532 P.2d 1226 (Cal. 1975).

Lloyd-Bostock, S. (1979). Common sense morality and accident compensation. In D. Farrington, K. Hawkins, & S. Lloyd-Bostock (Eds.), *Psychology, law, and legal processes* (pp. 93–110). Atlantic Highlands, NJ: Humanities Press.

Lloyd-Bostock, S. (1983). Attributions of cause and responsibility as social phenomena. In J. Jaspars, F. Fincham, & M. Hewstone (Eds.), *Attribution theory and research* (pp. 261–289). London: Academic Press.

Lloyd-Bostock, S. (1984). Fault and liability for accidents: The accident victim's perspective. In D. Harris, M. Maclean, H. Genn, S. Lloyd-Bostock, P. Fenn, P. Corfield, & Y. Brittan (Eds.), *Compensation and support for illness and injury* (pp. 141–163). Oxford, England: Clarendon Press.

Loftus, E., & Beach, L. (1982). Human inference and judgment: Is the glass half empty or half full? *Stanford Law Review, 34*, 939–956.

Loftus, E., & Palmer, J. (1974). Reconstruction of automobile deconstruction: An example of the interaction between language and memory. *Journal of Learning and Verbal Behavior, 13*, 585–589.

Longnecker, M., Berlin, J., Orza, M., & Chalmers, T. (1988). A meta-analysis of alcohol consumption in relation to risk of breast cancer. *Journal of the American Medical Association, 260*, 652–656.

Lord, C., Ross, L., & Lepper, M. (1979). Biased assimilation and attitude polarization: The effects of prior theories on subsequently considered evidence. *Journal of Personality and Social Psychology, 37*, 2098–2109.

Love, N. (1991). Why patients delay seeking care for cancer symptoms. *Postgraduate Medicine, 89,* 151–158.

Lucy Webb Hayes National Training School v. Perotti, 419 F.2d 704 (D.C. Cir. 1969).

Lupfer, M., Cohen, R., Bernard, J. L., Smalley, D., & Schippmann, J. (1985). An attributional analysis of jurors' judgments in civil cases. *Journal of Social Psychology, 125,* 743–751.

Lyons v. McCauley, 675 N.Y.S.2d 375 (App. Div. 1998).

MacCoun, R. (1986). *Getting inside the black box: Toward a better understanding of civil jury behavior.* Santa Monica, CA: RAND Institute for Civil Justice.

MacCoun, R. (1996). Differential treatment of corporate defendants by juries: An examination of the "deep-pockets" hypothesis. *Law and Society Review, 30,* 121–161.

Mackie, D., & Worth, L. (1991). Feeling good, but not thinking straight: The impact of positive mood on persuasion. In J. Forgas (Ed.), *Emotion and social judgments* (pp. 201–219). Oxford, England: Pergamon Press.

Macneil, I. (1983). Values in contract: Internal and external. *Northwestern University Law Review, 78,* 340–418.

Macrae, C. N. (1992). A tale of two curries: Counterfactual thinking and accident-related judgments. *Personality and Social Psychology Bulletin, 18,* 84–87.

Macrae, C. N., & Milne, A. (1992). A curry for your thoughts: Empathic effects on counterfactual thinking. *Personality and Social Psychology Bulletin, 18,* 625–630.

Macrae, C. N., Milne, A., & Griffiths, R. (1993). Counterfactual thinking and the perception of criminal behaviour. *British Journal of Psychology, 84,* 221–226.

Maes, J. (1994). Blaming the victim: Belief in control or belief in justice? *Social Justice Research, 7,* 69–90.

Major, B., & Deaux, K. (1982). Individual differences in justice behavior. In J. Greenberg & R. Cohen (Eds.), *Equity and justice in social behavior* (pp. 43–76). New York: Academic Press.

Malouff, J., & Schutte, N. (1988). Shaping juror attitudes: Effects of requesting different damage amounts in personal injury trials. *Journal of Social Psychology, 129,* 491–497.

Mandel, D., & Lehman, D. (1996). Counterfactual thinking and ascriptions of cause and preventability. *Journal of Personality and Social Psychology, 71,* 450–463.

Mann, B., Giuliano, A., Bassett, L., Barber, M., Hallauer, W., & Morton, D. (1983). Delayed diagnosis of breast cancer as a result of normal mammograms. *Archives of Surgery, 118,* 23–24.

Manzo, J. (1993). Jurors' narratives of personal experience in deliberation talk. *Text, 13,* 267–290.

Manzo, J. (1994). "You wouldn't take a seven-year-old and ask him all these questions": Jurors' use of practical reasoning in supporting their arguments. *Law and Social Inquiry, 19,* 639–663.

Marder, N. (1987). Gender dynamics and jury deliberations. *Yale Law Journal, 96,* 593–612.

Marder, N. (1997). Deliberations and disclosures: A study of post-verdict interviews of jurors. *Iowa Law Review, 82,* 465–546.

Marder, N. (1999). The interplay of race and false claims of jury nullification. *Michigan Journal of Law Reform, 32,* 285–321.

Margolis, H. (1996). *Dealing with risk.* Chicago: University of Chicago Press.

Martin, C., & Oshagan, H. (1997). Disciplining the workforce: The news media frame a General Motors plant closing. *Communication Research, 24,* 669–697.

Martin, L., Abend, T., Sedikides, C., & Green, J. (1997). How would I feel if . . . ? Mood as input to a role fulfillment evaluation process. *Journal of Personality and Social Psychology, 73,* 242–253.

Mason, J. (1993). *Melodrama and the myth of America.* Bloomington: Indiana University Press.

Mason, L., & Klein, J. (1997, April 16). *Enter the jury room* [Television broadcast]. New York: Columbia Broadcasting System.

Mauet, T. (1992). *Fundamentals of trial techniques* (3rd ed.). Boston: Little, Brown.

Mayer, J., & Hanson, E. (1995). Mood-congruent judgment over time. *Personality and Social Psychology Bulletin, 21,* 237–244.

Mayer, J., & Salovey, P. (1988). Personality moderates the interaction of mood and cognition. In K. Fiedler & J. Forgas (Eds.), *Affect, cognition, and social behavior* (pp. 87–99). Toronto, Ontario, Canada: Hogrefe.

McCaffery, E., Kahneman, D., & Spitzer, M. (1995). Framing the jury: Cognitive perspectives on pain and suffering awards. *Virginia Law Review, 81,* 1341–1420.

McClure, J. (1998). Discounting causes of behavior: Are two reasons better than one? *Journal of Personality and Social Psychology, 74,* 7–20.

McKee, R. (1996). *Story: Structure, substance, style, and the principles of screenwriting.* New York: Harper Collins.

Meisel, M. (1994). Scattered chiaroscuro: Melodrama as a matter of seeing. In J. Bratton, J. Cook, & C. Gledhill (Eds.), *Melodrama: Stage, picture, screen* (pp. 65–81). London: British Film Institute.

Menon, T., Morris, M., Chiu, C., & Hong, Y. (1999). Culture and the construal of agency: Attribution to individual versus group dispositions. *Journal of Personality and Social Psychology, 76,* 701–717.

Mercer, P. (1972). *Sympathy and ethics.* Oxford, England: Clarendon Press.

Merritt, D., & Barry, K. (1999). Is the tort system in crisis? New empirical evidence. *Ohio State Law Journal, 60,* 315–398.

Meyer, L. (1997). Just the facts? *Yale Law Journal, 106,* 1269–1312.

Meyer, P. (1994). "Desperate for love": Cinematic influences upon a defendant's closing argument to a jury. *Vermont Law Review, 18,* 721–749.

Mikula, G., Scherer, K., & Athenstaedt, U. (1998). The role of injustice in the elicitation of differential emotional reactions. *Personality and Social Psychology Bulletin, 24*, 769–783.

Mill, J. S. (1864). *A system of logic.* New York: Harper & Brothers.

Miller, D., & Turnbull, W. (1990). The counterfactual fallacy: Confusing what might have been with what ought to have been. *Social Justice Research, 4*, 1–19.

Miller, D., Turnbull, W., & McFarland, C. (1990). Counterfactual thinking and social perception: Thinking about what might have been. In M. Zanna (Ed.), *Advances in experimental social psychology* (Vol. 23, pp. 305–331). San Diego, CA: Academic Press.

Miller, J. (1984). Culture and the development of everyday social explanation. *Journal of Personality and Social Psychology, 46*, 961–978.

Miller, W. (1997). *The anatomy of disgust.* Cambridge, MA: Harvard University Press.

Moller, E. (1996). *Trends in civil jury verdicts since 1985.* Santa Monica, CA: RAND Institute for Civil Justice.

Monson, T. (1983). Implications of the traits v. situations controversy for differences in the attributions of actors and observers. In J. Jaspars, F. Fincham, & M. Hewstone (Eds.), *Attribution theory and research* (pp. 293–313). London: Academic Press.

Moor-Ede, M. (1995, January). When things go bump in the night. *American Bar Association Journal, 81*, 56–60.

Moore, S., Smith, R., & Gonzalez, R. (1997). Personality and judgment heuristics: Contextual and individual difference interactions in social judgment. *Personality and Social Psychology Bulletin, 23*, 76–83.

Moran, G., Cutler, B., & De Lisa, A. (1994). Attitudes toward tort reform, scientific jury selection, and juror bias: Verdict inclination in criminal and civil trials. *Law and Psychology Review, 18*, 309–328.

Morris, M., & Larrick, R. (1995). When one cause casts doubt on another: A normative analysis of discounting in causal attribution. *Psychological Review, 102*, 331–355.

Moscovici, S., & Doise, W. (1994). *Conflict and consensus.* London: Sage.

Mueller, C. B. (1994). Is breast cancer "curable"? In L. Wise & H. Johnson (Eds.), *Breast cancer: Controversies in management* (pp. 53–60). Armonk, NY: Futura.

Myers, D., & Lamm, H. (1976). The group polarization phenomenon. *Psychological Bulletin, 83*, 602–627.

Nagareda, R. (1998). Outrageous fortune and the criminalization of mass torts. *Michigan Law Review, 96*, 1121–1198.

Narby, D., Cutler, B., & Moran, G. (1993). A meta-analysis of the association between authoritarianism and jurors' perceptions of defendant culpability. *Journal of Applied Psychology, 78*, 34–42.

National Safety Council. (1997). *Accident facts.* Itasca, IL: National Safety Council.

Neuberg, S., & Newsom, J. (1993). Personal need for structure: Individual differences in the desire for simple structure. *Journal of Personality and Social Psychology, 65,* 113–131.

N'gbala, A., & Branscombe, N. (1995). Mental simulation and causal attribution: When simulating an event does not affect fault assignment. *Journal of Experimental Social Psychology, 31,* 139–162.

Niedenthal, P. (1992). Affect and social perception: On the psychological validity of rose-colored glasses. In R. Bornstein & T. Pittman (Eds.), *Perception without awareness* (pp. 211–235). New York: Guilford Press.

Niedenthal, P., Halberstadt, J., & Setterlund, M. (1997). Being happy and seeing "happy": Emotional state mediates visual word recognition. *Cognition and Emotion, 11,* 403–432.

Niedenthal, P., Setterlund, M., & Jones, D. (1994). Emotional organization of perceptual memory. In P. Niedenthal & S. Kitayama (Eds.), *The heart's eye* (pp. 85–113). San Diego, CA: Academic Press.

Niedenthal, P., & Showers, C. (1991). The perception and processing of affective information and its influences on social judgment. In J. Forgas (Ed.), *Emotion and social judgments* (pp. 125–143). Oxford, England: Pergamon Press.

Niedermeier, K., Kerr, N., & Messé, L. (1999). Jurors' use of naked statistical evidence: Exploring bases and implications of the Wells effect. *Journal of Personality and Social Psychology, 76,* 533–542.

Nisbett, R. (1993). *Rules for reasoning.* Hillsdale, NJ: Erlbaum.

Nisbett, R., & Ross, L. (1980). *Human inference: Strategies and shortcomings of social judgment.* Englewood Cliffs, NJ: Prentice Hall.

Nisbett, R., & Wilson, T. (1977). Telling more than we can know: Verbal reports on mental processes. *Psychological Review, 84,* 231–259.

Nowell-Smith, G. (1987). Minelli: and melodrama. In C. Glendhill (Ed.), *Home is where the heart is* (pp. 70–79). London: British Film Institute.

Nussbaum, M. (1992). Emotions as judgments of value. *Yale Journal of Criticism, 5,* 201–212.

Nussbaum, M. (1995). *Poetic justice.* Boston: Beacon Press.

O'Connell, V., & Barrett, P. (1999, February 16). Open season: How a jury placed the firearms industry on the legal defensive. *Wall Street Journal,* A-1, col. 6.

Oregon Revised Statutes, Or. Rev. Stat. §§ 18.470, 18.475 (1975, 1995).

Ortony, A., Clore, G., & Collins, A. (1988). *The cognitive structure of emotions.* Cambridge, England: Cambridge University Press.

Osuch, J., & Bonham, V. (1994). The timely diagnosis of breast cancer. *Cancer, 74*(Suppl.), 271–278.

Otto, A., Penrod, S., & Dexter, H. (1994). The biasing impact of pretrial publicity on juror judgments. *Law and Human Behavior, 18,* 453–469.

Palfai, T., & Salovey, P. (1994). The influence of depressed and elated mood in deductive and inductive reasoning. *Imagination, Cognition, and Personality, 13,* 57–71.

Palsgraf v. Long Island R.R., 162 N.E. 99 (N.Y. 1928).

Parkinson, M. (1981). Verbal behavior and courtroom success. *Communication Education, 30*, 22–32.

Parrott, G. (1993). On the scientific study of angry organisms. In R. Wyer & T. Srull (Eds.), *Perspectives on anger and emotion* (pp. 167–177). Hillsdale, NJ: Erlbaum.

Pelham, B., & Neter, E. (1995). The effect of motivation on judgment depends on the difficulty of the judgment. *Journal of Personality and Social Psychology, 68*, 581–594.

Pennebaker, J. (1989). Confession, inhibition, and disease. In L. Berkowitz (Ed.), *Advances in experimental social psychology* (Vol. 22, pp. 211–244). San Diego, CA: Academic Press.

Pennington, N., & Hastie, R. (1991). A cognitive theory of juror decision making: The story model. *Cardozo Law Review, 13*, 519–551.

Pennington, N., & Hastie, R. (1992). Explaining the evidence: Tests of the story model for juror decision making. *Journal of Personality and Social Psychology, 62*, 189–206.

Peterson, M. (1984). *Compensation of injuries: Civil jury verdicts in Cook County.* Santa Monica, CA: RAND Institute for Civil Justice.

Petrie, K., Booth, R., & Pennebaker, J. (1998). The immunological effects of thought suppression. *Journal of Personality and Social Psychology, 75*, 1264–1272.

Petty, R., & Cacioppo, J. (1979). Issue involvement can increase or decrease persuasion by enhancing message-relevant cognitive responses. *Journal of Personality and Social Psychology, 37*, 1915–1926.

Petty, R., & Cacioppo, J. (1986). The elaboration likelihood model of persuasion. In L. Berkowitz (Ed.), *Advances in experimental social psychology* (Vol. 19, pp. 123–205). Orlando, FL: Academic Press.

Petty, R., Cacioppo, J., & Heesacker, M. (1981). The use of rhetorical questions in persuasion: A cognitive response analysis. *Journal of Personality and Social Psychology, 40*, 432–440.

Petty, R., Gleicher, F., & Baker, S. (1991). Multiple roles for affect in persuasion. In J. Forgas (Ed.), *Emotion and social judgments* (pp. 181–200). Oxford, England: Pergamon Press.

Petty, R., & Wegener, D. (1993). Flexible correction processes in social judgment: Correcting for context-induced contrast. *Journal of Experimental Social Psychology, 29*, 137–165.

Petty, R., & Wegener, D. (1999). The elaboration likelihood model: Current status and controversies. In S. Chaiken & Y. Trope (Eds.), *Dual-process theories in social psychology* (pp. 41–72). New York: Guilford Press.

Petty, R., Wegener, D., & White, P. (1998). Flexible correction processes in social judgment: Implications for persuasion. *Social Cognition, 16*, 93–113.

Pillsbury, S. (1989). Emotional justice: Moralizing the passions of criminal punishment. *Cornell Law Review, 74*, 655–710.

Pittman, T. (1998). Motivation. In D. Gilbert, S. Fiske, & G. Lindzey (Eds.), *Handbook of social psychology* (Vol. 1, pp. 549–590). Boston: McGraw-Hill.

Plotkin, D., & Blankenberg, F. (1991). Breast cancer—biology and malpractice. *American Journal of Clinical Oncology, 14,* 254–266.

Plutchik, R. (1994). *The psychology and biology of emotion.* New York: Harper Collins.

Polinsky, A. M. (1983). *An introduction to law and economics.* Boston: Little, Brown.

Polisar, D., & Wildavsky, A. (1989). From individual to system blame: A cultural analysis of historical change in the law of torts. *Journal of Policy History, 1,* 129–155.

Posner, R. (1981). The concept of corrective justice in recent theories of tort law. *Journal of Legal Studies, 10,* 187–206.

Posner, R. (1992). *Economic analysis of law* (4th ed.). Boston: Little, Brown.

Priest, G. (1993). Justifying the civil jury. In R. Litan (Ed.), *Verdict: Assessing the civil jury system* (pp. 103–136). Washington, DC: Brookings Institution.

Pyszczynski, T., & Wrightsman, L. (1981). The effects of opening statements on mock jurors' verdicts in a simulated criminal trial. *Journal of Applied Social Psychology, 11,* 301–313.

Quattrone, G. (1982). Overattribution and unit formation: When behavior engulfs the person. *Journal of Personality and Social Psychology, 42,* 593–607.

Quigley, B., & Tedeschi, J. (1996). Mediating effects of blame attributions on feelings of anger. *Personality and Social Psychology Bulletin, 22,* 1280–1288.

Quinlan, R., & Ernst, C. (1982). Diseases of the breast. In L. Barker, J. Burton, & P. Zieve (Eds.), *Principles of ambulatory medicine* (pp. 947–957). Baltimore: Williams & Wilkins.

Quinn, N. (1987). Convergent evidence for a cultural model of marriage. In D. Holland & N. Quinn (Eds.), *Cultural models in language and thought* (pp. 173–192). Cambridge, England: Cambridge University Press.

Rabin, R. (1997). Restating the law: The dilemmas of products liability. *University of Michigan Journal of Law Reform, 30,* 197–214.

Rachlinski, J. (1996). Gains, losses, and the psychology of litigation. *Southern California Law Review, 70,* 113–185.

Rachlinksi, J. (1998). A positive psychological theory of judging in hindsight. *University of Chicago Law Review, 65,* 571–625.

Raitz, A., Greene, E., Goodman, J., & Loftus, E. (1990). Determining damages: The influence of expert testimony of jurors' decision making. *Law and Human Behavior, 14,* 385–395.

Rapping, E. (1997). The movie of the week: Law, narrativity, and gender on prime time. In M. Fineman & M. McCluskey (Eds.), *Feminism, media, and the law* (pp. 91–103). New York: Oxford University Press.

Reifman, A., Gusick, S., & Ellsworth, P. (1992). Real jurors' understanding of the law in real cases. *Law and Human Behavior, 16,* 539–554.

Reintgen, D., Cox, C., Greenberg, H., Baekey, P., Nicosia, S., Berman, C., Clark, R., & Lyman, G. (1993). The medical legal implications of following mammographic breast masses. *The American Surgeon, 59,* 99–105.

Reskin, B., & Visher, C. (1986). The impacts of evidence and extralegal factors in jurors' decisions. *Law and Society Review, 20*, 423–438.

Reyes, R., Thompson, W., & Bower, G. (1980). Judgmental biases resulting from differing availabilities of arguments. *Journal of Personality and Social Psychology, 39*, 2–12.

Ritov, I., & Baron, J. (1994). Judgements of compensation for misfortune: The role of expectation. *European Journal of Social Psychology, 24*, 525–539.

Robbennolt, J. (in press). Outcome severity and judgments of "responsibility": A meta-analytic review. *Journal of Applied Social Psychology.*

Robbennolt, J., & Sobus, M. (1997). An integration of hindsight bias and counterfactual thinking: Decision-making and drug courier profiles. *Law and Human Behavior, 21*, 539–560.

Robbennolt, J., & Studebaker, C. (1999). Anchoring in the courtroom: The effects of caps on punitive damages. *Law and Human Behavior, 23*, 353–373.

Roberts, C., Cox, C., Reintgen, D., Baile, W., & Gibertini, M. (1994). Influence of physician communication on newly diagnosed breast patients' psychologic adjustment and decision-making. *Cancer, 74*(Suppl.), 336–341.

Robinson, E., Mohilever, J., Zidan, J., & Sapir, D. (1984). Delay in diagnosis of cancer. *Cancer, 54*, 1454–1460.

Robinson, M. (1998). Running from William James's bear: A review of preattentive mechanisms and their contributions to emotional experience. *Cognition and Emotion, 12*, 667–696.

Robinson, P., & Darley, J. (1995). *Justice, liability, and blame.* Boulder, CO: Westview Press.

Robinson, R., Keltner, D., Ward, A., & Ross, L. (1995). Actual versus assumed differences in construal: "Naive realism" in intergroup perception and conflict. *Journal of Personality and Social Psychology, 68*, 404–417.

Roese, N. (1997). Counterfactual thinking. *Psychological Bulletin, 121*, 133–148.

Roese, N., & Olson, J. (1995). Counterfactual thinking: A critical overview. In N. Roese & J. Olson (Eds.), *What might have been: The social psychology of counterfactual thinking* (pp. 1–55). Hillsdale, NJ: Erlbaum.

Roese, N., & Olson, J. (1996). Counterfactuals, causal attributions, and the hindsight bias: A conceptual integration. *Journal of Experimental Social Psychology, 32*, 197–227.

Rorty, A. (Ed.). (1980). *Explaining emotions.* Berkeley: University of California Press.

Rose-Ackerman, S. (1991). Tort law in the regulatory state. In P. Schuck (Ed.), *Tort law and the public interest* (pp. 80–102). New York: Norton.

Roseman, I., Antoniou, A., & Jose, P. (1996). Appraisal determinants of emotions: Constructing a more accurate and comprehensive theory. *Cognition and Emotion, 10*, 241–277.

Rosen, J., & Schulkin, J. (1998). From normal fear to pathological anxiety. *Psychological Review, 105*, 325–350.

Rosenberg, J. (1978). *Dictionary of business and management.* New York: Wiley.

Rosenblatt, A., Greenberg, J., Solomon, S., Pyszczynski, T., & Lyon, D. (1989). Evidence for terror management theory: I. The effects of mortality salience on reactions to those who violate or uphold cultural values. *Journal of Personality and Social Psychology, 57*, 681–690.

Ross, L., & Anderson, C. (1982). Shortcomings in the attribution process: On the origins and maintenance of erroneous social assessments. In D. Kahneman, P. Slovic, & A. Tversky (Eds.), *Judgment under uncertainty: Heuristics and biases* (pp. 129–152). Cambridge, England: Cambridge University Press.

Ross, L., & Nisbett, R. (1991). *The person and the situation*. Philadelphia: Temple University Press.

Rothman, A., & Hardin, C. (1997). Differential use of the availability heuristic in social judgment. *Personality and Social Psychology Bulletin, 23*, 123–138.

Royak-Schaler, R., Stanton, A., & Danoff-Burg, S. (1997). Breast cancer: Psychosocial factors influencing risk perception, screening, diagnosis, and treatment. In S. Gallant, G. Keita, & R. Royak-Schaler (Eds.), *Health care for women* (pp. 295–314). Washington, DC: American Psychological Association.

Rozin, P., Lowery, L., Imada, S., & Haidt, J. (1999). The CAD triad hypothesis: A mapping between three moral emotions (contempt, anger, disgust) and three moral codes (community, autonomy, divinity). *Journal of Personality and Social Psychology, 76*, 574–586.

Rudolph, U., & Försterling, F. (1997). The psychological causality implicit in verbs: A review. *Psychological Bulletin, 121*, 192–218.

Ruprecht, C. (1997). Are verdicts, too, like sausages?: Lifting the cloak of jury secrecy. *University of Pennsylvania Law Review, 146*, 217–267.

Ruscher, J., Hammer, E. Y., & Hammer, E. D. (1996). Forming shared impressions through conversation: An adaptation of the continuum model. *Personality and Social Psychology Bulletin, 22*, 705–720.

Russell, J. (1994). Is there universal recognition of emotion from facial expression? A review of the cross-cultural studies. *Psychological Bulletin, 115*, 102–141.

Russell, J. (1995). Facial expression of emotion: What lies beyond minimal universality? *Psychological Bulletin, 118*, 379–391.

Russell, J., & Barrett, L. (1999). Core affect, prototypical emotion episodes, and other things called *emotion*: Dissecting the elephant. *Journal of Personality and Social Psychology, 76*, 805–819.

Rustad, M. (1998). Unraveling punitive damages: Current data and further inquiry. *Wisconsin Law Review, 1998*, 15–69.

Ryan, J. (1998). Risk management and breast cancer: A defense attorney's perspective. *Risk Management Foundation Forum, 19(2)* [On-line]. Available: http://www.rmf.org/www/rmf/b9705.html.

Rylands v. Fletcher, [1861–1873] All E. R. Rep. 1.

Saks, M. (1992). Do we really know anything about the behavior of the tort litigation system—and why not? *University of Pennsylvania Law Review, 140*, 1147–1289.

Saks, M., & Kidd, R. (1980). Human information processing and adjudication: Trial by heuristics. *Law and Society Review, 15*, 123–160.

Saks, M., & Marti, M. (1997). A meta-analysis of the effects of jury size. *Law and Human Behavior, 21*, 451–467.

Salovey, P., Hsee, C., & Mayer, D. (1993). Emotional intelligence and the self-regulation of affect. In D. Wegner & J. Pennebaker (Eds.), *Handbook of mental control* (pp. 258–277). Englewood Cliffs, NJ: Prentice Hall.

Salovey, P., & Mayer, J. (1990). Emotional intelligence. *Imagination, Cognition, and Personality, 9*, 185–211.

Sanders, J. (1998). *Bendectin on trial.* Ann Arbor: University of Michigan Press.

Schaller, M., Asp, C., Rosell, M., & Heim, S. (1996). Training in statistical reasoning inhibits the formation of erroneous group stereotypes. *Personality and Social Psychology Bulletin, 22*, 829–844.

Schank, R., & Abelson, R. (1977). *Scripts, plans, goals and understanding.* Hillsdale, NJ: Erlbaum.

Schatz, T. (1981). *Hollywood genres.* Philadelphia: Temple University Press.

Schelling, T. (1960). *The strategy of conflict.* Cambridge, MA: Harvard University Press.

Scherer, K. (1984). On the nature and function of emotion: A component process approach. In K. Scherer & P. Ekman (Eds.), *Approaches to emotion* (pp. 293–318). Hillsdale, NJ: Erlbaum.

Scherer, K. (1993). Neuroscience projections to current debates in emotion psychology. *Cognition and Emotion, 7*, 1–41.

Scherer, K. (1997). The role of culture in emotion-antecedent appraisal. *Journal of Personality and Social Psychology, 73*, 902–922.

Schkade, D., Sunstein, C., & Kahneman, D. (1999). Are juries less erratic than individuals? Deliberation, polarization, and punitive damages (John M. Olin Law & Economics Working Paper No. 81, 2nd Series). Chicago: University of Chicago Law School.

Schmid, J., & Fiedler, K. (1998). The backbone of closing speeches: The impact of prosecution versus defense language on judicial attributions. *Journal of Applied Social Psychology, 28*, 1140–1172.

Schmidt, G., & Weiner, B. (1988). An attribution–affect–action theory of behavior: Replications of judgments of help-giving. *Personality and Social Psychology Bulletin, 14*, 610–621.

Schul, Y., & Goren, H. (1997). When strong evidence has less impact than weak evidence: Bias, adjustment, and instructions to ignore. *Social Cognition, 15*, 133–155.

Schultz, T., Schleifer, M., & Altman, I. (1981). Judgments of causation, responsibility, and punishment in cases of harm-doing. *Canadian Journal of Behavioral Science, 13*, 238–253.

Schwartz, G. (1978). Contributory and comparative negligence: A reappraisal. *Yale Law Journal, 87*, 697–727.

Schwartz, S. (1994). Heuristics and biases in medical judgment and decision making. In L. Heath, R. S. Tindale, J. Edwards, E. Posavac, F. Bryant, E.

Henderson-King, Y. Suarez-Balcazar, & J. Myers (Eds.), *Applications of heuristics and biases to social issues* (Vol. 3, pp. 45–72). New York: Plenum.

Schwartz, V. (1986). *Comparative negligence* (2nd ed.). Indianapolis, IN: Allen Smith.

Schwarz, N. (1990). Feelings as information: Informational and motivational functions of affective states. In E. T. Higgins & R. Sorentino (Eds.), *Handbook of motivation and cognition* (Vol. 2, pp. 527–561). New York: Guilford Press.

Schwarz, N. (1996). *Cognition and communication*. Mahwah, NJ: Erlbaum.

Schwarz, N., & Bless, H. (1991). Happy and mindless, but sad and smart? The impact of affective states on analytic reasoning. In J. Forgas (Ed.), *Emotion and social judgments* (pp. 55–71). Oxford, England: Pergamon Press.

Schwarz, N., & Bless, H. (1992). Constructing reality and its alternatives: An inclusion/exclusion model of assimilation and contrast effects in social judgment. In L. Martin & A. Tesser (Eds.), *The construction of social judgments* (pp. 217–245). Hillsdale, NJ: Erlbaum.

Schwarz, N., Bless, H., Strack, F., Klumpp, G., Rittenauer-Schatka, H., & Simons, A. (1991). Ease of retrieval as information: Another look at the availability heuristic. *Journal of Personality and Social Psychology, 61,* 195–202.

Schwarz, N., & Clore, G. (1983). Mood, misattribution, and judgments of well-being: Informative and directive functions of affective states. *Journal of Personality and Social Psychology, 45,* 513–523.

Schwarz, N., & Clore, G. (1988). How do I feel about it? The informative function of affective states. In K. Fiedler & J. Forgas (Eds.), *Affect, cognition, and social behavior* (pp. 44–62). Toronto, Ontario, Canada: Hogrefe.

Selvin, M., & Picus, L. (1987). *The debate over jury performance: Observations from a recent asbestos case.* Santa Monica, CA: RAND Institute for Civil Justice.

Severance, L., & Loftus, E. (1982). Improving the ability of jurors to comprehend and apply criminal jury instructions. *Law and Society Review, 17,* 153–197.

Shalowitz, D. (1991, May 6). McDonald's seeks retrial of "fatigue" suit. *Crain's Business Insurance,* 73.

Shanley, M., & Peterson, M. (1987). *Posttrial adjustments to jury awards.* Santa Monica, CA: RAND Institute for Civil Justice.

Shaver, K. (1970). Defensive attribution: Effects of severity and relevance on the responsibility assigned for an accident. *Journal of Personality and Social Psychology, 14,* 101–113.

Shaver, K. (1985). *The attribution of blame.* New York: Springer-Verlag.

Sherman, S., & Corty, E. (1984). Cognitive heuristics. In R. Wyer & T. Srull (Eds.), *Handbook of social cognition* (Vol. 1, pp. 189–286). Hillsdale, NJ: Erlbaum.

Sherwin, R. (1994). Law frames: Historical truth and narrative necessity in a criminal case. *Stanford Law Review, 47,* 39–83.

Sherwin, R. (2000). *When law goes pop.* Chicago: University of Chicago Press.

Shestowsky, D., Wegener, D., & Fabrigar, L. (1998). Need for cognition and interpersonal influence: Individual differences in impact on dyadic decisions. *Journal of Personality and Social Psychology, 74,* 1317–1328.

Shuman, D. (1993). The psychology of deterrence in tort law. *Kansas Law Review, 42,* 115–168.

Shweder, R. (1994). "You're not sick, you're just in love": Emotion as an interpretive system. In P. Ekman & R. Davidson (Eds.), *The nature of emotion* (pp. 32–44). New York: Oxford University Press.

Siemer, M., & Reisenzein, R. (1998). Effects of mood on evaluative judgements: Influence of reduced processing capacity and mood salience. *Cognition and Emotion, 12,* 783–805.

Sigal, J., Braden-Maguire, J., Hayden, M., & Mosley, N. (1985). The effect of presentation style and sex of lawyer on jury decision-making behavior. *Psychology, A Quarterly Journal of Human Behavior, 22,* 13–19.

Sim, D., & Morris, M. (1998). Representativeness and counterfactual thinking: The principle that antecedent and outcome correspond in magnitude. *Personality and Social Psychology Bulletin, 24,* 595–609.

Sinclair, R., & Mark, M. (1992). The influence of mood state on judgment and action: Effects on persuasion, categorization, social justice, person perception, and judgmental accuracy. In L. Martin & A. Tesser (Eds.), *The construction of social judgments* (pp. 165–193). Hillsdale, NJ: Erlbaum.

Sinclair, R., & Mark, M. (1995). The effects of mood state on judgmental accuracy: Processing strategy as a mechanism. *Cognition and Emotion, 9,* 417–438.

Sindell v. Abbott Laboratories, 607 P.2d 924 (Cal. 1980).

Singer, E., & Endreny, P. (1987). Reporting hazards: Their benefits and costs. *Journal of Communication, 37,* 10–26.

Singer, E., & Endreny, P. (1993). *Reporting on risk.* New York: Russell Sage Foundation.

Singer, J., & Salovey, P. (1991). Organized knowledge structures and personality: Person schemas, self schemas, prototypes, and scripts. In M. Horowitz (Ed.), *Person schemas and maladaptive interpersonal patterns* (pp. 33–79). Chicago: University of Chicago Press.

Slovic, P., Fischhoff, B., & Lichtenstein, S. (1982). Facts versus fears: Understanding perceived risk. In D. Kahneman, P. Slovic, & A. Tversky (Eds.), *Judgment under uncertainty: Heuristics and biases* (pp. 463–489). Cambridge, England: Cambridge University Press.

Slovic, P., Fischhoff, B., & Lichtenstein, S. (1985). Characterizing perceived risk. In R. W. Kates, D. Hohennemser, & J. Kasperson (Eds.), *Perilous progress: Technology as hazard* (pp. 91–123). Boulder, CO: Westview Press.

Slovic, P., Fischhoff, B., & Lichtenstein, S. (1987). Behavioral decision theory perspectives on protective behavior. In N. Weinstein (Ed.), *Taking care: Understanding and encouraging self-protective behavior* (pp. 14–41). Cambridge, England: Cambridge University Press.

Smith, A. (1982). *The theory of moral sentiments.* Indianapolis, IN: Liberty Fund. (Original work published 1759.)

Smith, B., Gadd, M., Lawler, C., MacDonald, D., Grudberg, S., Chi, F., Carlson,

K., Comengo, A., & Souba, W. (1996). Perception of breast cancer risk among women in breast center and primary care settings: Correlation with age and family history of breast cancer. *Surgery, 120,* 297–303.

Smith, C., & Ellsworth, P. (1985). Patterns of cognitive appraisal in emotion. *Journal of Personality and Social Psychology, 48,* 813–838.

Smith, H., & Tyler, T. (1997). Choosing the right pond: The impact of group membership on self-esteem and group-oriented behavior. *Journal of Experimental Social Psychology, 33,* 146–170.

Smith, S., & Petty, R. (1996). Message framing and persuasion: A message processing analysis. *Personality and Social Psychology Bulletin, 22,* 257–268.

Smith, S. (1984). Rhetoric and rationality in the law of negligence. *Minnesota Law Review, 69,* 277–323.

Smith, V. (1991). Prototypes in the courtroom: Lay representations of legal concepts. *Journal of Personality and Social Psychology, 61,* 857–872.

Smith, V. (1993). When prior knowledge and law collide: Helping jurors use the law. *Law and Human Behavior, 17,* 507–535.

Smith, V., & Studebaker, C. (1996). What do you expect? The influence of people's prior knowledge of crime categories on fact-finding. *Law and Human Behavior, 20,* 517–532.

Smith v. National R.R. Passenger Corp., 856 F.2d 467 (2d Cir. 1988).

Solomon, R. (1990). *A passion for justice.* Reading, MA: Addison-Wesley.

Spencer, J. W., & Triche, E. (1994). Media constructions of risk and safety: Differential framings of hazard events. *Sociological Inquiry, 64,* 199–213.

Spratt, J., von Fournier, D., Spratt, J., & Weber, E. (1993). Mammographic assessment of human breast cancer growth and duration. *Cancer, 71,* 2020–2026.

Srull, T., & Wyer, R. (1979). The role of category accessibility in the interpretation of information about persons: Some determinants and implications. *Journal of Personality and Social Psychology, 37,* 1660–1672.

Stachenfeld, A., & Nicholson, C. (1996). Blurred boundaries: An analysis of the close relationship between popular culture and the practice of law. *University of San Francisco Law Review, 30,* 903–916.

Stallings, R. (1990). Media discourse and the social construction of risk. *Social Problems, 37,* 80–95.

Stapel, D., Martin, L., & Schwarz, N. (1998). The smell of bias: What instigates correction processes in social judgments? *Personality and Social Psychology Bulletin, 24,* 797–806.

Stapel, D., & Winkielman, P. (1998). Assimilation and contrast as a function of context-target similarity, distinctness, and dimensional relevance. *Personality and Social Psychology Bulletin, 24,* 634–646.

Stasser, G., Kerr, N., & Bray, R. (1982). The social psychology of jury deliberations: Structure, process, and product. In N. Kerr & R. Bray (Eds.), *The psychology of the courtroom* (pp. 221–256). San Diego, CA: Academic Press.

Steyskal, R. (1996). Minimizing the risk of delayed diagnosis of breast cancer.

Medscape Women's Health 1(7) [Online]. Available: http://www.medscape.com/
Medscape/womenshealth96/v01.n07w65.steyskal/w65.steyskal.html.

Stone, C. (1998). The doubling-time defense in failure-to-diagnose-cancer cases. *Medical Malpractice Law and Strategy, 15*(3), 1–3.

Strack, F., & Musweiler, T. (1997). Explaining the enigmatic anchoring effect: Mechanisms of selective accessibility. *Journal of Personality and Social Psychology, 73*, 437–446.

Strier, F. (1994). *Reconstructing justice.* Chicago: University of Chicago Press.

Strodtbeck, F., James, R., & Hawkins, C. (1957). Social status in jury deliberations. *American Sociological Review, 22*, 713–719.

Sunstein, C., Kahneman, D., & Schkade, D. (1998). Assessing punitive damages (with notes on cognition and valuation in law). *Yale Law Journal, 107*, 2071–2153.

Tanford, J. A. (1990). The law and psychology of jury instructions. *Nebraska Law Review, 69*, 71–111.

Tanford, J. A. (1991). Law reform by courts, legislatures, and commissions following empirical research on jury instructions. *Law and Society Review, 25*, 157–175.

Tanford, J. A. (1993). *The trial process: Law, tactics and ethics.* Charlottesville, VA: Michie.

Tanford, J. A., & Tanford, S. (1986). Closing argument procedure. *American Journal of Trial Advocacy, 10*, 47–140.

Tanford, J. A., & Tanford, S. (1988). Better trials through science: A defense of psychologist-lawyer collaboration. *North Carolina Law Review, 66*, 741–780.

Tanford, S., & Penrod, S. (1986). Jury deliberations: Discussion content and influence processes in jury decision making. *Journal of Applied Social Psychology, 16*, 322–347.

Taragin, M., Willett, L., Wilczek, A., Trout, R., & Carson, J. (1992). The influence of standard of care and severity of injury on the resolution of medical malpractice claims. *Annals of Internal Medicine, 117*, 780–784.

Tarasoff v. Regents of University of California, 551 P.2d 334 (Cal. 1976).

Taylor, S. (1982). The availability bias in social perception and interaction. In D. Kahneman, P. Slovic, & A. Tversky (Eds.), *Judgment under uncertainty: Heuristics and biases* (pp. 190–200). Cambridge, England: Cambridge University Press.

Taylor, S. (1991, September). Behind a jury's crazy verdict: The law made them do it. *The American Lawyer*, pp. 86–91.

Tetlock, P. (1985). Accountability: A social check on the fundamental attribution error. *Social Psychology Quarterly, 48*, 227–236.

Theberge, L. (Ed.) (1981). *Crooks, conmen, and clowns: Businessmen in TV entertainment.* Washington, DC: Media Institute.

Thomas, E., & Parpal, M. (1987). Liability as a function of plaintiff and defendant fault. *Journal of Personality and Social Psychology, 53*, 843–857.

Thompson, L., Valley, K., & Kramer, R. (1995). The bittersweet feeling of success:

An examination of social perception in negotiation. *Journal of Experimental Social Psychology, 31*, 467–492.

Thorburn, D. (1981). Television as melodrama. In R. Adler (Ed.), *Understanding television: Essays on television as a social and cultural force* (pp. 73–90). New York: Praeger.

Tice, D., & Baumeister, R. (1993). Controlling anger: Self-induced emotion change. In D. Wegner & J. Pennebaker (Eds.), *Handbook of mental control* (pp. 393–409). Englewood Cliffs, NJ: Prentice Hall.

The T. J. Hooper, 60 F.2d 737 (2d Cir. 1932).

Turnbull, W., & Slugoski, B. (1988). Conversational and linguistic processes in causal attribution. In D. Hilton (Ed.), *Contemporary science and natural explanation* (pp. 66–93). New York: New York University Press.

Turow, J. (1989). *Playing doctor: Television, storytelling, and medical power.* New York: Oxford University Press.

Tversky, A., & Kahneman, D. (1981). The framing of decisions and the psychology of choice. *Science, 211*, 453–458.

Tversky, A., & Kahneman, D. (1982a). Availability: A heuristic for judging frequency and probability. In D. Kahneman, P. Slovic, & A. Tversky (Eds.), *Judgment under uncertainty: Heuristics and biases* (pp. 163–178). Cambridge, England: Cambridge University Press.

Tversky, A., & Kahneman, D. (1982b). Judgment under uncertainty: Heuristics and biases. In D. Kahneman, P. Slovic, & A. Tversky (Eds.), *Judgment under uncertainty: Heuristics and biases* (pp. 3–20). Cambridge, England: Cambridge University Press.

Tyler, T., & Cook, F. (1984). The mass media and judgments of risk: Distinguishing impact on personal and societal level judgments. *Journal of Personality and Social Psychology, 47*, 693–708.

Tyler, T., Degoey, P., & Smith, H. (1996). Understanding why the justice of group procedures matters: A test of the psychological dynamics of the group-value model. *Journal of Personality and Social Psychology, 70*, 913–930.

Tyler, T., & Smith, H. (1999). Justice, social identity, and group processes. In T. Tyler, R. Kramer, & O. John (Eds.), *The psychology of the social self* (pp. 223–264). Mahwah, NJ: Erlbaum.

United States v. Carroll Towing Co., 159 F.2d 169 (2d Cir. 1947).

U.S. Preventive Services Task Force. (1989). Screening for breast cancer. In *Guide to clinical preventive services* (pp. 39–46). Baltimore: Williams & Wilkins.

van der Keilen, M., & Garg, R. (1993). Moral realism in adults' judgments of responsibility. *Journal of Psychology, 128*, 149–156.

Velasco, C., & Bond, A. (1998). Personal relevance is an important dimension for visceral reactivity in emotional imagery. *Cognition and Emotion, 12*, 231–242.

Vesely v. Sager, 486 P.2d 151 (Cal. 1971).

Vidmar, N. (1993). Empirical evidence on the deep pockets hypothesis: Jury awards for pain and suffering in medical malpractice cases. *Duke Law Journal, 43,* 217–266.

Vidmar, N. (1995). *Medical malpractice and the American jury.* Ann Arbor: University of Michigan Press.

Vidmar, N. (1998). The performance of the American civil jury: An empirical perspective. *Arizona Law Review, 40,* 849–899.

Vidmar, N., & Crinklaw, L. (1974). Attributing responsibility for an accident: A methodological and conceptual critique. *Canadian Journal of Behavioral Science, 13,* 112–130.

Vidmar, N., Gross, F., & Rose, M. (1998). Jury awards for medical malpractice and post-verdict adjustments of those awards. *DePaul Law Review, 48,* 265–299.

Vidmar, N., Lee, J., Cohen, E., & Stewart, A. (1994). Damage awards and jurors' responsibility ascriptions in medical versus automobile negligence cases. *Behavioral Sciences and the Law, 12,* 149–160.

Vidmar, N., & Rice, J. (1993). Assessments of noneconomic damage awards in medical negligence: A comparison of jurors with legal professionals. *Iowa Law Review, 78,* 883–911.

Vinson, D. (1982). Psychological anchors: Influencing the jury. *Litigation, 8,* 20–22, 57–58.

Viscusi, W. K., & Moore, M. (1991). Rationalizing the relationship between product liability and innovation. In P. Schuck (Ed.), *Tort law and the public interest* (pp. 105–126). New York: Norton.

Visher, C. (1987). Juror decision making: The importance of evidence. *Law and Human Behavior, 11,* 1–17.

Visser v. Packer Engineering Assoc., 924 F.2d 655 (7th Cir. 1991).

The Wagon Mound (No. 1), [1961] A.C. 388 (P.C. Aust.).

The Wagon Mound (No. 2), [1967] 1 A. C. 617 (P. C. Aust.).

Walker, D. (1980). *The Oxford companion to law.* Oxford, England: Clarendon Press.

Walster, E. (1966). Assignment of responsibility for an accident. *Journal of Personality and Social Psychology, 3,* 73–79.

Walster, E., Walster, G. W., & Berscheid, E. (1978). *Equity: Theory and research.* Boston: Allyn & Bacon.

Watts, C. (1990). *Malpractice defense: Breast cancer.* Oradell, NJ: Medical Economics Books.

Wegener, D., & Petty, R. (1995). Flexible correction processes in social judgment: The role of naive theories in corrections for perceived bias. *Journal of Personality and Social Psychology, 68,* 36–51.

Wegner, D. (1989). *White bears and other unwanted thoughts.* New York: Guilford Press.

Wegner, D., Erber, R., & Zanakos, S. (1993). Ironic processes in the mental control of mood and mood-related thought. *Journal of Personality and Social Psychology, 65,* 1093–1104.

Weiler, P. (1991). *Medical malpractice on trial*. Cambridge, MA: Harvard University Press.

Weiner, B. (1980). A cognitive (attribution)-emotion-action model of motivated behavior: An analysis of judgments of help-giving. *Journal of Personality and Social Psychology, 39,* 186–200.

Weiner, B. (1995). *Judgments of responsibility*. New York: Guilford Press.

Weiner, B., Graham, S., & Chandler, C. (1982). Pity, anger, and guilt: An attributional analysis. *Personality and Social Psychology Bulletin, 8,* 226–232.

Weinstein, N. (1984). Why it won't happen to me: Perceptions of risk factors and susceptibility. *Health Psychology, 3,* 431–457.

Weinstein, N. (1987). Unrealistic optimism about susceptibility to health problems: Conclusions from a community-wide sample. *Journal of Behavioral Medicine, 10,* 481–500.

Wells, G. (1992). Naked statistical evidence of liability: Is subjective probability enough? *Journal of Personality and Social Psychology, 62,* 739–752.

Wells, G., & Gavanski, I. (1989). Mental simulation of causality. *Journal of Personality and Social Psychology, 56,* 161–169.

Wells, M. (1992). Scientific policymaking and the torts revolution: The revenge of the ordinary observer. *Georgia Law Review, 26,* 725–756.

Wiener, R. (1993). Social analytic jurisprudence and tort law: Social cognition goes to court. *Saint Louis University Law Journal, 37,* 503–551.

Wiener, R., Habert, K., Shkodriani, G., & Staebler, C. (1991). The social psychology of jury nullification: Predicting when jurors disobey the law. *Journal of Applied Social Psychology, 21,* 1379–1401.

Wiener, R., & Pritchard, C. (1994). Negligence law and mental mutation: A social inference model of apportioning fault. In L. Heath, R. S. Tindale, J. Edwards, E. Posavac, F. Bryant, E. Henderson-King, Y. Suarez-Balcazar, & J. Myers (Eds.), *Applications of heuristics and biases to social issues* (Vol. 3, pp. 117–136). New York: Plenum.

Wiggins, E., & Breckler, S. (1990). Special verdicts as guides to jury decision making. *Law and Psychology Review, 14,* 1–41.

Wilkerson v. McCarthy, 336 U.S. 53 (1949).

Wilkins, L., & Patterson, P. (1987). Risk analysis and the construction of news. *Journal of Communication, 37*(3), 80–92.

Williams, C., Lees-Haley, P., & Brown, R. (1993). Human response to traumatic events: An integration of counterfactual thinking, hindsight bias, and attribution theory. *Psychological Reports, 72,* 483–494.

Williams, C., Lees-Haley, P., & Price, J. R. (1996). The role of counterfactual thinking and causal attribution in accident-related judgments. *Journal of Applied Social Psychology, 26,* 2100–2112.

Williams, R. (1975). *Television: Technology and cultural form*. New York: Schocken.

Wilson, D., & Donnerstein, E. (1977). Guilty or not guilty? A look at the "simulated" jury paradigm. *Journal of Applied Social Psychology, 7,* 175–190.

Wilson, J., & Bornstein, B. (1998). Methodological considerations in pretrial publicity research: Is the medium the message? *Law and Human Behavior, 22*, 585–597.

Wilson, T., & Brekke, N. (1994). Mental contamination and mental correction: Unwanted influences on judgments and evaluations. *Psychological Bulletin, 116*, 117–142.

Wilson, T., Lisle, D., Kraft, D., & Wetzel, C. (1989). Preferences as expectation-driven inferences: Effects of affective expectations on affective experience. *Journal of Personality and Social Psychology, 56*, 519–530.

Wispé, L. (1986). The distinction between sympathy and empathy: To call forth a concept, a word is needed. *Journal of Personality and Social Psychology, 50*, 314–321.

Wispé, L. (1991). *The psychology of sympathy.* New York: Plenum.

Wissler, R., Evans, D., Hart, A., Morry, M., & Saks, M. (1997). Explaining "pain and suffering" awards: The role of injury characteristics and fault attributions. *Law and Human Behavior, 21*, 181–207.

Wissler, R., & Saks, M. (1985). On the inefficacy of limiting instructions: When jurors use prior conviction evidence to decide on guilt. *Law and Human Behavior, 9*, 37–48.

Wober, M., & Gunter, B. (1988). *Television and social control.* New York: St. Martin's Press.

Wright, D., & Ankerman, W. (1993). *Connecticut jury instructions (Civil)* (4th ed.). West Hartford, CT: Atlantic Book.

Wrightsman, L., Nietzel, M., & Fortune, W. (1994). *Psychology and the legal system* (3rd ed.). Pacific Grove, CA: Brooks/Cole.

Yerkes, R., & Dodson, J. (1908). The relation of strength of stimulus to rapidity of habit-formation. *Journal of Comparative Neurology and Psychology, 18*, 459–482.

Zacharias, F. (1986). The politics of torts. *Yale Law Journal, 95*, 698–753.

Zajonc, R. (1980). Feeling and thinking: Preferences need no inferences. *American Psychologist, 35*, 151–175.

Zaller, J. (1992). *The nature and origins of mass opinion.* Cambridge, England: Cambridge University Press.

Zickafoose, D., & Bornstein, B. (1999). Double discounting: The effects of comparative negligence on mock juror decision making. *Law and Human Behavior, 23*, 577–596.

Zillmann, D. (1983). Transfer of excitation in emotional behavior. In J. Cacioppo & R. Petty (Eds.), *Social psychophysiology* (pp. 215–240). New York: Guilford Press.

Zillmann, D. (1994). Cognition-excitation interdependencies in the escalation of anger and angry aggression. In M. Potegal & J. Knutson (Eds.), *The dynamics of aggression* (pp. 45–71). Hillsdale, NJ: Erlbaum.

AUTHOR INDEX

An italicized page number indicates where that name is found in the references.
An n following a page number indicates location in a footnote.

Aagard, T, 177n, 177, 245
Abel, R., 3, 6, 37, 245, 253
Abelson, R., 46, 128, 272
Abend, T., 117n, 265
Adler, S., 4, 226, 245
Affron, C., 91n, 245
Ajzen, I., 58n, 245
Alexander, N., 232, 245
Alfini, J., 34, 253
Alicke, M., 17, 56, 57, 106, 245
Altman, I., 60n, 272
American College of Obstetricians and
    Gynecologists, 175, 245
American Law Institute, 25, 28n, 29,
    160n, 245
Amsterdam, A., 114, 120–21, 121n, 122,
    245
Amundson, D., 223, 263
Anderson, C., 57, 73, 271
Anderson, M., 73, 106, 245
Ankerman, W., 35, 280
Antoniou, A., 71, 270
Aristotle, 37, 38, 84, 245
Arkes, H., 65, 245
Aronson, E., 152, 245
Aronson, P., 209, 227n, 227, 245
Asp, C., 45n, 272
Athenstaedt, U., 17, 266
Averill, J., 71, 74, 81, 82, 84, 245, 262
Azevedo, D., 78, 246

Babin, B., 99, 250
Baile, W., 180n, 270
Bailis, D., 8, 230, 246
Baker, S., 72, 268
Balon, J., 175, 177, 184, 246
Banaji, M., 140n, 246, 247
Bandura, A., 108, 246
Bargh, J., 140n, 246
Baron, J., 16, 54n, 104, 246, 270
Baron, R., 83, 246
Barrett, L., 70, 271
Barrett, P., 226n, 267
Barry, K., 7, 8, 265

Batson, C. D., 51n, 75n, 75, 76, 77, 246
Baumeister, R., 74, 108, 246, 277
Beach, L., 60n, 263
Beitel, D., 129, 255
Bell, P., 37, 246
Benedict, K., 63, 249
Bennett, E., 189n, 250
Bennett, W. L., 117, 141n, 246
Benyamini, Y., 185, 246
Berlin, J., 184n, 263
Bernard, J. L., 100, 264
Berry, D., 115n, 247
Berscheid, E., 38, 278
Beyth, R., 62, 254
Biek, M., 84, 247
Bix, B., 40, 247
Black, J., 118, 129, 247
Blackmar, C., 25, 251
Blair, I., 140n, 247
Blanck, P., 43, 247
Blankenberg, F., 177, 269
Bless, H., 144, 240, 241, 247, 273
Bobbitt, P., 217n, 217, 229, 249
Bodenhausen, G., 82, 237, 247
Bonazzoli, J., 13n, 42, 247
Bond, A., 81, 277
Bonham, V., 176, 190n, 267
Booth, R., 74, 90n, 268
Bordens, K., 15, 33, 228, 259
Bornstein, B., 11, 14, 42n, 43, 51, 56n,
    65, 66, 78, 99, 100, 101, 106,
    122, 165, 247, 249, 279, 280
Bovbjerg, R., 14, 78, 100, 101n, 248
Bower, A., 230, 255
Bower, G., 14, 236, 237, 238, 239, 248,
    255, 270
Braden-Maguire, J., 14, 43, 274
Branscombe, N., 53n, 56, 116, 237, 248,
    267
Braver, S., 108, 249
Bray, R., 35, 44, 248, 275
Breckler, S., 35, 279
Brekke, N., 44–45n, 44, 280
Brewer, M., 152, 245
Brooks, P., 89, 90n, 159n, 248

281

Brown, R., 63, 115, *248*, *279*
Bruce, C., 40, *248*
Bruner, J., 45, 97, 117, 118, 122, 145, *248*
Bryan, T., 74, *252*
Buck, M., 77, *248*
Burger, J., 85, *248*

Cacioppo, J., 116n, 122n, 190n, *248*, *268*
Calabresi, G., 39, 140n, 216, 217n, 217, 218n, 229, *248–249*
Cantor, N., 46, 49, 50, 116, 140n, 140, 240, *249*
Caplan, L., 176n, 196n, *249*
Cardozo, B., 27n
Carroll, J., 43, 71, *249*, *261*
Carroll, S., 14, *257*
Carson, J., 100, *276*
Casper, J., 60n, 63, 228, *249*, *251*
Cecil, J., 110, *249*
Chaiken, S., 84, *247*, *263*
Chalmers, T., 184n, *263*
Chandler, C., 76, *279*
Chapman, G., 65, 66, 106, *249*
Charrow, R., 34, *249*
Charrow, V., 34, *249*
Chin, A., 14, 99, 101n, 115n, *249*, *265*
Chiu, C., 58n, 265n
Choi, I., 58n, *249*
Christianson, S., 95n, *249*
Cialdini, R., 108, *249*
Citron, R., 178, 189, *249*
Clermont, K., 7n, 7, 32, 96n, 103n, *249*
Clore, G., 71, 82, 86, 235–237, 239, 240, *247*, *250*, *255*, *267*, *273*
Coburn, E., 222, *250*
Cohen, B., 237, *248*
Cohen, E., 14, *278*
Cohen, R., 78, 100, *250*, *264*
Cohn, S., 176, *250*
Coleman, J., 38, 56, 104, *248*, *250*
Collins, A., 71, *267*
Conklin, L., 76, *251*
Conley, J., 18, 108, 115n, 156n, *250*
Conley, T., 114, *250*
Conway, M., 235, *250*
Cook, F., 183n, *277*
Cooper, J., 189n, *250*
Cordell, L., 43, *247*
Corneille, O., 58n, *263*
Cornell, D., 232, *245*

Corty, E., 46, 58, *273*
Cover, R., 107, *250*
Cox, C., 180n, *269*, *270*
Crinklaw, L., 85, *278*
Curran, N., 91n, *261*
Cusimano, G., 212, *250*
Cutler, B., 11, *266*

Damasio, A., 70, *250*
Dane, F., 43, 78, 115n, *250*
Daniels, S., 4, 6, 7n, 7, 8, 9, 16, 96, 111, 212, 225, 226, 230, *250*
Danoff-Burg, S., 193n, *271*
Danzon, P., 100, *250*
Darden, W., 99, 100, *250*
Darley, J., 44, 119, *260*, *270*
Davidson, R., 235, *250–251*
Davies, M., 73, *251*
Davis, M., 75n, 75, 76, 77, 123, *251*
Dawes, R., 48, *251*
De Lisa, A., 11, *266*
de Sousa, R., 72, *251*
Deaux, K., 75n, *264*
DeConinck, J., 99, *150*
Degoey, P., 107, *277*
Dennis, C., 166, 184, *251*
Denove, C., 13n, 14, 43, *251*
Deutsch, M., 38, *251*
Devine, P., 140n, *251*
Devitt, E., 25, 61n, 140n, *251*
Dewar, M., 176, *251*
Dewees, D., 3, 8, 16, 36, 37, 224, 229n, *251*
Dexter, H., 43, *267*
Diamond, S., 11, 33, 35n, 42, 43, 44, 152, 228, *251*
Dijksterhuis, A., 52n, *251*
Dobbs, D., 12, *261*
Dodson, J., 72, *280*
Dodd, M., 196n
Doise, W., 207, *266*
Donnerstein, E., 101n, 152, *279*
Dooley, L., 232, *251*
Dor, A., 14, *248*
Dorfman, A., 213, *251*
Douglas, M., 99, 212, 213, *251*
Downey, C., 65, *256*
Dreier, P., 223n, 224n, *252*

Marder, N., 35, 109, 152, 232, 233, *265*
Margolis, H., 16, 67, 219*n*, 226*n*, *265*
Mark, M., 240, *274*
Marti, M., 35, *272*
Martin, C., 223, *265*
Martin, J., 4, 6, 7*n*, 7, 8, 9, 16, 96, 111,
    212, 225, 226, 230, *250*
Martin, L., 45*n*, 117*n*, 237, *265*, *275*
Marx, K., 214*n*
Mason, L., 9*n*, 89, 171, *265*
Mauet, T., 33, *265*
Mayer, D., 73, *272*
Mayer, J., 73, 239, 240, *265*, *272*
Mayseless, O., 52*n*, 52, *261*
McCaffery, E., 67, *265*
McCann, M., 8*n*, 98, 230, *257*
McCloskey, A., 105, *253*
McClure, J., 52*n*, *265*
McFarland, C., 54, *266*
McGlynn, R., 58*n*, *258*
McKee, R., 106, 119, 120, *265*
Meleis, A., 196*n*
Meisel, M., 89, *265*
Menon, T., 58*n*, *265*
Mercer, P., 74, *265*
Merritt, D., 7, 8
Messé, L., 56*n*, *267*
Meyer, L., 38, 168*n*, 222*n*, *265*
Meyer, P., 14, 118, *265*
Mikula, G., 17, 81, 107, *266*
Mill, J. S., 51*n*, 51, *266*
Miller, D., 53, 54*n*, 54, 76, 77, 121*n*,
    248, 260, *266*
Miller, J., 58*n*, *266*
Miller, W., 74*n*, *266*
Milne, A., 54*n*, 76, 77, *264*
Mischel, W., 116, *249*
Mohilever, J., 177, *270*
Moller, T., 7, 8, 96, *266*
Monson, T., 58*n*, *266*
Monteith, M., 140*n*, *251*
Moore, M., 229*n*, *278*
Moore, S., 43, *266*
Moor-Ede, M., 220*n*, *266*
Moran, G., 11, 42, *266*
Moreland, R., 207, *262*
Morris, M., 49, 52*n*, 58*n*, 95, *265*, *266*,
    274
Morry, M., 8, *280*
Mort, N., 35*n*, *257*
Moscovici, S., 207, *266*
Mosley, N., 14, 43, *274*

Mott, N., *258*
Mueller, C. B., 190, *266*
Mueller, J., 115*n*, *247*
Munsterman, T., 34*n*, *257*
Musweiler, T., 65, *276*
Myers, D., 207, *266*

Nagareda, R., 17, 31, 86*n*, 106, 110, 190,
    218, 222, 228, *266*
Narby, D., 11, *266*
National Safety Council, 3, *266*
Nelson, W., 149*n*
Neter, E., 42*n*, 116*n*, *268*
Neuberg, S., 41*n*, 52*n*, *267*
Newsom, J., 41*n*, 52*n*, *267*
N'ghala, A., 53*n*, *267*
Nicholson, C., 16, 104, *275*
Niedenthal, P., 76, 239, 240, *257*, *267*
Niedermeier, K., 56*n*, *267*
Nietzel, M., 77, *280*
Nikolopolou, A., 90, *258*
Nisbett, R., 5, 11, 15, 16, 41–42*n*, 44–
    51, 45*n*, 52*n*, 57, 58, 58*n*, 67, 68,
    102, 103, 109, 122, 147, 152,
    164, 172, 249, *267*, *271*
Nowell-Smith, G., 90*n*, 90, 213*n*, *267*
Nussbaum, M., 72, 75*n*, 259, *267*

O'Barr, W., 18, 108, 115*n*, 156*n*, *250*
O'Connell, J., 37, *246*
O'Connell, V., 226*n*, *267*
Olson, J., 54, 55, 63, *270*
Ortony, A., 71, 72, 76, 81, 82, 85, 91,
    157*n*, *267*
Orza, M., 184*n*, *263*
Oshagan, H., 223, *265*
Osuch, J., 176, 190*n*, *267*
Otto, A., 43, *267*
Owen, D., 12, *261*
Owen, S., 55, *248*

Palfai, T., 240, *267*
Palmer, J., 147, *263*
Panter, A., 43, *256*
Park, J., 14, 79, *253*
Parkinson, M., 122, *268*
Parpal, M., 14, 100, 101, 121*n*, *276*
Parrott, G., 81, 237, 250, *268*
Patterson, P., 13, 215, *279*

Thorburn, D., 90n, 90, 277
Tice, D., 74, 277
Tomlinson, T., 105, 253
Town, J., 58n, 258
Traynor, M., 8, 260
Trebilcock, M., 3, 251
Triche, E., 215, 275
Trope, Y., 263
Trout, R., 100, 276
Turk, C., 76, 246
Turnbull, W., 54n, 54, 58n, 266, 277
Turow, J., 182n, 182, 277
Tversky, A., 11, 47–49, 53, 54, 55n, 65–
      68, 77, 86, 132, 236, 259, 260,
      277
Tyler, T., 17, 107, 183n, 275, 277

U.S. Preventative Services Task Force,
      175, 177, 277

Valley, K., 94n, 276
van der Keilen, M., 85n, 277
van Knippenberg, A., 52n, 251
Van Voris, B., 209, 245
Velasco, C., 81, 277
Vidmar, N., 4–6, 8, 9, 14, 16, 35, 36, 85,
      97, 100, 101n, 102, 108, 110,
      209, 226, 229, 278
Vinson, D., 185n, 278
Viscusi, W. K., 229n, 229, 258, 278
Visher, C., 13, 14, 42, 270, 278
von Fournier, D., 177, 275

Walker, D., 37, 278
Walster, E., 38, 64, 278
Walster, G. W., 38, 278
Ward, A., 111, 270
Watts, C., 177n, 278
Weber, E., 177, 275
Webster, D., 35, 52n, 261
Wegener, D., 35, 45n, 116n, 238, 268,
      273, 278
Wegner, D., 73, 239, 253, 278
Wehrwein, T., 175, 177, 184, 246
Weiler, P., 7, 26, 38, 40, 104, 219n, 219,
      225n, 279
Weiner, B., 3, 11, 41n, 58n, 75n, 76–77,
      81, 129, 256, 272, 279

Weinstein, N., 41n, 261, 279
Weinstock, M., 43, 261
Wells, G., 55, 56n, 279
Wells, M., 140n, 279
Wesley, M., 176n, 249
Wetzel, C., 95, 280
White, P., 45n, 268
Wiener, R., 50, 55, 279
Wiggins, E., 35, 110, 249, 279
Wilczek, A., 100, 276
Wildavsky, A., 99, 156n, 269
Wilkins, L., 13, 215n, 215, 279
Willett, L., 100, 215, 276
Williams, C., 54, 63, 82, 279
Williams, R., 118, 225, 279
Wilson, D., 101n, 152, 279
Wilson, J., 43, 279
Wilson, T., 44–45n, 44, 95, 152, 245,
      267, 280
Winkielman, P., 144n, 275
Wispé, L., 74, 75n, 75, 76, 78n, 85, 280
Wissler, R., 8, 11, 44, 62, 65, 103, 258,
      280
Wober, M., 182, 185n, 280
Wolff, M., 25, 251
Wood, W., 84, 247
Worth, L., 20, 237, 240, 264
Wright, D., 35, 280
Wrightsman, L., 4, 11, 35, 42, 43, 77,
      78, 115n, 115, 151, 201, 250,
      260, 269, 280
Wyer, R., 140, 144, 275

Yarkin, K., 58n, 258
Yerkes, R., 72, 280
Young, M., 240, 253
Yzerbyt, V., 58n, 263

Zacharias, F., 230, 280
Zajonc, R., 72, 280
Zaller, J., 15, 280
Zanakos, S., 73, 278
Zeisel, H., 4, 7, 16, 42n, 78, 109, 229,
      260
Zickafoose, D., 100, 280
Zidan, J., 177, 270
Zillmann, D., 72, 82, 280
Zucker, G., 75n, 76, 256

SUBJECT INDEX

An n following a page number indicates that information is found in a footnote.

Biases, juror (*continued*)
    attitudinal, 42
    demographic, 42
    extra-legal, 42, 43
    pro-plaintiff, 6, 14, 98, 100
    See also Habits of mind
"Blame the victim" defenses, 108, *see also*
        Belief in a just world
Blameworthiness; *see* Blaming; Negli-
        gence; Responsibility
Blaming
    dehumanization of subject, 78n; *see
        also* Belief in a just world
    mediated by anger, 83
    mediated by anxiety, 85
    mediated by sympathy, 77
    multidimensional nature of, 5, 10–13,
        232
    See also Causation; Responsibility
Blaming, melodramatic
    and "bad guy," 14, 16–17, 88, 92–94,
        110, 119, 155–159, 213
    as argumentative strategy, 118–120
    cultural implications, 212–216
    legal implications, 217–222
Bobbitt, Lorena, 108
Bobbitt, P., 217
Bornstein, B., 51, 56n, 66, 78
Bower, G., 236
Branscombe, N., 53n
Breast cancer
    causation of harm, 177–178
    delayed diagnosis, 171–210
    doubling time defense, 177–178, 189
    law governing, 175, 176–177
    loss of chance, 173, 176–177, 190,
        198–200
    size-of-the-lump heuristic, 179, 182–
        185, 188, 194, 197
    standards of medical care, 175–176
    See also Mock jury deliberations
Brooks, P., 89
Burden of proof, 24, 121, 137, 188
Butler v. Revere Copper & Brass, Inc.,
        123–136
    facts and issues, 123–124
    lawyers' arguments, 124–126, 131
    as workplace slip and fall accident,
        218–219, 226n

Calabresi, G., 39, 217, 217n–218
Carcinogens, 27, 31, 51, 86n, 219n, 222
Cardozo, Benjamin, 27n
Carelessness. *See* Negligence, breach of
        duty
Case selection effects, 7n, 96n, 103n
Case type hypothesis, 102–103
Causation
    acts versus omissions as affecting attri-
        butions of, 54, 130, 156, 160
    but-for causation, legal rule of, 26–27,
        28n, 176
    commingled with fault, 17, 106, 130,
        132n, 188, 190, 199n, 200, 218
    counterfactual thinking and attribu-
        tions of, 52–54, 130, 156, 166,
        190; *see also* Norm theory
    joint, 27
    logical fallacies, 55n
    loss of chance, legal rule of, 27, 173,
        176–177, 190, 198–200
    prima facie negligence, 26–28
    proximate cause, legal rule of, 12, 27–
        28, 137–138, 160n, 217
    social and systemic, 213, 216–219,
        222–223
    substantial factor, legal rule of, 28n
Chapman, G., 66
Clore, G., 236–237, 239
Closure
    jurors' desire for, 18, 120, 156
    need for, 41n, 52
Cognitive dissonance theory, 107
Cognitive heuristics, 11, 45–68
    See also Habits of mind
"Cold" cognitions, 41, 64, 69
Common sense, 10–11
    contradictory nature of, 5, 13–15, 18–
        19, 95–104, 167
    features of, 5, 13–14, 88n
    See also Habits of mind; Melodrama
Comparative negligence
    emotions, role of, 83, 85, 96–97
    fault apportionment, 38, 96, 100, 136–
        138, 157n, 200–209
    law of, 30–31, 137, 157n
    limited, 31, 201, 205, 208–209
    melodrama and, 87, 96–97
    split-the-difference heuristic, 173, 201,
        206–207

Dispositional attribution (*continued*)
cultural derivation of, 58n, 215–216
legal judgment and, 59–62, 106
See also Fundamental attribution error
Dorfman, A., 213–214
Dreier, P., 223n, 224n

Economic efficiency
accident cost reduction, 25–26, 36, 38–40, 229
cost-effectiveness of specific precautions, 132, 166n, 168, 220–221n
justice and, 37n
negligence defined as, 25–26
See also Hand, Learned; Risk *entries*
Elaboration likelihood model of persuasion, 116n, 122n, 190n, 238
Elsaesser, T., 213
Emotional intelligence, 73
Emotions, 69–86, 235–241
associative network model, 236, 237
cognitive aspects of, 71–74, 93n
complementarity of, 94, 104
control of, 73–74
gender differences, 75
intensity, influences on, 76, 93–95, 157–158
intelligence, 73
lawyers' use of, 123, 157–158
and legal judgment, 71–86, 96–97, 100, 104, 157–158, 163–164, 225, 228
melodrama and, 90–92, 94, 157
moods distinguished, 235
and social judgment, 235–241
See also Anger; Anxiety; Fear; Sympathy
Empathy, 74–75n, 76, 84, 180
Endowment effect, 66, 67
Evidence
emotion-provoking, 74
inadmissible, jurors' consideration of, 17, 61, 74, 105, 227
importance for juror decisions, 13, 42
jurors' organizing into story form, 117
presentation of, 33–34, 91, 110, 123
rules of, 217, 227
Expectations
affective expectancies, 94–95, 117n
knowledge structures and, 46

regarding lawyer arguments, 119–120, 123
melodrama and, 89, 216
"Expert" (non-juror) analysis of cases
jury verdict agreement with, 4–5, 7, 16, 109–110, 199–200, 210, 227, 229
jury verdict divergence from, 5, 16, 35n, 79, 110, 229
Expert discourse, 12–13, 36–40
Expert testimony, 65, 189–190n

Facial expressions
emotion recognition, 71, 90n
sympathy, arousal of, 76
sympathy, measurement of, 75n
Fairness. *See* Justice
False consciousness, 224n
Fault, *see* Blaming; Negligence; Responsibility
Faverty v. McDonald's Restaurants of Oregon, Inc., 152–169
blaming the defendant, compared with "expert" analysis, 219–222
facts and issues, 152, 153–154
jurors' views, 162–163
lawyers' arguments, 154–155, 159–160
Fear, 70–71, 74, 83–86
Federal Employers' Liability Act (FELA), 137
Feelings, 16, 17, 106–107; *see also* Emotions; Moods
Feldman, M., 117, 141n
Fiedler, K., 237
Fletcher, G., 108
Foreseeability, *see* Negligence, foreseeability and
Forgas, J., 238
Friedman, L., 224
Fundamental attribution error, 56–62
actor-observer effect, 57
anger and, 82
lawyers' use of, 61–62, 133–135, 158, 218
melodrama and, 15–16, 87, 93, 119, 135, 228
negligence definition and, 61n
sympathy and, 78
total justice and, 106

Juries, civil (*continued*)
    See also Mock jury deliberations; Total
        justice
Juror interviews
    as data, 9, 151–152
    Faverty jury, 153, 162–164
    self-presentation bias, 152, 164, 167
Jurors
    as active decision makers, 120–123,
        135–136, 143, 146–148, 156
    demographic characteristics, 42–43,
        115n, 231–232
    gender of, 35, 201, 231–232
    selection of, *see* Jury selection
    See also Total justice
Jurors, influences on
    anxiety or fear, 84
    desire to perform well, 42n
    evidence, 13, 17, 42
    expert opinions, 13, 23, 65, 66, 226
    extralegal factors, 43
    instructions from judge, 12, 61n
    law, 11–12; *see also* Instructions from
        judge, juror comprehension of;
        jurors' tendency to follow or not
    prior beliefs, 66, 117n, 172–173, 178–
        185; *see also* Prototype effects
    sympathy for victim, 77–80, 158–159
    See also Biases, juror; Deviance; Habits
        of mind
Jury consultants, 11
Jury nullification, 109
Jury selection, 33, 52n
Just world theory, 78n, 85n, 98, 101; *see*
    also Belief in a just world
Justice
    corrective, 12, 37–38, 104, 156, 227
    distributive, 12, 37, 38, 101n, 207
    policy oriented, 12
    public perception of, 225–226
    "relational" view of, 156n
    See also Total justice

Kahneman, D., 53, 54, 55n, 66, 132
Kalven, H., 78
Kanouse, D., 52
Keltner, D., 82, 111
Kleinhans, C., 214n, 214
Knowledge structures, 45–46

category exemplars, 117
cultural models, 14, 46
nature of, implicit and intuitive, 45,
    72–73
scripts, 11, 46, 72, 128, 182
stories as, 116–118
See also Prototype effects; Schemas
Kruglanski, A., 52n

Law of accidents. *See* Negligence; Proce-
    dural law; Strict liability; Tort
    law
Lawyers' arguments
    closing arguments as data, 10, 114–
        116, 153
    evidence, presentation of, 33–34, 91,
        103
    examples of, 124–126, 131, 138–139,
        145–146, 148, 154–155, 159–
        160
    expert reasoning, incorporation of, 13
    juror comprehension of, 42
    as melodrama, 97, 118–119, 123, 147,
        155, 158–159
    opening statements, 10, 33, 114–115
    paradigmatic reasoning, 97, 145–146
    persuasiveness of noncontent features
        of, 115n
    prototypes, use of, 136–144
    psychology and strategies of, 116–123
    summations, *see* closing arguments
Lawyers' rhetorical techniques
    active verbs, 135–136, 146
    analogies, 131–132, 141, 143, 154
    metaphors, 133–134, 141–143, 149,
        157
    primacy effect, 126–127
    rhetorical questions, 148
    second- and first-person plural, 122,
        135, 146, 148, 156
    story creation, 116–123, 140, 145–146
Lawyers' words, *see* Lawyers' arguments,
    examples of
Lazarus, R., 84n
Lehman, D., 53n
Lerner, J., 82
Leyens, J. P., 58n
Liability, vicarious, 30, 60n
    See also Products liability; Strict liabil-
    ity

Lichter, L., 224n
Lichter, S. R., 224n
Litan, R., 229n
Litigation and success rates, 7, 96, 103n, 191
"Litigotiation," 6, 32, 103n

Mandel, D., 53n
Marx, K., 214n
Mayer, J., 239
McDonald's Restaurants case. *See Faverty v. McDonald's Restaurants of Oregon, Inc.*
McKee, R., 120
Media
    availability heuristic and, 47, 48
    belief reinforcement, 182, 185n, 223
    blaming patterns, 8, 13n, 98, 215, 223, 223n, 224n
    expert opinions aired on, 13, 231
    fundamental attribution error, 215n
    information availability, 193, 195n
    knowledge structures, as source of, 14, 182, 223
    melodramatic content, 89–92, 215, 223–225
    novelty and exceptional cases, focus on, 8, 215n, 230
    pretrial publicity, 43
    purposeful editing of jurors' views by, 152
Medical malpractice
    breach of duty, 175–176, 186–188
    causation, 176–178, 189–191, 196–200
    delayed diagnosis, *see* Breast cancer, delayed diagnosis
    iatrogenic medical injuries, 100, 219n
    jury competence in deciding, 110, 209
    loss of chance rule, 27, 173, 176–177, 190, 198–200
    negligence, *see* breach of duty
    pro-plaintiff bias, 100, 209
    technology and "nondurable precautions," 225n
    See also Breast cancer; Mock jury deliberations
Medical treatment
    caring physician prototype, 172, 179–182, 186–188

causal efficacy attributed to by common sense, 55n
customary (ordinary) care standard, 26, 172, 174–176
Melodrama
    defined, 89–92
    "good" vs. "evil," 13–14, 16–17, 88–90, 92–94
    jurors' conception of accidents as, 14, 19, 20, 87–95, 151–169, 211–216, 223–226
    limitations of, as explanation for jurors' conception of accidents, 96–98
    personality-driven, 5, 15, 88, 212, 213
    social psychology of, 92–95, 119
    victim, focus on, 90, 94, 119, 158–159
    See also Blaming, melodramatic
Menendez brothers trial, 108
Mental shortcuts. *See* Habits of mind
Meyer, L., 168n, 222n
Mill, J. S., 51n, 51
Mock jury deliberations, 9–10, 151, 171–210
    anchoring and adjustment, jurors' use of, 206–207
    blaming the patient, 191–198
    blaming the physician, 185–191
    culpable causation, jurors' use of, 190
    as data, 173–174
    fault apportionment, 173, 196n, 200–209
    group decision making, 201–209
    norm theory, jurors' use of, 188, 190, 197
    prior beliefs, influence of, 172, 178–185
Monocausality, 51–52
    discounting of alternative causes, 52n
    incentives for behavior, 51–52n
    lawyers' use of, 157
    melodrama and, 14, 87, 88, 92
    need for closure and, 41–42n, 52, 120
    plausible sufficient cause, 51–52
Moods
    affect priming theory, 236–237, 238
    angry, persistence of, 82
    emotions distinguished, 235
    memory and, 239
    modification of, 73, 93n
    mood-as-information theory, 82, 236–237, 238, 240

Social utility, 36, 38–40; *see also* Economic efficiency
Solomon, S., 74*n*
Statistics, jurors' comprehension of, 48–49, 67–68, 110
Stereotypes, negative, 100, 121, 157, 223, 225, 232
  See also Protoype effects; Prototypes; Racial bias
Strict liability
  abnormally dangerous activities, 29
  described, 12, 24, 29–30
  economic efficiency and, 39–40
  fault standard, compared to, 217–218*n*
  respondeat superior, 60*n*
  ultrahazardous activities, 29
Strier, F., 226
Substantive law. *See* Negligence; Tort law
Sukel, H., 189*n*
Sympathy, 74–80
  action tendency, 78
  biasing effect, 100, 101*n*
  cognitive dimensions of, 74–75
  intensity of, influences on, 76, 93–95, 148
  and legal judgment, 69, 77–80, 91, 100, 121, 123, 127, 163

Tarasoff rule, 64
Taub, S., 186*n*, 196*n*
Taylor, S., Jr., 153, 162*n*, 164, 167
Terror management theory, 86
Tort law
  expert discourses regarding, 12–13, 36–40
  goals of, 3, 16, 36
  juror comprehension of, 4, 16, 34, 109
  melodramatic blaming and, 217–223
  See also Justice; Negligence; Procedural law; Strict liability
Tort reform, 11, 32, 230
Total justice, 16–18, 104–111, 226–233
  account squaring, 5, 16, 88, 104–105, 108–109, 227
  anger at injustice, 81, 107
  common sense and, 13–18, 104–111
  elements of, 5, 16–17, 88
  emotions and, 17, 106–107
  holistic decision making, 17–18, 88,

105–107, 200, 228–230; *see also* Causation, commingled with fault
  in lawyer's argument, 149
  legal rules and rationales compared with, 226–230
Trials
  bench (judge), 32
  popular perception of jury, 230–232
  unitary vs. bifurcated, 33, 228
Tversky, A., 53, 54, 55*n*, 66, 132

Vehicle-related accidents
  alcohol use and, 25, 32, 154, 215, 218*n*, 220–221*n*
  counterclaims, 32*n*
  other examples of, 28, 31*n*, 53–54, 55, 56, 106
  sleep-deprivation and, 152–155, 159–160, 220–221
  See also Faverty v. McDonald's Restaurants of Oregon, Inc.
Verdicts
  with jury interrogatories, 35, 228
  rejection of by judge, 35–36
  special, 12, 35, 126*n*, 191*n*, 228
  See also Expert analysis of cases
Viscusi, W. K., 229*n*
Voir dire, 33, 52*n*

Walster, E., 64
Ward, A., 111
Weiner, B., 76–77
Wells, G., 55*n*
Williams, C., 82
Wispé, L., 78*n*
Workers' compensation, 7*n*, 9
Workplace accidents
  other examples of, 28*n*
  railroad, 79, 80*n*, 83, 113, 136–149
  slip and fall, 123–136, 130, 226*n*
Wrongful death statutes, 28–29

Yzerbyt, V., 58*n*

Zeiberg, M., 220*n*
Zeisel, H., 78

ABOUT THE AUTHOR

Neal Feigenson, JD, is Professor of Law at Quinnipiac College School of Law in Hamden, CT, where he teaches torts, civil procedure, and jurisprudence, as well as a research affiliate in the Yale University Department of Psychology. Before joining the Quinnipiac faculty in 1987, Professor Feigenson received his law degree from Harvard, practiced law in Boston, and taught at the University of Chicago Law School and the New York University Law School, where he was senior research instructor and director of the Lawyering Program. His interest in tort law and practice has led Professor Feigenson to pursue both quantitative and qualitative inquiries into the psychology of jurors' decision-making in negligence cases, on which this book is based. In addition to his work in psychology and law, Professor Feigenson has published articles in the fields of legal history, constitutional law, and legal writing.